# A Catholic New Deal

# A Catholic New Deal

## Religion and Reform in Depression Pittsburgh

### Kenneth J. Heineman

The Pennsylvania State University Press
University Park, Pennsylvania

Library of Congress Cataloging-in-Publication Data

Heineman, Kenneth J., 1962–
    A Catholic new deal : religion and reform in Depression Pittsburgh /
Kenneth J. Heineman.
        p.   cm.
    Includes bibliographical references and index.
    ISBN 0-271-01895-X (cloth : alk. paper)
    ISBN 0-271-01896-8 (pbk. : alk. paper)
    1. Church and labor—Pennsylvania—Pittsburgh—History—20th century.
2. Church and social problems—Pennsylvania—Pittsburgh—Catholic Church—
History—20th century.   3. Depressions—1929—Pennsylvania—Pittsburgh.
4. New Deal, 1932–1939—Pennsylvania—Pittsburgh.   5. Social reformers—
Pennsylvania—Pittsburgh—History—20th century.   6. Anti-communist
movements—Pennsylvania—Pittsburgh—History—20th century.   7. Catholic
Worker Movement—History—20th century.   8. Congress of Industrial
Organizations (U.S.)—History.   I. Title.
HD6338.2.U52P574   1999
331.88'09748'86—dc21                                             98-44026
                                                                      CIP

It is the policy of The Pennsylvania State University Press to use acid-free paper for
the first printing of all clothbound books. Publications on uncoated stock satisfy
the minimum requirements of American National Standard for Information
Sciences—Permanence of Paper for Printed Library Materials, ANSI Z39.48-1992.

*For*
*Theresa Ann Heineman*
*and our children,*
*Natalie MacKenzie Heineman*
*and*
*Grace Ann Heineman*

# Contents

# List of Illustrations

# Preface and Acknowledgments

*A Catholic New Deal* is a history of religiously based social reform, ethnic politics, and labor organizing in Pittsburgh. To help orient the reader without, at the same time, interrupting the narrative flow, I have led off each chapter with a brief summary of its contents. Having written an academic monograph based upon my doctoral dissertation, as well as a more free-wheeling book of broad social commentary and political history, I am now trying to arrive at a compromise between "lab report–style" writing and a journalistic type of narrative that is more interested in telling a story than worrying about whether readers see up front that there is a point to it all. Professional historians rightly complain that nonacademic "popularizers" are wont to sacrifice analysis if it gets in the way of telling a good tale. On the other hand, most readers of history and biography tend to avoid dry, linguistically inaccessible academic monographs. My hope is to bridge the gap· between academia and the general reading public.

In the first chapter of *A Catholic New Deal*, we will meet Father James Cox, a Catholic priest and champion of the unemployed who, in 1932, led what was then the largest protest march on Washington in American history. Chapter 2 offers a discussion of Catholic social teaching and the New Deal. Between 1933 and 1935, the reform wing of the American Catholic Church struggled on behalf of pensions for the elderly, public works projects and compensation for the unemployed, and championed the right of workers to bargain collectively. At the same time, the Church reformers warned against the moral dangers of workers becoming too dependent upon the federal government. Meanwhile, Catholic clergy and laity matched wits with Communists and conservative corporate representatives who had their own vision of what constituted a just relationship between labor and management. Here we will meet Philip Murray and John Brophy, devout Catholics and labor leaders. Such working-class Catholics founded the Committee for Industrial Organization (CIO), America's first great industrial union. At the 1938 CIO convention in Pittsburgh, the union officially split from the American Federation of Labor (AFL) and became the Congress of Industrial Organizations.

In the third chapter, I will explore the ways in which class, race, and religion influenced the history of organized labor and the New Deal. As David Lawrence forged an electoral alliance with blacks, Catholics, and Jews, Phil Murray established the Steel Workers Organizing Committee (SWOC). Meanwhile, Catholic priests such as Charles Owen Rice and Carl Hensler of Pittsburgh joined forces with Dorothy Day's Catholic Worker movement. The activist priests sought to combat discrimination and assist in the building of a strong steel union. Feeling threatened by SWOC and the growing Democratic Party, Pittsburgh industrialists such as J. Howard Pew Sr. (Sun Oil) and Ernest Weir (National Steel) helped found the Liberty League. They hoped to undermine the New Deal and move the Republican Party further to the right in 1936.

Chapter 4 offers a discussion of the great steel war of 1937, a year in which over four thousand strikes occurred nationally and mill towns from Johnstown, Pennsylvania, to Chicago became combat zones. Many industrial communities in Illinois, Michigan, Ohio, and Pennsylvania were placed under martial law by local or state officials. Although U.S. Steel capitulated to Murray, Bethlehem, Republic, and Youngstown Sheet and Tube resisted SWOC with private security forces and machine guns. Determined to break the strike, the Little Steel companies accelerated their practice of recruiting southern blacks and Appalachian whites to replace Catholic workers. Reformist priests and bishops entered the fray, offering great assistance to the union. Out of this struggle came a landmark Supreme Court decision that had arisen from a bloody contest between Jones & Laughlin and SWOC in Aliquippa, just outside Pittsburgh. In the *National Labor Relations Board v. Jones & Laughlin Steel Company*, the court upheld the constitutionality of the New Deal's labor legislation.

In the fifth chapter, activist Church clergy and laity come under attack by the newly established House Special Committee to Investigate Un-American Activities. Blaming SWOC for the violence of 1937 — and upset with Roosevelt's faltering efforts to achieve economic recovery — middle-class Americans in 1938 turned away from the New Deal. The bishops of the industrial heartland, and the region's Catholic politicians, rallied behind organized labor. As the Church reformers squared off against corporate conservatives, a battle was being waged within the ranks of labor. Concerned with the influence exercised by the Communist Party in the CIO, Murray, Hensler, and Rice helped establish the Association of Catholic Trade Unionists (ACTU). Father Rice became ACTU chaplain, championing labor while combating Communist leaders in the Pittsburgh-based SWOC and the United Electrical (UE) Workers Union. At odds with CIO president John L. Lewis, Murray and clergy activists struggled for control of the union while war approached in Europe.

Chapter 6 addresses the Catholic Church's varied responses to political developments overseas from 1939 to 1941. Although critical of corporate executives who red-baited the CIO, the reform wing of the American Catholic Church was no less opposed to any kind of military alliance with the Soviet Union. Against this backdrop, the ACTU fought American Communists while Murray replaced Lewis as CIO president in late 1940. Homestead's Father Clement Hrtanek, an advocate of organized labor since the 1919 Steel Strike, as well as a national Slovak-American leader, did not respond well to the rise of European fascism. Convinced that the Czechs were atheistic Communists, Hrtanek demanded Slovak independence. His cousin, Monsignor Joseph Tiso, who twice visited Pittsburgh in the 1930s, received great support from Hrtanek in his bid to become the premiere of an independent Slovakia. After World War II, Monsignor Tiso was executed for Nazi war crimes, having sent sixty thousand Slovakian Jews to German gas chambers.

Fathers Hensler and Rice, who had embraced the pacifism of the Catholic Worker movement, broke with Dorothy Day. Viewing Nazi Germany and the Soviet Union as equally evil societies, Rice thought it best to temper his Irish nationalism and Anglophobia. Prior to America's entrance into the war, Rice urged Americans to give military aid to Great Britain. Murray quickly followed his friend's lead, becoming the only prominent Irish Catholic labor leader in America to champion the British. Once Hitler invaded the Soviet Union, Rice and Murray reluctantly embraced Stalin as an ally. However, the Catholic reformers never abandoned their anti-Communist principles. The events of World War II, particularly the Soviet occupation of Eastern Europe, provoked a Catholic backlash that endangered the political viability of the New Deal coalition.

Beyond telling the story outlined above, this work intends to illustrate the ways in which activist clergy and laity championed a distinctively Catholic vision of social justice. Their vision was anti-Communist, but never anti-Semitic. Catholics certainly did much to lay the groundwork for American opposition to Communism. However, the Catholic clergy who embraced the cause of social justice were equally concerned with an "exploitative" capi-

talist economy. They believed that Communists, as well as irresponsible capitalists, were impediments to the creation of a better society.[1]

Further, *A Catholic New Deal* hopes to persuade the reader that clergy
and laity activists did not use anti-Communism in the 1930s as a way to become Americanized; nor was Catholic anti-Communism motivated by Nazi
sympathies. Rather, Pittsburgh's reformist clergy sought to transform American society in line with their Church teachings. They were opposed to
Nazism, Communism, and a capitalist system unresponsive to the needs of
working-class citizens. Their mission was one of social reconstruction, not
cultural assimilation.[2]

The Catholic labor priests considered the Communists who joined the CIO
to be just as opportunistic as many capitalists, albeit loyal to Moscow rather
than Wall Street. Catholic reformers were determined to resist both. Historians who have written informed accounts of Catholic social activism in the
1930s frequently failed to give full credence to the labor priests' critique of
laissez-faire capitalism. Pittsburgh's labor priests supported much of the New
Deal but were highly selective in what federal programs they embraced, rejecting initiatives that enhanced federal power too much. As David O'Brien
observed in comparing the American and European Catholic responses to
the Great Depression:

> In Europe, Catholic leaders were willing to use the power of the au-
> thoritarian state to impose moral values in the vain hope that, once
> society had been restored to its Christian basis, the need for state in-
> tervention in the social sphere would disappear. In countries where
> the Church was a minority, Catholics hesitated to give such power to
> the secular state and hoped instead for the development of au-
> tonomous groups by organization from below.[3]

This notion of organization from below or, to use the terminology of Pius
XI, "subsidiarity," would form an important component of the Catholic New
Deal. Subsidiarity was the idea, as sociologist Andrew Greeley wrote, that a
democratic and moral society required "the maximization of participation in
decision making in every sector of society." Catholics should participate directly in shaping the kind of society that would serve the common good. If
Catholic activists perceived that particular New Deal policies circumvented
input by ordinary citizens, then they would express opposition to those programs. In this manner, reformist Catholic clergy and laity in the 1930s created their own definition of what it meant to be American citizens, as well

as to be members of a religious minority that had moved to the center of the nation's political debates. They would abandon neither their Catholicism nor their notion of what constituted social justice to appease critics.[4]

Being born in a small Michigan town and coming from a working-class Protestant background, I came to Pittsburgh in 1984 with great anticipation. I fell in love with the city and admired her sturdy, fascinating people. Even though the last of the great steel mills were closing as I entered graduate school, Pittsburghers were not defeated. I will always retain an abiding affection for the city and its good-natured shot-and-a-beer people.

While in graduate school I made two friends who have greatly influenced my thinking—Kevin Dunphy and Curt Miner. Kevin, whose grandmother was Mayor Richard Daley's secretary in Chicago's glory days, has provided me with research sources, ideas, and, most important of all, friendship. It took me some time to understand how Kevin could simultaneously admire Dorothy Day and William F. Buckley Jr., but Catholic social thought defies secular ideological boundaries. It is too bad Kevin decided to become a lawyer—the historical profession could use more quirky thinkers.

Curt Miner, my best friend and sounding board, has produced wonderful studies on Pennsylvania labor, religion, and cultural values. His museum exhibitions on Homestead and Johnstown, Pennsylvania, have been informative and entertaining. Curt's exhibition scripts, articles, and his film on the 1937 steel strike in Johnstown have broken new, important ground. His influence on this book is enormous. I expect his work at the Pennsylvania Museum Commission will be outstanding.

The following individuals and institutions merit my great thanks: Denise Conklin and the Penn State Archives, Father Edward McSweeney and Burris Esplen of the Diocese of Pittsburgh Archives, the staffers at the Archives of an Industrial Society at Pitt, the Carnegie Library of Pittsburgh (Oakland), and the Ohio Historical Society. My editors and peer reviewers at the *Pennsylvania Magazine of History and Biography* and Penn State Press were also immensely helpful. I must thank several other individuals for providing various insights and much to think about: Thomas Blantz, Andy Dowdle, John Faulkner, Ed Fitzgibbon, Fred Hetzel, Lon Hamby, Bill Hixson, Dan Ingram, Larry Kerr, Helen Killoran, Dennis Lupher, Steve Miner, Peter Potter, John Reiger, Kyle Sinisi, Ken Waltzer, Bob Whealey, Paul Yuckman, and John Zimmerman. Finally, I thank Theresa Heineman for reading my manuscript drafts, distracting our little girls so that I could work, and being an all around good sport.

# Advent

In the eighteenth century, George Washington came to the confluence of the Allegheny, Monongahela, and Ohio rivers to wrest control of America's western gateway from the French. Several decades later, Thomas Mellon and Andrew Carnegie struggled to make Pittsburgh more than a strategic outpost on the edge of the wilderness. The financier and the iron maker envisioned Pittsburgh as the hub of a vast industrial empire. Connected by navigable rivers and the Pennsylvania Railroad, their empire extended from Johnstown to Youngstown (Ohio). Amid the hills of Western Pennsylvania, nineteenth-century entrepreneurs built America's industrial heartland. In the mill towns of Duquesne, Pennsylvania, Steubenville, Ohio, and Weirton, West Virginia, the cultural outlines of twentieth-century America came into focus. The Protestant Republicans who built Pittsburgh could not have foreseen that their city would become a hotbed of Democratic politics, industrial unionism, and Catholic social activism.[1]

Entrepreneurial vision and seemingly unlimited natural resources conspired to make the twentieth century the American Century. In 1890, the United States emerged as the leading industrial power on the earth. Western Pennsylvania made that achievement possible. In 1900, Pittsburgh manufactured 64 percent of America's structural steel and 26 percent of its steel rails. Between Connellsville and Greensburg could be found thirty thousand beehive coke ovens, the greatest collection of such equipment on the planet. The beehive ovens, supplied by nine hundred mines in the area, processed coal into coking fuel for the steel mills. Upon such abundance, Bethlehem Steel, Carnegie Steel, Jones & Laughlin, Republic, and Youngstown Sheet and Tube built immense, profitable mills. When Carnegie sold his interests to New York banker J. P. Morgan in 1901, the new U.S. Steel Corporation became

America's grandest enterprise. By 1910, thanks in large measure to the steel corporations, Pittsburgh was the nation's chief industrial center.[2]

Continuing Carnegie's practice of securing raw materials and transportation routes, U.S. Steel acquired 20,000 acres of ore in the Mesabi iron range of Minnesota and 113,000 acres of coal fields in Pennsylvania, West Virginia, and Ohio. U.S. Steel also bought fifty-three ships to carry its ore on the Great Lakes, built 1,100 miles of railroad line, and erected seven hundred mills. By 1904, the corporate behemoth produced 65 percent of the nation's steel. Meanwhile, Bethlehem Steel, the chief rival to U.S. Steel, made Johnstown its greatest center, producing two million gross tons of steel in 1922. During World War II, the Pittsburgh District, excluding Johnstown, manufactured more steel than the Axis Powers combined. If one sought to locate President Franklin Roosevelt's "arsenal of democracy," then one had to look no further than the banks of the Allegheny and Monongahela rivers.[3]

As Carnegie built an empire of coal and steel, George Westinghouse erected an impressive string of factories in the region. The Westinghouse Electrical and Manufacturing Company, along with its New York rival, General Electric, made 90 percent of America's electrical equipment. In 1920, Westinghouse established the first commercial radio station in the United States, KDKA Pittsburgh. But of all the region's business titans, none could compare in stature to Thomas Mellon's ambitious son, Andrew. With the assets of the Mellon National Bank & Trust to draw upon, Andrew Mellon directed the Pittsburgh-based Aluminum Corporation of America (ALCOA) and Gulf Oil. ALCOA possessed a global monopoly on the production of aluminum. Additionally, Mellon exercised control over Westinghouse, the Chicago-based Pullman Sleeping Car Company, Pan American Airways, and the Pennsylvania Railroad. In all, Andrew Mellon owned oil fields in Venezuela, an aluminum die-casting corporation in Germany, and the street rail cars of Youngstown. Gulf Oil alone in the 1920s had assets of $744 million.[4]

Not content merely to be a multibillionaire, Andrew Mellon served as treasury secretary in the administrations of Warren Harding, Calvin Coolidge, and Herbert Hoover. Republicans credited Mellon's income and corporate tax reductions with stimulating capital investment and productivity. Mellon's policies did not, however, promote general prosperity. Between 1923 and 1929, the income share of the top 1 percent of the population increased by 6 percent while the bottom 93 percent of Americans saw their portion of the wealth decline 4 percent. At the height of the Mellon boom, 60 percent of the American people lived near or below the level of subsistence. In 1932, with the collapse of capitalism around the world, the Left depicted the Republicans as selfish men who did not pay their fair share of taxes. Worse, Republican industrialists paid low wages and destroyed labor unions. Businessmen such as Mellon, the Left charged, deprived workers of a decent living standard.[5]

Andrew Mellon's tribe, flinty Scotch-Irish men and women from Ulster, built immense fortunes in nineteenth-century Pittsburgh. Other clansmen disappeared into the Appalachian mountains; they occasionally appeared in the history books as colorful, marginal figures. To the frugal and industrious Scotch-Irish, poverty and unemployment were the result of individual sin and laziness. The local, state, and national government must not aid the unworthy poor. Conversely, wealth was a sign of God's approval. God wanted the Scotch-Irish to be fruitful. That meant building immense steel fabricating complexes, electrical works, and coking operations. Confronted with a shortage of inexpensive, pliable workers, industrialists looked to Southern and Eastern Europe. In a fifty-year period, Pittsburgh's population grew threefold, from 235,000 in 1880 to 670,000 by 1930. The great majority of this increase was due to immigration. In 1890, two-thirds of Pittsburgh's population was made up of foreigners and their children.[6]

In the first two decades of the twentieth century, fourteen million immigrants came to the United States. Eighty percent were Jews and Italian and Slavic Catholics. Most Russian Orthodox and Roman Catholics clustered in the urban-industrial states of Connecticut, Massachusetts, New Jersey, New York, and Pennsylvania. Thanks to the influx of Serbians and Ukrainians, the Pittsburgh District became the American center of the Russian Orthodox Church. The city also served as the overseas capitals of Croatia and Slovakia. Moreover, Pittsburgh ranked third, after New York and Chicago, in the number of foreign-language publications printed in America and had the highest circulation Slovak newspaper.[7]

The American Catholic Church was the chief beneficiary of early twentieth-century immigration. A despised religious minority, Catholics had gone from 3 percent of the population in pre–Civil War America to 18 percent by the 1920s. From the Gilded Age to the onset of the Great Depression, the Church established 2,626 new parishes. By 1940, with twenty-one million adherents, the American Church had founded 7,597 parochial schools which educated two million children. Brooklyn, Philadelphia, and Pittsburgh led the Church in the construction of parochial schools. Catering to 662,000 Catholics, the Pittsburgh Diocese in 1940 was the seventh largest in America. Its 366 parishes served a much more ethnically diverse collection of people than was the case for Boston, Hartford, and New York. Back east, Catholics were predominately of Irish, Italian, and Polish ancestry. In America's industrial core, Catholics were of Croatian, German, Hungarian, Irish, Italian, Polish, Slovakian, and Slovenian extraction. Only Chicago, the leading diocese in the American Church, had a comparably diverse mix of Roman Catholics.[8]

Of America's twenty-one thousand priests and one hundred bishops in 1921, most had humble origins. According to a survey of the Hartford Diocese, 48 percent of its seminarians were working class and 21 percent came from lower-middle-class families. Fewer than 2 percent of the young men had fathers in the professions. This was not a surprising development. In America, although the federal government did not sanction religious discrimination, most corporations would not knowingly employ Catholics and Jews in managerial positions. Many private and public universities and colleges similarly barred Catholics or imposed severe admissions quotas directed against religious minorities. Given the limited professional options available to ambitious Catholics prior to World War II, young men and women chose careers in the Church, law, and teaching. In actual practice, Catholic lawyers, trained at Catholic educational institutions, worked for their co-religionists. Similarly, since the Protestant-directed public schools often would not hire Catholics, lay teachers went to work in the parochial school system.[9]

America's Catholic laity was, like the clergy, overwhelmingly working class. As Catholics and Eastern European Jews entered the ranks of the urban working class, many Protestants moved up socially. In late nineteenth-century Pittsburgh, class and religious divisions overlapped nearly perfectly. Sixty percent of Pittsburgh's Protestants were businessmen and white-collar professionals. Less than 10 percent were working class. The class division between Catholics and Protestants, though greater in the industrial heartland than for the nation at large, was significant. By World War II, 55 percent of Catholics belonged to the working class. Just 9 percent enjoyed an upper-class lifestyle. Episcopalians and Presbyterians, in contrast, had the lowest representation in the ranks of the working class and the highest representation in the upper class. Americans who belonged to less affluent Protestant denominations, the Methodist and Baptist churches, usually came from rural and small-town backgrounds. They did not enter the steel mills and automobile factories in as high a proportion as Catholics. Only southern Protestants, a number of whom were black migrants to the northern cities, could match Catholic poverty rates.[10]

White Protestants who left their failed family farms for jobs in Detroit and Youngstown prospered no more than Catholics. However, they did not welcome the prospect of working with "foreigners." Thousands of them joined the anti-Catholic Ku Klux Klan in the 1920s. Religious tensions hindered efforts to form class-based labor unions prior to the Great Depression. Good intentions notwithstanding, the handful of Protestant clergy who concerned themselves with the material and spiritual lives of American workers were unsuccessful in reforming the economic order. Most Protestant clergymen and their middle-class flocks were hostile toward labor unions. Even in the ranks of less affluent Protestants, their suspicion of collective, as opposed to individual, action, and ingrained anti-Catholic religious beliefs, led them to reject the Social Gospel. God and social reform did not mix. Although the decade of the 1930s witnessed an explosion in labor organizing, Protestants tended to shun unions. Just one-third of working-class Baptists and Methodists joined a union. At the same time, 51 percent of working-class Catholics and 85 percent of blue-collar Jews enlisted in the labor movement.[11]

The Great Depression, in its unprecedented scope and duration, promoted Catholic labor and political mobilization. Within three years of the Wall Street Crash of 1929, fifteen million Americans, a quarter of the nation's work force, were unemployed. Bank failures numbered in the thousands until, in 1933, the financial structure of America collapsed. With the consumer demand for Detroit automobiles evaporating, the steel industry lost its largest client. Consequently, the steel industry was operating at a little more than one-tenth of its capacity and 40 percent of Pittsburgh's workers lost their jobs. Disaster also hit the electrical industry once automobile and steel companies reduced their equipment orders and financially strapped consumers chose not to buy new refrigerators. Westinghouse, which in 1929 employed nearly fifty thousand people, had thirty thousand working for it in 1933. Moreover, Westinghouse workers who had been making an average of $1,767 in 1929, had seen their wages slashed 32 percent in four years. They were fortunate. U.S. Steel imposed 60 percent wage reductions.[12]

Confronted with an economy that seemed to worsen rather than improve, the Democrats in 1933 launched a variety of federal programs to increase workers' income and thereby stimulate consumer spending. In 1929, the federal government had spent $21 billion, or 10 percent of America's Gross National Product (GNP). Such expenditures went to defense and other limited public endeavors. Eleven years later, thanks to President Roosevelt, the United States government was spending $40 billion a year, or 18 percent of the nation's GNP. Most of these funds went to support federal welfare and entitlement programs: Social Security and the Works Progress Administration (WPA), to list just two. Democratic reformers also placed the authority of the federal government behind the new industrial unions. The Democrats became the party of government; a government that extended itself into more areas of everyday life and demanded greater portions of the nation's income to give to favored constituencies. Ideological divisions that appeared in the 1930s over the role of the federal government in the regulation of industry, the imposition of greater taxes, and the expansion of programs designed to redistribute America's wealth, became deeper after the Great Depression.[13]

All of this is not to say that there were not serious problems in America even before the Great Depression. Prior to World War I, a group of social workers and economists, with a grant from the Russell Sage Foundation, compiled the first comprehensive study of an American city. The Sage Foundation's six-volume *Pittsburgh Survey* revealed that a seventy-two-hour work week was the norm in the steel industry. Additionally, 40 percent of the region's industrial fatalities occurred in the steel mills, while most workers did not make enough wages to support their families, forcing their children to leave school and seek employment. Andrew Carnegie's decision to break the iron worker's union at his Homestead, Pennsylvania, mill just outside Pittsburgh in 1892 had set a pattern for the entire industry. The steel barons paid low wages, demanded long hours, banned unions, and refused to improve the safety of the shop floor. Steel workers saw their skin burned by the blast furnaces, suffered various lung afflictions due to the iron particles floating in the air, and experienced some loss of hearing given the noise level of the mills. If one managed to avoid serious injury and reached an age when hard physical labor was no longer possible, then the worker could look forward to a bleak retirement. There were no pensions to draw upon and personal savings were often nonexistent, or quickly exhausted, since the bulk of the workers' income went to pay for shelter, food, and clothing. A society in which the majority of the people lived in virtual poverty was not one that bought automobiles and other high-ticket consumer goods on a great enough basis to sustain economic growth.[14]

It was the industrial worker, dependent upon meager wages for sustenance, who bore the brunt of the Great Depression. Most of those workers were Catholics, many of them the children or grandchildren of immigrants. The first generation of Slavic immigrants did not tend to join unions, become naturalized citizens, learn English, or vote. Their American-born children were not radicals. Each wanted a job, a home, and children. Unfortunately, the second generation came of age at a time when there were few or no jobs to be had. Frustrated, the young Slavic and Jewish workers became a considerable voting bloc. From 1920 to 1936, the American electorate increased 40 percent. The second generation accounted for almost all of that expansion. By 1940, the nation's twelve largest Catholic and Jewish cities provided nearly enough votes to elect the president. Having never voted before, the political loyalties of the second generation were up for grabs. The Democrats seized

their opportunity, offering a New Deal for the worker. Subsequently, the Democratic vote rose from nine million in 1920 to twenty-eight million in 1936.
Since Roosevelt never won the majority of middle and upper-class Protestant votes, working-class Catholics and Jews became the backbone of the
New Deal.[15]

In Allegheny County, the electorate increased 120 percent between 1924
and 1936. David Lawrence, the Irish boss of Pittsburgh's minuscule Democratic Party, saw an opportunity to forge a new coalition. In contrast to the
Irish political machines in Boston, New Haven, and New York, the Catholic
Democrats in Chicago, Cleveland, and Pittsburgh reached out to blacks, Italians, Jews, and Slavs. Having never held political power, and representing
working-class constituencies, Lawrence and his fellows stood in stark contrast to their East Coast counterparts. The Boston Irish had been in power
at the local level since the beginning of the twentieth century and claimed
many lower- and middle-class kinsmen. Such politicians did not support industrial unions and jealously kept the city government out of the hands of
Italians and Jews.[16]

Lawrence and the Irish Catholics of the heartland, confronting powerful
corporate interests, saw no advantage to the Boston and New York approach.
Making his machine open to all of society's marginal groups, Lawrence oversaw a political revolution. The 1924 Democratic presidential candidate in
Allegheny County had received 9 percent of the 225,000 votes cast. Twelve
years later, Roosevelt won 70 percent of the 562,000 votes cast. Lawrence's
power grew apace. In 1944, the Irish boss helped to deliver the Democratic
vice presidential nomination to Senator Harry Truman of Missouri. Convinced that Vice President Henry Wallace leaned too far to the Left, Lawrence
persuaded labor leader Philip Murray to abandon the incumbent. As a fellow Catholic and Pittsburgher, Murray went along with Lawrence.[17]

Many contemporary observers, and subsequent scholars as well, have
tended either to dismiss or distort the significant role American Catholicism
played in promoting the New Deal and building the industrial union movement. Indeed, a number of labor historians have criticized the anti-Communist priests who supported the 1930s union movement. According to
them, Catholic priests undermined the political power of American workers by purging their ranks of Communists. Moreover, as the labor historians contend, workers could not have formed successful industrial unions
without first severing their ties to their religious and ethnic communities.
To these scholars, workers' religious and cultural associations interfered
with the development of class consciousness and, therefore, stymied labor
organization.[18]

Other academics have depicted Catholic clergy and laity as foes of reform and as catalysts of America's anti-Communist foreign policy after World War II. Typically, they have argued that American Catholic anti-Communism in the 1930s "intertwined" with anti-Semitism. Additionally, the revisionist historians of the Cold War have asserted that anti-Communist political activism was the way by which Catholics proved "their American identity." In the same vein, one revisionist concluded that anti-Communism secured Catholics' place in American society: "A minority that had been subjected to a century of bigotry in Protestant America thus took out final citizenship papers." Even the otherwise sympathetic historian David O'Brien noted that in the 1930s "anti-Communism provided a device which could ease Catholic insecurity and allow for simultaneous assertion of loyalty to Church and nation."[19]

Contemporary actors were no less concerned with the political attitudes of American Catholics. Secretary of Interior Harold Ickes resented the Church's opposition to Joseph Stalin and its support of the Spanish fascist leader Francisco Franco. He also did not appreciate Catholics who argued that some New Deal programs dangerously enhanced federal power. At various points in 1939, Ickes observed that "the Roman Catholic Church has given its sympathy to the dictatorships because it feared Communism," while Pope Pius XII had undermined the Soviet Union's Popular Front against Hitler. In 1938, he accused the Catholic Church of pressuring Roosevelt to appoint former Michigan governor Frank Murphy to the Supreme Court: "It seems that the Catholics are after this appointment. They are not entitled to it, but the Roman Church is after all it can get." Ickes in 1937 recounted a conversation with the Episcopalian mayor of New York, Fiorello La Guardia, who observed that criticism of liberal child labor legislation by several Catholic bishops reminded him of "the Spanish Inquisition."[20]

The interior secretary and the New York mayor were not alone in castigating the American Catholic Church. Socialists and Communists, who viewed the Church as their chief rival for the affections of American workers, denounced Catholicism. In 1938, Socialist Party leader Norman Thomas, a former Protestant minister, accused Catholic bishops of "clandestinely or openly" working "for the fascist cause" in Europe and America. David Saposs, a socialist and member of Roosevelt's National Labor Relations Board, had contended in 1933 that the Catholic Church was "shaping the thought and aspirations of . . . the American labor movement," which is "why it has become more and more reactionary." Richard Rovere, a reporter for *The Nation,* was no less hostile. In 1941, Rovere argued that the Catholic Church was Machiavellian and implicitly un-American:

Catholics, like Communists, are often controlled by forces beyond the vision of most Americans; Rome, like Moscow, has its own interests, and although its political control over its followers is less absolute than Moscow's, it is always difficult to tell which way it plans to jump, particularly in the midst of a world in crisis. Moreover, the approach of both Catholics and Communists to the labor movement is millennial. While most labor leaders look to the here and now or to a plainly visible future in determining strategy, Catholics and Communist look to goals far in the distance, and the ends of both are so grandiose that almost any means seem justified for their attainment.[21]

On a superficial level, Rovere was correct. Many activist Catholic clergy in the 1930s were visionaries who influenced their parishioners politically. Such priests were crucial to mobilizing Catholics on behalf of social reform. New Dealers dared not ignore the Catholic Church. Additionally, the Catholic press, which in 1936 consisted of 134 newspapers and 198 magazines with a combined circulation of seven million, backed many of Roosevelt's economic programs, including the creation of Social Security. At the same time, publications such as the *Catholic Sentinel* (Portland, Oregon) and the *Catholic Telegraph-Register* (Cincinnati) castigated anti-Franco New Dealers and criticized some liberal initiatives—notably, the prohibition of child labor.[22]

Ickes, La Guardia, and the Left decried Catholic political clout but recognized that without it the New Deal, as well as their government jobs, would be jeopardized. They wanted Catholic votes, not Catholic leadership. In part, this explained their distaste for Catholic political activism. It was the strident denunciations of the New Deal and "international Jewry" by Michigan priest and radio personality Charles Coughlin, plus Franco's marriage of convenience with Nazi Germany, which enabled critics to disparage Catholicism.[23]

In reality, Coughlin's following, which was greatest among the Irish of Boston and New York, declined after 1936 when he became anti-Semitic and unreasonably critical of the New Deal. Moreover, many liberals failed to understand that a significant wing of the American Catholic Church was simultaneously anti-Communist and antifascist, as well as extremely critical of laissez-faire capitalism. Reformist clergy, largely to be found in the Slavic cities of Chicago, Cleveland, Toledo, Pittsburgh, and Youngstown, were imbued with the spirit of the papal encyclicals. In particular, they were inspired by Leo XIII's encyclical, *The Condition of Labor* (1891), and two written by Pius XI, *(After Forty Years) Reconstructing the Social Order* (1931) and *Atheistic Communism* (1937). Such clergy activists sought a political role in the 1930s. Having attained a position of influence within the Democratic Party and organized labor, the Catholic reformers fought Communist unionists and sought to build "a just and moral society" that would provide *all* citizens with economic security.[24]

There were members of the American Catholic Church hierarchy who were hostile toward the New Deal and viewed all reform efforts as Communist-inspired. Boston's William Cardinal O'Connor criticized New Dealers and ordered diocesan clergy not to promote lay instruction on *The Condition of Labor* and *Reconstructing the Social Order*. Father Robert Gannon, the president of Fordham University in New York, was no less suspicious of social reform. However, the majority of America's Catholic clergy, according to scholars Monroe Billington and Cal Clark, endorsed most of the New Deal's economic agenda. The Catholic Church of the industrial heartland was attuned to the material and spiritual needs of its working-class parishioners. Bishops Karl Alter (Toledo), Hugh Boyle (Pittsburgh), and Joseph Schrembs (Cleveland) placed their moral authority behind social reform and labor organizing. As members of the Administrative Council of the Washington-based National Catholic Welfare Conference, the bishops fought for the soul of the American Church. The bishops, and many of their clergy and laity, were determined to reconstruct the American social order. Without their efforts, there would have been no successful union for steel workers.[25]

# 1

# Pilgrimage

## Father James Cox and the Awakening of Catholic Social Activism, 1932

Father James Cox of Pittsburgh leads Catholic clergy and laity
into a new era of social activism and political mobilization.
Cox's march on Washington in 1932, and his subsequent
campaign for the presidency, galvanizes the unemployed of
Pennsylvania. President Herbert Hoover and the Republican
Party, having neglected the needs of working-class Catholics,
and having failed to deal adequately with the crisis of the
Great Depression, are on their way to electoral defeat in 1932.

As the Great Depression entered its third year, Pittsburgh residents marveled
at the pristine skies above their city. When the steel mills and coke ovens had
been operating at full capacity, the city's fathers turned on the street lamps
at noon so downtown office workers could find their way to diner and curb-
side vendor. Meanwhile, the white-collar employees of Mellon National Bank
& Trust used their lunch break to change soot-filled clothes. Pittsburgh was
known throughout the land as a three-shirt-a-day city and office workers
rarely left home without at least one change of clothing. However, life in
Pittsburgh had drastically changed since the 1929 stock market crash. Now
that the American steel industry was operating at 12 percent of capacity,
and 31 percent of white and 48 percent of black Pittsburghers were unemployed, the glorious days of full employment and foul air had become mock-
ing memories.[1]

Even though U.S. Steel had taken the lead in reducing wages, slashing workers' paychecks by 60 percent, chief executive officer Myron Taylor contended that blame for mounting economic hardship and social unrest could be pinned upon spendthrift workers and foreign-born radicals. Certainly there was no shortage of radicals in the region, foreign or otherwise, but spendthrifts were an endangered species. Gambling and illegal liquor trafficking in Pittsburgh, once the wide-open avenues of upward social mobility for many an immigrant's son, had become less accessible and more hazardous. The three Volpe brothers discovered this in the summer of 1932 when gun-toting rivals splattered the entrepreneurs from city hall to the county court-house.[2]

In Arnold City, near Uniontown, Pennsylvania, the Mellon-owned Pittsburgh Coal Company brought in scabs and sheriff's deputies to break a miners' strike. Deputies killed Michael Philipovich, a store owner who had turned his shop into a relief center for the Communist-organized National Miners' Union. He left behind a widow and five children. As Arnold City exploded, Milan Reshetar, a former Jones & Laughlin steel worker in Aliquippa, died of the tuberculosis he had contracted in the Allegheny County Workhouse. Reshetar had been serving a five-year sentence for distributing pro-labor union literature at the Jones & Laughlin mill. Pittsburgh police officials were just as concerned with radicalism, raiding the Ukrainian Hall on the city's South Side in November 1931. Police arrested six people who were attending a meeting of the Communist Party's Unemployed Council. Two months later, Pittsburgh police gunned down an unarmed man who had stolen a loaf of bread.[3]

And so it went. Braddock's U.S. Steel plant had once employed seven thousand workers. Now just five hundred were on the job; the bulk working two days out of every week. In a city where two-thirds of those remaining employed worked part time, Ray Webb seemed to be a fortunate young man with some measure of job security at Pittsburgh's Jones & Laughlin mill. That was true enough until his crane touched a 6,600 volt wire. The executive board of the International Brotherhood of Teamsters and Chauffeurs in November 1931 expelled the members of the Pittsburgh Taxi Drivers Union. Pittsburgh's cabbies, their desperate strike entering its sixth bloody month, had to choose between paying their union dues or feeding their families.[4]

By the spring of 1932, bankers and realtors evicted families who had fallen behind on their mortgage and rent payments. In the columns of the diocesan newspaper, the *Pittsburgh Catholic*, the editors angrily reported the story of three parochial school children who came home for lunch and found themselves locked out in the rain. The bank that held the property had evicted their parents and sold off all of their furniture and clothes. Not everyone, however, was experiencing hard times. Distributors of kerosene saw their sales increase by 700 percent in 1931. As Duquesne Light and Equitable Gas turned off Pittsburghers' utilities for nonpayment, citizens began relying upon kerosene for heat and light. The question *Harper's* had asked in 1930 was even more urgent by 1932: "Is Pittsburgh Civilized?"[5]

Andrew Mellon, patriarch of the Pittsburgh banking family and the U.S. Secretary of the Treasury, found himself torn between his distaste of Herbert Hoover and his party loyalty that compelled him to support the president. Consequently, Mellon issued frequent statements to the press emphasizing that Hoover was securing economic recovery. His credibility with the public evaporating with every bank failure and layoff, Mellon did himself no favors by declaring that if businessmen expected to survive, then they would have to reduce operating costs: "Liquidate labor, liquidate stocks, liquidate the farmers, liquidate real estate." If Mellon sounded like a capitalist Joseph Stalin, on the personal level he felt a sense of responsibility to his community. With brother Richard and Pittsburgh pickle prince Howard Heinz, Andrew Mellon raised one million dollars for city improvements. They intended to provide jobs to unemployed construction workers. Unfortunately, those funds quickly ran out and the additional $3 million he spent to build the East Liberty Presbyterian Church had little impact on the local economy. Worse, the church acquired a bitter nickname, "The Mellon Fire Escape."[6]

As businessmen slashed wages, production, working hours, and, eventually, contributions to charities, state government proved no more effective than Washington in responding to the social crisis. Gifford Pinchot, the independent Republican governor and former confidant of Theodore Roosevelt, failed to deal with the unprecedented public relief load. By the winter of 1932 and into the spring of 1933, over one million Pennsylvanians were jobless. Allegheny County accounted for 16 percent of Pennsylvania's unemployed and claimed nearly sixty-two thousand families who were dependent upon state assistance for food, clothing, and shelter. Unable to convince Mellon to extend a personal loan of $35 million to the Pennsylvania treasury, and failing to persuade the conservative legislature to raise income and corporate taxes, Pinchot advocated the imposition of higher sales taxes on groceries, gasoline, and tobacco to fund state relief efforts. It was not a popular strategy with strapped middle-class consumers.[7]

With the inability, or unwillingness, of corporation executives and politicians to alleviate suffering and provide inspirational leadership, Catholic clergy filled the void. At St. Ann's Church in Pittsburgh, the parish, watching as businesses reduced labor costs by firing men and hiring women at half the standard wage, founded a nursery for working wives. St. Ann's also ex-

Fig. 1.   Andrew Mellon, Pittsburgh industrialist and secretary of the treasury under three Republican presidents (1921–1932). His business empire included ALCOA, Gulf Oil, and Mellon National Bank & Trust. (Courtesy of the Carnegie Library, Pittsburgh.)

tended shelter and food to homeless women since the city's flophouses were intended only for men, and welcomed expectant mothers when city hospitals declined to accept charity cases. In the nearby mill town of Carnegie, Father Ercole Dominicis of the Holy Souls Church established a free barber shop and a soup kitchen. An Italian immigrant who had came to America in 1912, Father Dominicis had known grinding poverty on two continents. His soup kitchen, which opened in February 1932, served more than three thousand meals weekly in its sixteen-month operation.[8]

When the battered remnants of the "Bonus Army" passed through Pennsylvania, Dominicis fed the wretched World War I veterans. The former soldiers and their families had marched on Washington demanding early payment of their federal military service bonuses. President Hoover drove the unemployed veterans from the city at gun point. Dominicis, who, unlike Hoover, had served in the military, gave comfort to the scorned patriots. It was clergy such as Dominicis who led the journalist Lorena Hickok, in a 1933 fact-finding tour of Pennsylvania, to report confidentially to Washington Democrats that "the Catholic priests in some of these towns represent almost the last bulwark against riot and disorder among the unemployed."[9]

Before journalists became aware of the pivotal role Catholic clergy played in providing sustenance and hope to the unemployed, Father James Cox was preparing Herbert Hoover's excommunication from national politics. Born in 1886 in the Lawrenceville neighborhood of Pittsburgh, Cox grew up in a city experiencing rapid industrialization and a consequent influx of immigrants. In Cox's Lawrenceville, Irish Catholics could chart the advance of Polish settlement by the appearance of specially displayed lawn statues of the Madonna. To their consternation, the immigrants placed their Madonnas in up-ended claw-foot bathtubs.[10]

Raised in a working-class environment that stressed the virtues of faith and hard work, Cox found employment as a steel worker and taxi cab agent. He worked his way through Holy Ghost College (Duquesne University) and then attended the diocese's seminary school, St. Vincent's, in Latrobe. Ordained in 1911, Cox found himself in 1917 assigned to a hospital on the Western Front. Never one to permit himself to enjoy the comforts of rank, the priest shared in all of the hardships that American soldiers endured. By the end of his military tour in 1919, Father Cox had acquired severe bursitis and chronic pharynigitis. For the want of a dry place to sleep, sore joints and throat ailments would constantly remind him of peoples' need for good shelter.[11]

Returning to the Iron City, Father Cox earned a master's degree in economics from the University of Pittsburgh and received an appointment as pastor to Old St. Patrick's Church. Located between downtown and Lawrenceville in the produce market area known as the Strip District, Old St. Patrick's was in its third incarnation. The original structure had been completed in 1811, making St. Patrick's the oldest Catholic parish in the city. Burned to the ground in 1854 at the height of nativist riots directed against the Catholic minority, the second St. Patrick's succumbed to the expansionist whims of the Pennsylvania Railroad a decade later. The church that Cox inherited in 1923 was a walled fortress built in 1865 and nestled amid gritty warehouses and factories. Butchers and bakers, saloon keepers and prostitutes jostled for trade as respectable Irish Catholics moved to the middle-class Sacred Heart parish three miles across town. With just eighteen families attending Mass at Old St. Patrick's, Cox set out to raise membership by sponsoring plays and boxing matches in the diocese's poorest parish. Within a few years, the congenial priest performed Mass to ever larger crowds.[12]

When the Great Depression hit Pittsburgh, Cox established a soup kitchen. Between 1930 and 1934, with donated produce from the Strip District grocers, Cox served two million meals. He left nothing to chance, issuing appeals for food on the radio when not knocking on the doors of restaurants and bakeries. An inventive man, Cox worked out an arrangement with the Acme Coal and Coke Company. For every twenty tons of coal that Acme sold to the parish (at a reduced rate), one ton would be donated to the St. Patrick's Relief Fund. In this way, Cox distributed 2,120 tons of coal to the needy. The parish also collected wooden packing crates in order to construct housing for 250 men on the church grounds. By acclamation, Father Cox became the mayor of Shantytown, Pennsylvania.[13]

The mayor of Shantytown leapt into union organizing, helping the striking taxi cab drivers keep body and soul together in a labor war that killed one person and wounded 175 others. Cox realized that in a region where unions had either fallen apart or remained quiescent since the wrenching 1919 steel strike, other institutions would have to bear the responsibility for promoting workers' rights. Toward that end, Father Cox served as a vice chair of the Pennsylvania Civil Liberties Committee. Joining Cox on the state and city committees were B. J. Hovde, a Pitt professor, and Harvey O'Connor, the Pittsburgh correspondent of the *Federated Press*, a general labor news service. The Civil Liberties Committee took up the cause of a labor organizer in Stroudsburg who had been imprisoned on the charge of conspiring to organize a strike. Cox and Hovde also challenged the decision of Pitt chancellor John Bowman to ban the school's Socialist Club and to put a muzzle on faculty activists. The committee further urged the city government to

Fig. 2. Father James Cox feeds the unemployed in "Shantytown" Pittsburgh during the early years of the Great Depression. In 1932, he led what was then the largest protest march on Washington in American history. (Courtesy of the Archives of an Industrial Society, University of Pittsburgh.)

desist from breaking up meetings of the Communist Unemployed Councils, contending that the police were acting in a lawless manner that discredited American democracy.[14]

It was the activities of the Communist Party's Unemployed Councils that particularly caught Cox's attention. Established in 1929 under the auspices of the Communist Party's Trade Union Unity League, the Unemployed Councils organized demonstrations against rapacious landlords and indifferent politicians who were unwilling to increase public welfare expenditures. Beginning in 1930, the Unemployed Councils staged protests in Baltimore, Boston, Chicago, and Pittsburgh. Each successive wave of demonstrations became more violent, with the first fatality occurring after a clash with New

York City police in January 1930. Two years later, Dearborn, Michigan, police officers and the private security forces of the Ford Motor Company killed four more demonstrators.[15]

In 1931, the Unemployed Councils welcomed a new leader: Herbert Benjamin, a Lithuanian-Jewish immigrant. Benjamin soon organized a hunger march on Washington. The Communists planned to "fight for the streets." Unfortunately for Benjamin, the Communist Hunger March of December 1931 attracted just 1,600 participants who, as the conservative *Washington Star* angrily reported, sang "The Internationale, the hymn of Red Russia." The Unemployed Councils won few working-class converts to their cause.[16]

Although supporting the right of Communists to assemble and speak without police interference, Father Cox repudiated the movement's atheism and its subordination to the foreign policy objectives of the Soviet Union. He also believed that the Communists—intentionally or not—provoked violent confrontations with corporate security personnel and municipal police departments. In turn, the American Communist Party leadership denounced Cox as being part of the "national fascist tendencies lined up with Catholic religion." The Communist Party's newspaper, the *Daily Worker*, expressed great hostility toward the Catholic Church, claiming that it was "personally owned and controlled by the same class of multimillionaires who own and control American industry." In the same vein, Communist International (Comintern) functionary Otto Kuusinen urged college students not to follow the lead of Catholic priests who, he warned, were the true enemies of the working class.[17]

Alarmed by the behavior of the Communists and the Republicans, Cox decided to organize his own march on Washington. His inspiration was Social Gospel enthusiast Jacob Coxey. In 1894, the Massillon, Ohio, native led a thousand economically dispossessed followers to Washington. Coxey had called his movement "The Commonweal of Christ." Civil liberties attorney Henry Ellenbogen became an early recruit to Cox's army of the jobless. A graduate of Duquesne University, Ellenbogen was an emissary of David Lawrence, the Democratic Party chair of Allegheny County. Educated by Catholics, raised in a Jewish home, Ellenbogen moved comfortably between Hill District *shtetl* and Oakland neighborhood pub. Lawrence asked Ellenbogen to accompany Cox in case Hoover decided to have the priest arrested; a reasonable concern since President Grover Cleveland had jailed Coxey for walking on the White House lawn.[18]

Another notable pilgrim to join Cox had no roots in the city. Born in 1903, Elmer Cope was the son of a Protestant iron worker. Cope followed his father into the Amalgamated Association of Iron, Steel, and Tin Workers. Their union that had not seen good days since the 1892 Homestead strike. Cope found employment in a Warren, Ohio, steel mill, attended Ohio Wesleyan University on a football scholarship, dropped out, drove trucks for a living, and then paid his own way through Swarthmore College. At Swarthmore, Cope became a Quaker and joined the League for Industrial Democracy, a socialist organization critical of both Communism and capitalism. Desiring to become a union organizer, Cope enrolled at the Brookwood Labor College in Katonah, New York. Founded in the 1920s by United Mine Workers Union (UMW) insurgent John Brophy, railroad worker Clinton Golden, and defrocked Congregationalist minister A. J. (Abraham John) Muste, Brookwood trained a considerable number of trade unionists. Cope graduated from Brookwood in 1930, wrote for the *Federated Press*, and served as a national officer of Muste's Conference for Progressive Labor Action. In 1931, he moved to Pittsburgh and organized the Allegheny County Unemployed Citizens League, the Socialist Party's alternative to the Communist Unemployed Councils. Cope made frequent organizing trips to the mill towns of Western Pennsylvania, Ohio, and West Virginia.[19]

As Elmer Cope made his way to the Strip District on January 5, 1932, to observe the beginning of Father Cox's march on Washington, he did not expect a crowd of more than twenty-five hundred people. But the closer Cope came to Liberty and Penn Avenues, the more difficulty he had making his way through the pilgrims. A reporter for the *Pittsburgh Sun-Telegraph*, a Hearst publication that was still in its populist phase, estimated that Cox's followers numbered twenty-five thousand. The marchers came from the idled steel towns of Carnegie, McKeesport, Millvale, and beyond. Six hundred trucks and cars, as well as two brass bands, surrounded Old St. Patrick's. Many of the men were clothed in their World War I uniforms; others wore ragged overcoats and blankets. Father Casimir Orlemanski of Brackenridge marched with his ethnic Polish parishioners as the bands launched into the "Star-Spangled Banner." Given that 80 percent of the marchers were Catholic, and wishing to avoid any public perceptions of sexual impropriety, Cox had asked the unemployed women to remain at home. Although it meant separating husbands and wives for several days, he did not want Republican Protestants depicting the march as an occasion for roadside trysts. Cox was not just being prudish. Republicans in the 1928 presidential election had employed every anti-Catholic canard they could summon to smear Democratic nominee Al Smith.[20]

Cope did not know what to make of Father Cox. He wrote to a fellow socialist that "the more I witness the utter bankruptcy of the church and all organized religion during these days of tremendous suffering and injustice, so much the more am I convinced that it has outlived its usefulness, if it had any." Despite his suspicion of organized religion, Cope found himself drawn to Cox. Cope tried to maintain a critical stance toward Cox in his correspondence with Muste, describing the priest as politically unsophisticated. At the same time, Cope was greatly impressed with Cox and informed Muste that "there is little doubt that he is sincere and that he has the workers truly at heart." Cope also expressed awe at Cox's ability to create and motivate a following, something that the Conference for Progressive Labor Action had thus far failed to do in Pittsburgh.

> I went down to see the gang off thinking that only a small crowd would be there. I was completely stunned when I saw that milling mob, lining Penn Avenue for twelve solid squares, and clamoring for a way to get to Washington. When I left home I had no intention of doing more than see the gang off but the turn-out was so intriguing that I went on to Wilkinsburg, then to Johnstown, and later Harrisburg and Washington, as you know. All along the road were thousands of jobless workers walking toward Washington hoping that trucks and cars would pick them up. One group of men arrived at Blairsville, about twenty-five miles from Pittsburgh, on foot and, giving up all hope of getting rides on trucks, boarded freight trains. When this gang reached Washington two days later they had increased in number to 600 strong.[21]

Six thousand men began the trek to Washington. Every mile the procession walked or drove, more men poured in from the countryside. By early afternoon when Cox arrived in Johnstown, twenty thousand men were in line. Democratic mayor Eddie McCloskey, who had recently defeated the Bethlehem Steel candidate, effusively greeted Cox. Side by side, the Irishmen paraded through town and then held a rally in Point Stadium. As the crowd roared its approval, Mayor McCloskey denounced Bethlehem Steel's attempts to evade payment of property taxes. The city needed that money to feed unemployed steel workers and their families. Father Cox was no less critical of big business. He also condemned Hoover's Reconstruction Finance Corporation, which funneled federal revenue to banking institutions. In turn, bankers were supposed to loan the money to industrialists. Such loans would encourage businessmen to step up production and put everyone back to work.

> Our president is still trying to give money to the bankers, but none to the people. If I had my way it would go to the people, who need it badly. There is plenty of money in this country, but try and get it. I do

think that our mission to Washington will have its effect. The government sent Al Capone to jail for cheating it out of $100,000, yet John D. Rockefeller is giving $4,000,000 to his son to escape the inheritance tax.

We are going to rededicate this country to the principle that every man has a right to life, liberty, and the pursuit of happiness. We have that old Liberty Bell yet in Philadelphia and it's still ringing for us.[22]

Rested, and fed by generous residents, Cox's pilgrims continued on to Harrisburg. McCloskey and a local contingent of the unemployed entered the petitioners' ranks. Meanwhile, Henry Ellenbogen combed the state in search of more trucks and automobiles. An additional twenty thousand Pittsburghers wished to join the exodus.[23]

Reaching Huntingdon by nightfall, the ill-clad marchers were chilled to the bone by winter rain. To Cox, what happened that night in Huntingdon would have qualified as a miracle. In the region's coal patches of just a few years ago, Protestant ministers, merchants, and sheriff's deputies had maimed and murdered Catholics. Pennsylvania's 150,000 Klansmen, members of the fourth largest state organization of the Invisible Empire, were tireless in their efforts to terrorize immigrant Catholics and their children. Yet four years after the Ku Klux Klan burned crosses to protest Al Smith's presidential campaign, Protestants gave Father Cox quite a different greeting. As Cox stood in the mud and rain praying for dry shelter and coffee, Owen Poulson, the pastor of Huntingdon's Methodist Episcopal Church, appeared with the news that he and his friends would provide breakfast. Police officers opened the town's campground and courthouse to Cox while restaurant owners poured hundreds of gallons of free coffee for the multitude.[24]

The next day, more than two thousand trucks and automobiles crossed the Susquehanna River into Harrisburg. Initially, a toll-bridge officer had reduced the line to a crawl as he busily collected dimes. To Cope's great amusement, one truck load of jobless men, tired of sitting in the pouring rain, decided that this exercise of government power was a waste of time. They sped past the toll booth, cheerfully waving to the dumbfounded toll collector. The remainder of the eight-mile long caravan followed suit.[25]

In Harrisburg, Cope found even more cause for merriment. As Cox and Eddie McCloskey located a parking space downtown, Governor Pinchot made his way down the Capitol building's steps, his voice booming, "Command me! Whatever you want me to do I will do; you are the master of ceremonies." This represented quite a change for the man who hoped to defeat Mellon's candidate for senator in 1934. Just a few days ago, Pinchot had dodged Cox's request to secure food and shelter for the marchers when they reached Harrisburg. Moreover, the governor had recently lobbied against a bill to provide $10 million in direct relief to the state's unemployed, believing that his political rivals would use the money to bribe voters in the next election. Then, the legislature shot down his requests for regressive sales taxes to fund public works projects. With state government deadlocked, Pinchot had given Cox the brush off. He never expected Cox to bring more than a few hundred people through Harrisburg. Surveying the mass of registered voters crossing the Susquehanna, and reassessing his electoral prospects, Pinchot invited them to eat in the legislature's private restaurant at his expense. The governor also urged Cox to demand *federal* relief for the unemployed.[26]

Joining McCloskey at the rear of Cox's automobile, which was equipped with radio loudspeakers, Governor Pinchot assured the unemployed men that he was concerned with their plight. He also made a point of blaming the Republican machine of Philadelphia boss Joe Grundy for sabotaging his legislative program. After McCloskey and Cox hailed Pinchot as a worthy successor to Theodore Roosevelt, the pilgrims continued on their way to Washington.[27]

Night had fallen by the time Cox's army passed through the Civil War battlefield of Gettysburg. In a solemn mood, he recorded his thoughts amid the monuments and tombstones:

> It [is] a dramatic spectacle as the column [speeds] past the fields of Gettysburg in the darkness. Those monument-dotted farm lands are peopled by the specters of an army that fought to free civilization from slavery.
>
> The men in the long, tired column behind me [are] fighting a different kind of war. Theirs is a war that has only just begun—a struggle to free civilization from the curse of poverty and unemployment; a battle that will end in final victory when every man has a job that will permit him not only to exist, but to enjoy a real American standard of living.[28]

Crossing into Maryland, Cox's army finally arrived at Wisconsin Avenue, District of Columbia. Catching sight of the illuminated dome of the Capitol, the men, Cox reported, "forgot they were hungry; they forgot their clothes had not dried from the rain. They stared at [the dome] like pilgrims viewing some sacred shrine—and it was a shrine for them. It was the symbol of all they hope and believe that America should mean to its citizens." Three police inspectors and a contingent of officers escorted the men to Maryland Avenue where the United States Army had set up field kitchens. Pennsylvania senator James Davis, who had more savvy than his fellow Republicans, used his political influence to feed the men and shelter many in the District National Guard Armory. Meanwhile, the Hoover White House was in a dither.[29]

Before Father Cox had departed for Washington, Hoover's aides had been gathering information on the priest, clipping Pittsburgh newspapers even as supporters of the administration wrote letters describing Cox as "a blatherskite" and leader of "the hoodlum element." Lawrence Richey, the president's secretary, wrote an internal memorandum expressing Hoover's position in no uncertain terms: "We will not see this man. If he has a petition we will be glad to receive [it], but he cannot see the president." Once Cox arrived in Washington on January 7, another Hoover aide contacted a detective of the Metropolitan Police Force for assistance. Hoover wanted the aide to observe the "mob," ascertain if there really were any ex-servicemen with Cox, and determine if this march was merely another Communist propaganda ploy. He reported to Hoover that 20 percent of Cox's army had fought in World War I and 10 percent had served in the Spanish-American War. All of the marchers, he observed, were respectable citizens, not Communists.[30]

Confronted with what was then the largest protest march on Washington in the nation's history, with police and newspaper estimates of the milling crowds ranging from twelve thousand to twenty-five thousand, Hoover tried to hold firm in his desire to avoid a face-to-face meeting with Cox. Even if the men outside the White House gates were Catholics, and not Communists, that distinction mattered little to the president. Below him were thousands of working-class Catholics waving American flags and incongruously singing the fight song of evangelical Protestantism, "The Battle Hymn of the Republic." To the *Pittsburgh Catholic* those men represented retribution; retribution for having waged a campaign in 1928 that fanned the flames of religious hatred, as well as for having refused to appoint a Congressional Medal of Honor recipient, William Donovan, to the office of United States Attorney General. Catholics, even the few who were Republicans like Donovan, Hoover argued, could not be trusted to uphold the nation's Prohibition laws. If Hoover believed that the religious practices and the alleged criminal propensities of Catholics disqualified them from public office, then he should have not been surprised that they held him in no higher esteem.[31]

To Washington's political establishment, and to the city's Republican newspapers, which in their mounting disgust with Hoover were giving the jobless army extensive, favorable coverage, Cox issued a heart-felt plea as well as a warning:

We are not Red demonstrators. We are real honest American citizens and the people I represent here, as well as millions of others throughout the country, are entitled to work. In a country bursting with wealth there is no reason why employment and other relief should not be provided.

. . . This country is seething with revolt. The so-called representatives of the people are not helping the country. They are bound to their masters. We are going to have a change unless our people are the most supine the world as ever seen. . . .

We urge that money be appropriated to be used in direct relief of distressed families; that inheritance and other taxes on the wealthy be imposed; that large public work construction be undertaken. These are some of the things necessary to raise revenue and bring about relief.[32]

Hoover relented, agreeing to see Cox and a delegation of thirteen that included Senator Davis and Henry Ellenbogen. Cox told Hoover bluntly that "the administration was acting like an ostrich that sticks its head in the sand, believing that if he cannot see the hunter pursuing him or the trouble that is nearby, that the hunter or the trouble does not exist." Hoover expressed sympathy for the unemployed. He then read a terse statement contending that the Depression had nearly run its course and that his administration had a program in place to complete America's economic recovery. The president rejected massive federal spending on public works projects and blamed Congress for not cooperating with the White House's legislative initiatives. Hoover remained silent on the issue of providing federal assistance directly to those dependent upon exhausted state relief funds. Moreover, Hoover did not respond to the broader social concerns that Cox raised. The priest wanted the federal government to secure medical care for "undernourished and unhealthy children," construct more roads and schools, and provide affordable electrical power to the nation's rural poor. To pay for all of these federal initiatives, Cox urged Hoover to raise the taxes accessed on corporations and wealthy individuals.[33]

Although Hoover had not been overjoyed to receive Cox, Pittsburgh greeted the priest with an enthusiasm not seen since her sons had marched down the newly christened Boulevard of the Allies in 1919. With thousands of people cheering Cox and the men who made the seven-hundred-mile round-trip through rain, snow, and mud, he decided to keep applying pressure on Hoover. On January 16, Cox and Ellenbogen held a rally at the University of Pittsburgh football stadium that attracted sixty-five thousand spectators. Bundled in blankets against the biting cold, repeated rounds of singing and hand clapping quickly warmed the crowd. Ever the builder of coalitions and champion of Protestant society's outsiders, Cox had Rabbi Herman Halperin of the Orthodox Tree of Life Congregation give the invocation. If the significance behind the selection of Halperin was unclear to most Catholics, the city's Eastern European Jews, discontented with the leadership of the assimilated, German-Jewish Republicans, recognized a gesture of fellowship.[34]

Governor Pinchot, whose political ambitions had increased exponentially following Hoover's inept response to Cox's march, now aimed his sights higher than Capitol Hill. He believed Cox would endorse his clandestine efforts to wrest the Republican presidential nomination away from Hoover. After all, why should Cox not support his good friend Pinchot? In 1930, the governor had appointed Cox to the Public Utilities Investigating Committee and to the Pennsylvania Unemployment Commission. Pinchot had hoped to mute Cox's criticism of his administration by appointing the priest to powerless state offices. But then again, both men had worked together unsuccessfully to check the power of the Coal and Iron Police, an antilabor union army supported by Bethlehem Steel, Jones & Laughlin, and the Pennsylvania Railroad. To remind Cox of their shared history, Pinchot sent a telegram of personal greetings as well as a press release to be read at the rally.[35]

Father Cox dashed Pinchot's presidential ambitions, announcing that he planned to run for the White House on the Jobless Party ticket. Although Cox had no chance of winning the election, he wanted to use the campaign to compel the Republican and Democratic parties to address, rather than evade, the economic issues. Not in the mood to receive political instruction from a priest, Hoover launched a full-scale offensive against Cox. The Republican National Committee accused Cox of being a tool of Democratic operatives, as well as being an irresponsible demagogue only interested in embarrassing the president. Hoover's operatives also announced that they were trying to determine how the marchers were able to purchase such great quantities of gasoline to make the trip to Washington. The Republicans implied that either the Vatican, or Democratic supporters of Al Smith, had funded the entire operation.[36]

Hoover's well-publicized investigation of Cox backfired. He had been correct in one sense: a shadowy figure did provide assistance to the priest's caravan. Unfortunately, the figure in question was Andrew Mellon, who had quietly ordered his Gulf Oil service stations to dispense gasoline without charge. If not a fan of Father Cox, the treasury secretary was not one to follow Hoover into a political sewer. After all, the family patriarch, Thomas

Mellon, as pure a Scotch-Irish Ulster man as could have been found in Civil War–era Pittsburgh, never indulged himself in the unprofitable pursuit of Catholic baiting. Even if St. Patrick had not driven *all* of the snakes from Ireland, ranting against Catholic priests was an occupation best left to poorly bred, ignorant people. With Andrew Mellon no longer on speaking terms with the president, Hoover finally had a pretext to remove him from the Treasury Department and replace him with Ogden Mills, one of his few remaining loyalists.[37]

Pittsburgh Bishop Hugh Boyle—himself a product of working-class Pennsylvania—defended Cox, viewing his race for president as an effort to give substance to the encyclicals of Leo XIII and Pius XI. Washington pilgrim Casimir Orlemanski was more direct in his response to Hoover. The Polish priest fired off a long, blistering letter to the president, informing him that social injustice, not Father Cox, was at the root of his troubles:

> A system which can in the span of a few days add ten billions of dollars to the worth of securities on Wall Street when in the same time thousands of men are thrown out of work and the industry as a whole added not one bit to the appreciation of the values of securities, is a system which cannot long endure. . . .
>
> The wages are being cut right and left. The six-hour day has really become a twelve and sixteen hour day because not only that the working man must work for less hourly wages, but he is driven like a beast to do the work of twelve hours in six hours. This is not local but is generally practiced all over the country. Men are cringing from asserting their God-given rights from fear of losing whatever chances they might have of earning a miserable piece of bread for themselves, wives, and the poor kiddies. Dear President: they are cringing and lying low now but down deep they are inscribing indelibly this injustice for future reference. As the days go on the conditions are getting worse and worse.
>
> Now people want help from their government. *The government does not belong to the president or any legislators, it belongs to them; their good is to be the supreme good.*[38]

Although appreciative of such support, Cox could not rest; he had to contend with many other critics than just the president. Whenever Cox mentioned the Rockefellers, WJAS cut off his radio sermon broadcasts. More malicious than craven, *The World Tomorrow*, a left-wing Protestant magazine, accused Cox of having gone to Europe to meet with fascist dictators Benito Mussolini and Adolf Hitler "in an effort to familiarize himself with their technique of controlling masses of voters." A. J. Muste and *Federated Press* correspondent Harvey O'Connor believed that Cox was a fascist, given his penchant for imposing military-style discipline upon Shantytown's residents and what they perceived to be the Vatican's collaboration with Mussolini. Beyond those considerations, they also questioned Cox's establishment of the Blue Shirts, an organization of male and female workers who wore matching dress and army insignia. The Blue Shirts quickly grew to two hundred thousand and claimed members in Chicago, Cleveland, and New York.[39]

Since the German National Socialists donned matching brown shirts, and the Italian fascists wore black shirts, the American Left concluded that Cox's Blue Shirts were cut from the same cloth. But as John Jay Ewers wrote in *The Christian Century*, a liberal Protestant magazine, "This blue shirt army seeks no fascist dictatorship; it is the *people* as dictator that Father Cox seeks to set in power." To Ewers, Cox's movement was a truly democratic one, built from the bottom up and dedicated to achieving social justice and opportunity for all citizens regardless of creed and race. Moreover, Cox no doubt gained inspiration from Ireland where a Gaelic Blue Shirt movement had recently arisen. The Irish Blue Shirts were not anti-Semitic, though they unwisely held Mussolini in high regard. Cox's Irish cousins condemned Communism and capitalism, hoping for the day when the encyclicals of Leo XIII and Pius XI would become the law of the land. Unlike Cox, the Irish Blue Shirts could see themselves supporting a military-style dictatorship.[40]

Elmer Cope, having met with Cox, objected to branding the priest a Nazi. The problem with upper-middle-class socialists, Cope argued, was that they had no understanding of working-class Americans. As he had written to Muste in late 1931, Pittsburgh's Socialist Party chapter had astounded him: "I think it rather significant that a working-class party, self-professed, can work so many years in a community without having many contacts, not to mention groups, with workers themselves." Pittsburgh workers, who were overwhelmingly Catholic, had ignored the entreaties of the secular socialists. Not until Father Cox had announced his intent to organize on their behalf did the city's laborers become politically active. Contrary to Muste and O'Connor, rejecting Marxism, embracing the Sermon on the Mount, choosing to emulate a military organizational style, and seeking to bring about political change did not make that person a fascist.[41]

As Cox organized his Blue Shirt battalions and prepared for the August convention of the newly established Jobless Party, the priest lost whatever small amount of toleration he had for Hoover. First came the matter of Frank Phillips, utility baron and chair of Hoover's Committee on Unemployment. Phillips had told the president that Pittsburgh would not need any federal assistance to take care of its presumably small number of unemployed. Hoover concurred. Then there was the World War I veterans' Bonus March. Veterans from Erie, Pennsylvania, had invited Cox to address them in Washington. Arriving in Washington on June 9 in his chaplain's uniform, Cox lambasted the federal government for refusing to make good its financial obligations to the veterans, even as the Reconstruction Finance Corporation gave millions to bankers and industrialists. The veterans chose Cox to present their petition to Vice President Charles Curtis, Hoover being indisposed. After Cox departed, the president ordered General Douglas MacArthur to drive the Bonus Marchers from Washington. Thoroughly disgusted that Hoover had deployed tanks, sabers, and tear gas against defenseless, patriotic Americans, Cox wired the White House: "Told you last January there would be riots and probably revolution because of your attitude toward the unemployed . . . you are treading on dangerous grounds."[42]

In August, a thousand delegates journeyed to St. Louis to hold a joint convention of the Jobless Party and the Liberty Party. (The latter was an organization based in the Southwest and founded by the eighty-year-old Populist politician, William "Coin" Harvey.) St. Louis city officials threatened to seek a court injunction to prevent Cox and Harvey from holding their convention, while anonymous, conservative representatives of the diocese argued that Cox's efforts were futile. Even though the Jobless and Liberty Party delegates were unable to select a joint candidate since Harvey's Arkansas followers were uncomfortable with the notion of a Catholic presidential nominee, the convention was successful in one small way; Cox had brought many disillusioned, apathetic people back into the political process. Prophet and politician, Cox gave laissez-faire capitalism its last rites.

> Justice will have the bandage removed from her eyes, and America will be happy again if decentralization should be the order of the day; if we provide for our own protection and keep in mind that while the largest and most powerful nation on earth, we may become an easy victim to the avarice and cupidity of greedy enemies. Every attempt at monopoly or unfair trade practices, should be, in the interests of fair trade, strictly prohibited and punished. We have come to the end of an economic era. As a nation we are groping in the dark, awaiting the dawn of a better era than that which has passed. It must provide equal opportunities to all men, regardless of wealth.[43]

Equipped with a truck, trailer, and loud speakers, Father Cox and a small party intended to cross the continent. Possessing scant funds, Cox launched one of history's most quixotic presidential campaigns. Leaving Pittsburgh on August 28, the group reached Liverpool, Ohio, that afternoon where they rallied one thousand supporters. In Massillon, fifteen hundred people gathered to listen to Cox and Mayor Jacob Coxey. The mayor pledged his support in the struggle to drive Hoover from Washington. Cox's campaign staff then pushed on, traveling to Joliet, Illinois, Kansas City, Kansas, and Albuquerque, New Mexico, before arriving in San Francisco on October 1. In all, Cox spoke to more than fifty-seven thousand alternatively curious and enthusiastic people. Although his largest crowds, with the exception of the eight thousand who came to hear him in Oklahoma, tended to be in the Midwest, Cox had stirred keen interest on the prairie. Cox's reception in Iowa, however, was hostile. Herbert Hoover's home state—Republican, Protestant, and fearful of urban workers—hung out an unwelcome sign. In Davenport, which had some Catholic population and a Catholic college, local officials refused to allow Cox to speak.[44]

As Cox organized his presidential campaign, Allegheny County Democrats struggled to deal with an alien political concept: victory. There was, however, one obstacle to winning the White House and possibly preparing for the capture of the state legislature and the city of Pittsburgh. The national Democratic Party did not have any credible candidates to run against Hoover. Given Hoover's poor public image, the Democrats did not require a stellar candidate. Still, having only won the White House twice in the past generation, and then only because the Republican Party had temporarily split, securing an acceptable Democratic nominee in 1932 was a tall order. The editor of the *Pittsburgh Catholic*, expressing the views of many Catholic journalists and machine bosses, championed Al Smith. Unfortunately, the southern wing of the party threatened to bolt, just as it had in 1928 when Hoover made great inroads into Democratic Dixie. Unable to offer Smith the nomination, the convention chose New York governor Franklin D. Roosevelt. To the *Pittsburgh Catholic*, Roosevelt's selection was one of expediency over moral principle.[45]

The *Pittsburgh Catholic* criticized Roosevelt as a man who, with his personal fortune and the support of prejudiced southerners, had usurped Smith's place as titular head of the Democratic Party. David Lawrence, on the other hand, chose to embrace the Hyde Park patrician. At the Chicago convention, the Pennsylvania delegation remained steadfast in its support for Smith. Quietly, Lawrence informed Roosevelt's supporters that he would do everything within his power to deliver Pennsylvania to him in the fall. Back in Pitts-

*1930 just 5000 registered Democrats in Pittsburg*

burgh, Lawrence reserved Forbes Field for a Roosevelt address, hoping to fill the 35,000–seat stadium. This was a bold move on Lawrence's part. As recently as 1930 there were just five thousand registered Democrats in Pittsburgh. Indeed, since 1860, the city and the state had elected fifteen Republican governors to two Democratic ones and had never gone Democratic in a presidential election. With this history weighing heavily upon Lawrence, he had his operatives working overtime to fill Forbes Field for Roosevelt's October appearance.[46]

To neutralize the hostile *Pittsburgh Catholic*, Ellenbogen had to persuade Cox to end his campaign and endorse Roosevelt. Ellenbogen's profession of faith in Roosevelt, in addition to the speech that the New Yorker had made October 2 to a Detroit audience, swayed Cox. Roosevelt was the first and only major presidential candidate to quote Pius XI's encyclical *Reconstructing the Social Order* and condemn laissez-faire capitalism. Duly impressed, Cox went beyond endorsement and came close to making the Episcopalian a saint of the Church.

> Mr. Roosevelt has pledged himself to the protection of the interests of the common man. . . . He has pledged himself definitely to policies which will aid in the economic recovery and the re-creation of work.
>
> He has endorsed the principle of large public construction by the federal government in times of depression.
>
> This is not only an economic crisis, it is a human crisis. The old system is broken down. A new order must come. The opportunity to help was presented to Mr. Hoover a thousand times, but never did he lift a hand nor raise his voice to relieve the suffering American people.
>
> Now he comes to us with something about his sympathy for mankind and about measures of relief—measures which were forced on him. Words, words, words. Nobody believes these words. He had his chance. . . .
>
> America must reject Herbert Hoover and all that he represents if she means to continue as a democracy.[47]

With Cox giving rousing political speeches in the Catholic wards, Lawrence set out to array Republican blacks behind Roosevelt. To that end, national Democratic committeeman Joseph Guffey, a rare Scotch-Irish Democrat whose wealth gave him much clout in the Pittsburgh party, went to work. He approached *Pittsburgh Courier* publisher Robert Vann. A graduate of the Pitt Law School, as well as the owner of the largest circulation black newspaper in America, Vann proved a willing ally. He was ready to lead Pennsylvania's 181,000 registered black voters into the Democratic column. Certainly Vann had made no secret during the 1928 presidential election that he resented the bigotry underlying Hoover's campaign. Indeed, Vann had gone as far as to argue that Hoover hoped to carry Democratic Dixie through racist political appeals. The subsequent Depression and mounting economic hardship that Pittsburgh's fifty-five thousand blacks experienced made the politically ambitious publisher receptive to Guffey's overtures. While Vann did not have much influence in Philadelphia, the state's greatest black city, he managed to get 30 percent of its minority voters to support the Democrats. In Pittsburgh, Vann secured half of the black electorate for the Democrats. Although Hoover carried the majority of the northern black vote, Vann and the *Pittsburgh Courier* had cracked one of the Republican Party's most loyal constituencies. Moreover, in a speech to Cleveland blacks during the election, Vann captured national attention.

So long as the Republican Party could use the photograph of Abraham Lincoln to entice Negroes to vote a Republican ticket they condescended to accord Negroes some degree of political recognition. But when the Republican Party had built itself to the point of security, it no longer invited Negro support.

. . . The only true gauge by which to judge an individual or a party or a government is not by what is proclaimed or promised, but by what is done. . . .

It is a mistaken idea that the Negro must wait until the party selects him. The only true political philosophy dictates that the Negro must select his party and not wait to be selected. . . . I see millions of Negroes turning the picture of Lincoln to the wall. This year I see Negroes voting a Democratic ticket. . . . I, for one, shall join the ranks of this new army of fearless, courageous, patriotic Negroes who know the difference between blind partisanship and patriotism.[48]

Forging an alliance between Catholics and blacks required enormous effort since relations between the two groups had never been cordial. During the 1919 strike, U.S. Steel and Jones & Laughlin had recruited thousands of blacks. The steel corporations used the unwitting blacks as strikebreakers. Subsequently, blacks discovered that Eastern European immigrants and their children had little difficulty learning at least two words of English: "Goddamned niggers." So, too, blacks picked up on and then changed the derogatory nickname which the Protestant steel bosses had given Slavic Catholics.

The white Presbyterians' "Hunkies" became "honkies" to the black Baptists and Methodists. Father Cox would never figure out how to bridge this racial, as well as religious, gap. Other reformist priests in Pittsburgh would agonize over ways to overcome this tragic history.[49]

If Lawrence's Catholic-black coalition was tenuous, then the Democrats' appeals to organized labor, such as it was in 1932, seemed to offer even less promise. United Mine Workers leader John L. Lewis endorsed Hoover. Both men had worked together in the 1920s when Hoover, as the secretary of commerce, had helped Lewis arrive at a settlement with coal operators. More-over, Lewis was, like Hoover, a product of small-town Iowa, and a Protes-tant who supported Prohibition. Under Lewis' leadership, the UMW declined from five hundred thousand members in 1919 to eighty-four thousand by 1929, representing just 20 percent of the men who worked in the coal mines. In the 1920s, Lewis accused devout Catholics like John Brophy of being Com-munist operatives when they criticized his preference for choice hotels and restaurants. (Many miners lacked adequate shelter and their families often went hungry.) Lewis, however, found his match in Phil Murray. An Irish Catholic immigrant, former president of UMW District 5 (Pittsburgh), and current vice president of the national union, Murray lived humbly and was attuned to the needs of desperate workers. Murray and his personal secretary, David McDonald, met with Governor Roosevelt in Albany. Not wishing to bring about an outright breech with Lewis, Murray nonetheless led the min-ers into the Roosevelt camp.[50]

With Murray, Vann, and Cox gathered to champion Roosevelt, while El-lenbogen worked the Jewish neighborhoods in the Hill District, Lawrence was able to get a crowd of fifty thousand at Forbes Field to cheer the De-mocratic challenger. Roosevelt pledged to appropriate several billion dollars for public works projects, making Father Cox quite happy—if a little puz-zled when the candidate also promised to balance the federal budget by de-creasing government expenditures. The *Pittsburgh Catholic*, though placing no faith in Roosevelt, unleashed a broadside against Hoover in the last days of the election after he complained that the Democrats had been engaging in character assassination.

> The Republican candidate is so very regretful that little personal mat-ters have been brought into the campaign of 1932. May we rise to suggest that Herbert Hoover did not regret the personal things that were brought into the campaign of 1928? He was aware that a whis-pering campaign was conducted in that year. He knew that his chief advisers were going about from town to town telling things about

Catholics and the Catholic Church which he knew to be diabolical lies.

. . . Did Mr. Hoover raise one word in protest? After the election, we stated in this column that Mr. Hoover won the election at the price of bigotry and intolerance. Four years later, he comes back to the American people crying and bewailing that personal things of his life have been injected into the campaign of this year. Perhaps the present inhabitant of the White House realizes that the price of victory is sometimes a very dear one.[51]

There were no protestations on Hoover's behalf from Pittsburgh's Highland Park neighborhood where many members of the Mellon family lived. Indeed, from the Pittsburgh "Mellon Patch" to the governor's mansion in Harrisburg, Hoover heard not a word of encouragement. Once the election results came in, it was evident that Hoover had alienated a majority of Americans, collecting less than sixteen million votes to Roosevelt's total of nearly twenty-three million. Although Joe Grundy, as Republican boss and leader of the Pennsylvania Manufacturers Association, was able to deliver Philadelphia, and hence Pennsylvania, to Hoover, he did not foresee a bright future. Roosevelt had carried Allegheny County and Pittsburgh, the first Democratic candidate to win there since 1856. Less encouraging to Republican prospects, Roosevelt had received 189,000 votes in the county compared to 152,000 for Hoover. *There had barely been 200,000 Democratic and Republican voters in 1920.* The children of immigrant Catholics were coming of voting age and they were not supporting Republicans. A veritable demographic deluge was to follow. The Irish Democrats would finally get the attention of corporate Pittsburgh.[52]

For Father Cox, Roosevelt's victory was full of promise. He and the nation had journeyed far since his march on Washington. Sadly for the priest, his mother, who had come to Washington by train to greet the pilgrims, did not live to see the dawning of what Cox believed would be a new social order. Her body worn from a lifetime of struggle, proud of the one son who became a medical doctor and the other a servant of Christ, Julia Cox died in May. Hundreds of mourners came to Old St. Patrick's to pay their respects. Then the pallbearers carried her to Calvary cemetery. One young pallbearer and seminarian at St. Vincent's, Charles Owen Rice, had been inspired by the social activism of Father Cox. If Cox was prepared to devote his life to the cause of reform, then the son of working-class Irish immigrants could do no less.[53]

# 2

## Social Reconstruction

### The Moral Basis of Economic Reform, 1933–1935

Religious activists like Father Carl Hensler and the editors of the *Pittsburgh Catholic* cheer Franklin Roosevelt but warn New Dealers that improving the material conditions of ordinary people is not enough. Poverty, according to Pittsburgh's clergy and lay reformers, is a product of an unjust wage system *and* immoral, self-destructive behavior. Federal programs must be designed to nourish the body without, in the process, killing the spirit. Additionally, so far as Pittsburgh activists see matters in the first three years of the Roosevelt administration, Washington liberals and conservative industrialists should cease their bickering and, instead, embrace the encyclicals of Leo XIII and Pius XI.

The Scotch-Irish Presbyterians who settled Pennsylvania in the years before the American Revolution called their new home "The Best Poor Man's Country." For Ulster's indentured servants and tenant farmers Pennsylvania offered enormous economic opportunities. Ulster men such as James Laughlin, Thomas Mellon, and William Thaw prospered as iron makers, real estate speculators, and bankers. Subsequently, Pennsylvania became the American center of Scotch-Irish Presbyterianism. Best of all, deep in William Penn's Western Woods, there were few Irish Catholics. This was an important consideration given that the Irish had never accepted military defeat at the hands of John Calvin's faithful servants. Secure and prosperous, the Scotch-Irish annually celebrated their victory over the Papists at the Battle of Boyne. By the 1830s, the descendants of Protestant Ulster proudly proclaimed Pittsburgh to be "The Belfast of America."[1]

If inclined to consign Catholics to the fiery pits, the first generation of Scotch-Irish entrepreneurs was no less charitable toward its own clansmen. Drinking, smoking, and gambling were pursuits that led many an Ulster man astray. One could at least understand why the Irish were drunkards and thieves—it was their nature, as well as a consequence of their devotion to the Whore of Babylon. Protestants, however, had no such excuse. Presbyterians concluded that evil was ever present and that they must constantly guard against the moral debasement of society. Good men, through a government of their creation, had to promote morality. Since the Devil does his work among the idle, government must force the sinners to work for their keep. By the same reasoning, poverty and unemployment were signs of God's displeasure. Presbyterian Pittsburgh, in order to please God, would have to limit charity to the poor. The city's businessmen also recognized that their workers, who were members of that class precisely because they lacked ambition and good morals, should not be paid too much. They would only spend their money on sinful pursuits.[2]

Having lifted themselves out of poverty, the Scotch-Irish patriarchs passed their wisdom and real estate along to their sons. Although the sons discerned the value of applying Calvinist principles to the regulation of government, charity, and the work force, they found that the pursuit of wealth required most of their energies. Pittsburgh would have to do without their spiritual guidance. Meanwhile, the drive to build profitable iron and coal empires undermined Calvin's warnings against extravagant living. Every great mansion that appeared in the Sewickley and East End suburbs, and every advertisement placed for maids and cooks in the society newspaper, the *Bulletin Index*, testified to the Scotch-Irish quest for the good life. Paradoxically, as mansions and factories filled the Monongahela Valley, Pittsburgh looked less and less like Belfast. With each new iron mill and coal mine opened, tens of thousands of predominately Catholic immigrants from Ireland and Germany flooded into Western Pennsylvania.[3]

By the 1890s, Andrew Carnegie and Henry Frick of the Carnegie Steel Company were sending agents into Croatian, Italian, Polish, and Slovakian villages to recruit even cheaper Catholic labor. Belfast had become Babel. Just as unsettling, the industrialists transformed pastoral Pittsburgh into what the muckraking journalist Lincoln Steffens called "Hell with the lid off." The directors of the Pennsylvania Railroad, while untroubled by the industrial wasteland they had helped create, were not fools. They ordered their locomotive engineers not to fill their boilers with water drawn from the Allegheny and Monongahela rivers. The tainted water ate through the boilers.[4]

While Andrew Mellon built the Aluminum Corporation of America (ALCOA) into a global monopoly, other citizens sought to bring refinement to the city. The Heinz family proved instrumental in creating the Pittsburgh Symphony Orchestra and tried to provide recreational facilities and some measure of health care to their employees. Scotch-Irish Pittsburgh, however, did not choose to follow the civic example of the Heinzes, seeing in that family of German Lutheran immigrants a troubling streak of Continental paternalism.[5]

The Scotch-Irish could be little bothered with the Heinzes' efforts to promote cultural enlightenment. They had other pressing concerns. The industrialists could not consider themselves members of an elite until they had established their own social clubs. And what would be the point of having created the Duquesne Club if its board of directors permitted Catholics and Jews to join? There were additional considerations. While social clubs had their value, the children of the Pittsburgh elite still needed to acquire the trappings of an Ivy League education. The young men who had a knack for business would remain in the city to attend Western University (later renamed the University of Pittsburgh). Their other sons would go to Princeton and mingle with upper-class Bostonians, Philadelphians, and New Yorkers. Attending Princeton had its advantages. First, the curriculum was not demanding and sports received great emphasis. Second, Presbyterian Princeton, in contrast to other Ivy League schools, was highly successful in excluding Catholics and Jews.[6]

Having secured their status as members of a national elite, the Thaws and Laughlins joined the debate on unrestricted immigration. They endorsed the nativist statements of Senator Henry Cabot Lodge of Massachusetts. Senator Lodge fretted that uncivilized Catholics and Jews were out-breeding White Anglo-Saxon Protestants. The specter of advancing immigrant hordes became a major obsession in Pittsburgh. With the Irish and Italian population spilling out of the Hill District and into Oakland, Catholic churches and pubs sprang up amid the Victorian mansions. By the early 1920s, the headmistress of the Winchester girls' preparatory school watched in horror as the diocese erected the Central Catholic High School for Boys across from her establishment. The headmistress planted hedges around her school so that she would not have to look upon the Catholic school. Ultimately, she relocated Winchester further east into the Presbyterian neighborhood of Shadyside. Even household servants, recruited from Lutheran Scandinavia since good people did not want Irish Catholics in their homes, understood their place in the racial hierarchy. When their employers fell upon hard times and they had to seek new positions, servants placed advertisements in the *Bulletin Index* specifying that they would only work for Gentiles.[7]

The very industrialists who expounded upon the inferior racial qualities of

Poles and Slovaks, could not have secured their fortunes without the Eastern European immigrants. Such immigrants, or "Hunkies," to use the Scotch-Irish epithet, were an apparently perfect labor force. To begin with, they worked for a great deal less than native-born whites. Moreover, the immigrants were not a political threat to the industrialists since, even if eligible, they often failed to vote in national and local elections. Feeding their families was the most important duty to them; why should they waste their energy debating who should occupy the White House? In any event, whatever Republican candidate the steel bosses supported always won, so the "Hunkie vote" was superfluous. Finally, being divided by language and culture, the Eastern European immigrants proved unable, or unwilling, to build a powerful industrial union movement.[8]

Unfortunately for the Scotch-Irish, that docile and fragmented mass of Slavic workers changed the rules of the game. In 1919, two hundred thousand steel workers, primarily in the Pittsburgh District, went on strike. Nearly all of the Catholic laborers joined the strike while the handful of white Protestants who worked for U.S. Steel and Jones & Laughlin remained true to their employers. Coming hard on the heels of Communist uprisings in Hungary and Russia, the industrialists thought that they were witnessing a reprise of the October Revolution. Frightened, they responded with overwhelming physical force. The Polish steel workers referred to the subsequent occupation army of Pennsylvania state troopers as "Cossacks."[9]

In response to the Great Steel Strike of 1919, Pennsylvania senator David Aiken Reed approached the chair of the House Committee on Immigration, Albert Johnson of Washington State. Both men wished to write legislation to restrict immigration from Eastern Europe. Reed's father was one of the original organizers of U.S. Steel. A graduate of Princeton, Senator Reed belonged to the Duquesne Club and served on the board of the Mellon National Bank & Trust. Although the political representatives of the steel corporations had long opposed restricting immigration, desiring inexpensive, pliable labor, the events of 1919 had changed their minds. Moreover, the steel masters found a new source of labor that was Protestant, Republican, and willing to work for even less than their "Hunkies": southern black migrants. In 1919, steel towns from Buffalo to Homestead imported firty thousand southern blacks to replace the striking Slavs. Assured of this supply of black workers, and confident of their loyalties to the party of Lincoln, Reed and Johnson wrote the Immigration Act of 1924. The law established discriminatory national origins-based quotas. Subsequently, the number of Catholic and Jewish immigrants from Southern and Eastern Europe declined from 921,000 in 1914, to 21,000 annually after 1924.[10]

With the 1919 steel strike smashed, and America's Protestant purity advanced by immigration restriction and Prohibition, Scotch-Irish Pittsburgh seemed safe. Coal miner and UMW rebel leader John Brophy would not have suggested otherwise. As the decade of the 1920s progressed, Brophy witnessed one failed strike after another. Each time the miners put down their picks, the coal operators retaliated. Initially, the owners of Pittsburgh Coal expelled the miners' families from their company-owned housing. Then the miners moved into tents, living off the land and bracing for the cold Pennsylvania winters. If they had not returned to work at reduced pay by this point, then the shivering mining families would watch from the outskirts of town as the coal operators brought in scabs. Meanwhile, the person who was to inherit control of the Pittsburgh Coal Company, Paul Mellon, studied literature at Cambridge University.[11]

As Duquesne Club members sipped brandies and read the *Bulletin Index*, they surely could not help noticing the way in which society reporters wrote that Paul Mellon was the *only* son of Andrew Mellon. Even Harvey O'Connor of the *Pittsburgh Federated Press* noted, with relish, that Mellon's empire would likely pass on to Paul. It was not that Paul Mellon was a wastrel, as O'Connor slyly protested. Paul just did not share his father's interest in banking. Certainly, he did not inherit any of his father's political sense. In 1932, Homestead's landlords had turned off the water to five hundred unemployed families who had fallen behind on their rent payments. Now was the time for billionaires and their children to maintain a low profile. Yet as late as 1934, Paul Mellon took well-publicized sleigh rides through New York City, drank the best champagne, and gambled away small fortunes in the Central Park Casino.[12]

If Paul Mellon was too busy enjoying the New York social scene to notice the poverty around him, and if John Brophy was too immersed in the coal wars of the 1920s to see anything but despair, then it was up to other observers to discern the shape of things to come. During the 1919 steel strike, the Protestant Inter-Church World Movement, the forerunner of the reformist World Council of Churches, had sent economist David Saposs to Pittsburgh. Saposs met with Protestant clergy who contended that the strike was Communist-inspired. Then he sought out various Roman Catholic and Orthodox clergy for their opinions. What Saposs found would baffle him for the rest of his life. One Orthodox Greek priest in Braddock had opened his doors to union meetings. Expressing surprise at his support for the strike, the priest bluntly replied that "Protestantism and capitalism came into existence at the same time, and they are the ones that blocked the progress of our church. You destroy capitalism, you destroy Protestantism." This Braddock priest was not exceptional. Saposs found two Irish priests, assistants to the bishop of the Harrisburg Diocese, who expressed the same sentiment and then asked him if he had read any of the perceptive literature published by the radical Industrial Workers of the World.[13]

Saposs's bewilderment, a product perhaps of his close association with Protestant intellectuals, or a result of his Jewish upbringing, should not have been so great. After all, the Administrative Council of the National Catholic War Council had issued the "Bishops' Program of Social Reconstruction" in February 1919. In this pronouncement, the leading bishops of the American Catholic Church, among them Joseph Schrembs of the Toledo (later Cleveland) Diocese, argued that workers had the legal right to form labor unions and should expect "a living wage." The bishops then contended that women in the industrial work force were entitled to receive "equal pay for equal amounts and qualities of work." Schrembs and his colleagues also advocated that industry and the federal government provide for "insurance against illness, invalidity, unemployment, and old age." Once workers received better wages and access to education, then they could assume more responsibility for providing for their own health insurance and retirement. Finally, the bishops admonished both labor and capital that

> the laborer must come to realize that he owes his employer and society an honest day's work in return for a fair wage, and that conditions cannot be substantially improved until he roots out the desire to get a maximum return for a minimum of service. The capitalist must likewise get a new viewpoint. He needs to learn the long-forgotten truth that wealth is stewardship, that profit-making is not the basic justification of business enterprise, and that there are such things as fair profits, fair interest, and fair prices. Above and before all, he must cultivate and strengthen within his mind the truth which many of his class have begun to grasp for the first time during the present war, namely, that the laborer is a human being, not merely an instrument of production; and that the laborer's right to a decent livelihood is the first moral charge upon industry. The employer has a right to get a reasonable living out of his business, but he has no right to interest on his investment until his employees have obtained at least living wages. This is human and Christian, in contrast to the purely commercial and pagan, ethics of industry.[14]

Many Pennsylvanian Slovaks embraced the bishops' contentions and supported their efforts to establish a National Catholic Welfare Conference. The

National Catholic Welfare Conference continued the War Council's efforts to achieve social change. In Homestead, Father Clement Hrtanek of St. Anne's Church dismissed claims that the 1919 steel strike had its origins in Russia. Born in 1889 to Slovak immigrant laborers, and a graduate of St. Vincent's Seminary, Hrtanek knew his people well. Catholic workers, so Hrtanek told anyone who would listen, wanted decent wages, not Bolshevik Revolution. As Thomas Bell (Belejcak), a Slovak-American novelist from Braddock put it in 1941, his people sought to secure their full rights as citizens of the United States.

> It wasn't where you were born or how you spelled your name or where your father had come from. It was the way you thought and felt about certain things. About freedom of speech and the equality of men and the importance of having one law—the same law—for rich and poor, for the people you liked and the people you didn't like. About the right of every man to live his life as he thought best, his right to defend it if anyone tried to change it and his right to change it himself if he decided he liked some other way of living better. About the uses to which wealth and power could honorably be put, and about honor itself, honor, integrity, self-respect, the whatever-you-wanted-to-call-it that determined for a man which things he couldn't say or do under any circumstances, not for all the money there was, not even to help his side win. About human dignity, which helped a man live proudly and distinguished his death from an animal's; and, finally, about the value to be put on a human life, one's enemy no less than one's own.[15]

Beyond Hrtanek and Bell, other Catholics viewed Church teachings as blueprints to constructing a just society. Brophy, driven from the Pennsylvania coal fields by anti-union operators and John L. Lewis, came to Pittsburgh in 1927. Once there, he discovered Leo XIII's encyclical *The Condition of Labor*. According to Brophy, he had found Church support for his ideas on "democratic economic and social planning." Soon, Brophy joined Father James Cox in establishing a labor school. Here the coal miner trained unionists in Catholic social thought, a topic that A. J. Muste had ignored at the Brookwood Labor College—the very institution Brophy helped to found. Having seen such great human suffering in the Johnstown coal fields, Brophy despaired for the future. But Leo XIII and Father Cox reminded him of what, as a child, he had observed in Mass. Chiefly, that out of despair, ugliness, and persecution, even to the point of crucifixion, will come faith, beauty, and brotherhood.

On Sunday mornings at Mass I saw large numbers of adults I never saw at other times—working men, mostly Irish, who labored in the mills, factories, and pits of the community. I got my first sense of kinship with people as I watched those rough, hardworking people worshipping their God. I was moved by the divine mystery, the stately drama of the Mass, the momentary hush that falls upon the congregation at the moment of consecration. In this church I got my first feeling for the beauty of line and form, light and color. The statues, the paintings, the beauty of ritual, all combined to impress upon my mind an affection for this scene.[16]

Pat Fagan, who became president of UMW District 5 in 1922 when Phil Murray rose to national office in the miner's union, was no less inspired by Catholic social instruction. A friend of Brophy's, as well as an ardent member of the Ancient Order of Hibernians, a fraternal organization that the Pennsylvania coal operators had attempted to destroy in the 1870s, Fagan drew strength from Leo XIII.

One of the greatest things that ever happened for labor and management was the encyclical of Pope Leo XIII. To me it was one of the finest social documents that I've ever seen for social justice, for protecting the worker and management.

. . . I became aware of it because of my father's knowledge of the encyclical. It was called *Rerum Novarum* [*The Condition of Labor*]. My father used to read all encyclicals and talk to us about them. It was a result of going into the mine at the age that I did [12] and after starting to do a little more thinking than I did at first. I thought, "Is this all life means—to work, eat, and sleep? Have no recreation, no leisure, no time to spend with your family?" I said, "This really is a tough world."

Then, of course, naturally, I thought that the Pope was somebody I was responsible to. He was the vicar of Christ on Earth, and he was interested in not only the spiritual and moral, but the material welfare of people that have to work for a living.[17]

As the reminiscences of Fagan, Brophy, and Bell attest, the Pittsburgh Diocese did not lack Catholics who were prepared to bring their religious beliefs to bear on the transformation of labor-management relations. Moreover, Father Cox gave the diocese an activist cast, even as he encouraged other priests to speak out against social injustice. In 1933, Father Casimir Orlemanski, who had marched on Washington with Cox, exhorted the state legislature to prohibit sweatshops from employing child labor. Children, who should be in school, Orlemanski argued, had become trapped in a "monstrous peonage system, operated by those "greedy for gold and to whom the human being is less than the beast of the field." Similarly, Father J. Elliot Ross of the Sacred Heart Church declared in the spring of 1933 that corporations had made workers into slaves who starved amid the riches of the land.

> We do not know how many men are unemployed, but it is grotesque to say there is no work for these idle hands, when in reality there is more work than they could do in fifty years. It is a lazy alibi to say there is no work when our industries could be humming in wiping out slums, building roads, clothing the half naked. Every ton of steel Pittsburgh can produce could be used if we were wise enough and honest enough to devise a better social organization.[18]

While Father Orlemanski urged his parishioners to lobby the state legislature, other diocesan priests praised Franklin Roosevelt's moral leadership. When coal company guards in 1933 fired on a United Mine Workers' picket line, killing World War I veteran Louis Podrosky, the Slovak-born priest Michael Yesko presided at the funeral Mass. With twelve thousand mourners gathered at St. Mary's church in Brownsville, Pennsylvania, Yesko castigated the "classes of people that look down on the laboring man and when the smallest dispute arises say, 'That fellow is a foreigner, a Communist.'" Pleading for an end to violence, and grateful for the telegram of support from Roosevelt appointee Hugh Johnson, Yesko thanked God "for a president who takes care of all the country, the poor as well as the rich."[19]

Writing for the *Pittsburgh Catholic* and *The Commonweal*, a Catholic magazine, seminarian Charles Owen Rice in 1933 contended that American Catholics had to become more politically active. Granted, the Catholic minority, whenever it exerted itself at the ballot box, had suffered nativist reprisals. However, fear should not prevent Catholics from bringing their "matchless moral code, founded on reason and revelation" to bear upon national and local politics. Rice rejected the secular belief that the interests of church and state were separate and irreconcilable. On the contrary, Rice wrote, "Religion belongs in politics and is needed there. It alone can curb the unbridled greed that lies at the root of political corruption. Laws and systems of reform cannot stem the passions of men. Without religion every attempt at reform is doomed to failure."[20]

Bishop Hugh Boyle emphatically concurred. Since his installation as Pittsburgh bishop in 1921, Boyle had supported Cox's charitable and political initiatives and taken on the role of mentor to several young seminarians and priests who had enlisted in Dorothy Day's Catholic Worker movement. Boyle also operated on the national political level, joining Bishop Schrembs to become a persistent champion of organized labor in the National Catholic Welfare Conference. All of this is not to say, however, that he did not have his sore points. Sensitive to the popular image of the drunken Irishman, Boyle once sharply rebuked Father Thomas Lappan of Pittsburgh's St. Vincent de Paul Society. Lappan had organized a St. Patrick's Day floor show and cash bar in order to raise money for charity.[21]

According to the Pittsburgh bishop, the Great Depression threatened the survival of the most basic unit of human civilization: the family. In the spring of 1932, Boyle had helped secure aid for the families in Allegheny County who faced imminent starvation. Boyle appointed Father Lappan to a special committee of priests and then gave them their marching orders—raise another $8 million to replenish the funds that the Allegheny County Emergency Association had spent since the fall of 1931. The bishop and the *Pittsburgh Catholic* also pleaded with parishioners to give to the Catholic Welfare Fund. To underline the importance of the Welfare Fund, the diocesan newspaper in 1933 ran a full-page advertisement. The advertisement featured an illustration of a downcast woman holding her young daughter and baby. Presumably, her husband, who is absent from the picture, has temporarily left his family in order to search for work. Then again, perhaps he had died in an industrial accident, or, in panic, had abandoned his wife and children. The advertisement concluded with a call to end poverty and to save an ever growing number of families from permanent dependency upon public assistance.

> We have, then, for our neighbors, an increasing number of individuals who have not daily bread, nor roof over their head, nor shoes on their feet, nor decent covering for their bodies, nor a flame for their stove, nor medicine for their illness, except as they receive it by the grace of others. For two, three or four years they have faced the undermining necessity of paying for the bare necessities of life, not with money, but with their self-respect.
>
> The numbers rise. The days fly. And what move do we make to salvage the still unbeaten majority? Shall we in Allegheny County carry 60,000 to 80,000 beaten families—300,000 to 400,000 beaten individuals—with us into the future as our neighbors? Can we achieve recovery for any of us if we do?

. . . Shall we wait until we have by our own hand forced 300,000 good neighbors into permanent dependency, or shall we vote *now* for Family Reconstruction with an increased pledge to the Welfare Fund.[22]

Although supportive of federal efforts to aid the unemployed, and having no brief for Herbert Hoover's philosophy of rugged individualism that allowed the affluent to rationalize their neglect of the working poor, the American Catholic Church harbored at least one great fear. What would happen to Americans' sense of self-respect if the government assumed responsibility for supporting their families? Even Federal Emergency Relief Administration director Harry Hopkins was worried that welfare, if there was no obligation of work attached to it, could be deadly. "Give a man a dole," Hopkins warned, "and you save his body and destroy his spirit; give him a job and pay him an assured wage, and you save both the body and the spirit." The last thing Hopkins and Boyle wished to see was the creation of a class of spiritually dead welfare recipients who shunned their responsibilities to family and community. However, in 1933, neither the architects of the New Deal's social-welfare programs nor Catholic clergy knew at what point public assistance began to do more long-term harm than good.[23]

If leery of a federal dole, the Pittsburgh Diocese happily embraced quite a few of Roosevelt's relief programs—including the Civilian Conservation Corps (CCC), a legislative initiative that Roosevelt had submitted to Congress on March 21, 1933. Approved eight days later, the CCC created two thousand camps that employed 2.5 million youths in projects ranging from planting trees to restoring national park sites. Twenty thousand Pennsylvanians immediately enlisted in the CCC. Five hundred young men from Pittsburgh joined the CCC, grateful for the opportunity to work for their own support. Accompanying them was Father Francis Bailey of the St. Lawrence Church. His parish, located along Penn Avenue where County Cork met the Mississippi Delta, had its share of pool halls and saloons. St. Lawrence's assistant pastor was all too aware of the temptations idle city youths faced.[24]

Father Bailey's original mission was to provide moral direction to the boys, an understandable concern of the Pittsburgh Diocese since 70 percent of the CCC recruits in Western Pennsylvania were Catholic. Soon, however, Bailey was making work assignments for eighty CCC camps and had received a commission as a First Lieutenant in the U.S. Army Reserve Corps. The priest remained in the Pennsylvania CCC camps for several years, boasting of the twenty-six thousand miles of roads his young men had built, and making a point of holding Mass for the black Catholics that the federal government had placed in segregated camps. He also wrote regularly to the *Pittsburgh*

*Catholic*, noting that the $25 each boy made monthly went home to support their destitute families. The *Pittsburgh Catholic* praised all of the CCC chaplains and gave the program a ringing endorsement:

> Rescued from idleness and bad environment, in many cases saved from the physical and spiritual dangers that beset those unable to find employment, these youths have enjoyed the satisfaction of accomplishing things, of living under healthy and wholesome conditions, of coming close to nature, of sharing in a really constructive task. They have seen the countryside improve under their hands, even while they themselves were improving physically and mentally. They have become receptive to spiritual ideas, as is testified by the chaplains who have worked among them. Some of them, taken from congested city districts, had acquired a false outlook on life; many of the Catholics among them had become careless in the practice of their religion; but in their new surroundings they responded readily to the counsel and guidance of their spiritual leaders. In every way the "conservation" camps have been true to their name. They have helped conserve the material and spiritual resources of the nation.[25]

To the editor of the *Pittsburgh Catholic*, the CCC was but one part of a larger vision to reconstruct the American social order. In May 1933, John Collins, an admirer of Dorothy Day and Father John Ryan of the National Catholic Welfare Conference, became managing editor. In his first front-page editorial, Collins discussed the proper role of a Catholic newspaper in promoting the social encyclicals of Leo XIII and Pius XI. As Collins argued, Pius's 1931 encyclical *Reconstructing the Social Order* was a clarion call to overhaul the moral foundations of American society.

> We have seen, for instance, flagrant exploitation of the laboring classes: in the mines, the mills, the factories, the department stores, conditions have been exposed that shame civilization. The sweatshop, the company store, and starvation wages are only part of them.
>
> We know that political corruption exists and has existed here, and that it has brought a whole train of evils in its wake. The gangster, the racketeer, and the bootlegger have flourished under its protection; the material prosperity denied to the decent workman and the law-abiding business man is enjoyed by those in sinister alliance with law officers faithless to their trust.
>
> As if these intolerable conditions were not enough, our people must

endure constantly the debasing influence of the stage and screen, the daily papers, the magazines, the "circulating novel," and all the other carriers of immoral propaganda. . . . The proper Catholic position in each problem can be determined; we should determine it. The methods laid down in the social encyclical of Pope Pius XI should be invoked; if his words apply any place they apply here.[26]

While the *Pittsburgh Catholic* exhorted readers to participate in the social reconstruction of the city, the National Catholic Welfare Conference was, with some circumspection, urging the Roosevelt administration to take Pius XI's encyclical to heart. In April 1933, Hugh Boyle, John Noll (Fort Wayne, Indiana), Joseph Schrembs, and four other bishops issued a statement on behalf of the American Catholic hierarchy. In the "Present Crisis," the bishops reassured American Protestants that "the Catholic Church is not in politics. She is not allied with any political party." It was not an accurate claim, given that the "Present Crisis" called for Roosevelt to champion the rights of working people and to persuade industrialists that labor and capital "should, as brothers, sit down together at the council table. Unlimited, reckless, immoral competition and economic dictatorship will continue until this is done. Capital and labor should be convinced that greed is a vice, and that a just division of profits can and should be a virtue." In essence, the publicly nonpartisan National Catholic Welfare Conference was asking Republicans to abandon sixty years of laissez-faire capitalist practice and, instead, share the wealth with their employees. This was a message that only a Democrat with a strong belief in government activism, and a deep suspicion of business, could embrace.[27]

The Roosevelt administration did take a step toward curbing the excesses of capitalism with the passage of the National Industrial Recovery Act. One component of the act authorized the creation of the National Recovery Administration. Its director, Hugh Johnson, cajoled businessmen into adopting voluntary codes of conduct. In particular, Johnson wanted industrialists to eliminate what he colorfully called "eye-gouging and knee-groining" competition. One of the factors that had made the Depression grow progressively worse was the practice of industries to expand their share of a contracting market by slashing wages and thereby reducing the cost of their products. Unfortunately, with industries laying off workers and reducing the salaries of those who remained, consumer willingness to buy goods declined. In response, corporations fired more employees, increased the number working part time, and further slashed wages. Consumers who had seen their incomes cut, and feared that they would eventually lose their jobs, proved unwilling to buy marginally less expensive automobiles and refrigerators. This led corporate executives to fire more workers. Johnson hoped to halt wage reductions and layoffs by encouraging businesses not to undersell one another. Additionally, through a clause in the National Industrial Recovery Act, Section 7a, employers agreed to permit workers to bargain collectively. If workers could join unions and negotiate better wages, then they would be able to acquire more consumer goods and thus end the Depression.[28]

Most businessmen agreed to eliminate "eye-gouging" competition in exchange for the federal government's promise to suspend various antitrust laws. Many companies even gave assurances to Hugh Johnson that they would not interfere with their employees' attempts to form labor unions independent of company control. As it developed, businessmen backpedaled away from their agreements, even as they rejoiced in their exemption from federal antitrust prosecution. Their celebrations, however, were short-lived for they had not foreseen that Section 7a would become a major irritant. Perhaps their first, and worst, mistake had been to underestimate the federal government's commitment to some reform in labor-management relations. Shortly after Roosevelt had entered the White House in March, Labor Secretary Frances Perkins, a social worker and America's first female cabinet member, contacted Father John Ryan at the Catholic University. She wanted Ryan and the National Catholic Welfare Conference to participate in wide-ranging discussions of labor problems. If more centrist, cautious, and business oriented than Perkins, Roosevelt had few peers in the art of political mathematics. The recent presidential election had broken sharply along class lines, with the Democrats securing a solid majority of working-class voters. Moreover, the patrician president knew that there were more graduates of the school of hard knocks than there were Harvard alumni.[29]

The Roosevelt administration chose to express its concern for American workers in August when Frances Perkins made a tour of the Pittsburgh steel district. Suspecting that workers might not feel comfortable talking to an upper-middle-class Protestant social worker, Perkins asked Father Francis Haas of the National Catholic Welfare Conference to be her escort. Perkins chose Haas "because he was a friend of labor" and "because the cloth of his profession" would give her credibility with the workers. Before Perkins and Haas left for Homestead, Roosevelt told the labor secretary not to get arrested. He then chuckled, greatly amused by his jest. Too serious to share Roosevelt's gallows humor, Perkins departed Washington with great trepidation.[30]

Her concerns at first appeared to be exaggerated. Myron Taylor, the chair of U.S. Steel, and Eugene Grace, the leader of Bethlehem Steel, ordered their minions to extend every courtesy to Perkins and Father Haas. Subsequently, the two were able to enter mills and talk to workers in McKeesport and Pittsburgh without any company interference. When Haas and Perkins arrived in Homestead, Father Hrtanek offered them the use of St. Anne's Church. Five hundred workers met with Perkins and discussed conditions in the U.S. Steel plant. All had gone well up to that point. On Friday evening, Perkins and Haas held a second meeting, this time at the Borough Hall. After Perkins learned that the Homestead burgess, or mayor, had denied entrance to a few hundred men, she confronted him. Burgess John Cavanaugh refused to allow Perkins to speak to the workers. "These men are not any good," Cavanaugh protested, "They're undesirable Reds. I know them well. They just want to make trouble." When she insisted on talking to them, Cavanaugh ordered her to leave the hall and then shooed her out of the city park. Spotting a post office, Perkins and Haas held a third meeting on federal property over which Cavanaugh had no control.[31]

Perkins depicted Cavanaugh as a tool of a reactionary U.S. Steel and used the Homestead incident to push for an expanded federal role in regulating labor-management relations. Her view of Homestead was incorrect. The encounter also underlined the gap between what Washington thought ailed America and what Bishop Boyle and his allies in the hinterlands knew to be wrong with the country. As burgess, and before that, as a police officer, Cavanaugh regularly shook down Homestead's brothels, distilleries, and gambling joints. He may have trafficked in prostitution, bathtub gin, and numbers, but he was no toady of U.S. Steel.[32]

The New Dealers back in Washington viewed communities like Braddock, Carnegie, Duquesne, and Homestead as company towns. On one level they were correct. The fortunes of these towns depended upon the success of their leading industries. In economic terms, U.S. Steel and Jones & Laughlin did much to determine the quality of life in the mill towns. However, financial domination did not necessarily translate into political control. The Homestead politicians Perkins clashed with in 1933 were not representatives of U.S. Steel. According to the histories she had read, in 1892 Andrew Carnegie, with the assistance of several thousand Pennsylvania National Guardsmen, had broken the back of the Amalgamated Association of Iron, Steel, and Tin Workers. Not content to destroy the union, Carnegie's partner, Henry Frick, drove its officers from the town council. As far as Frick was concerned, it would be a cold day in a blast furnace before the president of a union was ever again elected town burgess.[33]

Once Carnegie sold off his business interests to J. P. Morgan in 1901, the new-born U.S. Steel Corporation endeavored to govern Homestead. The Corporation, as everyone in Pittsburgh succinctly called U.S. Steel, maintained a tight leash on Homestead for several years. However, The Corporation did not anticipate the rise of a rival locus of power. With the immigrant workers finding the Pittsburgh Symphony Orchestra too distant, both physically and culturally, they pursued their recreational pursuits in the town. By the 1920s, an upwardly mobile generation of Slovak, black, and Jewish entrepreneurs had been born. With their fortunes resting upon the gambling, liquor, and prostitution trade, this new middle class flexed its muscles, capturing Homestead's government. Cavanaugh's allies included four Slovaks who sat on the city council; one of them had married a prosperous whorehouse madam.[34]

This was Burgess Cavanaugh's power base: the vice trade, not The Corporation. With greater numbers of children opting to run errands for Cavanaugh, instead of passing their free time learning to become altar boys, the impetus behind the *Pittsburgh Catholic*'s crusade against vice was clear. Perkins thought that the only problems with the mill towns were inadequate wages and corporate oppression. Bishop Boyle and the diocesan newspaper dissented from that view. Giving people more money, but leaving the corruption, would only subsidize self-destructive behavior. This was why the *Pittsburgh Catholic* had observed that there could not be an improvement in the material condition of people without there also being a reformation in the spiritual values of the working poor. Beyond better incomes, people required a reason to live that transcended material concerns. They also needed to be taught that an abusive lifestyle sentenced their children to poverty. The New Deal could provide neither the instruction nor the sense of a greater purpose. That was a job for the clergy and laity—Catholic, Jewish, and Protestant.[35]

If Homestead was not the legendary company town Frances Perkins made it out to be, there were other industrial centers in the district that deserved the title. In Aliquippa, Jones & Laughlin ruled ruthlessly. The steel company owned Aliquippa's fresh water supply, held title to many workers' homes, and routinely purchased politicians and police officers. Since Jones & Laughlin employed one-third of the Aliquippa's thirty thousand residents, crossing the company would, at best, result in unemployment and the need to find another job elsewhere in the district. At worst, Jones & Laughlin dealt savagely with "troublemakers." Shortly after Perkins returned to Washington, John Mayer, a representative of the Amalgamated Association of Iron, Steel, and Tin Workers, attempted to convince Jones & Laughlin employees to join the union. The Amalgamated, an affiliate of the American Federation of Labor, hoped to awaken from the coma it had been in since 1892. AFL president William Green believed that Section 7a of the National Industrial Recovery Act protected labor organizers from company reprisals. Green was

Fig. 3.   Pittsburgh neighborhood darkened by Jones & Laughlin mill in the early 1940s. Before the economic crisis of the 1930s shut down Pittsburgh's smoke-spewing mills, the street lights would come on at noon. (Courtesy of the Carnegie Library, Pittsburgh.)

wrong. Two Jones & Laughlin operatives beat Mayer until he was nearly blind. With the beating finished, Aliquippa policemen arrested Mayer for disorderly conduct.[36]

The bloody response of Jones & Laughlin to union organizing efforts was not a surprise to UMW leaders. However, Phil Murray and his secretary, David McDonald, also believed that the union movement confronted enemies other than those who inhabited corporate boardrooms. In 1923, McDonald, attending his first AFL national convention, watched in amazement as a Communist Party operative denounced Murray. The president of a Virginian UMW district responded to the Communist:

> The Communists don't give a damn about the workers. In my state, the Communists are working hand in glove with the coal operators to wreck the United Mine Workers of America. They know they have no chance to establish their own union or to take over the UMW, so

they have joined with the people they say they hate to destroy the only organization that *really* works for the miners. And why are the Communists doing this? I'll tell you why. Because you think that by destroying our union you can wipe out all the gains we've made and then move into that misery and take over for the Communists. You don't care about the workers. All you care about is the party.[37]

McDonald claimed that the coal operators and the Communists had extensive ties. In 1926, a UMW official in Illinois, who was also a secret Communist Party organizer, allegedly received funds from the Peabody Coal Company. Peabody's owners may have wanted the Communist to seize control of the union, expecting him to drive it into the ground. The next year, several Communists, who called themselves members of the "Save the Union Committee," sponsored a convention in Pittsburgh. Murray exposed the committee, charging that the Pittsburgh Coal Company had given the Communist Party $50,000 to finance its efforts to wreck the UMW. The Communists denied the charge. As McDonald later claimed, the Pittsburgh Coal Company had actually given the "Save the Union Committee" $100,000. Defeated in their efforts to capture the leadership of the UMW, the Communists in 1928 established the rival National Miners' Union. John Brophy initially sympathized with the rebels, believing they offered a democratic alternative to John L. Lewis's rule. After he discovered the Communist role in forming the National Miners' Union, Brophy repudiated the organization and its leaders.[38]

In short order, the National Miners' Union became a magnet for industrial violence. Having no problem with shooting strikers, the coal operators counted upon the general public to confuse the National Miners' Union with the United Mine Workers. For quite different reasons, both the coal operators and the Communists wanted to create a political backlash against the UMW. In 1930, the Communists expanded their activities among workers, establishing the Steel and Metal Workers Industrial Union. The party hoped to finish off the decrepit Amalgamated. Three years later, Communist organizers and mill owners clashed in Ambridge, Pennsylvania. One person died. One participant in the Ambridge confrontation, Jessie Lloyd O'Connor, the wife of *Federated Press* correspondent Harvey O'Connor, quickly returned to Pittsburgh to avoid arrest.[39]

Since their arrival in Pittsburgh in 1931, the O'Connors had become leading members of the community's Left, their activities financed by Jessie's trust fund. (Her grandfather was the millionaire socialist Henry Demarest Lloyd.) Harvey O'Connor had gained some national attention with the 1933 publication of *Mellon's Millions: The Biography of a Fortune*. The muckraking book enjoyed brisk sales. Many Pittsburgh shopkeepers, their leases held by Mellon National Bank & Trust, preferred to keep the book hidden under their counters until customers asked for it. A. J. Muste thought that Harvey O'Connor was a valuable ally, but had written Elmer Cope in 1931 warning him that the O'Connors possessed strong Communist leanings. Harvey O'Connor's membership in the Communist-front Friends of the Soviet Union might have led Muste to that conclusion. However, if Muste was afraid that Cope would inadvertently pass along information to the Communists, he should not have worried. One member of the executive board of the Conference for Progressive Labor Action, the Oxford-educated Len DeCaux, was a secret Communist Party organizer. A second member of the board, Louis Budenz, became a major figure in the party.[40]

Cope did not have to be concerned that the Communist Party would successfully challenge the socialists for leadership of the unemployed. The Communist Unemployed Councils had made little headway in the Monongahela and Ohio valleys. In part this was because the Communists were never able to form a successful grassroots movement among the unemployed. Their style was to join an existing group and then move into its leadership, imposing direction from above. Most workers quit the Unemployed Councils once Communist leadership became obvious. Additionally, the Communists made few converts among the Catholic majority in the coal patches and steel towns of Pennsylvania, Ohio, and Illinois. Church teaching against Communism limited the party's reach.[41] Blacks 2nd choice/Sneaky methods

Unable to penetrate Catholic neighborhoods, the Communists focused their attentions on recruiting blacks. In the Homewood neighborhood of Pittsburgh, the Communists told blacks that the Unemployed Councils would fight discrimination. The Communists also supposedly resorted to other means to recruit blacks to the party. John Gillard, writing for *The Commonweal* in 1932, noted that Harlem Communists had purportedly used Jewish females to attract black males to party functions. Although not thrilled with such couplings, Gillard blamed discrimination and racial injustice for allowing Communism to paint "many a black man red." Catholics, Gillard concluded, had to become the champions of blacks and save them from the Communist embrace. After all, Catholics and blacks were both minorities and victims of discrimination.[42]

Ultimately, the Communists made little progress in Pittsburgh because the New Deal was bringing about some material improvement for working-class residents. Meeting with representatives of the National Recovery Administration and the coal industry in 1933, John L. Lewis grew irritated with vice president P. C. Thomas of the Mellon-owned Koppers Coal Company. Thomas refused to reach an agreement with the UMW. Shortly thereafter, Andrew Mellon called the chief executive officer of the Pittsburgh Coal Company, who was also at the meeting. He asked why a settlement had not been reached. Sitting in the anteroom, McDonald could hear a string of curses flying from the telephone. Weary of being blamed for every bit of bad economic news since 1929, Mellon was ready to cut a deal with Lewis. His recent conversation with Roosevelt may have also persuaded him that it was better to cooperate with the federal government lest vocal populists in Congress decided to take more drastic action. An agreement with the UMW was preferable to the nationalization of the coal fields—a course of action John Brophy had recommended in the 1920s and one which Mellon feared.[43]

Mellon's accommodation salvaged the fortunes of the UMW. Insisting that Section 7a of the National Industrial Recovery Act gave federal approval to labor organizing, Lewis told workers that Roosevelt wanted them to join the UMW. As the UMW marched from victory to victory, however, the Amalgamated Association of Iron, Steel, and Tin Workers remained hidebound. Resenting Elmer Cope's call for a more aggressive posture in the recruitment of unskilled workers, president Mike Tighe engineered his expulsion from the organization. The leadership of the Pittsburgh-based union had no sense that 1933 had been the harbinger of greater things to come.[44]

The *Pittsburgh Catholic* rang in 1934 by praising Roosevelt's message to Congress. If, as editor John Collins observed, Roosevelt had not embraced all of Pius XI's points in *Reconstructing the Social Order*, the president had pledged to fight "the ruthless exploitation of all labor" in 1934. To assist Roosevelt in that struggle, Bishop Boyle announced that a Catholic Conference on Industrial Problems would be held in Pittsburgh. For the past year, the Social Action Department of the National Catholic Welfare Conference had hosted discussions on *The Condition of Labor* and *Reconstructing the Social Order* in Chicago, Cleveland, Detroit, and New York. Boyle appointed Father Hrtanek to work with the Catholic University's new monsignor, John Ryan, on the conference.[45]

A thousand people attended the two-day conference in February, including union, business, and Church representatives. Economists from Notre Dame and the University of Pittsburgh also held sessions on the creation of old age pensions and unemployment compensation. The conference ran smoothly, blending academic, political, and religious points of view. Harmony prevailed up to the point when Ernest Weir, chair of the Pittsburgh-based National Steel Corporation, shared his thoughts with the assembly. Weir charged that the National Labor Board, created by Roosevelt in Au-

Fig. 4.   Ernest Weir founded the National Steel Corporation in 1929 after merging three companies, including his Weirton (West Virginia) Steel Company. Here Weir is standing with his attorneys in 1934 as they prepare to do battle with the Federal Government over collective bargaining.

gust 1933 to mediate disputes between workers and management, was "prejudiced, biased, and unfair to industry." He further accused AFL president William Green and UMW president Lewis of acting as judge and jury. According to Weir, the labor leaders controlled the National Labor Board and always reached settlements that undermined American business and democracy.[46]

Pat Fagan of the UMW defended Lewis while letters poured into the offices of the *Pittsburgh Catholic* charging Weir with having intimidated union organizers. The most thorough critique of Weir did not come from either labor leaders or anonymous National Steel employees. A week after the conference, Father Joseph Lonergan of the Clairton, Pennsylvania, St. Paulinus Church wrote a blistering column for the *Pittsburgh Catholic*:

> The stockholders [of the National Steel Corporation] are bound to-
> gether in a close, powerful, centrally controlled organization with a
> billion dollars of capital, with funds aplenty to hire the best brains
> that money can buy. This corporation is a member of the [American]
> Iron and Steel Institute binding the tremendous power of the various
> steel corporations in a super-organization, with a large amount of
> control over the legislation, courts, political office-holders, the very
> government.
>
>    . . . Standing alone [the worker] does not have the chance of a snow
> ball in a blast furnace. His only hope of entering into an agreement
> that will in any sense be free and equitable is to be represented by a
> person or a moral person of equal power. In other words, each and
> every steel worker to the last man will have to be bound together in
> an organization, a moral person, that is in every way as powerful as
> the steel industry. Then and then only will the steel worker be in a po-
> sition to enter into a free and equitable agreement with his employer.[47]

Father Lonergan made no impression on Weir. He had founded the National Steel Corporation in 1929 after merging three companies, including his
Weirton (West Virginia) Steel business. Focusing on a niche market, Weir
avoided direct competition with U.S. Steel which did a great portion of its
trade with the Big Three automobile makers. When Big Three sales sharply
declined after 1929, The Corporation fell upon difficult times. Meanwhile,
National Steel maintained its market share in the manufacture of cans. Consumers who would not purchase a car would buy canned goods. In 1932,
Weir's company was the only steel concern showing a profit. On Wall Street,
National Steel commanded attention since its stocks were a rarity on the exchange; their value increased nearly 41 percent between 1932 and 1933.[48]

National Steel also commanded attention in Washington. In 1933, Weir
and Bethlehem Steel's Eugene Grace met with Frances Perkins in order to
discuss NRA codes for their industry. As they entered her office, they noticed
AFL president William Green. Taken aback, Weir and Grace retreated to a
corner of the room. They reminded Perkins of "frightened little boys" who
would not move until Green had left. Once Green departed, Weir assured
Perkins that he would abide by the terms of Section 7a. However, Weir refused to deal with the AFL "racketeers," and, instead, established a subservient company union. As his feud with the AFL continued into the spring
of 1934, Weir instructed his legal counsel to invite seventy-five industrialists
from fifty mills to a special gathering. The representatives of National Steel
and Jones & Laughlin, among others, met to formulate strategies against the

AFL and the New Deal. Weir was notably upset with the efforts of Senator Robert Wagner, a New York Democrat, to "virtually outlaw company unions." This was "class legislation," Weir cried, that discriminated against the wealthy.[49]

Bishop Boyle rejected Weir's interpretation of the Wagner bill. At an April meeting of the Administrative Council of the National Catholic Welfare Conference, the bishops sent a letter to the Senate Committee on Education and Labor. They endorsed Senator Wagner's proposal to guarantee the right of workers to join unions. The bishops also pushed for the establishment of a stronger federal tribunal to adjudicate labor disputes. Boyle's colleagues spelled out the religious impulse behind their reasoning:

> The worker can exercise his God-given faculty of freedom and properly order his life in preparation for eternity only through a system which permits him freely to choose his representatives in industry. From a practical standpoint, the worker's free choice of representatives must be safeguarded in order to secure for him equality of contractual power in the wage contract. Undue interference with this choice is an unfair labor practice, unjust alike to worker and the general public.[50]

Father Carl Hensler, assistant pastor of Pittsburgh's St. Lawrence Church, recognized that the stakes in the dispute between Weir and organized labor were enormous. At issue was the kind of society the industrialists and the bishops hoped to construct. Hensler was not the type of clergyman to sit out such an important debate. Born in Carnegie at the turn of the century, Hensler's father had been a coal mine foreman who sired seven children. Carl's sister, Mary, became a nun while his brother Frank chose to serve God by becoming a labor organizer. The early deaths of Hensler's parents left Carl responsible for his younger siblings' support. Having personally seen how quickly people could fall from financial security to economic hardship, Hensler devoted himself to improving the lot of those who were less fortunate.[51]

A bright youth, Hensler's teachers directed him to St. Vincent's Seminary. Impressing the faculty at St. Vincent's, Hensler received a rare invitation to attend the North American College in Rome. Only those whom the Vatican was grooming for a position in the Church hierarchy studied at the North American College. In 1924, Hensler had the distinct honor of being ordained by the Cardinal Vicar of the Roman Diocese. Hensler spent the next six years as an assistant pastor in Braddock, before heading to China to establish the Catholic University of Peking. Boyle and Hensler corresponded frequently,

Fig. 5.   Father Carl Hensler, Pittsburgh labor priest. This photograph shows Father Hensler at the Catholic University of Peking in the late 1920s. (Courtesy of the Diocese of Pittsburgh Archives.)

with the priest discussing his efforts to build a social studies department and to place the university press on firm footing. Hensler also confided to Boyle that conditions in China were horrible, yet the people somehow persevered. "I am learning for the first time how really cold a winter can be. The poor, as usual, suffered more than others. The papers report many deaths from freezing. They were largely coolies, a class of people who bravely attempt to live on nothing, and look happy while doing it."[52]

Hensler returned to Pittsburgh in 1934. The shocked priest confronted conditions that he thought he had left behind in China. With the blessing and warm friendship of Bishop Boyle, Hensler became an assistant pastor, educator, and political activist. At St. Lawrence, Hensler lectured on the social encyclicals while in the columns of the *Pittsburgh Catholic* he discussed Christian ethics and economics. According to Hensler, selfish individualism and laissez-faire capitalism had committed suicide by bringing about a "bad distribution of the national income." Consequently, "wealthy individuals may sport yachts and Rolls Royce cars, but man for man they do not consume much more in the way of beefsteaks, shoes, and toothbrushes than do their poorer neighbors. On the other hand, the masses who could and would have consumed all that industry produces, were unable to do so because they lacked purchasing power." A society in which 60 percent of Americans did not have "enough income for health and decency," Hensler contended, required reconstruction.

> It is becoming increasingly evident that a proper distribution of the national income calls for a thorough reformation of the entire profit-system. An equitable allocation of income cannot be left to the functioning of purely natural forces. Experience teaches that it won't work. Men themselves must regulate the system under which they live. This means that profits, wages, and prices be made to conform to the demands of the common good and the principles of social justice.[53]

Beyond an equitable distribution of the nation's income, Hensler knew that the New Deal could not reconstruct the social order without first building a new ethical foundation for the nation. Humans, Hensler wrote, did not exist simply to acquire wealth. Rather, man's ultimate end in life was to obey the Supreme Law. God's law required people to recognize that achieving a good end through evil means was wrong. Those who followed God's instruction also knew "that the family is more sacred than the State and that men are begotten not for the earth, and for time, but for heaven and eternity."

*Important*

Opposed to the creation of a powerful federal bureaucracy that usurped God's place on earth, the Supreme Law also called upon people not to destroy their bodies through narcotics and alcohol abuse. Nor should people defile their minds by imitating the dissolute lifestyles often depicted on the movie screen. "Their example has made vicious speech and vicious conduct seem smart and good and desirable to young people everywhere in the country," Hensler said of many Hollywood actors. Further, "Their manner, their dress, the indecency of their speech, are imitated by little children, as well as by young people who should know better, and whose standards of right and wrong in the matters derive from other sources than Hollywood."[54]

The positions Hensler took on poverty, federal power, and morality were consistent with Church teaching, although they bewildered many secularized New Dealers. Was the Church liberal or conservative, or both? Liberals were hard pressed to explain how bishops Boyle and John Noll could endorse the rights of workers to organize and freely express themselves while simultaneously leading a new organization, the Legion of Decency, in a crusade to censor Hollywood. New Dealers were even more perplexed, when not enraged, by the Church's stance against a constitutional amendment to prohibit child labor. Throughout the winter and spring of 1934, the *Pittsburgh Catholic* condemned the amendment.

> It is an ingenuous attempt to make children responsible to the national government instead of to their parents. Its language is too broad, too indefinite, too general, in the face of principles of well-known construction to suggest otherwise. It is an attack upon the family. It strikes a blow at the home. It is opposed to the ideals, the traditions, of our American institutions.

Even if the amendment was ratified, the *Pittsburgh Catholic* concluded, businessmen would ignore the ban. The best course to follow, would be for the federal government and the Church to teach the public not to buy goods made in sweatshops that exploited children and women.[55]

Secretary of the Interior Harold Ickes, a leader of liberal opinion in Roosevelt's cabinet, privately expressed disgust with the Church's opposition to the child labor amendment. The reformist mayor of New York, the Episcopalian Fiorello La Guardia, shared Ickes's view, telling the interior secretary that Catholic criticism of the proposed amendment reminded him of "the Spanish Inquisition." Unwilling to consider the bishops' concerns about the relationship between the government and the family, Ickes was also prone to ignore the great support the Church gave to other New Deal initiatives. Given that most of the press was hostile to Roosevelt, Catholic newspapers provided a valuable forum to advance the New Deal. Certainly, the staid *New York Times* would not have published an editorial on the New Deal like the one the *Pittsburgh Catholic* carried on the one-year anniversary of Roosevelt's inauguration:

> The material depression has, to a marked, even though limited, degree, been lifted; the mental and spiritual depression, which was decidedly more serious, has been unquestionably conquered; there has been rooted out of the American mind, permanently, let us hope, the notion that the nation exists for the sole purpose of bringing material profit to those shrewd enough to acquire control of industry and commerce. The American people should long remember March 5, 1933, as the day that opened up a new and brighter era.[56]

The American Catholic Church also puzzled many New Dealers and socialists by simultaneously rejecting Communism and laissez-faire capitalism. Moreover, they could not understand why Church reformers urged Catholics to ignore those who red-baited the AFL. Surely, liberals and socialists countered, the Church was actively anti-Communist. Was there any difference between the anti-Communist stances of the Catholic Church and the anti–New Deal businessman? To the *Pittsburgh Catholic*, the answer to that question was obvious: Catholics opposed Communism because they believed in social justice. In contrast, Ernest Weir and other corporate leaders raised the specter of Communist influence in the labor movement and the New Deal as a way to thwart social justice.

> Hence it is clear that Catholics (and clear thinkers outside the Church see the matter in the same light) must not be misled by the specious claims of Communism or socialism, but neither must they be deterred from laboring for social justice by parrot cries of radicalism. For it is perfectly plain that Communism would have no chance of winning converts in a well-ordered, Christian society; it is only the obvious evils of the present system that have given the extremists a hearing among the suffering masses. Whoever helps to bring closer the era of Christian social justice is helping to build a strong wall against Communism; but he who aids in any way to perpetuate the "abominable abuses," the "injustices and frauds," the "unconscionable methods,"

the "enormous evils" which the Pontiff describes as associated with the prevailing economic order, is furthering the plans of those who would not reform, but destroy that order.[57]

At least two major institutions in Western Pennsylvania were not about to become friends of the labor movement: Jones & Laughlin and the University of Pittsburgh. Since John Mayer's beating at the hands of the Jones & Laughlin "goon squad," the Pennsylvania Department of Labor and Industry had dispatched Clinton Golden to Aliquippa. Born the son of a Southern Baptist minister in 1888, Golden's father had tended to the spiritual needs of black slaves before moving north after the Civil War. Orphaned at the age of nine, Golden found work in an iron ore mine. He later became a locomotive fireman as well as a machinist. Golden also joined the International Association of Machinists and read every book that came his way. By the 1920s, the self-educated union officer joined John Brophy in founding the Brookwood Labor College. A member of the executive board of the Conference for Progressive Labor Action, Golden became disturbed by A. J. Muste's flirtation with Trotskyism and advocacy of violent revolution. Although Golden did not make a formal break with Muste in 1930, he put some distance between himself and the Communists whom he felt were gaining control of Brookwood. After three years of farming in Bucks County, Pennsylvania, the sheriff came on behalf of Golden's creditors to seize his land and furniture.[58]

In debt, and with a family to support, Golden found himself in Aliquippa, secure in the knowledge that if Jones & Laughlin arranged for him to disappear, Governor Gifford Pinchot would call for an investigation. As Golden began talking to workers that fall, he discovered the existence of an extensive company spy network. He also had the privilege of listening to an anti-union rally led by the captain of the Jones & Laughlin security forces. The captain informed the two hundred people lining the sidewalks in front of a barbershop that he would "bust up" every "son of a bitch" who joined the Amalgamated. This was no idle threat. In early September, three company policemen confronted George Issoski and confiscated the union pledge cards that he had been distributing to steel workers. A few days later, other police officers arrested and beat Issoski. Jones & Laughlin then arranged to have the Slovak unionist committed to the State Hospital for the Insane. Issoski might have remained there had not Golden brought his case before Pinchot who then ordered his release.[59]

While Jones & Laughlin tried to cow its employees, Chancellor John Bowman of the University of Pittsburgh clashed with his activist faculty and students. When Bowman came to Pitt in 1921, he planned to make the provincial school into a major research institution. With twelve of the twenty-nine trustees of the university also serving as directors in Andrew Mellon's companies, Bowman was not shy about asking for money. One of Bowman's pet projects was the construction of a skyscraper classroom and administrative building in Oakland. The Cathedral of Learning, or, to the more cynical, "The Heights of Ignorance," was to cost $10 million and rise fifty-two stories—the tallest structure devoted to higher education in America. According to his socialist critics, Bowman was a racial theorist. Every ethnic group in Pittsburgh was to have a classroom dedicated to it and located in the cathedral. Bowman's foes claimed that proximity of the classrooms to the Anglo-Saxon Commons depended upon the racial worth of each group. The Slovak classroom was distant from the Medieval Commons. In reality, Bowman scattered classrooms hither and yon, his primary concern being financial, not racial. Playing to ethnic pride, Bowman solicited school children for their pennies. Bowman promised the "Hunkie" children that their donations would be used to decorate "their" classrooms.[60]

Construction of the cathedral began shortly before the onset of the Depression. With Bowman's funds drying up, the chancellor scaled back the height of his building to forty-two stories. To shame Mellon National Bank & Trust and U.S. Steel into donating more money, Bowman left the bottom three floors of the structure exposed, ordering his masons to begin their work from the top. The chancellor was making an inspired, desperate gamble, in effect extorting funds from the city's corporate elite by rendering "their" building uninhabitable and weird looking. If he was going to succeed in this endeavor, Bowman would have to give his trustees and donors something in exchange—a pledge to silence the Pitt students and faculty who criticized district businessmen.[61]

By no means could Pitt claim as many student radicals as the City University of New York. However, the extent of their activities belied their small numbers. In 1927, a few Pitt students had formed a Liberal Club to sponsor debates on socialist ideas. Bowman disbanded the club and expelled two student leaders. Uncowed, the remaining students founded a chapter of the Young People's Socialist League, a Socialist Party affiliate. In 1931, they were publishing *The Young Socialist* which attacked Jones & Laughlin for reducing workers' wages. Pitt students also wrote the *Voice of Revolt*, which was aimed at high school students. The *Voice of Revolt* intoned that there was little point in going to college since the crippled capitalist economy did not need more accountants, doctors, lawyers, and teachers. In 1932, students founded the Pitt Socialist Club and published *The Gadfly*, daring Bowman to suppress both. He did.[62]

Several Pitt professors objected to Bowman's treatment of the Liberal Club, prompting them to join the Pittsburgh branch of the American Civil Liberties Union. In 1933, economist Carroll Daugherty and sociologist Harold Phelps worked with the YMCA to sponsor an educational program on unemployment and poverty. A year later, economist Francis Tyson spoke at the Catholic Conference on Industrial Problems where he urged the creation of a federal unemployment insurance system. Tyson was also a member of the Pittsburgh League for Social Justice, a group Elmer Cope had founded in 1932 to organize the unemployed and reform the Amalgamated. Pitt professor and Civil Liberties leader B. J. Hovde served as chair of the League for Social Justice.[63]

Bowman regarded his activist faculty as Communists, a peculiar sentiment to Cope since in 1932 the Pittsburgh Communist Party had denounced the League for Social Justice as a fascist front. In 1934, Bowman purged his more troublesome faculty. His most notable target was Ralph Turner. The historian had incurred Bowman's wrath in 1933 by becoming the chair of the Pennsylvania Security League, a socialist organization that advocated the establishment of federal old-age pensions and unemployment insurance. One of Carroll Daugherty's former students, Harold Ruttenberg, leaped to Turner's defense, denouncing Bowman as a "Tory," as well as a tool of the city's "steel-munitions-oil rulers." Turner's dismissal soon came to the attention of leftist magazines across America. Rose Stein, a Pittsburgh socialist, reported to *The Nation* that Bowman's loyalists were "Academic Cossacks." Seeking sympathy outside the Pittsburgh Chamber of Commerce and the Duquesne Club, Bowman claimed Turner was an atheist. The positive reaction that Bowman expected from the city's Catholics did not materialize. After all, Duquesne, not Pitt, was "their" university. The *Pittsburgh Catholic*, which did not like Bowman, noted that Turner's religion, or lack of it, was not the issue. Rather, editor John Collins argued, the issue was academic freedom and Bowman's efforts to make higher education subservient to a discredited business ethos.[64]

Even as Bowman denounced the New Deal to Pitt trustee Ernest Weir, the chancellor did not pass up opportunities to acquire financial assistance—regardless of the source. Once Roosevelt established the Civil Works Administration in 1933 to provide temporary work to the unemployed, Bowman stood in line for federal aid. Stone masons employed by the Civil Works Administration put the final touches on the Cathedral of Learning. When the *Pittsburgh Post-Gazette* complained that the federal agency was hiring union labor to work on the cathedral, Bowman remained uncharacteristically quiet.[65]

The Pitt chancellor was not the only public figure trying to learn the fine art of discretion. Senator David Aiken Reed was up for reelection. A New Deal army formed to engage him in battle. Congressman Henry Ellenbogen joined Pat Fagan and diocesan secretary Father Andrew Pauley at Labor Day rallies. Reed sensed impending doom. Bishop Boyle never said anything directly critical of Senator Reed, but the National Catholic Welfare Conference had called his efforts to restrict Catholic and Jewish immigration "racist." The bishops did not use that epithet lightly. Reed also had to fend off Governor Pinchot who derived great pleasure in accusing the senator of being a front for the steel corporations. Desperate, Reed ran full-page advertisements in the *Pittsburgh Catholic*, emphasizing his World War I military record and giving the impression that he was a friend of the AFL. Fooling no one, Reed lost to Joseph Guffey by 128,000 votes. Although the Republican machine delivered Philadelphia to Reed, David Lawrence mobilized 143,000 Democratic voters in Allegheny County. Thanks to Pittsburgh, carrying Republican Philadelphia no longer meant winning the state.[66]

Reed's defeat was part of a larger Republican disaster at the polls. Democrats won twenty-two of Pennsylvania's thirty-two congressional seats, seized the state house, and elected a governor. Only the rural-dominated state senate and Philadelphia County remained Republican bastions. Nationally, Republicans lost thirteen congressional races, giving the Democrats 322 seats in the House, compared to 103 for the Republicans, and 10 for pro-New Deal independents. In the Senate, Democrats won nine races, giving them a majority of 69 seats. The Republicans retained seven governorships. Given the proportions of this electoral mandate, federal relief director Harry Hopkins saw 1935 as the year in which America would get a national system of pensions and strong labor legislation. The *Pittsburgh Catholic* tried mightily not to overstep the bounds of religious propriety by endorsing candidates. After the election, however, the newspaper tweaked Republicans for clinging to "rugged individualism," greed, and "other evils antagonistic to social justice."[67]

As the *Pittsburgh Catholic* had hoped, the seeds of social reconstruction that the Church and other activists planted in 1933 bore fruit in 1935. Reformers would have much to celebrate. Harold Ruttenberg, who became a typist for the Amalgamated in the hope of organizing resistance to the union's stand-pat leadership, moved to Harrisburg in 1935. There he served as a state organizer for the Pennsylvania Security League. Ruttenberg also coordinated the activities of Pennsylvania's Unemployed Citizens' Leagues, filling in the vacuum left by Cope when he parted company with A. J. Muste and returned to Ohio. To Ruttenberg's delight, the New Deal soon adopted many of the Pennsylvania Security League's causes: federal old age pensions, unemployment insurance, and a minimum wage. Much to his chagrin, the Communist Party tried to lay claim to the league's program. Indeed, that January the Communists held a National Congress for Unemployment and Social Insurance in Washington. At their Washington meeting, the Communists argued that they were now allies of the New Deal. (The sponsors of the unemployment congress represented a who's who of American Communism: Harry Bridges, president of the International Longshoremen's Association; Benjamin Davis, editor of *The Negro Liberator*; and Ben Gold, national secretary of the Fur Workers Industrial Union. Only Bridges denied that he was a Communist Party member.)[68]

Although the Communist Party took credit for inspiring every piece of New Deal legislation that it considered "progressive," it was a hollow boast. Communist Party chief Earl Browder in 1933 had said, "It is clear that fascism already finds much of its work done in America, and more of this is being done by Roosevelt." After two years of denouncing Roosevelt and the AFL, the party line shifted. By 1935, the Communists wanted to make common cause with the New Deal in order to influence government policies, particularly in regard to foreign policy. The Communist cadres also abandoned their efforts to build their own coal and steel unions. Instead, they returned to their original tactic of joining established labor unions. But for all of their expressions of friendship, the Communists never forgave Roosevelt for having saved American capitalism.[69] *Which ones?*

When Roosevelt entered the White House in 1933 his priorities had been to restore Americans' faith in the banking system and to put people to work on federal projects before they starved to death. To shore up American finance, Congress passed the Banking Act of 1933. This act gave greater powers to the Federal Reserve Board to prevent financial institutions from lending money for highly speculative business ventures that could drag the bank down with the borrower. This legislation also created the Federal Deposit Insurance Corporation in order to insure the deposits of ordinary people who would lose all of their savings if the bank failed. Two years later, the Banking Act of 1935 gave the Federal Reserve Board in Washington even more power. The Federal Reserve's new Board of Governors was authorized to review the books of lending institutions, set the prime interest rate, and determine how much money banks had to keep in reserve and how much of their funds could be used for loans.[70]

Confronted with millions of needy people, the Democratic Congress had established the Federal Emergency Relief Administration. Relief director Harry Hopkins funneled millions of dollars to the states between 1934 and

1935. With this federal aid, state governments built 240,000 miles of roads and provided immunization shots to one million people. A champion of work relief, Hopkins pushed Roosevelt to establish the Civil Works Administration in the fall of 1933. The Civil Works Administration employed four million people on projects ranging from laying sewer lines to building playgrounds. As a result of graft at the local level, the Civil Works Administration and the Federal Emergency Relief Administration gave way to the Works Progress Administration. Hopkins hoped that the WPA, which Roosevelt created by Executive Order in 1935, would be free of corruption and provide meaningful work to the 20 percent of the labor force that remained unemployed.[71]

Communists bemoaned the New Deal's relief programs, believing that they were restoring workers' morale and undermining the appeal of their Unemployed Councils. The Pennsylvania Security League and the socialist Unemployed Citizens Leagues viewed matters differently, shepherding their members directly on to WPA rolls. Welcoming the expansion of work relief programs, the *Pittsburgh Catholic* warned in early 1935 that federal welfare programs which required nothing in return from recipients were creating

> conditions that weaken self-respect, darkens family life, and affect evilly the moral fiber of young and old. The theory that "the world owes me a living" is being widely replaced by the cynical assertion that "the world owes me all I can get by fair means or foul," and to administer relief without developing a general moral breakdown is becoming a task more and more difficult.
>
> Without religion, of course, the task would be not only difficult but impossible, and it is clear that in so far as religion is permitted and urged to enter into any solution of the relief problem will that solution be successful. The churches are doing their best to maintain the morale of the people, to strengthen them against the dangers caused by present conditions.[72]

If poverty and welfare corrupted the spirit of household heads, then it followed that the children of the unemployed were in great peril. Father H. J. Huber, the superintendent of St. Joseph's Protectory for Homeless Boys, warned in February 1935 that juvenile crime was on the rise. While economic conditions contributed to the rise in delinquency, Huber contended that too many parents had "been neglectful in the care and supervision of their children. An all-wise God has made parents their children's keepers and theirs is an inescapable responsibility." J. William McGowan, Pittsburgh's presiding Morals Court magistrate, as well as the director of the Catholic Boy Wel-

fare Bureau, concurred with Father Huber. McGowan sadly observed that
of the 1,392 boys arraigned before Morals Court in 1934, 710 were Catholic.
Merely 44 of the boys were Jewish—good support for the proposition that
just because an ethnic group clustered in the ghetto did not mean that its
youths would become criminally inclined. When Roosevelt established the
National Youth Administration by Executive Order in the summer of 1935,
McGowan became the Western Pennsylvania director of the program.
Through the National Youth Administration, McGowan provided employment and job training to thousands of teenagers whose parents were without work.[73]

Work relief, job training, and reforms in the banking system were not
enough, according to Father Hensler, to protect the working poor and advance "their claims to the minimum amounts of goods and opportunities
that are required for a decent livelihood." A person could work for many
years at subsistence wages and then, upon infirmity or disability, find that
there were not enough savings with which to live decently in retirement. One
way to rectify this injustice, the Church contended, was for business, labor,
and government to cooperate in the creation of a pension system. The American Catholic bishops had embraced the idea of federal pensions in 1919.
Sixteen years later, Monsignor John Ryan, who had helped to write the
bishop's 1919 statement, represented the National Catholic Welfare Conference on a special federal advisory council. The advisory council recommended
that Congress establish a national retirement program. In consultation with
Harry Hopkins and Frances Perkins, Congress passed the Social Security Act
of 1935.[74]

In addition to providing pensions, the Social Security Act created a federal and state compensation fund for involuntarily unemployed workers and
allocated funds for single mothers. To ensure that Republicans would never
be able to abolish Social Security, Roosevelt suggested that employees be required to pay a token payroll tax. Having paid into the Social Security system, few workers would tolerate any politician who threatened to "take away
their money." This was an unnecessary safeguard since most people did not
believe Republican charges that Social Security would bankrupt the country.
There were not many Americans who lived to the retirement age of sixty-
five, and even fewer who continued much beyond that age. More people
would always be paying into the system than drawing money out of it. Nor
did many Americans in 1935 seriously consider Republican claims that the
act's provision for Aid to [Families with] Dependent Children would encourage women to have children out of wedlock. This entitlement was intended for women whose husbands had died or deliberately abandoned them.

Women, liberals protested, did not choose to become single mothers. The availability of federal assistance to support their children would not alter that reality.[75]

As the Catholic bishops had stated in 1919, while employers and the federal government should provide pensions, in the long run workers had to provide for their own retirement. To accomplish that, many clergy argued, the federal government would have to assist workers in raising their standard of living. In 1935, Hensler reiterated the bishops' proposition: "Labor's portion of the national income must be increased; that of capital decreased. This means, in effect, not only higher wages and salaries, but also lower dividend and interest rates. . . . Men must be rewarded more for what they do than for what they own." At the same time, Hensler did not want a highly centralized government dictating national economic policy and coercing business into raising wages. "State control of economic activity has generally proved a failure. It is either ineffective, or encroaches too heavily upon human liberty. . . . Social control by compulsion can enforce obedience only be means of inspectors, and nobody loves being inspected." Frightened by the possibility of federal dictatorship, Hensler had embraced the National Industrial Recovery Act. The priest believed in voluntary cooperation among representatives of business, labor, and the government. When the United States Supreme Court declared in 1935 that the act was unconstitutional, social reformers had to write new legislation.[76]

Even as the Supreme Court moved against the National Industrial Recovery Act, Senator Wagner sponsored a bill to retain and strengthen Section 7a. The Wagner Act created a National Labor Relations Board that guaranteed free union elections. Wagner prohibited management from intimidating employees who wanted to organize and would not allow business to evade the intent of the law by establishing company unions. The National Labor Relations Board became a bastion of unionism and—according to Soviet archives—Communism. (Not surprisingly, its first three board directors were extremely hostile toward business.) While the *Pittsburgh Catholic* and the National Catholic Welfare Conference lamented the decision of the Supreme Court to overturn the National Industrial Recovery Act, they endorsed Wagner's efforts. The National Labor Relations Board hired economist David Saposs as an advisor. Although a proponent of labor unions, Saposs had, in an article published in 1933 by *Modern Monthly*, warned that the "reactionary" American Catholic Church sought to gain control of the labor movement.[77]

Believing that the federal government would be an ally in organized labor's contest against management, John L. Lewis decided to take charge of the union movement. In October, at the Atlantic City convention of the AFL, Lewis played his hand. Challenging president William Green to organize the unskilled, largely Slavic workers in the automobile, chemical, rubber, and steel industries, Lewis became abusive. When Bill Hutcheson of the carpenters union allegedly made a comment concerning his parentage, Lewis replied with a punch that sent the labor leader flying and plunged the convention into chaos. When the shouting stopped, Lewis announced the creation of the Committee for Industrial Organization. With organizers and funds from the UMW treasury, the CIO prepared to enter America's industrial heartland. In Pittsburgh, Phil Murray and his friends in UMW District 5 plotted strategies to mobilize the steel workers.[78]

Born in Scotland of Irish Catholic parents in 1886, Murray became a coal miner at the age of ten. At sixteen, Murray and his father made their way to Irwin, Pennsylvania, near Pittsburgh. His twelve brothers and sisters eventually followed him to Western Pennsylvania. A devout Catholic and union man, Murray settled in Greenfield, a working-class neighborhood in Pittsburgh. No matter how far he rose in the ranks of organized labor, he never severed his blue-collar, Catholic roots. If John L. Lewis enjoyed a prodigal, combative lifestyle, Murray was frugal and soft-spoken. He also approached his role as a union leader with much more trepidation than was the case for Lewis. Murray knew all too well that the steel workers in the Monongahela and Ohio valleys were either completely cowed by the steel companies and too afraid to join a union, or were extremely resentful and waiting for the day to exact revenge upon bosses like Ernest Weir. To hate one's enemies so warped the souls of the oppressed. Moreover, today's victims could easily become tomorrow's exploiters if circumstances changed.[79]

In December 1935, Murray, Pat Fagan, Dorothy Day, and 128 other Catholic intellectuals, labor leaders, and politicians endorsed a statement issued by the National Catholic Welfare Conference. The statement, "Organized Social Justice," advocated a constitutional amendment to establish a national minimum wage, a standard forty-hour work week, and an "elementary regulation of industry." Its signers also praised the defunct National Recovery Administration, seeing in its attempt to have labor and management work peacefully together, a model for social reconstruction. Murray and Fagan preferred industrial harmony to class confrontation. Conservatives, however, had opted for battle and gave Lewis the opportunity he needed to become the commander-in-chief of a militant labor movement.[80]

While the National Catholic Welfare Conference hoped for a reconciliation between organized labor and industry, Monsignor John Ryan and the bishops had to contend with a bitter political division within the ranks of the Church. Since the early days of the New Deal, Father Charles Coughlin of Royal Oak, Michigan, had been making highly political radio broadcasts to a national audience. Coughlin, with the approval of his bishop, Michael Gallagher, expressed a desire to see the social reconstruction of the United States. He lambasted bankers, praised Roosevelt, and claimed to embrace the papal encyclicals on social justice. Coughlin's audience grew to several million, with his greatest support coming from Catholic laity in Boston and New York. His most fervent followers tended to be lower-middle-class Irish and German Catholics.[81]

At first, the *Pittsburgh Catholic* gave extensive, supportive coverage to Coughlin. But then, Coughlin became egotistical and vindictive. Feeling slighted by Roosevelt, and driven by the quest for political power, Coughlin began to criticize the New Deal in harsh terms. Bishop Noll of the National Catholic Welfare Conference had never liked Coughlin, viewing him as a self-serving publicity hound. Similarly, William Cardinal O'Connell of Boston, who was not a warm friend of Roosevelt, let it be known that he did not want his priests listening to Coughlin's broadcasts. As Monsignor Ryan saw it, Coughlin's hateful words represented a rejection of the spirit, as well as the message, of the social encyclicals. Once Coughlin turned against the New Deal in 1935, the *Pittsburgh Catholic* reduced its coverage of him and the bulk of his predominately Catholic audience tuned him out. Although Ryan would have liked to have restrained Coughlin, the only person who had the authority to do so was his bishop—and Gallagher embraced the strident priest.[82]

For all of the national publicity Coughlin generated, and for all of the fear he engendered among liberal circles in Washington, the Detroit priest never successfully penetrated the mill towns of America's industrial heartland. In the working-class Croatian, Italian, Polish, and Slovak precincts of Cleveland, Johnstown, and Pittsburgh, Coughlin seemed to be nothing more than a typical anti-New Deal reactionary, albeit one who wore a clerical collar. Moreover, though a few Irish laity in Pittsburgh praised Coughlin and criticized the diocesan newspaper for denouncing the Detroiter, the city's Catholic clergy and politicians repudiated the radio priest. Political boss David Lawrence wanted to build a coalition of black Protestants, Jews, and Slavs. He did not approve of Coughlin's style, and he had no tolerance for the way the priest's Irish followers in Boston and New York excluded blacks and other white ethnics from enjoying the benefits of Democratic rule. Similarly, Pittsburgh's reformist clergy looked not to Coughlin, but to the National Catholic Welfare Conference and to Dorothy Day for leadership. Coughlin was irrelevant, even if many Washington liberals thought that he was the

Never introduced her.

head of an incipient fascist movement and threatened the New Deal's electoral prospects in 1936.[83]

Dorothy Day was a strange counterpart to Charles Coughlin. In her early years she had been a socialist. Through various personal misfortunes, and by constant exposure to New York City's underside, Day experienced a profound spiritual awakening that led her to the Catholic Church. Her faith, however, was not the Catholicism of New York's conservative hierarchy. She had taken to heart Leo XIII's and Pius XI's teachings on social justice. In 1933, she acted upon her beliefs, founding the Catholic Worker movement and its newspaper, *The Catholic Worker*. Beginning with a circulation of 2,500 and selling for one cent, *The Catholic Worker* had 65,000 readers by 1935. In its columns Day explored labor and race issues, while her organization attracted a legion of former seminarians and jobless volunteers. Day established "a House of Hospitality"—a place where the jobless and homeless could find shelter, food, and, perhaps, hope in the knowledge that God lived among them.[84]

Father Charles Owen Rice had met Dorothy Day in 1933. Day's grace and determination inspired Rice to emulate her example in Pittsburgh. With Bishop Boyle's blessing, Rice and Hensler began in 1935 to formulate strategies to promote the cause of organized labor in the Monongahela and Ohio valleys. They were also concerned with race relations and poverty. Both priests sought to act upon one of the core principles of Catholic social theory—the belief in subsidiarity. In essence, subsidiarity was the proposition that economic, moral, and political decisions should be made, whenever possible, at the local level and by the people most directly affected by policy changes. While the federal government had a role to play in social reconstruction, it was up to ordinary people to participate in the political process. In consultation with Washington, the people decided how to build a better society. Federal bureaucrats did not impose their will upon the people. A government that did not listen to all of its people, poor and rich, Catholic and Protestant, white and black, was not worthy of popular support.[85]

Calvinism appeared to be dead. The New Deal had severely wounded it, while the Church reformers had—prematurely—administered the last rites. By 1935, the Scotch-Irish corporate elite could, only with difficulty, ascribe poverty to laziness and sin. Businessmen could no longer tout to the public that wealth was a reward—a gift from God or the secular free market. The Catholic Church and the New Deal viewed poverty as a result of an inequitable distribution of the wealth. Where the Church differed with the New Deal was in its belief that immorality perpetuated misery and increased the ranks of the poor. A few New Dealers in Washington, and certainly every

Communist, viewed wealth as a force for injustice. In contrast, the Church taught its followers that they should not hate the rich. Instead, Catholics had to educate affluent families like the Mellons and Weirs. With love, rather than hate, the working poor could help such people see that wealth was a social responsibility, not a license for exploitation. Of course, if love was not sufficient, then voting Democratic, and supporting legislation to regulate industry, might be necessary.

*Nice ending*

# 3

## City of God

### Class, Culture, and the Coming Together of the New Deal Coalition, 1936

Catholic reformers realize that forging an electoral coalition of Slavs, Jews, and blacks will not be easy. Each group bears the scars of decades of discrimination and has some cause to be suspicious of the other. Fortunately for reformers like Father Charles Owen Rice, Democratic boss David Lawrence, and labor leader Phil Murray, Roosevelt's economic reforms unite America's dispossessed. Moreover, Catholic politicians in the industrial heartland, unlike their counterparts in the East, offer their friendship and assistance to blacks and Jews. In 1936, in cities like Pittsburgh, a New Deal electoral majority is born.

Father Charles Owen Rice was not one to pull punches, particularly when it came to confronting what he viewed as hypocritical behavior among Catholics. And what could possibly be more hypocritical than for an impoverished minority to sanction discrimination against other less fortunate minorities? To Catholics who had "tasted the bitterest dregs of persecution," racial hatred was unconscionable. "Before any Catholic says, 'The Negro must keep his place,' let him find out just what right he or any other sinful lump of the slime of the earth has to assign any race an inferior place. Christ has something to say about those who pick the highest place for themselves and leave the lower places for others. They end up in the lowest place." No less critical of racism, the *Pittsburgh Catholic* endorsed the efforts of Democrats in the state legislature to prohibit discrimination in public accommodations. The diocesan newspaper further urged Catholics to join with their black and Jewish neighbors in a crusade to defeat bigotry. If Catholics failed to do so, then their neighborhoods would devolve into besieged fortresses—their defenders threatened by racial violence and social disorder. In such a race war, Rice believed, the only winners would be Ku Klux Klansmen and Communists.[1]

The region's Catholic political, labor, and clergy leadership agreed that racism had to be overcome if there was to be social reconstruction. However, the campaign to eradicate bigotry required great commitment and there was no guarantee of victory. First, even though Catholics, blacks, and Jews shared a history of persecution, the cultural differences among them were enormous. Differing cultural values influenced the amount and variety of opportunities for social advancement. Second, while each group may have had a shared history of persecution, their experiences were, upon closer examination, markedly different. Third, and perhaps most important of all, America's northern urban centers seemed to accelerate social disorganization. Those who learned the ways of the streets, the *Pittsburgh Catholic* lamented, often lost their souls in the process.[2]

With the outbreak of World War I in 1914, Eastern European immigration had come to a standstill. Desperate for workers, especially after the United States entered the war and the federal government initiated a military draft, northern corporations aggressively recruited in the South. Between 1916 and 1919, one million southern blacks migrated to the North. Subsequently, the black population of Chicago, Cleveland, and Pittsburgh more than doubled. In the Pittsburgh District, Jones & Laughlin, the Pennsylvania Railroad, U.S. Steel, and Westinghouse continued to import southern black laborers after the war in order to break the emergent industrial unions. As writer Thomas Bell recalled, the first generation of Slavic steel workers was never able to live comfortably with southern blacks. "It's too bad the niggers had to come," stated the fictional Slovak mill hand George Kracha. "They never bother me, but some of my neighbors have moved, especially the ones with daughters. The men are always getting drunk and fighting, and you hear women screaming during the night. They all live together like so many animals. And so dirty!" As Bell pointed out, many native-born Protestants had said the same things about the Slovak immigrants.[3]

The few thousand blacks who had lived in Pittsburgh before World War I were the very picture of respectability. Sixty-six percent traced their origins to Virginia, 74 percent had families, and 59 percent were over the age of thirty and, presumably, settled in front of the hearth. Fully 63 percent of Pittsburgh's black teenagers attended high school, compared to just 48 percent of the Slavs. Moreover, 20 percent of blacks, pacing the city's average, owned their own homes. Pittsburgh's black community included shopkeepers, doctors, lawyers, and journalists. Affluent blacks lived in Homewood, an exclusive East End neighborhood. Before the war there was no residential segregation based on race, although there were many private real estate arrangements to exclude Catholics and Jews from various neighborhoods. As Protestants, light-skinned blacks moved easily within Pittsburgh's elite circles. But blacks also lived comfortably in the city's working-class wards. Polish ethnics patronized black-owned stores in Lawrenceville and their children played together. There was some racial discrimination—the public schools would not hire black teachers. Then again, the nominally secular schools also chose not to employ Catholics and Jews. In Pennsylvania, applicants for positions in the public school system had to reveal their religious affiliation to the board of education. Catholic lay teachers had the option of working in the parochial schools. Blacks and Jews either had to reform the public education system or follow the Catholic example and establish their own schools.[4]

By the 1930s there were fifty-five thousand blacks living in Pittsburgh—8 percent of the city's overall population. Their circumstances had changed drastically. Fully 85 percent of the city's black citizens had came to the region after 1917. Fifty-two percent of the recent black migrants were under the age of thirty, 40 percent remained single, and 51 percent hailed from the Deep South. Lacking basic vocational skills, the Mississippi Delta blacks came to Pittsburgh as menial laborers, not as doctors and lawyers. Such migrants clustered in the Lower and Upper Hill District ghettos that had been home to every successive wave of poor sojourners. In the Hill District, where Italian day laborers, Jewish rag pickers, and dispossessed black tenant farmers rubbed shoulders, overcrowding was a fact of life. Each worn-out acre of the Hill housed 110 people, or four times the city's average. The Hill District's residents jammed into dilapidated houses, half of which did not have indoor plumbing.[5]

The Hill District was the city's most crime-ridden neighborhood in the 1930s. More than 38 percent of Pittsburgh's murders occurred in the Hill District. The black wards also claimed the greatest proportion of juvenile delinquents—a quarter of the city total. Quite a few contemporary social commentators, and others who followed, argued that racial discrimination and the lack of job opportunities explained why blacks experienced the highest crime and unemployment rates in the region. Racial discrimination, however, was not the sole factor in explaining the problems of the poor. Even though 54 percent of Lower Hill District blacks were unskilled and thus likely to be without work, a greater proportion of Italians and Poles similarly lacked skills and had few ways to secure better-paying jobs. Moreover, of the fifty-three labor unions that appeared in Pittsburgh after 1935, just five insignificant craft organizations barred blacks. The revitalized United Mine Workers prohibited racial discrimination and made it a point to recruit blacks. Further, the New Deal gave great attention to Pittsburgh's poor neighborhoods. Finally, the Lower Hill District ranked first in the city in the amount of public assistance granted and second in the number of WPA projects undertaken. Italian East Liberty and Polish Hill, in contrast, ranked twenty-second and twenty-third, respectively, in WPA funding. In terms of poverty rates, East Liberty and Polish Hill differed only slightly from the Hill District.[6]

If discrimination and the lack of advanced job skills were not entirely adequate explanations for black poverty, what other factors could have led to their plight? Perhaps, as the editors of the *Pittsburgh Catholic* and the *Courier* believed, the alternative reasons could be found in the destruction of the family. The Deep South blacks had the highest divorce rate in the region, while the Catholic neighborhood of Polish Hill ranked fifty-first in the number of dissolved marriages. In the Lower Hill District, single mothers represented one-quarter of black household heads, four times the figure for Catholics and Jews. (Single-parent households, as the sociologist Edward Banfield observed, are more likely to be poor and beset with social problems than intact families.) Additionally, Hill District blacks, unlike Jews and most Catholics, took in boarders who were not related to the family, often renting each bedroom to as many as six people at a time. Conditions such as these made for an unsettled home life. To make matters worse, 99 percent of Hill District blacks rented, and overall, less than 18 percent lived in the same house or neighborhood for any length of time. In comparison, 40 percent of Italians and 36 percent of Poles maintained residence in the same neighborhood for years, either as renters or as home owners. Intact families tended to take pride in home ownership, knew their neighbors, and maintained the peace. The *Courier* complained that a number of blacks in the Hill District had no respect for their neighbors.[7]

The Baptist and African Methodist Episcopal churches, like their Catholic counterpart, deplored vice and juvenile delinquency. Unfortunately, the Hill District's black churches were not in a strong enough position to combat the social corrosion poverty wrought. Although the Hill District in the 1930s claimed forty-five of Pittsburgh's fifty-six historically black churches, only four had enough funds to sponsor glee clubs, fellowship dinners, and sports teams. While the Slavs had the Catholic Youth Organization and the Jews established Hebrew schools, numbers of black children found their entertainment in the secular world. Pittsburgh's new black citizens created 250 social clubs whose major activities including drinking and gambling. "Blind Pigs" and "Honky Tonks" opened weekly on Wylie and Centre Avenues. To Steven Bochco, a son of Slavic Pittsburgh and later a Hollywood screenwriter, the blacks he saw as a child lived on "Hill Street Blues," a macabre place where inhumanity and indifference flourished.[8]

More harsh, novelist John Edgar Wideman, who had grown up in Homewood, angrily recounted the effect southern blacks had on his neighborhood in the Great Depression. Born into a family of light-skinned blacks who had settled in Pittsburgh prior to the Civil War, Wideman's family found itself engulfed in a sea of turbulent southerners. John French, a paper hanger and Wideman's grandfather, increasingly spent more time away from job and home, drawn to the "Bucket of Blood" tavern. The "Bucket of Blood" had acquired its name in part because its customers drank so much cheap "Dago Red" wine. Also, a patron had slashed a man's throat during a fight. French's wife, Freeda, did not hesitate to offer an opinion of her neighbors: "Every one of them shacks full of niggers. And they let their children run the street half-naked and those burr heads ain't never seen a comb. Let them children out in the morning and called 'em in at night like they was goats or something."[9]

The *Courier* accused the Hill District's residents of turning their neighborhoods into centers of crime and filth. In one garish series, the *Courier* breathlessly reported that the Hill District had seventeen juvenile gangs. "The kid gangs have taken over!," the black newspaper exclaimed. Young "Capones, Dillinger's, and down-and-out tough guys are spreading a reign of terror in the Hill District and other sections of Pittsburgh." Noting that the gangs claimed "uncontrollable youngsters ranging between the ages of nine and twenty-one," the *Courier* blamed juvenile delinquency not on white racism but rather on "adolescent egotism, encouraged by irresponsible parents." Other *Courier* reporters chastised the Hill District's southerners for what they viewed as antisocial behavior. That torrent of criticism came shortly after the establishment of the Works Progress Administration. Pittsburgh's WPA director announced that his large budget for civic improvements in the Hill District had gone entirely to clear rubbish off the streets. Daily, many of the Hill District's citizens threw garbage from the windows of their homes. Others urinated in the alleys and on their neighbors' front porches. Frustrated, the WPA gave up even attempting to collect rotting food and feces from the Hill District.[10]

Paradoxically, publisher Robert Vann had great cause to be more circumspect in his criticism of Hill District southerners. If on one page of the *Courier* Vann waged a crusade against crime, on the next page his newspaper raved about the Hill District's striptease joints. Not an issue went by that did not carry provocative photographs of scantily clad "exotic dancers." The *Courier* encouraged its readers to visit the Harlem Bar on Wylie Avenue. At this black nightclub, "Sandra, the savage dancer," performed while a blues band played the "Zonky" song. The *Courier* devoted far more of its pages to the entertainment schedules of the Hill District's honky-tonks than to black church events. Vann never noticed that nearly every knife fight and shoot out in the Hill District began or ended at a reefer-drenched blues club. Certainly, Vann's reporters chose not to question the callow white males who flocked to the Crawford Inn in search of their first interracial sexual encounter. Vann failed to understood that the *Courier* was promoting the very antisocial behavior he deplored.[11]

An aristocratic Virginian who could "pass as white," Vann was one of the black South's so-called "talented one-tenth." In the eyes of early twentieth-century black leaders, young men such as Vann, who possessed intelligence, drive, and light complexions, were destined for greatness. Receiving a degree in 1903 from Richmond's Virginia Union University, a racially segregated institution, Vann went north to attend Pitt. With instant entree into the black upper class, Vann earned the admiration of the middle-class white Protestant world as well. Students, faculty, and university administrators took note of Vann's oratory and literary accomplishments. Securing a second undergraduate degree from Pitt in 1906, Vann graduated from the university's law school as a member of the class of 1910. Quickly bored with his successful legal practice, he leapt at the opportunity to assist in the founding and publishing of the *Pittsburgh Courier*. Vann soon set his sights on becoming *the* political voice of black America. It was an ambition that Pittsburgh's black elite had lacked prior to World War I; they were content to allow wealthy white Republicans to speak for them.[12]

Throughout the 1920s and 1930s, Vann alternatively cajoled and castigated the Republican and Democratic Party chiefs. Disgusted with President Herbert Hoover's overtures to southern racists in 1928, and then with his subsequent refusal to alleviate the suffering of the black unemployed in 1932, Vann had moved into the Roosevelt camp. A vocal champion of the WPA and the National Youth Administration, both federal agencies providing work to impoverished urban dwellers without regard to color, the *Courier* occasionally rebuked the New Deal. Vann criticized Roosevelt's unwillingness to challenge the southern disfranchisement of black voters and to make the mob lynching of black criminal suspects a federal crime. Unfortunately for Vann, Roosevelt needed the support of the southern white Democrats who dominated the leadership of nearly every congressional committee that had oversight on New Deal legislation. The president found it difficult to appease white southerners and the increasingly important northern black voting bloc.[13]

In 1936, Vann resigned his position as an assistant to the United States Attorney General, protesting the Justice Department's reluctance to advance black civil rights. Having departed from the Roosevelt administration, Vann felt free to unleash stronger salvos against the white South: "It is manifestly unconstitutional for Negroes to be barred from the ballot by a system of terrorism which arouses the emulation of Hitler, Mussolini, and Stalin." The publisher also decried residential segregation in the northern cities and took the flagship Kaufmann department store in Pittsburgh to task for replacing black female maids with "foreign white women." Apparently Vann did not consider it inconsistent on his part to denounce southern white supremacy while expressing nativist sentiments in Pittsburgh. Then again, whenever the issue required Vann to choose between supporting black rights or the civil rights of all minorities, he opted for the former. In 1924, the *Pittsburgh Courier* had endorsed Senator David Aiken Reed's efforts to restrict immigration. According to Vann, the legislation would, by stemming Catholic and Jewish immigration, increase blacks' economic opportunities in the North.[14]

Vann's concern for black civil rights and economic opportunity had, as with his stand on crime, a highly contradictory quality. Quite rightly, the *Courier* criticized many Catholics and Jews for viewing blacks as an unsavory presence in their neighborhoods. Yet Vann chose to live away from the southerners in the Hill District. The black press baron moved twenty miles outside Pittsburgh, acquiring an estate complete with servants' quarters and a billiards room. His new residence, Oakmont, had long been off-limits to Catholics and Jews. Unwilling to live near the working class, Vann, and the black elite that followed, abandoned the Hill District. Perhaps even worse than depriving inner-city black youths of middle-class, law-abiding role models, the *Courier* widened the gulf between its words and deeds. Exhorting Pittsburgh's black southerners to take pride in their race, the *Courier* then undermined its stance by running reams of advertisements for cosmetic products designed to bleach dark skin white and to make kinky hair straight.[15]

If ambivalent toward southern blacks, Vann was no more consistent in his regard for Jews. On the one hand, the *Courier* vigorously defended Henry Ellenbogen. Hoping to discredit Ellenbogen, who planned to leave Congress in order to run for judge of the Allegheny County Common Pleas Court, Pittsburgh Republicans mailed a letter to voters contending that "one of every three Jewish citizens" was "on the federal, state, county, or city payroll with an estimated salary for these people in key positions to be $375,000 a month." Ellenbogen, the Republicans implied, was the reigning king of all

Jewish welfare recipients. But even as the *Courier* expressed antipathy for the Republicans, Vann accused Jewish merchants and restaurant owners in the Hill District of refusing to hire blacks. The *Courier* advocated a boycott of Jewish-owned businesses, urging blacks to "Spend Where You Can Work." To some children of immigrant Jews, the memory of Ku Klux Klan cross burnings in the 1920s, and the sight of their parents discriminating against blacks in the 1930s, confused them. How was it possible for Jews to be bigots?[16]

Pittsburgh's 53,000 Jews were, like blacks, sharply divided by class, culture, and regional origins. The district's first substantial Jewish immigration occurred during the 1840s when thousands of Germans, Gentile and not, left their homeland. To the Lutheran Heinzes, and the Jewish Kaufmanns, the petty rivalries among the dozens of independent German kingdoms hindered those with business ambitions. Seeking economic advancement, German Gentiles and Jews came to America's industrial frontier. For the Kaufmann brothers—Henry, Isaac, Jacob, and Morris—Pittsburgh became their treasured home. In 1871, the year in which Prince Otto von Bismarck proclaimed the birth of the Second Reich, the Kaufmanns opened their first clothing store.[17]

Prosperous German Jews established the Rodef Shalom Temple in 1854. Ten years later, a dispute within the temple over how far Jews should accommodate their religion to the Protestant American environment led to the founding of the Tree of Life Congregation. By 1885, Rodef Shalom had taken the lead in championing the Pittsburgh Platform, a call for the radical reorientation of Judaism worldwide. Reform Judaism, as its adherents called it, did away with many traditional Jewish rituals and dietary practices. Reacting to Rodef Shalom's practice of seating men and women together in the temple, as well as its abandonment of kosher, the Tree of Life Congregation became a center of Jewish Orthodoxy. One consequence of this schism was that the Tree of Life Congregation attracted poor Eastern European Orthodox Jews while Rodef Shalom took on an assimilated, prosperous German cast. Even before this division, the German Jews had acted upon their desire to avoid interacting too closely with their eastern co-religionists. When the German Jews founded the Concordia Club, they barred Lithuanian, Polish, Romanian, and Russian Jews from membership.[18]

The greatest Jewish exodus in modern times began as a result of a tragic murder. In 1881, six Russian radicals, among them a Jewish apostate, had assassinated Czar Alexander II. A relatively tolerant leader for his times, Alexander II appeared to be ameliorating social conditions in the Russian Empire. Concerned that such improvement in the lives of ordinary people would thwart their revolution against centralized government, conventional morality, and religious devotion, the nihilists had killed the Czar. The assassins welcomed the furious reaction of the new Czar, Alexander III, convinced that government repression would lead to a revolt. Unfortunately for the revolutionaries, there was no armed uprising. Worse, Alexander III initiated a special policy to deal with Jews, a group that he collectively blamed for murdering his father. Russia's Jews would either leave their ghettoes or die. In response to state-sponsored anti-Semitism, Jewish-American poet Emma Lazarus urged the "huddled masses" to come to the United States. Two million Lithuanian, Polish, and Russian Jews, the "wretched refuse" of the Czarist empire, accepted her offer of asylum.[19]

Unlike southern black migrants, two-thirds of the Eastern European Jews who trekked to America possessed some industrial skills. The Orthodox Jews also came to the American cities in family groups. While half of the Jewish immigrants chose to settle in New York City, the other half found their way to Boston, Chicago, Cleveland, Philadelphia, and Pittsburgh. For many of the easterners, Pittsburgh resembled Russia in some aspects, but mercifully did not in other, more important, ways. In Russia, as in Pittsburgh, the Jewish immigrants seldom, if ever, met any Gentiles. Yet if certain blocks in the Hill District became insulated Jewish enclaves, it was by choice, not by government decree. Moreover, though the Jewish sections of the Hill District had many impoverished tailors and cigar makers, they did not live in a ghetto surrounded by armed Cossacks and Gentile peasants seeking to punish "the Christ-killers." Every day, Jewish families arrived by train in Pittsburgh, lost and unable to speak any language other than Yiddish. With children in tow, mothers and fathers found their way to relatives with the help of strangers. In a city where, prior to World War I, two-thirds of the people were foreign-born or the children of immigrants, Croatians, Poles, Russian Jews, and Slovaks knew how to communicate with each other through a few simple gestures. The Jewish refugees who settled in Pittsburgh were fortunate to have found a place where its Slavic people, although not free of anti-Semitic prejudice, had no love for the Czarist Empire that oppressed non-Russian Gentile and Jew alike.[20]

Even though the easterners kept to themselves, often associating only with people who had come from their own village, the Kaufmanns took a dim view of the Orthodox Jews. Chiefly, the assimilated Germans were worried that the easterners would provoke an anti-Semitic backlash. After all, their prayer shawls, yarmulkes, and boisterous Yiddish made them look so obviously Jewish. The Germans also half-believed Czar Alexander III in his charge that the eastern Jews were dangerous radicals. This was no small concern on the Kaufmanns' part since a Jewish anarchist had attempted to assassinate industrialist Henry Clay Frick in 1892. Subsequently, the Kaufmanns set out to civilize the easterners. In 1895, with $150,000, Henry Kaufmann opened the Irene Kaufmann Social Settlement House. Located in the Hill District, and patterned after Jane Addams's Chicago Hull House, the Irene Kaufmann Settlement tried to persuade the easterners to learn English, forsake kosher, and become Reform Jews.[21]

The eastern Jews were never taken in by the Kaufmann Settlement's offers of free milk and bathing facilities. To the Orthodox, if the Germans had really been interested in their welfare, they would not have operated such miserable sweat shops and cigar-rolling businesses in the Hill District. Indeed, the tobacco used to make Pittsburgh cigars was so toxic that eastern Jews used the stogies to eradicate lice and roaches in their apartments. In 1913, the easterners had gone on strike against their German Jewish employers. As frequently happened in such disputes, the Germans replaced the strikers with a group of scabs fresh from the Old Country. Imitating Jones & Laughlin and U.S. Steel, the German Jews played one ethnic group off against another. While the steel corporations would replace Croatians with Serbians, or Catholics with blacks, the Germans pitted Lithuanian, Polish, Rumanian, and Russian Jews against one another.[22]

If unwilling to forsake kosher, the easterners were ready to take advantage of the settlement house's free courses in English, history, and mathematics. (Loathing upper-class Protestant social workers, Catholic Pittsburghers avoided the Kingsley Settlement House, a Presbyterian-funded establishment built in 1893 to proselytize the Strip District's Irish and Italians.) Choosing to ignore the anti-Orthodox bias in the settlement house and the public schools, the children of the Jewish immigrants acquired a great deal of education. Moreover, Jewish immigrant parents were prepared to sacrifice their own immediate standard of living in order to have their children graduate from high school and, perhaps, attend college. Thus most Jewish immigrants rented, rather than bought their own homes, and insisted that their children remain in school, even if that meant that the parents would have to work that much harder to support their families. Jewish immigrant parents also tended not to drink and gamble. All such recreational pursuits cost scarce financial resources that were better spent on their children's education. In any event, eastern Jews came from a culture that regarded excessive alcohol consumption as disgraceful. Their chief rebuke to Jews who drank and carried on said much about their view of the world: "You are shaming us in front of the Gentiles."[23]

While few immigrant Jews escaped the sweat shops, many of their children acquired high school diplomas and joined the ranks of the lower middle class. Nationally, 63 percent of Jews had graduated from high school by World War II; a proportion equal to that of the more privileged Presbyterians. In contrast, just 43 percent of Catholics and 35 percent of white Baptists, who hailed mainly from the South, were high school graduates. Moreover, 16 percent of Jews had earned college degrees, compared to 7 percent of Catholics and 6 percent of white Baptists. This despite the fact that Princeton, and many other universities, limited the number of Jews admitted to their institutions. In 1935, Jews accounted for three-tenths of 1 percent of the student body at Ivy League schools and represented nine-tenths of 1 percent of the enrollment at state universities. Meanwhile, at Catholic colleges, Jews were 15 percent of the student body. Disdaining the religious discrimination practiced by the state and Ivy institutions of higher education, Jews flocked to the Catholic colleges. It was, after all, Duquesne University that educated Henry Ellenbogen, himself an immigrant, and gave him a place in the Irish political machine. For Jews who did not live on the East Coast and thus did not have the option of attending the more tolerant City College of New York, Catholic universities were their salvation.[24]

Since most corporations, founded and managed by Episcopalians and Presbyterians, did not employ minorities in management positions, many Jews became independent professionals or businessmen. Others worked for small companies as accountants and bookkeepers. By World War II, just 27 percent of American Jews, compared to 55 percent of Catholics and 52 percent of black and white Baptists, remained members of the urban working class. For those Pittsburgh Jews who studied and worked their way out of poverty, migration from the Hill District ghetto to the more respectable neighborhood of Squirrel Hill was possible. Indeed, the number of Jewish children enrolled in Hill District public schools had fallen by one-third just before the onset of the Great Depression. Once the economy began to make a limited recovery, even more Jewish children would be going to school in their new Squirrel Hill neighborhood.[25]

As eastern Jews poured into Pittsburgh, three million Slavs came to America. By World War I, the coal and steel belt extending from Johnstown to Youngstown had become the center of "American Slavdom." The Slavs were a heterogeneous lot, counting among their number Bulgarians, Croatians, Lithuanians, Poles, Slovaks, and Slovenes. In an exercise of great futility, the U.S. Steel plant in Homestead, which had recruited Slavs from their Eastern European villages, posted safety signs in more than a dozen languages. Many of the Slavic immigrants, however, were illiterate in their own native tongues. Consequently, industrial accidents were the norm among the first generation

*Surely not the only reason!*

of Slavic steel workers. As Thomas Bell observed, Slovak wives never knew if their husbands would be coming home at the end of the twelve-hour shift. Prior to World War I, one-quarter of all steel workers could expect to be injured or killed annually. In one year alone, 127 Slavic immigrants in Allegheny County steel mills died in industrial accidents. These numbers improved only slightly after the war. This fact of life explained why the most popular investment Slavs made in America, next to buying a house, was life insurance. Destitute widows had no other way to cover funeral expenses.[26]

The Slavs were a conquered people. For years Poles and Slovaks had lived under the economic and political domination of at least one of three Central European power blocs: the Austro-Hungarian Empire of the Hapsburgs; the Prussian kingdom of the Hohenzollerns; and the Russian autocracy of the Romanovs. The Russians regarded their Polish subjects as cannon fodder for their army and as inexpensive peasant labor for their agricultural estates. In Germany, the Prussians placed enormous taxes upon the Poles. In the German empire's coal fields Polish miners wallowed in misery. On the other hand, the Prussians did not, like the Cossack marauders of the Czarist army, descend upon Polish villages with rape on their minds. Moreover, the Lutheran Prussians, having failed to make Roman Catholicism subordinate to the government in the 1870s and 1880s, reluctantly tolerated the Polish Church. Polish Catholics who lived under the sway of the Russian Orthodox Church were, like Polish Jews, no strangers to Czarist persecution. Not surprisingly, the majority of America's one and a half million Polish immigrants were from the Russian-occupied provinces of their homeland. Most Poles settled in Buffalo, Chicago, Detroit, Milwaukee, and Pittsburgh. By 1920, Pittsburgh was home to 125,000 Polish Catholics—the third highest concentration of Poles in the United States.[27]

Poles and Slovaks found that the Hapsburgs were the least offensive rulers to live under, Austrian inefficiency and a sense of irrelevancy in the affairs of the world making for a much more benign administration than was the case with Germany and Russia. If not feeling the full brunt of foreign rule, Slovak nationalists resented the Czechs who wanted to incorporate them into an independent Czechoslovakian federation. Desiring to remove themselves from Czech influence, and in desperate search for work, 20 percent of Slovakia's population, 530,000 people, came to America. More than 100,000 went to live in the mill towns of Allegheny County, making the Pittsburgh District the largest Slovak settlement outside Europe. The Croatians and Slovenes had similar reasons for leaving the Balkans. Dreading the imperialist intentions of the Serbian kingdom, 225,000 Croatians and Slovenes found their way to Pennsylvania's steel towns. Their loathing of Serbia was

considerable. In terms of culture and religion, the Serbs were tied to Orthodox Russia. Serbia's rulers acquired the autocratic ways of the Russian aristocracy, while its intellectuals followed the lead of the Bolshevik
revolutionaries. A Russian-style Serbian dictatorship, whether monarchist
or Communist, was not the dream of most Croatians and Slovenes. In short
order, Pittsburgh became Croatia's "Second City" and Slovenia's American
capital.[28]

Middle-class Protestants did not give the Slavs an enthusiastic welcome.
One Protestant school teacher, after administering an intelligence test to Johnstown's Slavic children in 1928, concluded that they were mentally deficient.
It seemed that when she asked the children to provide the English word that
best described their father's feelings toward them, they had written "pity."
The correct answer was "affection." In Steelton, a mill town near Harrisburg, middle-class Protestants accused the "Hunkies" of dining on their missing family pets. Working-class Protestants were no more kind, contending in
1905 that the Slavic "dog eaters" were "the incubators of nihilism, anarchy,
disease, and crime." As John Bodnar, a historian with Slavic forebears, observed, Steelton's black migrants "never became an object of ridicule to the
same degree as the white immigrants from Southern Europe." Black migrants
were Protestant and, to the cultural heirs of Republican abolitionism, worthy objects of Christian paternalism. Of course, Protestant sympathy for
blacks expressed itself in strange ways. During World War II, one Protestant
from Pennsylvania explained her preference for black neighbors:

> Why, I would just as soon live alongside a nigger family as some of
> these foreigners. I think that the niggers are whiter than the foreign-
> ers because at least they speak your own language. . . . [The foreign-
> ers] might be plotting to kill you and you wouldn't even know it. . . .
> They remind me of these old-time people back in the Bible. The
> women would have a shawl of some kind on their head. . . . They had
> a different look from us . . . couldn't talk our language.[29]

The Slavs committed other sins in the eyes of the white nativists: they drank
excessively and would not assimilate. Certainly, Slavs imbibed more hard alcohol than any other immigrant or native-born group in the United States.
Many also had no intention of planting roots. One-third of the Polish immigrants went back to Europe once they had saved enough money to acquire
some land. As far as the Slavs being profligate, it is useful to keep in mind
that, in 1907, Johnstown and Steelton's workers sent nearly $1.5 million to
their families who had remained in Central Europe. On the South Side of

Pittsburgh, Jones & Laughlin's Slavic laborers had deposited more than $600,000 into savings accounts in just one bank. This was a remarkable feat given that two-thirds of the Pittsburgh District's steel workers in 1908 earned $12.50 a week. The remaining one-third made less than $10 a week. According to the reformist Protestants who had compiled the *Pittsburgh Survey*, an economic analysis of working-class life published in 1914, the average steel worker needed to earn $15 a week to clothe, feed, and shelter his family. Slavic children often had no choice but to find work in order to keep the family from starvation.[30]

Despite their poverty, Slavs did not rush to the local and federal welfare agencies. Even in the midst of the Great Depression, Croatians, Poles, and Slovaks avoided public assistance. Slavic aversion to welfare in part stemmed from their appreciation of the much better life they enjoyed in America. By the standards of Protestant reformers, Pittsburgh's Slavs dwelled in misery. Most had no running water, while children, once over the age of twelve, and sometimes even younger, had to find employment. In Pennsylvania's coal patches and steel towns the off-spring of Polish immigrants provided one-third of the family's annual income. The steel mills also robbed Slavs of their health and cast a blanket of poisonous sulfur on their neighborhoods. All of this was true. However, the issue for Slavs was survival. In Croatia, Poland, and Slovakia, peasants had little hope that their families would endure from one harvest to the next. By coming to America, Slavs acquired shoes and regular meals. Understandably grateful, the first generation was not one to join industrial unions or to lead political crusades against social injustice. In 1919, it took a profiteering steel industry—an industry that was determined to drive wages well below the level of subsistence—to compel Slavs to strike.[31]

Persuaded by the suppression of the 1919 steel strike that social injustice was not only a European phenomenon, Slavs took comfort in their Church. The Roman Catholic Church in America gave its parishioners spiritual shelter, educated their children, and provided them with wholesome recreational activities. Additionally, the Church encouraged its ethnically diverse followers to develop their own fraternal organizations, preserve their cultural heritage's, and vote and join labor unions. Since Slavs were the most religiously devout of the Catholic immigrants who came to the United States in the years preceding World War I, the American Church found it relatively easy to strengthen their faith. Significantly, the word for "settlement" or "village" in Lithuanian, Polish, and Slovakian was "parish." Home and church were interchangeable concepts.[32]

For the four million Italian immigrants who journeyed to America between 1899 and 1924, the Catholic Church had a more challenging task. In Italy, anti-clerical sentiment was strong and many peasants viewed their parish priests as the religious representatives of the powerful landlords. Despite some initial friction between the Irish hierarchy of the American Catholic Church and the Italian immigrants, the clergy brought most of the new-comers, particularly their children, back to the faith. In Pittsburgh, where Italians numbered fifty-five thousand, or 8 percent of the total city population in 1930, Bishop Hugh Boyle made special efforts to renew their ties to the Church—including the recruitment of Italian-speaking priests to serve the *pisan*. It was a testament to the good will between Irish priests and Italian laity that Father James Cox collected much of the food to feed the unemployed from the shelves of Italian grocers in the Strip District.[33]

Pittsburgh's first bishop, Michael O'Connor, had found himself in the 1840s contending with rioting Scotch-Irish Presbyterians and, just as disturbing, beer-drinking German Catholics. Both groups gave O'Connor no end of trouble; the Presbyterians by burning down the district's Catholic churches and the Germans by keeping the Irish out of the affairs of their parishes. O'Connor's successors were just as busy, grappling with the financial and spiritual demands of a rapidly industrializing metropolis. Foremost among their concerns was the influx of Catholic immigrants from Central and Southern Europe. The Catholic population of the Pittsburgh Diocese increased from 280,000 in 1900 to 581,327 by 1930, while the number of clerics and sisters more than doubled in those years, giving the diocese 3,930 priests and nuns. Between 1904 and 1921, the Pittsburgh Diocese had to build a new church every month. Each ethnic group, whether Croatian, Italian, Polish, and Slovakian had to have a church and a pastor that reflected their national, and often provincial, origins.[34]

The diocese also had to overcome Slavic opposition to the construction of parochial schools. From his installation as bishop in 1921 to his death thirty years later, Boyle built fifty-eight diocesan parochial schools. Many Polish and Slovakian parents complained to Boyle that their children did not require more than a third grade education in order to work in the steel mills. Moreover, they felt that their scarce resources should go to buying their own homes instead of supporting parish schools. Other Slavic parents sent their children to the "free" public schools until, tired of being ridiculed by Protestant students and teachers, they quit. To the first generation of Slavic immigrants, economic security was paramount. One obtained that goal by working in the mill and purchasing a house, not by going to school and pursuing the precarious lifestyle of the independent entrepreneur. Greek diners and Jewish tailor shops failed at alarming rates; steel mills would never remain shut down for long. Additionally, to people starved for land, home ownership transformed the Slavic peasants into barons of their own estates. Education was unimportant, as well as a waste of time.[35]

While Bishop Boyle told his Central European parishioners that an education, particularly a Catholic education, was good for their children, the mill town of Duquesne became the center of the Orthodox Church in the United States. Although the Orthodox Serbs and Ukrainians, prior to the Russian Revolution, looked to Moscow, rather than Rome, for their religious leadership, there was not a great deal of friction between the historic rivals. One of the seeming glories of America, or at least of the nation's industrial cities, was that different ethnic, racial, and religious groups could easily avoid contact with one another. Italians, Jews, Poles, and Serbs lived in voluntarily segregated ethnic enclaves, attended their own "national" churches, belonged to different fraternal organizations, and married within their particular faith and cultural group. Members of the Lithuanian Roman Catholic Federation of Pittsburgh, the First Catholic Slovak Union of America, and the Polish Falcons did not attend each other's functions, let alone recreate with one another outside the workplace. Arguably, ethnic segregation promoted a great degree of social harmony in that people of different cultures got along best when they did not have to deal with each other. Of course, the drawback was that the Scotch-Irish political and corporate leadership counted upon such cultural divisions to thwart industrial unions and to maintain their influence in the local, state, and federal government.[36]

Beyond the promotion of social harmony and education, the Catholic Church had to contend with Protestant discrimination. Geno Baroni, who grew up in the coal fields near Johnstown in the 1930s, knew all too well the operators' attitude toward their Italian miners. As the future priest and civil rights activist recounted, one method the coal operators had to cut production costs was to use less lumber in bracing the mine shafts. Every time a shaft collapsed, Baroni would hear his father say in disgust, "Wops are cheaper than props." David McDonald, prior to becoming Phil Murray's secretary, once applied for a clerical job with the Pennsylvania Railroad. His interview had gone well. However, the railroad representative conducting the interview withdrew the job offer when he learned that McDonald was a graduate of Pittsburgh's Holy Cross High School. McDonald's experiences were not atypical. In 1933, the Wilkinsburg school district, just across the city limits from Pittsburgh, did not employ a single Catholic school teacher. At a school board meeting that year, a former Westinghouse engineer and member of the First Presbyterian Church of Wilkinsburg found such discrimination so distasteful that he could remain silent no longer: "I'm going to say things that will make the intolerant bigots of this community wince. Of 200 or more teachers in the Wilkinsburg public school system, not one is of the Catholic faith. Let's be fair—if we exempt Catholics from teaching in our schools, then let us exempt them from paying taxes to support those schools." His remarks were not appreciated.[37]

In Sewickley, a mostly Protestant suburb of Pittsburgh, Father William Curtin led a battle against the chief of police, Roy Barclay. As pastor of Sewickley's St. James Church Curtin exposed the police chief's Ku Klux Klan activities. In an impassioned address to the Sewickley City Council and one thousand spectators in January 1934, Curtin urged the town's elected officials to fire Barclay.

> He and his hooded companions kidnapped a Negro at Fallston [Pennsylvania], gagged and bound him hand and foot, brought him to Patterson Heights, put a noose around the Negro's neck, threw the other end of the rope over a tree limb and swung him into the air. They lowered the victim to the ground and beat and kicked him in a murderous frenzy. In extenuation he says that the Negro did not really die; that he thinks he is still alive!
>
> He was a grand marshal of the masked brigade [of 5,000] which marched into the peaceful town of Carnegie [in 1923], every man carrying a weapon of some sort, ready to riot. You remember what happened. Scores injured and one man shot to death. Don't you think that, before God, Barclay was responsible for that murder?
>
> Do you think this is the man to teach us respect for the law?

Unmoved, council members voted seven to one to retain the Klansman as their police chief.[38]

It was no coincidence that the Catholic clergy who defended the civil rights of religious and racial minorities were of Irish descent. Fleeing from British oppression and the infamous potato famine, nearly two million Irish immigrants came to America in the 1840s and 1850s. With little or no capital, the Irish mainly settled where their ships had landed: Boston, New York, and Philadelphia. Others secured jobs as railroad and iron workers, making their way to Chicago, Pittsburgh, and San Francisco. As the first great religious minority in America, the Irish provoked an anti-Catholic reaction. By the 1850s, nativists, desiring to restrict Catholic immigration, had elected one hundred congressmen and took over the Pennsylvania and New York legislatures. Confronted with political persecution and anti-Catholic riots in Philadelphia and Pittsburgh, the Irish counterattacked. Blessed with the advantages of speaking America's native language, and having a long history of political mobilization and a sense of cultural nationalism, both born in response to the British occupation of their homeland, the Irish entrenched themselves in the northern Democratic Party. The Irish also assumed control of the American Catholic Church. Although German Catholics claimed Cincinnati, Toledo, and Dubuque, Iowa, the Irish took everything else. In 1900, half of America's bishops were of Irish descent and only four of seventeen American cardinals were not Irish. Intent upon overcoming Protestant persecution, Irish clergy built the American Catholic Church and its system of parochial schools.[39]

In the 1880s and 1890s, Irish clergy such as Archbishop John Ireland of St. Paul, Minnesota, and James Cardinal Gibbons of Baltimore, became ardent advocates of workers' rights. They exerted enormous influence with Leo XIII who, at their urging, placed the Church firmly behind the cause of organized labor. Beyond strictly moral considerations, and a fear that the Church would lose members to the "atheistic" socialist cause, Catholic leaders had good reason to support labor unions: most American Catholics were working class. In the early years of the twentieth century, American corporations did not typically employ Catholics in white-collar positions. Consequently, career opportunities were often limited to municipal employment, the Church, politics, and, to the dismay of the clergy, organized crime. The leading profession for educated, second-generation Irish men and women in 1910 was the Church. This state of affairs changed very little and then only when Irish Catholic politicians captured the city councils of Boston and New York. Having conquered city hall, the Boston and New York Irish employed their own as police officers and firemen.[40]

It is a telling point that America's two wealthiest Irish Catholic businessmen in the 1930s, Joseph P. Kennedy of Boston and William F. Buckley Sr. of Sharon, Connecticut, had made their fortunes as *independent* entrepreneurs. In their respective fields of finance and oil, Kennedy and Buckley worked around the Protestant business establishment. Although successful, Kennedy and Buckley could not be considered representative of Catholic America. During the Great Depression, just 9 percent of Catholics, including the Irish, were upper class. At the same time, nearly a quarter of Episcopalians and Presbyterians were upper class. Kennedy and Buckley were outsiders and they conveyed that feeling of social exclusion to their children.[41]

Such was the history of the Irish, and that of the Pittsburgh District's blacks and Jews, when Phil Murray announced the formation of the Steel Workers Organizing Committee in June 1936. Having joined Murray, Monsignor John Ryan, and Dorothy Day in their 1935 call for social reform, Michael Tighe agreed to the absorption of the Amalgamated into SWOC. A devout

Catholic and Irishman himself, Tighe succumbed to the advancing legion of Celtic reformers. Murray called for the labor movement's exiles, notably those who had annoyed Tighe and CIO president John L. Lewis, to join his crusade. Surprised, and excited at the prospect of organizing the steel industry, John Brophy, Elmer Cope, and Harold Ruttenberg joined the CIO. To Brophy's amazement, Lewis did not openly object to his appointment as CIO director and troubleshooter in the steel and automobile industries. Meanwhile, Cope became a SWOC organizer for the Steubenville and Youngstown area, and Ruttenberg returned to Pittsburgh to serve as SWOC Research Director. With a cadre of UMW officers, including Pat Fagan, Murray built the foundation for a mass industrial union. From the onset, Lewis sought to interfere with Murray's management of SWOC. As one who believed that union officers had to spend great sums of money in order to impress businessmen, Lewis directed Murray to rent the most expensive office suites in downtown Pittsburgh. The union's new neighbors included the corporate headquarters of U.S. Steel. Although Lewis's move was inspired showmanship, SWOC did not have the money to cover future rent payments.[42]

Alarmed by the formation of SWOC, the steel industry's lobby group, the American Iron and Steel Institute, placed advertisements in 375 newspapers. The institute pledged that the steel industry would "protect its employees and their families from intimidation, coercion, and violence," as well as any other tactics that SWOC might adopt. Murray responded with his own press release to counter the steel lobby's $500,000 anti-union campaign. He made it abundantly clear that it was not SWOC that intimidated and coerced steel workers.

> The Bethlehem Steel Corporation at its Johnstown plant has given employment to 130 additional policemen during the past ten days. The duties of these policemen are confined to watching the employees of this corporation whilst at work, to listen in to their conversations, to follow them to and from their homes and to use every means of intimidation and coercion in order that the employees of the corporation may not join [the union]. This, we presume is what the American Iron and Steel Institute pledged to use its resources for when it promised to protect its employees and their families. In addition, this crew of special police and gunmen are openly walking the streets of the city of Johnstown following the representatives of the Steel Workers Organizing Committee who are now engaged in the legitimate work of organizing the employees of this corporation.[43]

Murray followed up his rejoinder to the American Iron and Steel Institute with a letter to Benjamin Fairless, the ironically named president of the Carnegie-Illinois Steel Corporation. Murray called upon the leader of this U.S. Steel subsidiary to improve the level of safety at his mills, adopt a forty-hour work week, and grant a 25 percent wage increase. The steel industry was not going to negotiate any of these issues, notably the one calling for improved wages. In 1912, Charles Schwab, the president of Bethlehem Steel, had appeared before a congressional committee and stated that even if the economy was booming, and workers increased their productivity, wages were never to be negotiated and certainly not increased. The other steel barons concurred with Schwab's contention that wages, productivity, and corporate earnings were unrelated matters. For the steel worker who, in Harold Ruttenberg's SWOC reports, lived in a "two-roomed tar-papered shack" and shared with seven other families a common outhouse, Fairless expressed his sympathy. However, he could not raise wages, even though U.S. Steel earned $46 million in 1935. Those profits belonged to the corporation's stockholders. Murray gave Fairless a measured response:

> You express "sympathy" for a wage raise. I am sure the men appreciate the "sympathy of the management." But when a steel worker goes to the clothing store, he is unable to cash the "sympathy of the management" for a new suit of clothes, a dress for his wife, or shoes for his children to go to school. The registrar at the university will not accept the "sympathy of the management" as payment for tuition for education of his children, nor will it put music in his house, a car in his garage, or a frigidaire in his kitchen. To purchase these things the steel worker and his family must have cash, and the "sympathy of the management" is an empty substitute.

SWOC's president noted that Myron Taylor, the current chair of U.S. Steel, made $166,786 in 1935. The mischievous Irishman then asked Fairless what the U.S. Steel executives had done with corporate profits since dividend payments to their investors were quite small. Perhaps, Murray suggested, U.S. Steel and its subsidiaries should open their books to investors, employees, and federal officials.[44]

While SWOC and the steel industry fought a public relations skirmish, a real battle was being waged in the region. At John Brophy's urging, Clinton Golden left his position with the Pennsylvania Department of Labor and Industry to become a regional director of SWOC. With the assistance of informants he had cultivated in the lower rungs of the Jones & Laughlin white-collar labor force, Golden learned that the Aliquippa plant was buying quantities of tear gas and submachine guns. Alarmed, Golden had contacted Wisconsin senator Robert La Follette Jr., the chair of the subcommittee on Education and Labor. An independent politician and ally of organized labor, La Follette relied upon Golden for information in his investigation of management-inspired violence against unions. La Follette's hearings on the steel industry, which commenced in April 1936, documented the existence of vast spy networks, goon squads, and private arsenals. Beyond exposing many corporate executives as gun-toting reactionaries, the hearings helped to make the American public more receptive to New Deal labor legislation. Enraged, congressional conservatives bided their time, waiting for the day when they had regained their political strength. Once they had improved their positions, the anti–New Deal congressmen could form a committee to attack unions with the same vigor that New Deal liberals assaulted businessmen.[45]

If, as Golden believed, Aliquippa seemed to be on the verge of civil war by the summer of 1936, Ohio had already crossed the threshold. In Steubenville, the security forces of Ernest Weir's National Steel corporation assaulted a SWOC field representative. On July 31, three men dragged the SWOC organizer from his car, fractured his skull, and beat him until he lost consciousness. The Steubenville police department, unwilling to challenge Weir's one hundred armed deputies who were patrolling the city, announced that it had no leads in the case. Meanwhile in Niles, a steel town close to Youngstown, Cope reported his situation to Harold Ruttenberg. Determined to undercut SWOC's organizing efforts, Carnegie-Illinois had authorized its plants to increase the number of company-sponsored unions. As Cope wrote to Ruttenberg, in the Youngstown area one of the most successful company union leaders was Colonel Fred Bohne. According to Cope, Bohne was "a pretty slick article" who seemed "more interested in fighting the onslaught of radicalism and Communism than he is in fighting the workers' cause." Many of the Ohio steel workers, Cope observed, were avoiding SWOC because of Bohne's efforts. Bohne depicted U.S. Steel and Youngstown Sheet and Tube as companies concerned with their workers' welfare. SWOC, on the other hand, might be part of a Communist conspiracy to capture control of American industry.[46]

Cope's warning that the steel companies would use "independent" workers to red-bait the union proved accurate. In Weirton, West Virginia, the Security League, a company-sponsored association of Weirton Steel employees, circulated leaflets denouncing SWOC. According to the Security League, which was a product of Ernest Weir's fertile imagination, the CIO organiz-

ers were "The Strangers in Our Midst." Led by John L. Lewis, "a labor rack-
eteer," and the "agents of the La Follette Committee," SWOC representatives were "beating and threatening honest citizens and preventing us from
earning a living." Similarly, in Brackenridge, Pennsylvania, James Finley, the
president of the Allegheny Steel Employees Union, distributed garish pam-
phlets to the workers. On the front page of the pamphlet workers found the
"Main Highway of Industrial Progress" that led to "security, industrial peace,
[and] industrial freedom." But along the way there was a warning sign: "No
Left Turn!" If workers took that left turn, then they would find "Strikes,
Reds, SWOC, Ruin, Racketeers, Riots, Communism, [and the] CIO." As
Finley wrote on behalf of his employer:

> These radicals have undertaken the wrecking of industrial America
> under the thin guise of what they have chosen to call industrial union-
> ism. Their CIO and SWOC are merely symbols under which they op-
> erate and use to lure us workers into industrial Communism. . . .
>
> The SWOC is even sending their vultures into the worker's home . . .
> to whisper promises into his ear . . . coaxing him to sign away his self-
> governing rights. Look at these men who come into your home. Ask
> yourself if they look as if they ever done a day's work themselves. You
> should realize they get paid for coming to your home . . . that they
> make a living preying on the man who really does work.
>
> Don't let these parasites wreck your home. Don't let your "man of
> the house" make the fatal mistake all of you would live to regret.[47]

Unfortunately for Allegheny Steel, larger numbers of workers were expressing an interest in SWOC. In part, their desire to join an independent
union stemmed from the Great Depression which had shattered their psy-
ches, as well as their assumptions about the American economy. The Slavs'
general quiescence in American political affairs and unwillingness to join labor unions were dependent upon their belief that economic security was attainable. Economic security, however, was premised on their belief that the
steel mills would never remain closed for long periods of time and that part-
time work and reduced wages would not supersede regular employment.
America's economic history, or at least the history that the Slavs had witnessed, indicated that depressions were brief. These were the lessons they
learned from the depressions of 1907 and 1921. Nothing in their experience
prepared them for a depression that, by 1936, seemed to be without end.
Frustrated, the second generation of Slavs, born in America, conversant in
English, and coming of voting age and entering the job market at a time when

there was little or no employment to be had, found SWOC attractive. Where the first generation of Eastern European immigrants had been slow to anger, their children, denied the same chance their parents had to acquire homes and jobs, were, in the words of one militant Johnstown steel worker, unwilling to be "treated like trash."[48]

Even if second-generation Slavs were tired of being regarded as human garbage, many would not have joined SWOC if they had believed that the union was Communist-led. Although the second generation of Slavic steel workers was more assertive than its parents, the children were no less Catholic and tribal. Recognizing that reality, Murray preferred to send Catholic organizers to the mill towns. Catholic SWOC representatives approached the local priests and fraternal presidents and asked them for their cooperation in holding union meetings. Often as not, the fraternals met in the only affordable and friendly place available to them: the Catholic Church. Consequently, supportive parish priests and bishops were central to the success or failure of SWOC. In Aliquippa, labor organizers met in the Polish Hall; safe from the attacks of the Jones & Laughlin security men who hesitated to invade a fraternal lodge or Catholic Church. By all accounts, Aliquippa's Monsignor Joseph Altany, "a man's man," according to Slovak steel workers, would have given the company goons a good pasting. In Homestead, Father Clement Hrtanek had opened his church to Labor Secretary Frances Perkins and SWOC organizers. As a leader of the National Catholic Slovak Federation, Father Hrtanek had access to, and influence with, tens of thousands of Slovak steel workers. His support meant much to the union. Finally, it did not hurt SWOC, and gave the steel union its shield against corporate red baiting, that the majority of SWOC's officers were devout Catholics. With McDonald, Fagan, and Vincent Sweeney, a SWOC publicist and former Pittsburgh newspaper reporter, at the helm, the union looked like an Irish College of Cardinals. Murray was the Pope.[49]

At the approach of the 1936 presidential election, Murray left no doubt as to which party deserved labor's benediction. In a nationally broadcast speech over the CBS radio network, Murray urged American workers to support Roosevelt against his Republican opponent, Alfred Landon:

> President Roosevelt has governed the country for the people, for labor, for the nation. He has given you political freedom. And he has given you—all the working men and women—the opportunity to win yourself economic freedom, by promoting legislation guaranteeing your rights to organize into whatever labor organization you choose, and without interference, coercion, or intimidation from your em-

ployer. President Roosevelt and the Democratic Congress have passed the National Labor Relations Act, which gives you your rights.

But the "economic royalists" who have violated this act—who have violated the law of the land—they are behind Landon. They want to take away from you the political freedom you enjoy under President Roosevelt and place you under political tyranny under their Mr. Landon.[50]

Landon, the governor of Kansas, was neither an economic royalist, nor a reactionary. However, his financial backers, notably Ernest Weir and the Pews of Pittsburgh's Sun Oil Company, were anti-New Deal wheel horses. In 1934, Weir, the Pews, and General Motors leader Alfred Sloan established the American Liberty League, a conservative lobby group. J. Howard Pew Sr., and his son spent $1.5 million to defeat Roosevelt in 1936 (the equivalent of $15 million in 1997). Al Smith, the 1928 Democratic presidential candidate, became a prominent member of the American Liberty League and campaigned against Roosevelt in 1936. His hatred of Roosevelt, and opposition to the reformist agenda of the National Catholic Welfare Conference, led the working-class Catholic politician to the Right. Smith had done much to mold Catholics into a potentially powerful voting bloc. However, his alliance with industrialists who had vigorously opposed the creation of Social Security and the WPA all but eliminated Smith's influence in Catholic circles. Beyond a few thousand middle-class Irish Catholics in Boston and New York who had no use for labor unions and social reform, Smith claimed no great political clout.[51]

The *Pittsburgh Catholic* and the Allegheny County Democratic Party, both of which had supported Smith in 1928, severed their ties to the New Yorker. If Smith had retained any political savvy, he would have noticed an important phenomenon. Since 1933, Catholic politicians in communities like Pittsburgh never passed up the opportunity to feature a photograph of Roosevelt in their campaign literature. In 1934, judging by the enormous Democratic Party advertisements placed in the *Pittsburgh Catholic*, Democratic senatorial candidate Joseph Guffey and other Pennsylvania political personalities appeared to have met with Roosevelt in the Oval Office and to have received his endorsement. The American public did not yet appreciate the miracles of composite photography.[52]

Smith was not the only Catholic political figure to have lost stature among his co-religionists. Hoping to exploit public frustration with the limited economic recovery, and viewing the New Deal as an agency of Communist-inspired change, Father Charles Coughlin had helped to found the Union

Party in 1936. Coughlin was convinced that he could rally anti-Roosevelt forces. There was some basis for Coughlin's belief that the New Deal political coalition might be stillborn. Boston's William Cardinal O'Connor, while no friend of Coughlin's, had, in a July 4, 1934, radio address, criticized New Dealers as people who "will dictate to us even against our will . . . [and] will rule us as if they had a divine right to rule. That is autocracy." To Cardinal O'Connor, who despised Monsignor John Ryan, the National Catholic Welfare Conference, and Dorothy Day's Catholic Worker movement, social reformers were Communists. The cardinal ordered diocesan clergy not to promote the teachings of the National Catholic Welfare Conference and not to give the New Deal any support. Coughlin had some cause for hope in 1936 given O'Connor's opposition to the New Deal and the priest's friendship with Boston mayor James Michael Curley. However, Italian Catholics resented Cardinal O'Connor's anti-union stance, leading them, along with the city's Jews and blacks, to back Roosevelt. Moreover, while 16 percent of Boston's Irish voters defected to Coughlin's party, the majority would not abandon the Democrats.[53]

New York provided more fertile ground for Coughlin than was the case for Boston. Unwilling to share power with Italians and Jews, the Irish Democrats insisted upon maintaining control over municipal jobs. Frustrated, Italians and Jews had elected a nominal Republican, Fiorello La Guardia, to the mayor's office in 1933. Three years later, both ethnic groups established the American Labor Party. In this way, they could place Roosevelt at the top of their ticket and then nominate Italians and Jews for various other offices. This eliminated the need to vote for Irish Democrats. Speaking for many discontented New York Irishmen, Father Robert Gannon, the president of Fordham University, gave his assessment of New Deal liberals after the 1936 presidential election.

> What [liberals] want is not so much our money as our children. They want our schools and colleges. They want key positions in the civil service. They want control of relief and all the social agencies and they are getting what they want. Later they hope, when they have the youth of the nation in their power, to eliminate all religion and all morality that does not conform to their peculiar ideology.[54]

Coughlin fed off such cultural and economic rivalries. However, as was the case in Boston, he did not gain the support of more than several thousand Irish and German Catholics. New York's Church hierarchy proved no more supportive of Coughlin than it was of the laity-dominated Catholic Worker movement. Most Irish Catholics in New York set aside their distaste of Italians and Jews to vote for Roosevelt on the Democratic ticket. Moreover, Coughlin's anti-Semitism prevented him from exploiting the racial tensions between the blacks and Jews of New York.[55]

The greatest shortcoming of Coughlin, Al Smith, and many of the Irish clergy in Boston and New York, was their inability to understand the aspirations of working-class Catholics. This failure, and their fear that they were losing social position relative to Italians, Jews, and blacks, made most of the Irish political and religious leaders of the East Coast irrelevant to the Catholic reformers of America's industrial center. Catholic clergy, labor, and political activists from Johnstown to Chicago drew inspiration from their own local experiences and from the pronouncements of the National Catholic Welfare Conference. The grievances that animated Boston and New York politics were of little concern to labor and Church activists in Pittsburgh. As Geno Baroni's father believed, the Catholic Church must administer to the social needs of working people. Guido Baroni wanted a Catholic New Deal for the Pennsylvania coal fields. To Baroni, a Catholic Church that failed to serve its working-class majority had no religious authority.[56]

While the Baroni family viewed the New Deal as the political expression of American Catholic religious belief, Pittsburgh Croatians were developing their own sense of the relationship among Church, self-image, and social reform. Shortly before World War I, a mythic figure named Joe Magarac had appeared in the mill towns of Western Pennsylvania. Magarac was a Croatian steel worker who could bend bars of iron with his enormous hands. One day, a man called Mestrovic announced a contest to determine who would marry his daughter. From as far away as Johnstown and Ohio Croatians came to see how much steel they could make. Joe Magarac, with broad peasant shoulders and a fire burning in his heart, defeated his competitors. A great worker among his peers, this Paul Bunyan of the Monongahela Valley was not his own man. Stronger than steel, Magarac was, unlike his Protestant counterpart, subservient to the mill bosses: "Sure! Magarac. Joe. Dat's me. All I do is eatit and workit same lak jackass donkey." In Croatian, Magarac means "jackass."[57]

Such was the cultural ambivalence of the first generation of Croatian steel workers. They admired strength and hard work, but rightly suspected that to their employers they were poor dumb jackasses. The American-born generation of Croatian steel workers, while cherishing Joe Magarac's determination, developed an identity that was more politicized. Magarac's children were not content just to eat and work, especially in an time when both were difficult to accomplish. The second generation sought a new image. That

Fig. 6.   A Croatian-American worker is sacrificed on the altar of greed as the Madonna of the Monogahela Valley mourns. 1937 painting from St. Nicholas Church, Pittsburgh. (Photo by Theresa Heineman.)

quest came to be realized in St. Nicholas, the first Croatian Catholic Church built in America. Located across the Allegheny River, and made possible through the financial sacrifice of the Millvale parish, St. Nicholas stood apart from Pittsburgh's industrial landscape in 1900. Pristine and humble, St. Nicholas was in the world but not of the world. A generation later, St. Nicholas could no longer resist becoming involved with secular concerns. Although good Catholics, as St. Augustine had written centuries earlier, should live in the City of God, secular influences compelled most to be beaten down by the City of Man. Father Albert Zagar of the St. Nicholas Church told his people that while one's soul belonged in the City of God, people had to exist, at least temporarily, in the City of Man. It was time to reconstruct the social order so as to prepare people to live in the City of God.[58]

Father Zagar and WPA artist Maxo Vanka wanted to make a statement about social justice and the Church. Week after week, from high ceilings and along the walls of St. Nicholas's interior, Vanka painted murals to reflect the historical experiences and religious vision of the Croatians. Behind the altar, in greater-than-life-size representation, there were two murals. On the left, Croatian peasants in a pastoral setting prayed to God for a bountiful harvest. On the right side of the altar, the Croatian peasants are in Pittsburgh and dressed in workers' clothes. In the background, the valley's steel mills spew smoke. Father Zagar kneels, asking God to remember his people in their new and forbidding land. At the rear of St. Nicholas, a coal miner lies dead. His mother, the Madonna of the Monongahela Valley, weeps over his broken body while the young man's friends return to the mines to await their own crucifixion. Near the holy water font, a rotund businessman glories in his prosperity while the poor shudder underneath the capitalist's well-stocked dining table. Zagar and Vanka's messages were unmistakable. The Croatian peasants became industrial workers destined to be sacrificed on the altar of greed and injustice. As Jesus Christ preached hope in this world and the next, so Croatians who vote for justice will realize God's peace in heaven and on the earth. These were the parishioners of St. Nicholas: Croatian-American Catholics and registered Democrats.[59]

On the national level, the Roosevelt administration attracted Slavic votes by embracing much of the reform agenda set forth by the National Catholic Welfare Conference. Roosevelt's "Fireside Chat" commemorating Labor Day 1936 could have been scripted by Bishop Boyle:

> In this country we insist, as an essential of the American way of life, that the employer-employee relationship should be one between free men and equals. We refuse to regard those who work with hand or brain as different from or inferior to those who live from their own property. We insist that labor is entitled to as much respect as property. But our workers with hand and brain deserve more than respect for their labor. They deserve practical protection in the opportunity to use their labor at a return adequate to support them at a decent and constantly rising standard of living, and to accumulate a margin of security against the inevitable vicissitudes of life.[60]

Moving beyond rhetoric, Roosevelt chose a number of Catholics, from Monsignor Ryan to Joseph P. Kennedy, to serve in various federal agencies. One-fourth of Roosevelt's judicial appointments were Catholic. In 1920, just 5 percent of the judges President Warren Harding had chosen were Catholic, while Herbert Hoover tried not to appoint any Catholics to positions of influence. David Lawrence identified his political machine with the New Deal. Indeed, *The New York Times* commented in 1933 that one would have thought that Roosevelt, rather than the erratic Mennonite William McNair, was running for mayor of Pittsburgh. Of course, though Roosevelt had his charms, McNair endeavored to be colorful. He enjoyed going on one-man vice raids of the city's gambling establishments and aspired to play the fiddle on radio's "Major Bowes Amateur Hour."[61]

In 1933, Lawrence had felt that Catholic Democrats were not sufficiently organized to champion one of their own in the mayoral race. Consequently, he settled for McNair, a conservative Democrat who preferred Theodore Roosevelt to Franklin Roosevelt and whose scourging of Andrew Mellon elicited great approval among Protestant liberals. Lawrence hoped McNair would attract independent Republican votes, not yet realizing that there were fewer and fewer such people to be found in the city. Although McNair appointed Father James Cox as city assessor, and in 1934 went to Rome to receive the blessing of Pius XI, the mayor did not get along with Lawrence. McNair refused to give city jobs to blacks and Italians, preferring to reward his core constituency of upper-middle-class Protestant reformers. In 1934, McNair showed his true political colors by campaigning for the state Republican ticket. He also limited WPA projects in Pittsburgh, citing a fear of political graft and vote buying. McNair's fears were justified, but that was beside the point. Since the Civil War, Republicans had used their corporate wealth to influence elections. Now the Pennsylvania Democrats had the federal government to draw upon for funds. WPA jobs were necessary to building an army of grateful New Deal voters.[62]

Determined to force McNair out of office, Lawrence turned to allies in the state legislature. As a result of a Progressive-era law designed to punish an Allegheny County politician, the legislature had the authority to remove Pittsburgh mayors from office. Lawrence, however, did not have to deploy the aptly named "ripper" act to McNair. In a showdown with Lawrence in 1936, McNair tendered his resignation to the Pittsburgh city council. To McNair's chagrin, the city council promptly accepted it. With councilman Cornelius Scully elevated to the mayor's office, federal assistance flowed into Pittsburgh. At the direction of the city's new Irish Catholic mayor, the Pittsburgh Department of Public Works employed hundreds of adults and youths in revitalizing the city's deteriorating parks.[63]

Having abandoned Oakland, and then much of the city, to the Catholics and Jews, the Scotch-Irish Presbyterians had no interest after World War I in maintaining the city's recreational facilities. In Schenley Park—designed to serve affluent East Enders before World War I—the Works Progress Administration and the National Youth Administration built seven stone bridges and 15,500 feet of curbs. The hitherto unemployed men and teenagers also planted 13,500 trees. Meanwhile, Schenley Park became home to a magnificent, fully restored carousel. In Lawrence's efforts to build an electoral majority, a carousal may have seemed immaterial to the political struggle. But to at least one Jewish child in the Hill District, that carousal meant rare, inexpensive entertainment. Her impoverished father, who supported the family by collecting discarded rags with which to make clothes for resale, could not afford to take his children to theaters. Schenley Park offered the only attainable source of recreation to Oakland's Catholics and the Hill District's Jews. Carousels and public works projects—such were the ways that Lawrence and Mayor Scully made life-long New Deal Democrats.[64]

While the German Jews clung to the Republican Party, the second generation of Eastern European Jews moved enmasse into the Democratic camp. In the 1928 presidential election, Al Smith received the majority of Jewish votes cast. Two years later, six Jewish Democrats, compared to two Jewish Republicans, were elected to Congress. A rising generation of Democratic Jews had entered the political arena by the Great Depression. In addition to Henry Ellenbogen, the Pittsburgh District claimed a second Jewish congressman, Samuel Weiss of McKeesport. Captain of the 1923 Duquesne University football team, Weiss served in the Pennsylvania House of Representatives from 1935 to 1938. Subsequently, Weiss represented his Catholic district in Congress from 1941 to 1946. Of all of the white ethnic groups in America, the eastern Jews proved to be the most loyal New Deal Democrats. Roosevelt routinely captured 90 percent of the Jewish vote, compared to an average of 80 percent of the Italian and Polish vote. This phenomenon was not lost on the president who appointed numerous Jews to public office; most notably, Supreme Court justice Felix Frankfurter.[65]

The second generation of eastern Jews was, by virtue of cultural and historical experience, more comfortable with political and labor union activism than was the case for its Catholic counterpart. Eighty-five percent of blue-collar Jews belonged to unions, compared to 51 percent of working-class Catholics. Irish Catholic social reformers from Bishop Hugh Boyle to Phil Murray had to overcome the Slavic desire to retreat from the secular world of labor unions and politics. Then again, Catholic theology had always stressed that the spiritual world was more important than temporal existence. Second-generation Slavic Americans lived with a theological paradox. Irish reformers urged Catholics to fight social injustice, but reminded them that they should not to become too absorbed with the secular world. If that happened, they would become materialistic and lose sight of the afterlife where politics and labor organizing were irrelevant. The second generation of Slavic Catholics wanted to be more politically assertive than its parents, and, indeed, was, yet remained uncomfortable with the wider secular world. Slavic Catholics began to vote and join labor unions in the 1930s. They did not generally choose to run for political office or lead unions.[66]

Jews did not have to confront the Catholics' theological paradox since their religion did not dwell upon the hereafter. Focused on the here and now, Jews inclined toward secular activities that aimed to improve temporal existence. If poor, then labor union organizing and the promotion of government-sponsored social welfare programs were natural Jewish undertakings. Additionally, given their historical experience in Europe and the Middle East, Jews had learned the value of placing allies within the State's governing apparatus. If the Jews wished to avoid religious persecution, then it made sense for some of them to become indispensable advisors to the government. For that reason, the Kaufmanns embraced the Republican Party, while their Eastern European rivals joined the Democrats. A smaller number of Eastern European Jews, convinced that the capitalist State was the cause of their economic and political oppression, enlisted in the American Socialist or Communist parties. Catholics maintained an ambiguous posture toward the federal government, fearing centralized secular power on the one hand, yet desiring some reforms that could only be brought about by centralized secular power.[67]

Unable to gain the allegiance of Catholic and Jewish voters in 1936, the Republicans were in the process of losing the support of northern blacks. The Roosevelt administration shrewdly cultivated middle-class black leaders. More than fifty blacks received federal political appointments. Meanwhile, Interior Secretary Harold Ickes, who was the former president of the Chicago branch of the National Association for the Advancement of Colored People (NAACP), desegregated his department. Beyond symbolic gestures, the WPA and the National Youth Administration in the North operated on a color-blind basis, providing employment to working-class blacks. Moreover, David Lawrence had vowed to help the city's blacks. Mayor Scully kept Lawrence's promise. Pittsburgh blacks appreciated a city government that did not practice racial discrimination. For the first time in Pittsburgh's history blacks served on the public school board. It took a Catholic to reform the public school system and give teaching jobs to blacks and Jews.[68]

Although Lawrence and Scully worked hard to forge an interracial political alliance, Robert Vann and other middle-class blacks were never at ease in the working-class, Catholic-oriented Democratic Party. Vann's discomfort stemmed from Lawrence's friendship with a younger black political activist, Paul Jones. A graduate of the Duquesne University Law School, Jones would become the first black elected to the Pittsburgh city council. Vann viewed Jones, the state organizer for the Democratic Party, as a threat to his own power. Petty jealousies aside, Vann was suspicious of Catholics, remaining culturally attached to the white Protestant world. When Andrew Mellon died in 1937, the *Pittsburgh Courier* lauded the billionaire for his efforts to provide jobs to blacks. The *Courier* did not mention that Mellon's companies imported blacks from the South in order to serve as strikebreakers and, subsequently, displace Catholic workers.[69]

Vann's reservations notwithstanding, the Democrats scored stunning victories in 1936. Nationally, Roosevelt won 60 percent of the popular vote and carried every state except Maine and Vermont. Just eighty-eight Republicans remained in the House and sixteen in the Senate. In Pennsylvania, Roosevelt won every major and medium-sized city, decisively cracking the Republican stronghold of Philadelphia. Pennsylvania Democrats claimed a 154 to 54 majority in the state house, captured the state senate, and racked up six hundred thousand more votes than the Republicans. Seventy-five percent of Pittsburgh's black voters chose Democrats, a percentage second only to that of New York (81 percent). Elated, Democratic governor George Earle made a widely publicized vow to give Pennsylvania a "Little New Deal." Less publicized were the Democratic campaign slogans used in black neighborhoods: "Let Jesus lead you and Roosevelt feed you!" and, "When the time come, I ain't got a cent. You buy my groceries, and pay my rent. Mr. Roosevelt, you're my man!" Black gratitude toward the New Deal was understandable. However, as the *Pittsburgh Catholic* had lamented, the New Dealers in Washington seemed not to care if they lifted people out of poverty through the provision of jobs or by making greater funds available for relief checks. As Pittsburgh's Catholic clergy realized, welfare could destroy a man's self-image, undermine the family, and perpetuate poverty.[70]

The Pittsburgh Diocese joined Catholic politicians in their efforts to secure civil rights and jobs for blacks. As the *Pittsburgh Catholic* editorialized, while "white members of the Church have not taken part in the demonstrations of race hatred that have disgraced this country," Catholics "have stopped short of realizing their full obligation to concern themselves with the welfare, spiritual and temporal, of their Negro neighbors." The failure of Catholics to embrace their "Negro brother" could, the editor of the *Pittsburgh Catholic* contended, lead blacks to join the Communist Party. Moving beyond a condemnation of racism, Charles Owen Rice and Carl Hensler announced the birth of the Catholic Worker movement in Pittsburgh. The followers of Dorothy Day would attempt to do something concrete about reconstructing the lives of the poor. Father Thomas Lappan of the St. Vincent de Paul Society and Monsignor Barry O'Toole, a philosophy professor at Duquesne University and former rector of the Catholic University of Peking, joined Rice and Hensler. An Irish son of blue-collar Toledo, O'Toole had served as a secretary to Cleveland Bishop Joseph Schrembs. Given his experiences in Toledo and China, O'Toole was no stranger to destitution. Through Schrembs, O'Toole had also been immersed in the reformist politics of the National Catholic Welfare Conference.[71]

One hundred clergy and laity gathered at the St. Agnes Church in November 1936 to found the Pittsburgh branch of the Catholic Worker movement. William Callahan, the managing editor of *The Catholic Worker*, which now had a circulation of 125,000, stressed the importance of aiding the awakened labor movement and directing it away from Communism.

> When there is a strike, for instance, with picket lines established, men worried, women in distress, you will find the Communists on hand, giving the strikers material aid and helping them win their fight—and presenting them with Communist literature as they do so. Instead of this, Catholics ought to be in these places, helping the strikers' families, doing all they can to support the workers' cause, if it is a just one—and handing out extracts of the Papal Encyclicals showing how the Church supports the laborer in his rights on the basis of the divine law.[72]

On a swing through the Pittsburgh District shortly before Callahan's talk, Dorothy Day had met with Phil Murray, John Brophy, and Bishop Boyle. Day's tour of the region made a lasting impression upon her. Father Joseph Lonergan, who had clashed with Ernest Weir in 1934, greeted her with enthusiasm. In addition to championing SWOC, Father Lonergan and his parishioners were building a new church that would house their specially designed stations of the cross. All worked for the love of God, not for money. In Braddock, Day watched in admiration as a Polish priest implored the steel workers not to "let the Carnegie [Illinois] Steel Company crush you." At her meeting with Murray, Day praised SWOC's cause:

> Pope Leo XIII and Pope Pius XI spoke of how necessary it was for the workers to organize in order to achieve a modest living and in order to be treated as men and not as "chattels." But though Catholic teaching has been in favor of the organization of workers in unions

of their own choosing these last forty-five years, the industrialists of Pittsburgh have opposed these Christian teachings, and in their ruthless materialism have been as atheistic as the Communists they condemn. Inasmuch as they have degraded the worker, they have degraded Christ.

As Day concluded, the federal government had a moral obligation to assist workers in their efforts to achieve a better standard of living. Workers, however, should not depend solely upon Washington. Only "a sense of personal responsibility, instead of a sense of State responsibility," she argued, could eradicate poverty. Workers who gave themselves wholeheartedly to the government, were simply exchanging one spiritually empty master—their corporate employers—for another.[73]

Dorothy Day and her voluble assistant, the French-born Peter Maurin, were, as Rice contended, modern-day saints of the Church. Certainly, their voluntary vow of poverty and commitment to racial equality, as symbolized by the illustration of a white and black laborer on the masthead of *The Catholic Worker*, placed them in a realm apart from their fellow mortals. In their own way, Pittsburgh's activist clergy sought to embrace Day and Maurin's idea of "Christian personalism." According to one student of the American Church,

> Christian personalism stressed the necessity of each individual Christian's responsibility to live out the faith by assisting one's neighbor at a personal sacrifice. Personal holiness, grounded in the liturgy, expressed in practical action and dedicated to self-reform as a means of social regeneration was the hallmark of the Catholic Worker movement. Radical social change could never be accomplished without personal cooperation with supernatural grace and that always entailed moral regeneration manifested in voluntary poverty and the evangelical virtues of faith, love, and hope. The reformed Christian individual, rather than social legislation, was the primary key to a Christian society of love, justice, and peace.[74]

To Maurin, New Deal programs allowed nominal Christians to eschew their moral obligation to the poor. Since the federal government had assumed responsibility for the less fortunate, many citizens did not feel any need to assist in the nation's spiritual reconstruction. Ultimately, Maurin and Day worried, the "Welfare State" could become the "Servile State," with both the poor and the comfortable having surrendered their initiative and souls to the government. Arguing that the federal government was by its nature oppressive and flawed, given its temporal, as opposed to Godly, origins, Day rejected political activism. She argued that Christians could not give their loyalty to God and to the secular State. Although Hensler and Rice sympathized with Day's distrust of the State, they would not reject electoral and legislative means to achieving social reconstruction. Shortly before the presidential election, the *Pittsburgh Catholic* ran an editorial succinctly entitled "Justice Through Politics." Stopping short of endorsing Roosevelt, the *Pittsburgh Catholic* urged its readers to vote for candidates who championed progressive legislation. That, the diocesan newspaper implied, eliminated Republicans. The diocese also removed Father Coughlin's movement from consideration. Father Patrick Rice, the younger brother of Father Charles Owen Rice, argued that while Catholic clergy must participate in the political process, an exception should be made for Coughlin. The Catholic Church, Patrick Rice contended, would be better off if the Michigan clergyman expended his efforts on saving souls.[75]

Having rejected a political solution to the social crisis of the 1930s, Day and Maurin had found a more spiritual way to assist their impoverished neighbors and promote moral regeneration. The Catholic reformers created a House of Hospitality in New York City "where," Day observed, "men poor and in need find more than the mere hospice affords, bed and board; they find a warm welcome and a comfortable conversation and loving brothers and sisters." Day's House of Hospitality was the first of thirty established in the United States. With Bishop Boyle's support, Hensler and Charles Rice founded a House of Hospitality in Pittsburgh. Committed to the moral reformation of the poor, as well as to the success of the labor movement, the priests named their house after St. Joseph—the patron saint of the worker and a humble man who spent his life as a poor carpenter far from the seat of power. Determined to live among the poorest of the poor, Hensler and Rice placed the St. Joseph House of Hospitality in the Hill District. Bishop Boyle provided whatever meager funds the diocese could spare, while Frank Hensler—Carl's brother—Patrick Fagan, and Alan Kistler, a young, idealistic labor organizer, led group discussions on social justice and equality.[76]

The clientele of the St. Joseph House of Hospitality ran the gamut from unemployed coal and steel workers to alcoholics and drug addicts who had never held a steady job. Sometimes the people who appeared on the doorstep were teenagers locked out of the job market by older men who warned away hungry youngsters. One day, a Polish Catholic youth named Jock Yablonski came to the St. Joseph House. He found friendship and succor. Rice, who performed Yablonski's marriage ceremony, filled the young man with a crusading zeal that would compel him to seek social justice in the coal fields and, thirty years later, lead to his martyrdom. At the St. Joseph House, blacks and Italians dined together and learned from the "Christian personalism" of Hensler and Lappan that poverty did not have to mean degradation. With money raised from donations to the St. Vincent de Paul Society and the sale of the *Pittsburgh Catholic*, as well as from gifts of food by Strip District bakers and grocers, the St. Joseph House was soon serving 1,000 meals daily and providing shelter to 250 men—all of that on a budget of $150 a month. The Catholic Workers also gave regular lectures on charity, labor organizing, racial and religious fraternity, and the quest for social justice. Rice, as director of the St. Joseph House, acquired regular radio shows on KDKA, WCAE, and WWSW in order to discuss the Catholic Worker movement with a broader audience.[77]

Being a member of the Catholic Worker movement was not easy, and responsibility for dispensing limited Church charity exacted an enormous emotional toll. It seemed as if every destitute family eventually found its way to Father Lappan, pleading for help and believing that the coffers of the St. Vincent de Paul Society were bottomless. The missives addressed to Lappan and the Pittsburgh Diocese could be heart-rending.

> I have been working on the WPA project, up until a month ago. Was laid off on account of the work on that project was finished. I am now on relief.
>
> Right now, we are threatened with having our gas and electric turned off, no coal and Sister Sylvester of the school can tell you the condition of shoes and clothing my boys go to school in.
>
> Everywhere I go for aid I'm told that there is no funds for aid. Our church here (St. Peters) has helped me a little on food but they have not the funds to help me any more.
>
> So I write to you this letter, Father, in the hopes that you may aid me in the way you think best. My wife and children and I alone know what we are suffering.
>
> Sometimes my children even go to school hungry.

Upon investigation, Lappan learned that the man's family, though receiving $11 a week in public assistance, was renting a fashionable house for $18 a month and making $3 weekly payments for very stylish furniture. Catholics, Bishop Boyle had observed earlier, were no more immune to the charms of welfare than Protestants.[78]

Catholic labor, political, and religious reformers in 1936 were in agreement that if everyone was entitled to just treatment, regardless of race or creed, then everyone was also obligated to live a moral life. Corporations should pay a living wage and cease their war against organized labor. Workers were obliged to labor honestly. Catholics must not spew racial epithets at fellow minorities. However, Pittsburgh's Catholic activists believed, blacks should not blame their economic woes entirely on discrimination. Family dissolution and vice, so Catholic reformers thought, were among the factors that forced many urban whites and blacks into poverty. Catholics, allied with Jews and blacks, should organize politically, join SWOC, and support most New Deal reforms. That did not change the fact that individuals had to accept the consequences of their behavior. Ernest Weir deserved to be forgiven for his sins. However, that did not absolve him from the responsibility of running a moral corporation.

The Slovaks' desire to own a home led them to withdraw their children from school. Even if someday, thanks to the union, they did not need their children's earnings, Slavs would continue to prize home ownership above all else. They would remain working class. The first generation of eastern Jews, as poor as the Slavic immigrants, chose to educate their children at great sacrifice. Jews and Slavs had made their own choices. Catholic reformers believed that the government should no more force Slavs to go to college than it should provide relief to the undeserving poor. While the pre–New Deal social order could be blamed for many injustices, the Catholic reformers recognized that a balance had to be found. Society and the individual often shared in the perpetuation of human misery. If more willing to embrace the New Deal than Dorothy Day, Pittsburgh's Catholic activists were no less concerned that federal welfare undermined the ethic of personal responsibility. In the City of God, laziness and greed recognized no religious, racial, or class boundaries.

# 4

# Working-Class Saints

## Catholic Reformers and the Building of the Steel Workers' Union, 1937

Buffeted between militant Communists and red-baiting industrialists like Ernest Weir of National Steel and Thomas Girdler of Republic Steel, the CIO wins a few notable victories in 1937 but loses the struggle to unionize most of Little Steel. Violence erupts on picket lines from Chicago to Johnstown, Pennsylvania, as strikers, national guardsmen, and company security personnel clash. The Roosevelt administration, aware of a mounting public backlash against the CIO, distances itself from organized labor. Phil Murray and the steel workers sorely need friends like fathers Charles Owen Rice and Carl Hensler and Bishop Hugh Boyle to rally blue-collar Catholics and reassure workers that their cause is untainted by Communism.

In 1913, Phil Murray had an appointment at the Pittsburgh Labor Temple on Webster Avenue. He was to meet with John L. Lewis, a rising organizer for the American Federation of Labor. When Murray arrived at the rendezvous, he found a hulking Welshman beating up two men. The battle was nearly finished. One combatant had gone down for the count while the other desperately sought an exit. Overcoming his amazement, Murray asked, "Is there a fellow by the name of John Lewis here?" Lewis, disinclined to interrupt his important business, replied, "Yes, but I'm busy now, see you in a few minutes." It seemed that two representatives of the Westinghouse Corporation had waylaid Lewis in nearby Turtlecreek. Licking his wounds, Lewis had made some inquiries in Pittsburgh and then located his friends.[1]

Lewis and Murray were an odd duo. The Welshman thought nothing of threatening powerful corporations, as well as the leaders of the rival AFL. Indeed, Lewis was not above playing the strong man with Roosevelt. In 1936, Lewis, seeking to gain influence in the White House, presented a $250,000 campaign donation to Roosevelt. To Lewis's surprise, the president knew how to handle ambitious courtiers. He waved the check aside. However, a smiling Roosevelt said to Lewis that he would be happy to "call you if and when any small need arises." Small needs did arise, ones which cost the United Mine Workers more than $250,000. As Lewis ruefully told a colleague, "You don't know politicians. They stay under the golden drip from the honey barrel until no drop is left."[2]

Upon establishing the Committee for Industrial Organization, Lewis hired his relatives. Although Murray received the CIO vice presidency, Lewis's daughter, Kathryn, became the UMW secretary-treasurer. Denny Lewis, John Lewis's brother, served as the chair of the United Construction Workers Organizing Committee. By World War II, Lewis and ten members of his family were drawing $112,500 annually, plus expenses, from union accounts. Lewis's salary as UMW president in 1942 was $25,000 (the equivalent of $225,000 in 1997). In contrast, Murray drew $18,000, once he had replaced Lewis as the president of the CIO. It was typical of Murray that, even though as CIO president he had become the leader of the United Automobile Workers (UAW), the United Steel Workers, and numerous other affiliated unions, Murray made significantly less than the president of the mine workers. Moreover, Murray did not practice nepotism, choosing to employ people on the basis of their abilities. Lewis, as John Brophy observed, "was strong for his family, and always backed them to the limit."[3]

If a stalwart champion of the Lewis family, the union boss was also a firm believer in comfort. Lewis had servants and tailor-made suits. He took vacations in trendy European locales, collected antiques, lived in the suburbs, and associated with businessmen. Harold Ruttenberg suspected that Lewis would have preferred to have been a banker instead of a labor leader. Certainly, Lewis spent little of his life working as a miner and he disdained the company of beer-drinking Catholics. In contrast, when Murray was not trying to improve working conditions and wages for his miners, he remained close to his simple Pittsburgh home and beloved wife. As early as 1915, Murray had gained the trust and admiration of Pennsylvania coal miners when he lobbied on behalf of a workmen's compensation law. His efforts were successful and Pennsylvania became one of the few places in the United States that provided some assistance to disabled workers.[4]

Lewis and Murray embarked upon their productive, albeit strained, partnership in the early 1920s when the former became national president of the UMW and the latter assumed the vice presidency of the miners' union. The UMW leader brooked no criticism, purging Clinton Golden and John Brophy. According to Brophy, Murray was not comfortable with Lewis's extravagant lifestyle, but recognized him as someone who had the drive to build the union. The UMW's experiences in the 1920s, however, demonstrated just the opposite. Lewis oversaw the virtual dissolution of the UMW. Only the New Deal saved the miners. As CIO vice president, and as president of the Steel Workers Organizing Committee, Murray charted an independent course. Murray brought Lewis's exiles home and, with the assistance of honest UMW organizers, sought to make SWOC the voice of common people. While Lewis viewed the CIO as a vehicle for his own political ambitions, Murray considered himself to be an ordinary coal miner, immigrant, and Roman Catholic who served a just cause.[5]

Beyond personal differences, there was a basic question of tactics that separated Lewis and Murray. Lewis had made a point of recruiting Communists into the CIO. For CIO general counsel, Lewis had picked Lee Pressman while Len DeCaux became CIO publicity director. Both men were high-ranking members of the American Communist Party, though they denied their political affiliations. Brophy expressed wonderment at how easily Pressman, a Jew, rationalized Joseph Stalin's alliance with Hitler in 1939. For his part, DeCaux held the SWOC leadership in contempt. To DeCaux, whose father was a prominent Protestant minister in Australia, SWOC was "a setup—a Catholic setup. . . . In national CIO and most other new unions, religion didn't stick out as it did in SWOC." (DeCaux had reason to be resentful. Although sixty of SWOC's two hundred organizers were Communists, their influence among the rank and file became negligible once Catholic clergy denounced them.) In the CIO at large, Communists led 40 percent of its affiliates. Pressman and DeCaux played to Lewis's vanity. Meanwhile, they placed their allies throughout the CIO. Lewis thought he could use the Communists to build the CIO and thereby increase his power. In turn, the Communists used the CIO enhance their political position.[6]

Among labor leaders, Murray was the conciliator. This had not always been so. As a young man, Murray had a quick temper.

> Years before . . . I had discovered one of the less attractive sides of life in America. Miners in the Pennsylvania coal pits earned better wages than we'd been paid in Scotland. But they were forbidden to form unions, and no machinery existed for considering their complaints against crooked or overbearing bosses.

> In the shaft where I worked, the men were convinced they were be-
> ing cheated out of a portion of their wages by a dishonest weight man.
> [American coal operators paid miners on the basis of how much coal
> each produced daily and its quality.] One night I lodged a protest and
> suggested that the men be permitted to hire a weight man of their
> own — a common practice in the Scottish mines. But here I was called
> an agitator, a dirty foreigner, and other uncomplimentary names. For
> the first and only time in a labor dispute, I lost my temper. A bloody
> fight ensued.
>
> Next morning I was fired for engaging in a brawl on company prop-
> erty. Five hundred miners forthwith walked off the job. The strike
> lasted three weeks. During part of that time the Murray family lived
> in a tent, having been evicted from their company-owned house, while
> I was held a prisoner in the company store. Hunger finally drove the
> men back to the pits; but deputy sheriffs and members of miner oper-
> ators' police escorted me to Pittsburgh and warned me never to return.

Murray vowed not to lose his composure in the future.[7]

So long as "employers demonstrated a reasonable spirit of cooperation,"
Murray was content to avoid strikes. Unfortunately for the labor organizer,
there was little in the way of a cooperative spirit to be found among workers and managers. Late in December 1936, Walter Reuther and his energetic
brothers had begun a grueling contest to establish the UAW. What started as
a small demonstration in a Flint, Michigan, automobile factory escalated
into a full-blown labor war. Soon, nearly five hundred thousand workers at
sixty General Motors (GM) plants had gone on strike, many barricading
themselves inside the factories. As a favor to the UAW, Murray went to Detroit in an effort to bargain with Henry Ford. The SWOC leader hoped that
an agreement with Ford would bring GM in line. Bemused at the plight of
his business rival, Ford proved a congenial host. In fact, Ford felt so comfortable with Murray that the old fellow curled up on the thick carpet of his
office and slept for an hour. When he awoke, Ford said he would be happy
to recognize the UAW if the Reuthers would allow his private security forces
to join as well. Murray doubted that the UAW would want Ford's goon squad
in its ranks.[8]

While Murray dickered with Ford, two SWOC organizers went to Flint
to assist the UAW. They disappeared. Alarmed, Murray contacted Frank
Murphy, the governor of Michigan. Many middle-class citizens did not approve of workers taking over their places of employment, even if their intent
was to prevent strikebreakers from gaining entrance. The workers were not,

Fig. 7.　Philip Murray of Pittsburgh. Founder of the Steel Workers Organizing Committee (1936) and president of the CIO (1940–1952). A devout Catholic, Murray embraced the labor encyclicals of Leo XIII and Pius XI. (Courtesy of the United Steelworkers of America Archive, Pennsylvania State University Libraries.)

as GM charged, part of a sinister Communist conspiracy to seize American industry. As the first Catholic governor of Michigan, and the first Democrat to occupy the office in a generation, Murphy's sympathies were with the UAW. Viewing the sit-down strike as a no-win proposition, Roosevelt put some distance between himself and the union. Left to his own devices, Murphy requested the Michigan State Police to locate the missing SWOC organizers. The officers found the men in a hotel where GM was keeping them under armed guard. By February, believing that the strikers and GM's private army were about to shoot one another, Murphy ordered the Michigan National Guard to place itself between the two factions. GM capitulated to the UAW, but not after Murphy had alienated a considerable portion of the Michigan electorate.[9]

In Pittsburgh, Murray faced a formidable task. With a limited economic recovery, the American steel industry in 1937 employed 479,000 blue-collar workers. U.S. Steel accounted for 222,000 of those men, followed by Bethlehem Steel (80,000), Republic Steel (49,000), and Jones & Laughlin (29,000). Youngstown Sheet and Tube was the baby sibling of what constituted Little Steel—every mill other than U.S. Steel. The steel companies were bastions of the open shop and had broken unions and organizers' skulls with equal ease since 1892. U.S. Steel had been so opposed to any type of worker organization that even as Little Steel established company-controlled unions in the early 1920s, the behemoth refused to accept any small compromise of the open shop. It took the economic crisis of the 1930s, and the fear of Section 7a of the National Recovery Act, to prompt U.S. Steel to create a company union. U.S. Steel hoped to co-opt its restless work force. The Corporation miscalculated. SWOC soon dominated the company union.[10]

Myron Taylor, the chair of U.S. Steel, had changed since the early days of the Depression when he blamed radicals and immigrants for social unrest. Realizing that the best way to deal with a powerful rival was to give him a government job, Roosevelt had appointed Taylor to the advisory board of the National Recovery Administration. Taylor, and the industrialists and Republican politicians who followed him, felt obliged to defend the New Deal policies that they had helped formulate. Subsequently, Taylor became an ally of Roosevelt. While the DuPonts, Pews, and other wealthy contributors to the Liberty League were depicting Roosevelt as a Communist agitator in the 1936 presidential election, the chair of U.S. Steel kept a low profile. The president, and a SWOC-controlled company union, had made Taylor see the light.[11]

In February 1937, Taylor invited Murray to dine at his Park Avenue home. Having just returned to New York, Taylor was in a reflective mood. Gesturing to some artifacts he had collected while cruising the Mediterranean, the U.S. Steel chief told Murray and David McDonald that he wished to talk about ancient Babylon.

> Babylon traded throughout the known world and she had all kinds of businesses. She even had labor unions, and there were strikes and people fighting, just as there are today. As I crossed the same waters that the Babylonian ships used to sail, I did a lot of thinking about what you fellows are doing back here in trying to organize my employees into a union. And it occurred to me that one day we will be just as extinct as Babylon, and a thousand years from now, nobody is going to know or care about the decisions we make today. I have to make a decision about you. I either have to fight you or bargain with you. I have

no desire for a fight. I don't want a strike and I don't want to see people hurt and killed on picket lines. So on that ship, I made up my mind. I want to make a labor agreement with you men for the employees of U.S. Steel.

McDonald was in shock, not believing that SWOC's largest opponent had really capitulated. The union won a forty-hour work week, a $5 daily minimum wage, paid vacations, and a pledge to work out labor-management disputes peacefully.[12]

Taylor's conversion to the cause of unionism was not entirely selfless. The canny lawyer suspected that Little Steel would fight SWOC, thereby crippling his competitors. Certainly, SWOC's experiences with Jones & Laughlin seemed to confirm Taylor's point of view. In Aliquippa, Murray's organizers had been dodging company goons and city police for nearly a year. The SWOC organizers had also been engaged in daring games of cloak and dagger. Concerned about the many company agents who had infiltrated SWOC, Clinton Golden built his own spy bureau. Golden's agents tailed corporate security personnel in Aliquippa, Braddock, and Pittsburgh. There was no shortage of tense moments as SWOC's agents stalked Jones & Laughlin and National Steel representatives through the Carnegie Library and the lobby of the Hotel Webster in Oakland. Invariably, they would happen upon a rendezvous between the security men and the steel companies' union infiltrators. This was the stuff of high drama, made more exciting by Golden's success in placing an agent within the management of Jones & Laughlin. SWOC's covert operative even took a code name: "M."[13]

Thanks to Golden's counter-espionage efforts, and to the courage of SWOC's organizers and Aliquippa's priests, the majority of steel workers indicated their desire to join the union. Just as a civil war was about to break out, the United States Supreme Court made a stunning ruling. On April 12, 1937, the Republican-dominated court addressed the constitutionality of the New Deal's labor reforms. In *National Labor Relations Board v. Jones & Laughlin Steel Company*, the court concluded that the company's actions against labor organizers in Aliquippa had been illegal. Bowing to the law, Jones & Laughlin promised to schedule an employee vote on unionization.[14]

Having signed an agreement with U.S. Steel, and being in no small part responsible for presenting a test case to the Supreme Court on the legal merits of the Wagner Act, SWOC appeared unbeatable. Lieutenant Governor Thomas Kennedy, a former UMW official, pledged state protection to SWOC organizers. Meanwhile, Pittsburgh mayor Cornelius Scully waxed eloquent on the SWOC-U.S. Steel accord:

[SWOC and U.S. Steel] have cast aside old shibboleths to achieve collective bargaining under the letter and spirit of the law of the land and in accordance with the true American way.

Pittsburgh will not flourish as a low-wage city. It does not profit a city to gain a sweatshop, and lose the health and well-being of its people.

"Big Steel" and SWOC have set an example to the nation.

They have put an imperative injunction upon management and labor.

That injunction is, "Go thou and do likewise."[15]

John L. Lewis claimed credit for the U.S. Steel accord. Ignoring the work Murray's organizers had done among U.S. Steel's rank and file, Lee Pressman spared no praise for his boss. The Harvard Law School graduate told reporters that Lewis alone was responsible for bringing Taylor to the negotiating table. Although Murray did not object to Lewis's performances before the press, he was alarmed by reports coming out of Minnesota. In the Duluth mills, SWOC organizers demanded that workers join the Communist Party when they signed their union cards. Worse, Gus Hall (a.k.a., Arvo Holberg), an Ohio SWOC organizer, and later a perennial Communist Party presidential candidate, was generating negative publicity. Hall had been caught dynamiting the homes of anti-union workers in Warren. Given these developments, Murray feared a backlash against the CIO, especially if the public became aware of its ties to the Communist Party.[16]

The American Catholic Church was not of one mind when it came to the CIO in the winter of 1937. In New York, the *Brooklyn Tablet* contended that the leaders of the UAW sit-down strike were Communists. Similarly, Father Edmund Walsh of Georgetown University believed that the CIO strikers had taken orders from their Soviet masters. Father Charles Coughlin, his party resoundingly defeated in the 1936 elections, but unwilling to admit that his hour had passed, argued that good Catholics could not join the Communist-led CIO. In Chicago, George Cardinal Mundelein and Auxiliary Bishop Bernard Sheil thought that Catholics had a "duty" to join the CIO and fight for social justice. Across the continent in Seattle, Bishop Gerald Shaughnessy defended the automobile strikers and observed that "the right of the working man to a living wage takes precedence over the right of the stockholder to his dividends."[17]

In a January editorial, the *Pittsburgh Catholic* praised the CIO and urged the public to broaden its definition of property rights.

Capital has dominated, and still insists on trying to dominate, the industrial world; there has not yet been a whole-hearted acceptance of the principle of collective bargaining, which is essential if the position of labor is to be above that of a mere commodity. Before we say that workers, who have suspended work in protest against terms of employment with which they are dissatisfied, as a group, have no "right" to remain at "their" machines and in "their" plant, we must remember that these are tools of production to which the workers have a relation closer than that of accessories. The employer who thinks himself on safe ground when he asserts that "no one is going to dictate to me how to run my business" forgets that "his" business exists only as part of the general economic system, and that he has an obligation to society that transcends what he calls his "property rights."[18]

Pittsburgh's Catholic labor organizers received special praise from a variety of Church representatives. San Antonio Archbishop Robert Lucey wrote an effusive letter to John Brophy, noting that "in the Providence of God a better day has dawned on the teeming masses of people. By enormous efforts the Committee for Industrial Organization is lifting labor from its lethargy." The *Pittsburgh Catholic* described Brophy and Murray as

men who have devoted themselves to the cause of improving the lot of their fellow-workers: splendid motives inspire them, selfishness is not corrupting them. They are more serious students of the problems that face them, more conscious of their responsibilities. They have learned to make personal sacrifices; they stand out as men of high probity in life. What they need, and what they should receive from the Catholic body as a whole, is not criticism, but help; not suspicion, but support. Not aloofness, but cooperation. They are our representatives in a trying and difficult situation today; through them Catholic principles are being applied, definitely and constructively. Through them the opportunity presents itself now to make far reaching gains in the cause of Catholic social justice.

Given that Murray kept a copy of Leo XIII's labor encyclical in his office for ready reference, it is no wonder that the Church reformers called him a working-class saint.[19]

Charles Owen Rice and Carl Hensler eagerly embraced SWOC. Unlike Dorothy Day, who feared that a successful labor movement could become corrupted, the Pittsburgh priests did not hesitate to champion the CIO. Day admired Murray and spoke well of the CIO. However, she was concerned that organized labor would succumb to the false charms of materialism. Rice and Hensler appreciated the allures of capitalist materialism and recognized that workers were not immune to their effects. Mindful of human frailties, but also painfully aware of the spiritual costs of poverty, the clergy advocated a sweeping change in the relationship between labor and management. As Rice and Hensler announced in April 1937, they were founding the Catholic Radical Alliance because they wanted

> a changed and reformed social order that will be Christian and just in every sense of the word. We are not Utopians looking for a perfect set-up for perfect men. The set-up we want is one that will work with imperfect men. For one thing we believe in every man having and being protected in ownership, and control of his means of making a living. That's the only way that a man can be free and secure. As for the big factories that can't be broken down to small holdings, we believe that workers should share in their control, ownership, and profit.[20]

With Hensler, Rice, and Monsignor Barry O'Toole as instructors, the Catholic Radical Alliance established an educational program devoted to training workers for social action. Fifty male and female workers learned a new catechism. "Is the present economic and social system a good one," queried the priests. "Is it Christian?" The response of the laity was, "Emphatically no! It is materialistic and Godless." On the subject of Communism, the Pittsburgh catechism was no less critical: "[Communism] is Godless and materialistic. It looks to the well-being just of men's bodies and is nothing more than capitalism carried to extremes. Also, it is spark-plugged by hatred of persons, which must result in evil." To reassure Catholics that religion and reform did mix, the catechism asked, "Why does the Church bother with economic and social matters? Is it any business of hers, since she is a religious and moral society?" Hensler wrote this response:

> In the first place, the Church has the right and duty of being interested in everything that affects the well-being of her children. In the second place, the Church is the boss, appointed by Christ, of the moral law; and these things, social and economic matters, like everything else, are under the moral law, the law of right and wrong. Most important, for another thing, a just social system helps people to save their souls; while an unjust one works the opposite.[21]

By early May, Rice inaugurated a half-hour radio program on KDKA. His first address, "The Dynamite of the Encyclicals," praised the social teachings of Leo XIII and Pius XI. Rice also chided Communists, anti-New Deal Catholics, and "irresponsible" capitalists:

> There are Catholics . . . who act, not like followers of Christ, but like followers of the devil in their dealings with, and attitude toward, the problem of social justice, toward the workers and the poor. They are children not of the Church but of the unjust economic and social system that has warped their minds and their conduct. . . .
>
> There are many other Catholics who impede the advance of the truth by their blundering . . . They rant and rave against the menace of Communism, against its Godlessness; with never a word about the menace and Godlessness of finance capitalism. They let hatred of Communism, which is proper, blind them into breaking Christ's law against hatred of persons.
>
> The Communists are . . . much like the finance capitalists. Neither can see beyond his nose. They both rule out God—the finance capitalist when he says business is business, I'm not running a charitable concern, what do I care if they are not getting enough wages, let them go elsewhere if they don't like it.
>
> The best system in the world will go on the rocks if individualism and materialism are the ruling ideas. Individualism is, simply, the doctrine of every man for himself. Materialism is the doctrine that we are just animals; that there is no other life but this one, no other values but those we find on earth. These ideas have been in the saddle of modern life and they are what have made such a mess out of civilization. . . . They rule the present system; they rule business today, and they will rule in the Communist or fascist super-state, and don't fool yourself.[22]

As Aliquippa's workers prepared to vote on whether or not to affiliate with SWOC, Rice spoke to Jones & Laughlin employees at the Romanian Hall and the Sons of Italy Hall. He told the steel workers that the Church was with them in their struggle for social justice. Hundreds of workers gave the priest a hearty ovation. Seventy percent of the steel workers chose SWOC as their legal bargaining agent. Meanwhile, Father Thomas Lappan, who had joined the Catholic Radical Alliance, wrote to Murray pledging to use the resources of the St. Vincent de Paul Society to assist striking workers and their families.

We are ready to use all of resources to relieve any such hardships. We are not going to stand by and see hunger and suffering used as weapons for the settlement of differences between employees and employers. We shall not inquire into the "reasonableness" of the strike, or the religion or politics of those who are affected. Wherever there is distress, we shall do our best to supply whatever is needed.[23]

Lappan's offer of assistance was well-timed. Tom Girdler, the chair of Republic, soon fired the first salvo in Little Steel's battle against SWOC. In South Chicago, on Memorial Day, several thousand strikers and their families were picketing a Republic mill. Suddenly, five hundred police officers charged into the crowd. As men, women, and children fled the officers' swinging nightsticks, the police, a number of whom were on Republic's payroll, began shooting. The officers killed ten people and wounded ninety more. Girdler had developed this approach to labor-management relations as a superintendent at Aliquippa's Jones & Laughlin mill. A devout Episcopalian and vestryman of his church, Girdler was, in his own mind, doing God's work.[24]

With Chicago workers taken care of, Little Steel's campaign against SWOC shifted to Ohio. In Niles and Warren, SWOC pickets besieged the Republic mills. No scabs were going to cross the picket lines and take away their jobs. Determined to feed the workers who had remained in the mills, Girdler sent a squadron of planes to eastern Ohio. As the Republic aircraft buzzed overhead, several CIO planes attacked. Awestruck, the pickets watched the ensuing dogfight. Suffering several casualties, the Republic pilots retreated. Girdler's men had not expected to be exchanging gun fire while cruising several hundred feet off the ground.[25]

Determined to break the strike in Warren—a community of forty-five thousand people—hundreds of black men crawled through the swamps in order to evade SWOC pickets. As one black steel worker informed George Schuyler, the *Pittsburgh Courier*'s outstanding labor reporter, the CIO was "a Bolshevik movement." Warren's black clergy, as well as the Urban League—a civil rights organization—praised Republic Steel and denounced the strikers. Only six blacks in Warren, standing up to their ministers' censure, joined SWOC. Grateful for the support of black workers, Girdler dramatically increased their pay. Many scabs were making $20 a day, bringing great prosperity to the city's three thousand blacks. Angry, hungry, and desperate, the Italians and Slavs began to shout "black bastard!" whenever they saw a scab.[26]

In Canton and Massillon, pimps, gamblers, and prostitutes from Cleveland and Detroit came to share in the black community's new-found wealth.

Every night at one Canton honky-tonk a three-piece orchestra played jazz as hookers and steel workers guzzled liquor and danced the "Suzy Q." Schuyler, a northern-bred black who admired Phil Murray, was visibly upset with what he found in Ohio's mill towns. Surveying the black steel workers in Massillon, Schuyler disdainfully reported on their spending habits and lifestyles: "Most of the money is being spent for new cars which usually have no garage and sit in the back yards surrounded by high weeds. There are few home owners." Little did the blacks and Appalachian whites who crossed the picket lines realize that once the strike was defeated they would be fired.[27]

Demoralized by the onset of the Depression and the election of Jacob Coxey to the mayor's office, Republic had soon regained its bearings. By the mid-1930s, Republic ousted Coxey from office. Desiring to solidify their power, Massillon's white businessmen made common cause with blacks. This was no mean feat given that in the 1920s the Mahoning Valley Ku Klux Klan—led by Protestant ministers and businessmen—had posted racist signs at area train depots: "Niggers, [don't] let the sun set on [your] heads." Once the steel strike began, middle-class Protestants and company executives organized the Law and Order League of Massillon. Within a few weeks, forty members of the Law and Order League became sworn deputies of the city police department, their salaries paid by Republic. On the night of July 11, the police fired on SWOC's local headquarters, killing three people. By early morning, Republic's police officers had arrested 165 supporters of the CIO. Republic won the battles of Canton, Massillon, Niles, and Warren.[28]

The struggle for Youngstown ended on a similar note. Republic and Youngstown Sheet and Tube arranged for the county sheriff to deputize ninety-four of their employees, while the city hired an additional 144 police officers. Fifty-nine of the special officers worked for Republic and Youngstown Sheet and Tube. Steel representatives also established the Mahoning Valley Citizens' Committee—a group of Protestant businessmen—to combat SWOC. Disturbed by Little Steel's Ohio offensive, Rice, Hensler, and O'Toole arrived in Youngstown to address two SWOC rallies. The priests prayed for the success of the union. O'Toole, who had participated in the great 1919 steel strike, hoped that this time the forces of law and justice would be on the side of the workers. A few days after the Pittsburghers departed, 250 deputies fired into a picket line, killing two strikers and wounding forty-two more. Ohio governor Martin Davey, an antilabor Democrat from Kent, ordered the National Guard to occupy Youngstown. Davey declared martial law and arrested hundreds of SWOC members. Girdler's supporters gleefully announced that the initials CIO stood for "Collapsed in Ohio."[29]

To anyone who knew the recent history of eastern Ohio, the violence that characterized the 1937 Little Steel strike was not unexpected. In 1923, weary of violent Klan attacks, a group of Catholics in Niles and Steubenville had formed the Knights of the Flaming Circle. Whenever Klansmen burned crosses in front of Slavic homes and churches, the Knights of the Flaming Circle would go to a hooded-member's home and set fire to a tire. The self-defense organization found eager members as far away as Johnstown, Pennsylvania. To Catholics, the tire represented the circle that often is depicted above the Virgin Mary's head. Protestants, apparently, did not view the burning tires as harmless halos and set out to ban the Knights.[30]

Dismayed by the course of events in Ohio, George Schuyler argued that the blacks who sided with Republic had poisoned race relations for generations to come. Trying to make the best of a bad situation, Schuyler stressed that many black workers in Chicago, Cleveland, Detroit, and Pittsburgh had either joined SWOC or staged sympathy strikes in support of the steel union. Schuyler also reassured blacks that Murray would not tolerate racial discrimination in the union. Murray personally secured the endorsement of A. Philip Randolph, the president of the International Brotherhood of Sleeping Car Porters and the most prominent black unionist in the United States. Swayed by Randolph and Schuyler's impassioned pleas on behalf of SWOC, *Courier* publisher Robert Vann took a break from his feud with machine boss David Lawrence. Vann's editorial line was blunt: "When labor has a decided voice in government, police will not shoot workers in the back for wanting to live like human beings."[31]

Ironically, there had been far more white than black scabs. In Warren, twenty-one hundred whites had remained on the job. Many of these whites were poor Protestant migrants from the southern reaches of Appalachia. Indeed, eastern Ohio had become the home of so many Appalachian whites that in the 1920s one West Virginian gubernatorial candidate made a campaign tour through the area. He expected the transplanted West Virginians to return home to vote. Such were the people, deeply suspicious of Roman Catholicism and labor unions, who tried to break the 1937 steel strike. Nonetheless, many Slavs focused their resentments on blacks, perhaps because they stood out from their southern white brethren. Beyond racial considerations, blacks had a clergy that often denounced labor unions and courted the favor of paternalistic white employers. In that regard, the ministers were acting upon the injunction that the great nineteenth-century black leader, Booker T. Washington, had proclaimed in 1895. Addressing himself to southern (and northern) businessmen, Washington made common cause against unions and immigrants:

To those of the white race who look to the incoming of those of foreign birth and strange tongue and habits for the prosperity of the South, were I permitted I would repeat what I say to my own race, "Cast down your bucket where you are." Cast it down among the 8,000,000 Negroes whose habits you know, whose fidelity and love you have tested in days when to have proved treacherous meant the ruin of your firesides. Cast down your bucket among these people who have, without strikes and labor wars, tilled your fields, cleared your forests, built your railroads and cities, and brought forth treasures from the bowels of the earth. . . .

While doing this, you can be sure in the future, as in the past, that you and your families will be surrounded by the most patient, faithful, law-abiding, and unresentful people that the world has seen. . . . [W]e shall stand by you with a devotion that no foreigner can approach, ready to lay down our lives, if need be, in defense of yours, interlacing our industrial, commercial, civil, and religious life with yours in a way that shall make the interests of both races one.[32]

The spirit of Booker T. Washington, Schuyler wrote, was alive and well in Johnstown. As Schuyler reported, just a half-dozen black steel workers, out of some four hundred, had gone on strike. They were pariahs in their own community and the subjects of some initial suspicion among Catholic strikers. At one SWOC rally in Point Stadium, there were twenty-thousand whites to four hundred blacks—nearly every African-American present was an out-of-town UMW member. According to Schuyler, the black miners were "shocked and puzzled" by the absence of their brethren.

Their amazement was not without foundation. Johnstown, to say the least, is unprepossessing. The mean, tawdry, dun-colored rookeries in which the workers are forced to dwell are in marked contrast to the vivid green of the steep hills that hem in the town. For eight miles along the tortuous Conemaugh Valley, the rusty mills sprawl like some puffing, Mesozoic monster stuffed with the blood and bones and hopes of men, women, and children.[33]

Sadly, the journalist concluded, the Bethlehem Steel Corporation had secured the loyalties of Johnstown's blacks, contributing money to their churches and civil rights organizations and giving them jobs on the city police force. Indeed, Johnstown's first black police officer, who was appointed at the beginning of the steel strike, had worked as a chauffeur for a number of wealthy Protestant families. In what became a familiar pattern in John-stown race relations, a group of white pickets in early July attempted to throw five black scabs into the Conemaugh River. At another racial alterca-tion, a group of white strikers, armed with pick handles, attacked a black as he tried to cross the picket line. Prepared for action, the black steel worker stabbed three whites. His wife had told him that Satan stood behind SWOC.[34]

Johnstown's Protestant clergy cultivated the cultural ties that bound white and black against SWOC. Their efforts proved successful. Seventy-five per-cent of the workers and businessmen who supported Bethlehem Steel were Protestant, while 70 percent of the strikers were young Slavs and Italian eth-nics. One Johnstown minister, who had helped form a committee of com-munity leaders to defend the steel corporation, penned a jeremiad against the CIO:

> The fruits of the CIO have been lawlessness, riots, bloodshed, kid-napping, threats, and great losses in wages to the working man. There is no question but that the CIO is paving the way for a Soviet Amer-ica. Surely Mr. Lewis claims he is not a Communist, for if he did make that claim all thinking American citizens would be against him at once, but as he claims otherwise he has been able to deceive many into think-ing that he is truly the "savior of the laboring classes." If John L. Lewis is not a Communist, then why are all the Communist leaders taking their orders from him? We can see that months before there was even a suspicion of unrest in the prosperous, high-wage-paying auto industry, a very significant step was taken in Moscow. In order to overthrow our government and establish a Soviet America in its place, the map of the United States was re-drawn and the names of its principal cities changed. The city of Detroit was changed or renamed, Lewistown—in honor of John L. Lewis, who holds the fourth place on the *Communist Honor Role* for 1937. This map is proudly dis-played in the Moscow Museum of Revolution.
>
> O! Christian America—wake up—put on the whole armor of God. . . . Satan has no army so large that cannot be put to rout by the prayers and power of God's people. . . . This is an hour when Chris-tians everywhere should stand together and by God's help defeat the foe.[35]

Anthony Lorditch, a member of the Johnstown SWOC, thought he was a good Catholic, not a Communist. Johnstown's Protestant clergy made no distinction between the two. The son of a Croatian immigrant, Lorditch had entered the city's steel mills in 1917. A participant in the 1919 Steel Strike, he had left town for a while, working for the Pennsylvania Railroad. By the 1930s, Lorditch was ready to attempt another union organizing drive.

> In 1936, when they started organizing the SWOC, we weren't too sure after the 1919 fracas what to expect. But one of the fellows in the mill got interested in it, Mike Neary, and he got us to go to a meeting that they had down at the SWOC headquarters on Main Street, up where the garment workers had their headquarters for a long time. We went down to a couple meetings and the organizer was a fellow by the name of Jim Gent. And I think what made most of feel a little safe about it was that Jim was a practicing Catholic, he went to church every morning and of course we found it out, most of us were Catholics. He got us interested and we all signed up.
>
> . . . They [SWOC] brought some organizers in, most of them were coal miners and some of them came from Pittsburgh. . . . Phil Murray came to me, called me over by myself. . . . I never knew anybody I respected like that man. The way he acted, the way he talked, never got excited.
>
> . . . I believed [in the union] because I heard Phil Murray, and being a Catholic, I read the encyclical of Pope Leo XIII, saying that human justice should allow people to join together in order to get fair deals and everything.[36]

Bethlehem Steel was not about to permit Lorditch to realize his vision of Catholic social justice. By threats and lavish spending, as well as through calls of Protestant solidarity directed toward Johnstown's blacks, Bethlehem had fought populist Mayor Eddie McCloskey to a standstill. By 1936, Bethlehem had elected a new mayor. To no one's surprise, Mayor Daniel Shields gave his all to Bethlehem Steel. With $30,000 provided by the steel corporation, Shields acquired an army and an arsenal to combat SWOC. Excited at the prospect of battle, Shields and his minions posed before newsreel cameras. The jaunty crew playfully bashed their clubs on each other's heads, demonstrating the strength of their combat helmets. If the resulting film resembled a "Three Stooges" comedy short, it was no more malicious than what was occurring in Johnstown's streets. As a photographer for *Life* magazine recorded the scene, a number of Slavic women stripped the clothes off a white scab.[37]

Desiring to assist Catholic unionists like Lorditch, Rice and Hensler contacted Murray. They offered to go to Johnstown. When Democratic governor George Earle declared martial law in Johnstown, hoping the state police could disarm Shields's army and the angry strikers, the priests were unable to enter the city. Rice subsequently delivered a pro-CIO radio address that was heard in Johnstown, as well as in Harrisburg and Baltimore. Despite the efforts of the Catholic Radical Alliance and SWOC, the Bethlehem strike fell apart.[38]

The Catholic Radical Alliance had been busy throughout the summer of 1937, fighting valiantly on behalf of SWOC and other labor unions. In Pittsburgh, Hensler, Rice, and Lappan had been assisting workers in their efforts to form unions at H. J. Heinz and the Loose Wiles Biscuit Company. Father Lappan was feeding the strikers at both companies while distributing five hundred copies of Dorothy Day's *Catholic Worker* to the families of Jones & Laughlin workers. Angry with Rice and his growing number of friends in the labor movement, representatives of Loose Wiles threatened to relocate the plant if their Pittsburgh employees joined the CIO. Meanwhile, John Brophy addressed a meeting of the Catholic Radical Alliance, reassuring the laity who had joined the group that the CIO opposed Communism and violence. As Rice informed the readers of the *Pittsburgh Catholic*, he did not want people to regard his anti-Communism as a defense of laissez-faire capitalism:

> We support the labor unions, the drives for higher wages, better working conditions, security of employment, etc., but we say that is not enough. We look and work for the day when workers will work WITH and not FOR the boss; when there will be a partnership and sharing in ownership, profits, and control between labor and management. We want to see private property as widely distributed as possible among all the people.[39]

At the beginning of the Heinz strike, Hensler and Rice joined the picket line that the Canning and Pickle Workers Union had set up on Pittsburgh's North Side. Their presence greatly heartened the strikers. Responding to the anti-AFL propaganda put out by Heinz, the priests distributed a leaflet criticizing the company union. Hensler, O'Toole, and Rice also urged employees to vote for the Canning and Pickle Workers in the union certification elections being conducted by the National Labor Relations Board. "Why does the Catholic Radical Alliance support the Heinz strike?" the activists asked,

> Because it believes with Pope Pius XI and Pope Leo XIII that workers have the right, nay the duty, to organize, and to organize as they

see fit, within the moral law, under whatever leader they wish, without coercion. Organization of the workers is the first step toward a just and workable, Christian social order.

. . . We appeal to the employers to cease interference with the workers' natural rights. The workers are not cattle, they are not a commodity; but they are human beings with bodies and souls and human dignity. They must be treated with respect as responsible persons.[40]

The spectacle of priests joining a picket line, and then addressing a crowd of six hundred Heinz employees, attracted the attention of *Time* magazine and the national press. Closer to home, Howard Heinz was annoyed. His employees, who had not been comfortable with the AFL organizers, fell into line behind Hensler, O'Toole, and Rice. Consequently, the Heinz workers, as well as those employed by Loose Wiles, voted in favor of affiliation with the Canning and Pickle Union. One North Side priest, whose church had been the beneficiary of Heinz donations, denounced the activist clergy. Describing the union organizers as "agitators from the outside" with "a Communistic background," Father Cosmas Minster went on to brand Hensler and Rice as "unpriestly and uncharitable." Minster noted that "Mr. Heinz and his company are held in the highest esteem by the priests in the neighborhood of the factory." While publicly offering to extend his "hand of fellowship in the true spirit of Christ's charity" to Minster, privately Rice complained about clergymen who acted like corporation employees. Bishop Hugh Boyle did not directly comment on this incident, but he had already made his position known by having given the Catholic Radical Alliance his blessing.[41]

Two prominent Pittsburgh priests were no more favorably disposed toward the Catholic Radical Alliance and the CIO. One would have expected Father Thomas Coakley of the Sacred Heart Parish to have condemned labor unions and reformist clergy. Born in the Irish wards of the Hill District in 1880, the priest used the Church as his exit from poverty. Intelligent and ambitious, Coakley had graduated from Rome's North American College, served in World War I, and became the chaplain of the Allegheny County chapter of the Ancient Order of Hibernians. In 1921, Coakley had informed a reporter for the *New York World* that

the Ku Klux Klan had its rise in Alabama and South Carolina, and now has its headquarters in Georgia. . . . South Carolina is the most illiterate state in the Union, next comes Alabama. Georgia is 44th in the list of states where ignorance reigns. You don't hear of the KKK in the territory influenced by Harvard, Yale, Princeton, Columbia, Cornell, or Chicago Universities.

Actually, Harvard and Princeton had thriving Ku Klux Klan chapters.[42]
Having left the Catholic working class behind when he moved from Old St. Patrick's to Sacred Heart, Coakley did not approve of Roosevelt. In 1934, Coakley had called the New Deal "pagan." Three years later, Coakley stood in his pulpit and decried SWOC "labor racketeers," and Senator Robert Wagner for having written the 1935 National Labor Relations Act. Coakley then called for Congress to amend the New Deal's labor legislation to protect employers from Lewis and Murray.[43]

Although Coakley was consistent in his opposition to social activism, many people were surprised that Father James Cox also castigated the Catholic Radical Alliance and SWOC. Father Casimir Orlemanski did not agree with his old comrade. He enlisted in the Catholic Radical Alliance. Indeed, Orlemanski, who in 1932 had marched shoulder to shoulder with Cox in Washington, became such a vigorous champion of the CIO that the Federal Bureau of Investigation placed him under surveillance. When Rice discovered that the FBI was keeping tabs on Orlemanski, he assured the government agents that the priest was no Stalinist.[44]

Father Cox did not relish being in the same company with Coakley. He thought that the cleric was full of himself. Then again, Cox had come to feel the same way about Rice. In part, Cox's hostility toward the Catholic Radical Alliance stemmed from his gratitude to Howard Heinz. Since the beginning of the Depression Heinz had donated food to Cox's soup kitchen. Cox did not appreciate Hensler and Rice's assault on the company. If the great Pittsburgh benefactor did not want his employees to belong to an independent union, that was his own business. Additionally, the erstwhile presidential candidate was a man of no small ego. Cox felt that Pittsburgh was not big enough for more than one high-profile priest—himself. Beyond jealousy, Old St. Patrick's pastor was not comfortable with the younger labor organizers who had displaced the older, ineffective union men he had worked with in the 1920s. Cox felt particularly alarmed by Lewis's Communist organizers. Betraying a hint of nativism (and no little irony), Cox angrily observed that some of the CIO representatives—presumably the Marxist Serbians—were "unable even to speak English."[45]

Such considerations, as well as a propensity to blame SWOC, instead of Little Steel, for promoting violence, might explain the bitter broadside Cox directed against the CIO in June 1937. Speaking at Old St. Patrick's on a radio link-up with station WJAS, Cox held nothing back:

I am, always have been and always will be a union man, one who believes in unionism. . . . But the tactics being employed today by so-called "union-racketeers" are as unjust and repugnant to me as the injustice of child labor and the sweatshop of other days. The pendulum of injustice has swung from the five percent of the unjust old privileged class who ruled before the Depression, to the fifteen percent represented in the 1937 mushroom labor ranks of today. . . . Labor racketeerism in America today is mobocracy led by fanatics, directed and controlled by aliens.[46]

The *Pittsburgh Catholic*, the *Post-Gazette*, and Pittsburgh's high-society newspaper, the *Bulletin Index*, recorded Rice and Hensler's rebuttals. Although the first two newspapers softened their accounts, the defender of upper-class Republicanism did not intend to tone down its coverage. How could the *Bulletin Index* resist reporting in squalid detail a priestly donnybrook involving three of Pennsylvania's most important social activists? To Rice went the award for employing the most aggressive grammar just short of profanity:

If snobbery and propaganda succeed in keeping the white-collar people hostile or suspicious of labor in this country, the result will be class war. Labor wants to cooperate with management and wants to join forces with the middle class. If the advances of labor be repulsed, then will the twin dangers of Communism and fascism be realities. . . .

Every union leader in United States history has faced the vilification that is being showered on the leaders of today. It is an old story. Its result is bitterness and class hatred. I pray God that it is a story that will soon end, and I regret the day that a religious representative has seen fit to add to the flood of hatred and misrepresentation.[47]

Unlike Rice, Hensler was conciliatory on the radio. At a subsequent meeting of the Catholic Radical Alliance, however, he disclaimed the "innuendo, half-truths, and whole lies" put forth by the CIO's critics. Instead of promoting violence, as Cox and Coakley contended, the CIO was simply "securing for the workers of the country some voice in determining the conduct of their working lives. If that aim is not achieved we shall have a dictatorship; indeed, our financial overlords will become our rulers politically as well as economically." Addressing himself to the various citizens' committees that had formed on behalf of Little Steel, Hensler stated,

> Many who are taking part in the current attempt to arouse middle-class public opinion against the aspirations of organized labor are doing so under the mask of patriotism. These would-be vigilantes are shouting "save the flag." If they succeed in killing the movement to organize fully the workers of the country the flag may be saved, but it will be a sorry, tattered banner. Instead of industrial democracy and a new social order, we may get a taste of real class warfare. And the middle class will fare as ill as it has in other countries where it permitted itself to be made the tool of the vested interests.[48]

Most working-class Catholics dismissed claims that the CIO was directed from Moscow. Propaganda leaflets—written by "fellow workers"—warned that labor organizers wanted employees "to join the CIO and help establish a Soviet America." More serious was Roosevelt's reaction to the Little Steel strike. In his efforts to appoint additional, pro–New Deal judges to the Supreme Court, Roosevelt had aroused a dormant conservative opposition in Congress. Rightly criticized for his unwillingness to wait for Republican justices to retire or die, the president did not need more trouble. Sensing that a southern and middle-class backlash against the New Deal was in the making, partly because of the Little Steel strike, Roosevelt lost his composure. At a press conference on June 29, Roosevelt wished "a plague on both" the CIO and Republic Steel.[49]

For the newspaper reporters who went to Lewis for a response, the labor leader coldly stated that "it ill behooves one who has supped at labor's table . . . to curse with equal fervor and fine impartiality both labor and its adversaries when they become locked in deadly embrace." Finding it difficult to restrain himself further, Lewis assaulted a desk. Lee Pressman informed anyone who would listen that Murray, not Lewis, had been behind the disastrous Little Steel strike. According to Pressman, Murray was an emotionally stunted individual who had to "prove his manhood" by taking on Republic and Bethlehem. In reality, it was Lewis who had directed the Johnstown-area UMW to organize a strike at the Bethlehem mill. Murray did not believe that the steel workers were adequately prepared for a lengthy confrontation with Bethlehem, but Lewis figured that the UMW could win the battle by itself.[50]

With Roosevelt seeking to distance himself from the CIO, organized labor was in great need of friends. Pittsburgh's Catholic clergy and laity came to Murray's rescue. In July, the *Pittsburgh Catholic* responded to the critics of the CIO. Looking at Dixie, the newspaper observed, "Some southerners consider it 'proof' of Communism that the CIO admits Negroes to membership. Then Christianity is Communistic." The *Pittsburgh Catholic* also urged workers to unionize Republic Steel.

> Mr. Girdler, in short, gives an exhibition of ruthless arrogance which demonstrates positively that no unprotected worker, no "company union" need expect justice or consideration; that the rights of the worker, the welfare and prosperity of the country as a whole, can be secured only by collective bargaining through a genuine labor union strong enough to meet Mr. Girdler and his kind on a footing of equality. Mr. Girdler's convincing display of what unregulated employer domination means, should clarify in the minds of his employees the course that is demanded of them in the name of their human dignity and their obligations to their families: that they can make themselves free of such arrogant domination, protect themselves against such ruthless intimidation, and peaceably bring order and fairness into industry only by genuine unionization.[51]

Other Catholic clergy joined the fray. In Cleveland, Monsignor Joseph F. Smith, the vicar general of the diocese, spoke to twenty-five hundred SWOC strikers. At the beginning of his speech, Smith rebutted Girdler's charges that Lewis and John Brophy were Communists: "I will believe that Lewis and Brophy have joined the Communist Party when it is proved to me that a good Irish Catholic has joined the Ku Klux Klan." Seeking to boost the spirits of the workers who had been fighting Republic, the clergyman envisioned a day

> when the first money paid out of profits will go to the workers in addition to their wages. When God placed the iron, the coal, the gold, the oil, and all the other minerals in the earth, He did not intend that they should be owned by two or three men and that all the rest should work to make them rich. God intended a fair division of all these riches and that is why, when a man gains more than his share, it is his duty to share it with his fellow men.[52]

Trapped between militant SWOC organizers and Girdler's troops, Bishop Joseph Schrembs of Cleveland was desperately seeking a union victory and an end to labor violence. (By the summer of 1937 Cleveland was an armed camp. Both Republic Steel and the Ohio Communist Party were based in the city.) The steel workers, Schrembs realized, needed the support of the Catholic Church if they were to triumph over corporate repression and turn aside

Communist entreaties. Praising the labor encyclicals of Leo XIII and Pius XI, Schrembs informed his diocese that

> as a Bishop of God's Church it is both a privilege and a duty to champion the cause of labor. This I shall do as long as God spares me to serve my people.
>
> My ears are not open to those who would prejudice me against God's humble and God's people shall always vindicate their rights not only to a living wage but to a competence sufficient to live in the dignity befitting their status with enough remaining to care for their old age or unforeseen illness.[53]

To coordinate the activities of pro-CIO clergy, Monsignor John Ryan of the National Catholic Welfare Conference organized a Summer School for Social Action. Held in Toledo from mid-July to mid-August, fifty priests from Baltimore, Detroit, Fort Wayne (Indiana), and Louisville (Kentucky) discussed ways in which to support union organizing initiatives. Father John Cronin of Baltimore, an instructor at the summer school, criticized scabs and private enterprise:

> There is a moral pressure, if not an obligation, on a workman to join a workers' organization. No man can morally take a job under conditions that damage his fellows, provided he has real freedom of choice.
>
> The right to work is intimately bound up with the social system under which we live, and must be fitted in with the system of private property and private enterprise prevailing today. Because of large population, and therefore of industrial specialization, all industry is intimately connected with the community and government. Accordingly, the earning of bread is tied up with the social order and the individual's life is qualified by and must qualify the social system.[54]

Toledo Bishop Karl Alter who, with Bishops Schrembs and Boyle, had been a champion of labor, gave the Social Action school great support. He also made it a point to repudiate Father Charles Coughlin. The Michigan priest, circumscribed on the national political stage, had been championing a company-dominated automobile workers' union in Toledo and Detroit. Hensler and Rice had earlier condemned Coughlin for crusading against the UAW. Angered, Coughlin fired off a letter to the *Pittsburgh Catholic* explaining that his labor organization, the Workers Council for Social Justice, was open to any Christian who repudiated the Communist leadership of the CIO. He was not, the Detroit priest insisted, undermining the union drive at Ford Motor Company. Hensler and Rice answered Coughlin in the columns of the *Pittsburgh Catholic*. The latter was greatly annoyed when Coughlin followed up his attack on the CIO by denouncing the Catholic Worker movement. As Rice pointed out, Dorothy Day was simply too good a Christian to respond to Coughlin's mean-spirited broadsides. The Pittsburgher, however, managed to set aside his sense of Christian charity to rebuke Coughlin. Edward Mooney, the new archbishop of Detroit, informed Michigan Catholics that Coughlin was mistaken in his view of the UAW and Dorothy Day.[55]

Clearly indicating where his sympathies could be found, Archbishop Mooney encouraged Day, Hensler, and Rice to come to Detroit in September. The three spoke at a convention of the Detroit Catholic Study Clubs. At that meeting, one woman declared from the convention floor that "I've been through the sit-down strikes in Flint and I know they were led by Communists." Rice dismissed her claims and noted that the CIO was not radical enough for his tastes. The woman later admitted that her husband had been the judge who had issued an injunction against the UAW during the Flint confrontation. Another member of the audience contended that UAW "rowdies" had "terrorized" the great majority of workers. Most workers, she asserted, had opposed the automobile strike. Rice gave her a very pointed response: "Did you ever see terrorism put over by employers?" She promptly sat down.[56]

Beyond contesting issues with Coughlin's vocal following, as well as their work for SWOC and the Heinz employees, Hensler and Rice moved from one union and Church forum to the next. Toward the end of summer and into the fall the Pittsburghers went to New York with John Brophy, lending their moral authority to a mass meeting of the American Radio Telegraphers' Union. Back in Pittsburgh, the priests exhorted all nine hundred employees of the Heppenstall company, a Lawrenceville steel works firm, to join the CIO. Believing, in Father Lappan's words, that "when men are fighting for their rights, every true Christian must rally to their aid," the St. Vincent de Paul Society was feeding twenty-one of the families whose household heads had gone on strike. Rice praised the Heppenstall strikers and their employer, a good Catholic who would no doubt see the error of his ways. Certainly, Rice continued in his references to William Heppenstall, a devout Catholic such as he would not follow the "bad example" of Tom Girdler. Heppenstall surrendered.[57]

Following an address to the United Electrical and Radio Workers who were seeking union recognition from Westinghouse, Hensler joined John

Lewis at a Labor Day rally. One hundred and ten thousand people gathered in Pittsburgh's South Park to hear the CIO speakers. Father Orlemanski teamed up with Lewis at a smaller labor rally near Natrona Heights later that day. Perhaps finding it easier to ridicule Lewis than a priest, the *Pittsburgh Sun-Telegraph* and *Post-Gazette* did not report Hensler's words. The *Pittsburgh Catholic*, however, devoted considerable space to Hensler's vision of American democracy, social justice, and the CIO.

> It is not merely those who actually produce goods by the toil of their hands who have a stake in a strong and progressive labor movement. It belongs to all of us; not only as individuals, but as members of groups such as the family, the community, and the Church. In its essence, the organized labor movement, especially since the coming of the CIO, is a drive to preserve and to extend American democracy. Government of the people, by the people, for the people, is on trial throughout the world today. It is extinct in many lands. We still have a measure of it here, but it steadily grows less, and may also disappear. Anything that can stop this lessening of our fundamental liberties should enlist the sympathy and active support of every true American.
>
> Democracy doesn't consist merely in marking ballots, and sending men to assemblies and Congress. It really consists in having a voice in deciding the conditions under which we live our daily lives. It is most needed at work, where men spend the best part of their waking hours. And it is precisely democracy or self-government in work that is the objective of the American labor movement. If it is not attained, we move rapidly in the direction of the servile state. We may remain politically free for a time, but always in a precarious condition. We can be really free if the organized labor movement is successful in bringing about democracy in American industry.[58]

After Labor Day, Rice presented a paper on collective bargaining at the regional Catholic Conference on Industrial Problems. Held in Indianapolis, Bishop Joseph Ritter, with the assistance of the National Catholic Welfare Conference, invited a variety of clergy and lay activists. Unlike the industrial conference held in Pittsburgh four years earlier, there were no clashes between representatives of labor and management. Taking little time out for rest, Rice and Hensler received an invitation from Patrick Fagan to attend a banquet sponsored by UMW District 5. The priests next talked to meat cutters who were deciding whether or not to join the AFL, and to workers of the Westinghouse Air-Brake Company in Wilmerding, outside Pittsburgh. Rice also sent a telegram to Murray urging the CIO to make peace with the AFL, gave a talk on radio station WWSW about Catholic theories of social justice, and sponsored a lecture by SWOC's publicity director, Vincent Sweeney. His lecture, "A Catholic CIO Man Looks at the Record," received much praise from the diocesan newspaper.[59]

Beyond the activities already noted, Hensler spoke to a SWOC local in Duquesne. Elmer Maloy, the president of SWOC's Duquesne local, wanted to make sure that the company union remained buried; one-third of that union's representatives had been "stool pigeons" for management. Meanwhile, Rice roused a mass meeting of Westinghouse workers and took to the witness stand at a hearing before the National Labor Relations Board. The NLRB was investigating Heinz's refusal to sign a contract with his union workers. In the first week of December, Hensler and Orlemanski went to Johnstown, exhorting one thousand workers and their families not to lose hope. In spite of what Protestant clergy and businessmen said, unionism, Hensler argued, had a Christian basis. During all of Hensler and Rice's travels to union and fraternal hall, their House of Hospitality was feeding nine hundred men weekly. Soup, coffee, and a dose of union homily were what every man, white and black, could expect to find in that sanctuary from Hill District vice and despair.[60]

The efforts of Hensler and Rice to promote social reform did not go unnoticed or unappreciated. Letters from workers as far away as Canada poured into the St. Joseph House of Hospitality and the respective rectories of Rice (St. Agnes) and Hensler (St. Lawrence). A Milltown, New Brunswick, worker asked Rice for assistance:

> We have had organizers here from Waterville, Maine, representing the Textile Workers' Organizing Committee of the CIO.
>
> They commenced organizing here, but were called back to Waterville expecting a strike.
>
> In the meantime, our local parish priest, Rev. C. P. J. Carleton, has attacked the CIO in a most vicious manner. Here are some of the things he said: "If you want your churches torn down, join the CIO; if you want your priests shot down, join the CIO; if you want the Blessed Sacrament thrown about the streets, join the CIO."
>
> . . . The result has been a blow to the cause of organized labor in this locality. . . .
>
> The [CIO] organizer is himself a member of the Knights of Columbus so we need not fear his activities.

What I would like you to do is this:

Drop a line to Father Carleton informing him of the work you are doing in the cause of the laboring classes, and your support, as well as the Church itself, of the CIO. Particularly stating the sanction of Rome toward the CIO.[61]

Despite the general failure of Catholic Radical Alliance and SWOC to recruit blacks into the CIO, the few who did join spared no praise for Murray and Rice. James McCoy, a black steel worker, fondly recalled Rice's interracial organizing efforts:

I think the Roman Catholic Church itself played a very important role toward the successful organizing campaign, the Steel Workers Organizing Committee in the steel industry. We find men who are today [1968] high up in the, should I say, Catholic hierarchy, that have been identified actively with the labor movement in those days, they were on the front lines when the battle was hot. When bricks were being thrown and when guns were being fired against the workers because they wanted to organize and have a union. One man whom I admire and admire deeply, happened to be Father Charles Owen Rice. In those days he was commonly known as the "labor priest." He had a glorious record of achievement and sacrifice in the labor movement and in particular, the steel workers union. Father Charles Owen Rice is still identified and he can always be relied on to lend his body, his intellect, and his knowledge when it comes to a problem, resolving a problem concerning the labor movement or when it comes to the race issue. He is always there. He seems to be a man who was born to be devoted to the cause of the underdog and the under-privileged.[62]

Bolstered by the aid of the Pittsburgh labor priests, SWOC's first national convention in December offered a mixture of defiance and sobriety. Responding to a recession that had began that year—and which wiped out many of the New Deal's gains—Harold Ruttenberg suggested in a confidential report that the CIO "[p]lace the blame and responsibility for the present severe slump . . . on the doorsteps of industry and finance." SWOC's research director also argued that those in the federal government who had sought to reduce social welfare expenditures and balance the budget had "withdrawn huge sums of purchasing power from the country and catapulted us into the present slump." Obviously, he concluded, the CIO must pressure Roosevelt to see that workers' wages were increased, while consumer prices remained flat. The president should also increase funding for the WPA, Social Security, and other programs designed to distribute the nation's wealth more widely. Ruttenberg did not feel bound by Catholic social teaching to worry about the enormous expansion of federal power he was advocating. He also did not sense that the American middle class, registering disgust with the CIO in the wake of the GM and Little Steel confrontations, might not appreciate the heavier tax burden Ruttenberg was implicitly hoping to impose upon it.[63]

Eight hundred and seventy-five delegates gathered in Pittsburgh on December 14. After a Catholic priest gave the invocation and Mayor Cornelius Scully proclaimed his high regard for registered Democrats, Murray tried to put the best light on SWOC's situation:

*end 1937*

> We have almost one-half million members in this organization; we have 1,080 lodges created, and have negotiated 445 collective bargaining agreements. Our efforts have resulted in the bringing about of annual wage increases to the employees amounting to $200 million, the work-week has been shortened from forty-eight-hours to forty-hours. Seniority rights, vacations, and grievance machinery have been recognized. Our record speaks for itself.[64]

The SWOC convention skirted the agenda Ruttenberg had advanced, choosing, instead, to pass resolutions condemning Tom Girdler, Governor Martin Davey of Ohio, and Johnstown mayor Daniel Shields. Such resolutions were meaningless unless labor could deny reelection to such politicians. This had already occurred to Murray which was why he became the chair of Pennsylvania Labor Coordinating Committee. Murray also established a local industrial council to coordinate labor and political activities in the region. Patrick Fagan and SWOC secretary David McDonald became key players in the industrial council. Both were determined to see the CIO solidify its grip on regional and state government. To that end, the industrial council endorsed Congressman Henry Ellenbogen as a candidate for Judge of the Common Pleas Court and gave financial assistance to union men running for various offices in Clairton, Duquesne, and McKeesport. Meanwhile, Lewis sought to influence congressional races and legislation through Labor's Non-Partisan League. In 1936 Roosevelt had solicited votes from the grossly misnamed organization. By the end of 1937, however, he was less inclined to be identified publicly with organized labor.[65]

Nineteen thirty-seven had been an exhilarating and frustrating year for Catholic activists. The labor war had taught Murray, Hensler, and Rice many valuable lessons. First, building the CIO was not going to be an easy, or necessarily successful task. Organized labor confronted bitter foes in management, the churches (Protestant and, to a lesser extent, Catholic), and politics. These opponents did not hesitate to brand every labor organizer a Communist. Second, there were serious tensions within the ranks of labor, pitting Catholics against Communist organizers. That struggle, which came out into the open in 1937, was bound up in the personality and ideological differences that separated Murray and Lewis. Third, New Deal politicians trimmed their sails with the prevailing winds. To be fair to Roosevelt, he had won re-election in a landslide in November 1936, only to see his public approval ratings and clout in Congress slip from his hands just a year later. The UAW and SWOC were fueling a backlash that was undercutting the New Deal. Unfairly, middle-class Protestants blamed the CIO for promoting violence.

All of these factors, not to mention a legacy of mutual mistrust between blacks and white ethnics, weighed heavily upon the Catholic reformers. How could they save the union movement, champion social reform, and combat the Communists in their ranks? This last dilemma was particularly acute. The Communists, Murray and Rice believed, were more interested in serving Moscow than the American worker. Further, the presence of Communists in the CIO made it all that much easier for Protestant businessmen, clergy, and politicians to discredit organized labor. Additionally, Catholics, who made up the bulk of the industrial work force, would not join unions if they thought that they were under Communist control. The Catholic clergy activists had given great respectability to the CIO, at least in the eyes of the ethnic Italians and Slavs. There was, however, much work remaining to be done if clergy and laity were to realize a true Catholic New Deal.

# 5

# Christian Democracy

## Anti-Communism, Social Justice, and the End of New Deal Reform, 1938

In the wake of the disastrous 1937 Little Steel Strike, Pittsburgh's Catholic clergy and labor reformers find themselves defending the CIO against critics within the Church, in Congress, and in corporate America. The House Committee on Un-American Activities smears SWOC while Catholic clergy like Fulton Sheen red-bait the CIO. At the same time, fathers Charles Owen Rice and Carl Hensler combat Communist Party organizers who are intent upon moving the CIO further to the left. Hensler and Rice advocate Christian Democracy, a new kind of religiously informed politics that embraces the social encyclicals and rejects capitalist and Communist materialism. Sensing that they have been abandoned by the Roosevelt administration, Pittsburgh's Catholic labor leaders become firmly attached to their clerical champions. By the end of 1938, Roosevelt and his New Deal allies in Congress and in industrial states like Pennsylvania are in trouble. The 1938 midterm elections signal the end of New Deal reform.

During the Depression, one million Americans, convinced that capitalism was the root cause of discrimination and economic exploitation, passed through the Communist Party and its many front organizations. There they found a political home seemingly free of the racism and anti-Semitism that tainted factions of the Democratic and Republican parties. A movement of the alienated, the Communist Party geared its message to society's outsiders:

blacks, Jews, unassimilated immigrants, and Anglo-Saxon intellectuals. Though a party of the proletariat, the Communists attracted a number of highly educated people. John Abt, a member of the WPA's legal staff, was born into a middle-class Chicago family. He graduated from the University of Chicago Law School. His father was a product of Yale. In 1937, Abt served as chief counsel for the La Follette Committee, where he coordinated the congressional investigation of anti-CIO employers. Abt was also a member of the (Harold) Ware Group: a Soviet espionage ring.[1]

A second member of the Ware Group, Lee Pressman, was the son of Jewish immigrants and a graduate of Harvard Law School. As legal counsel for the CIO, Pressman occupied a position of enormous influence with John L. Lewis. At CIO meetings, Pressman delivered contemptuous lectures to John Brophy. Pressman's associate in the CIO, the Oxford-educated Len DeCaux, was no less imperious. DeCaux contended that the CIO could be divided into three factions. The first faction was made up of Communists or, as they referred to themselves outside party circles, progressives. Catholics made up the second faction and Jews the third. In DeCaux's opinion, the leaders of the Catholic and the Jewish factions, Phil Murray and Sidney Hillman, were insipid. It was DeCaux and Pressman's mission to undercut their power. To that end, the Communists played to Lewis's belief that other labor leaders were untrustworthy rivals. A vain man who, in DeCaux's words, "could strut sitting down," Lewis was receptive to flattery.[2]

DeCaux claimed that he had no "particular religious prejudices," but his disdain for Catholic SWOC officials called that proposition into doubt. This was the same man who denied that he was a Communist and in 1938 threatened to sue the Scripps-Howard newspaper chain for libel when a reporter exposed his political ties. (It was a party directive that Communists who entered government service or became CIO representatives were not to reveal their political affiliations.) Worried about red-baiting, many Communists made efforts to appear "more American." Thus Morris Poberski, a Lithuanian-Jewish immigrant and secretary of the Communist Party's Western Pennsylvanian district, became George Powers, a McKeesport SWOC organizer. (Powers later claimed that he moved away from the party once his loyalty to the CIO became more important to him.) Similarly, Stjepan Mesaros, a Serbian immigrant and 1931 graduate of the Lenin School in Moscow, changed his name to Steve Nelson. He became a central figure in the Pittsburgh party. Nelson later moved to Los Angeles, where he coordinated West Coast operations and earned a position on the Communist Party's national board.[3]

Isolated from mainstream society, and lacking a strong religious grounding upon which to build their political philosophy, numbers of immigrants and blacks were drawn to Marxism. In Pittsburgh, according to subsequent congressional investigations, the majority of the party's membership was Serbian. Many Serbian immigrants looked to Moscow for guidance and, as Russian Orthodox apostates, maintained an abiding distrust of Roman Catholics. The party also made inroads among Pittsburgh blacks in the early 1930s, with the city claiming more African-American Communists than were to be found in Harlem. (New York's share of black Communists surpassed Pittsburgh's by the mid-1930s.) Benjamin Careathers was Pittsburgh's most prominent black Communist. By day, Careathers was a SWOC organizer. At night, from a Hill District candy store that served as a cover for his political activities, he led the region's black radicals. Respectable society appeared to be simultaneously resentful of, and titillated by, the black Communists. In the summer of 1937, the *Bulletin Index* ran a feature on an interracial Communist dance held at the Hill District Elks' Temple. Beneath the photographs of white women and black men in tight embrace, the captions read: "At a Communist party, black boys dance with white girls," and "Like all good Communists, she [Communist activist Carolyn Hart] draws no color line in selecting her dance partners."[4]

Jews accounted for the remaining membership of the Communist Party. Although a minority in the Pittsburgh chapter, Jews were the largest, most influential ethnic group in the national party. Better educated than the bulk of second-generation Americans, and inculcated from birth in the importance of political mobilization to resist discrimination, Eastern European Jews flocked to parties that championed social justice: the American Labor Party of New York, the Socialist Party, and the Communist Party. Seeking federal relief from the Great Depression, envisioning a day when religious discrimination would be outlawed, and fearing the rise of right-wing, anti-Semitic social movements in Europe and America, secularized Jews sought shelter in liberal and radical ranks. Religiously observant Jews enthusiastically embraced the New Deal Democrats, but balked at the strident atheism of the Communists.[5]

In the years preceding World War I, Pittsburgh's Jewish socialists had established the National Radical Peoples' School. Ninety students annually received lessons in Marxist dialectics. As a rebuke to the Hill District's Hebrew Schools, pupils at the socialist institution did not study the Torah. After all, religious devotion undermined the class struggle. One socialist flatly told his son, "I want you to be a good Jew. Stay out of the synagogues." In 1904, Pittsburgh socialists created a branch of the Workmen's Circle. This New York-based group served as a fraternal organization for the Pittsburgh Jews who belonged to the cigar, bakery, and garment workers' unions. Once the

Russian Revolution broke out, the Hill District's socialists split into several factions, out of which emerged a pro-Soviet group. By 1930, Jewish Communists withdrew from the Workmen's Circle and created the International Workers Order (IWO). One hundred and twenty people belonged to the Pittsburgh IWO chapter. Bill Gebert, a Polish immigrant, was the Pittsburgh IWO organizer. He was also a founder of the American Communist Party.[6]

The International Workers Order, which by 1938 had 141,000 dues-paying members, was unique among Communist-front organizations. Its leaders, Rubin Saltzman and Max Bedacht, were open members of the party. In 1929, Bedacht had gone to Moscow to receive political instruction. The mission of the IWO was twofold. First, Bedacht sought to increase the Communist Party's presence among Catholic Croatians and Poles who had thus far eschewed Marxist palliatives. Second, the IWO was to establish itself in America's steel belt. Although the IWO made enormous efforts to recruit Slavs into the party, not many joined. The Communists found that the Catholic Church blocked their path. Their success in building cadres in the industrial heartland, however, was unquestionable. Thirty-eight percent of the IWO's cadres lived in Pennsylvania, Ohio, and Illinois. It was from the IWO ranks that Lewis recruited labor organizers for the electrical and steel industries.[7]

In the United Electrical, Radio, and Machine Workers union, or UE, Julius Emspak emerged as a powerful labor official. The son of Hungarian immigrants, Emspak received a bachelor's degree from Union College in Schenectady, New York. After a stint in graduate school at Brown University, he went to work for General Electric and the Communist Party. As secretary-treasurer of the UE, Emspak worked closely with James Matles, a Rumanian immigrant and organizer of the Communist Party's Steel and Metal Workers' Industrial Union. After Matles brought his rump union into the UE in 1936, the Communists, who publicly disavowed their party affiliation, went into action. By 1937, the UE had 137,000 members and was the largest Communist-dominated union in the United States. General Electric president Gerard Swope signed a union contract with the UE in 1938. Swope regarded Roosevelt as the savior of capitalism and hoped that the CIO would promote harmonious labor-management relations.[8]

James Carey, the twenty-seven year-old president of the UE, had joined the union movement at an early age, rising rapidly in the ranks of the AFL and then the CIO. As one of ten children in a family of practicing Catholics, Carey was a favorite of Phil Murray. His youthful enthusiasm and naiveté, however, often placed him in embarrassing situations. For example, although opposed to Communism, Carey served as vice president of the American

Youth Congress and belonged to the League Against War and Fascism. Both organizations were fronts for the Communist Party. Carey was unfamiliar with Communist tactics and inattentive to behind-the-scenes maneuvering. Emspak and Matles dominated the UE through sheer tenacity. Communists came to union meetings in force and talked issues into the ground. Tired from working all day and politically uninitiated, the rank and file went home when meetings dragged on far into the night. Before Carey realized what was happening, Emspak and Matles stacked the executive board of the union with their allies. Even though the majority of UE members were Catholic, many believed Emspak and Matles when they denied that they were Stalinists. The UE's Communists retained rank-and-file loyalties by accusing their critics of being corporate stooges. Only when the gap between their words and deeds grew great enough would most of the UE's members repudiate their leadership and join a rival union.[9]

The Communist Party failed to gain dominion over the Steel Workers Organizing Committee, but not for lack of trying. John Williamson, a Communist district leader in Ohio, brought senior party members to SWOC's Buckeye staff. Bill Gebert, who had once directed the party's Unemployed Councils, became liaison between SWOC and the International Workers Order. Murray allowed Gebert to become a SWOC organizer, not realizing that Gebert loathed Catholic reformers. Within a year of SWOC's founding, Murray had grown leery of "progressives." In 1937, during the Little Steel war in Ohio, he had chastised Gus Hall. Murray would not tolerate any SWOC organizer who terrorized scabs. A year later, Murray fired a Communist from the Minnesota SWOC staff who had been requiring steel workers to join the party as a precondition for belonging to the union. To his disgust, the Communist became secretary-treasurer of the Minnesota CIO.[10]

By 1938, eighteen of the forty-five CIO affiliates either had Communist leaders or were under subtle forms of party direction. This gave the party access to the union dues of 1,370,000 CIO members, a considerable pot from which to dole out patronage. The IWO alone contributed $110,000 a month to the party. In addition to the UE, the Communists were a strong force in the United Automobile Workers union. Of the great industrial unions, only SWOC remained independent of the party. Party chief Earl Browder reported to Moscow that the CIO provided "the basis of the Communist advances" in various federal agencies. Communists dominated the National Labor Relations Board and held influential jobs in other parts of the New Deal bureaucracy. At no other time in American history had a political organization that received its inspiration from a foreign power achieved such prominence. The Right used that development to bash New Deal politicians and non-

Communist labor leaders. This placed Murray in the awkward position of having to dispute the extent of Communist power in the CIO so as not to permit conservatives to smear the labor movement. Murray would have been even more agitated had he known the full story. As recently opened Soviet documents have revealed, Lewis had undertaken secret negotiations with the Comintern. He requested Browder to select Communists to organize and lead the CIO's unions.[11]

American Catholics had been concerned for some time with Communism. In 1935, laity at the Church of the Immaculate Conception in Brooklyn founded the Catholic War Veterans. A patriotic group with a more prominent religious coloration than the American Legion, the Catholic War Veterans launched an assault on Communism. According to Father Edward Higgins, "Communism is a religion of hatred toward all religions and all peoples except Communists." The *Pittsburgh Catholic*, in quoting the Brooklyn priest, added that "the Communists, by abolishing God from a place in life and by destroying marriage and the family—hope, if possible, to force their followers to forget God." Catholic clergy had ripped into Roosevelt for establishing diplomatic relations with the Soviet Union in 1933 and resented his wife's support for a Spanish government that they viewed as atheist. Wishing to avoid more grief from Catholics, Roosevelt sent a warm greeting to Higgins. The president heartily concurred with him that the New Deal had, through economic reforms and the provision of federal jobs, "killed Communism by one stroke."[12]

Monsignor Fulton Sheen, the star of a national radio program called "The Catholic Hour," presented an apocalyptic picture of the moral contest between Christianity and Communism. In 1935, the former Catholic University professor predicted:

> In the future there will be only two capitals in the world, Rome and Moscow; only two temples, the Kremlin and St. Peter's; only two sanctuary lamps, the red flag and the red sentinel of the altar; only two tabernacles, the Red Square and the Eucharist's; only two hosts, the rotted body of Lenin and the Mystical Body of Christ; only two hymns, the Internationale and the *Panis Angelicas*.
>
> But there will be only one victory, for if Christ wins, we win; and if Christ—Ah! But Christ cannot lose.

A year later, Al Smith changed some of Sheen's wording for an address he gave to the right-wing Liberty League. The New Yorker suggested that Roosevelt was making America sick with "the foul breath of Communistic Russia."[13]

Unsettled by the efforts of the Liberty League to destroy the New Deal, Monsignor John Ryan contended "that our beloved America is in less danger from the preaching of the Communists than from certain professedly anti-Communist propaganda which is, in reality, directed against social justice." Ryan also denounced an effort in the District of Columbia to require teachers to sign a pledge that they were not Communists. As the monsignor noted in 1936, the proposed legislation was "a gratuitous insult to the patriotism of the entire body of teachers in the public schools of the District of Columbia. . . . If any of the teachers have actually defended or inculcated Communism in the classroom, they will have no scruples about denying the fact." The *Pittsburgh Catholic* concurred with Ryan and questioned a similar initiative in Massachusetts:

> The administering of an oath presupposes a belief in a Supreme Being to Whom the one swearing owes a first loyalty. If there is not such a belief and such a loyalty, then the oath is a meaningless form. Where such a belief and such a loyalty are present an oath to support any human institution should be unnecessary, for man's duty to his God requires that he faithfully respect his obligations to his fellow men. What is needed today is not loud-mouthed protestations of patriotism (some of those advocating oaths for teachers are undoubtedly sincere and some are unquestionably scheming scoundrels) but reviving and intensifying of religion that will make oaths binding when they are taken and unnecessary except for the most solemn purposes.[14]

Like Ryan, the *Pittsburgh Catholic* believed that "social injustice gave rise to Communism; our failure to adjust the wrongs of the economic system provides fuel for the incendiary doctrines of radicalism; and there will be no stopping of Communism unless and until we secure social justice." Believing that the Hearst press was using the public fear of Communism to block social reconstruction, the diocesan newspaper urged readers to be sane opponents of the Left. Catholics must remember to despise the sin, not the sinner. Moreover, working-class Catholics should neither move to the right in their reaction against Communism nor abandon their support for the CIO. Casting an eye on Nazi Germany, the *Pittsburgh Catholic* in 1936 argued that

> it will not do to war against Communism in favor of some other destructive system. In Germany, for instance, the State and the State-controlled press are, for the present, opposed to Communism, but they uphold a system which denies natural rights and would make the

citizen a slave of the State. Even in this country a certain section of the secular press, loud in its denunciation of Communism, is a supporter of the vicious plan by which the poor are exploited to make the rich more wealthy, by which class is set against class, by which immorality of all kinds is promoted in order to keep the people debased and in subjugation.[15]

Addressing the laity of the Pittsburgh Diocese in 1936, Bishop Hugh Boyle exhorted Catholics to combat Communism by being good Christians and unionists. "If we lived our lives as Catholics should," Boyle contended, "there would be no Communism." The Communist, Boyle believed, "is often only wrong-headed, not wrong-hearted" in his desire for a just social order. "Sometimes I don't blame him for his radicalism," Boyle told his diocese. "We Catholics fail so often and to such an extent in doing what we profess, that he is led to think we are wrong or insincere. We think too much as the world does, act as the world does, ape the world altogether too thoroughly." Materialism, a desire to pursue profit at the expense of the soul, spawned social injustice. For that reason, Pittsburgh's bishop concluded, Communism grew. Social reform, guided by religious faith, was God's response to misery and Marxism. Pius XI's 1937 encyclical, *Atheistic Communism*, expressed the same critique of Marxist materialism.[16]

Boyle was careful not to permit his anti-Communism to become strident. His priests, however, were another matter. Father Francis Bailey, who continued his service with the Civilian Conservation Corps, held a rousing Mass at Fort Meade, Maryland. The priest informed civilians and soldiers in 1937 that subversives of the Left and Right were about the land:

> In the United States, there are many who are not satisfied with our form of government. They are warring against us, not in open warfare, nor with weapons that kill the body. Their war is a war of propaganda; they seek to poison our minds; they seek to destroy our flag and all those things for which it stands. They want us to exchange our hard earned liberty for the shackles of slavery; they want us to give up our domestic tranquillity and happiness for the suspicion and hatred and bloodshed that is rending so many of the nations of the world today.[17]

While Father Casimir Orlemanski gave pro-CIO speeches to working-class Slavs, Hensler and Rice fought for the soul of organized labor. Their vehicle for reform became the Association of Catholic Trade Unionists. Founded in

New York in 1937 by members of the Catholic Worker movement, the ACTU, in Hensler and Rice's words, was

> not to be in any sense a rival labor union. Its purpose will not be to set Catholic against non-Catholic, but to set Catholics working for the common good and to bring the Charity of Christ into the labor arena. This association will encourage unionization of all Catholic workers in accordance with the mind of the Pope.
>
> . . . We propose to instruct Catholic employers, and others if they will listen to us, in their duties to us, in their duties toward labor and the common good. We propose to instruct the rich in their duties toward the poor and to emphasize that their wealth has been loaned them by God, Who will one day ask an accounting of it.[18]

Paradoxically, the ACTU became much stronger in Pittsburgh than in its place of origination. In part this stemmed from the fact that the Catholic Worker movement in the East had few ties to labor unions. Second, although Dorothy Day criticized Communism, New York's Catholic Workers would not engage in the type of bare-knuckled politics necessary to wrest various unions away from the party. Third, New York was the bastion of American Communism, with party leaders entrenched in city and state political office and in organizations such as the Transport Workers' Union. Conversely, the Catholic Church of the East, even if more affluent than its poor sister in the industrial heartland, was not as respected among parishioners. The New York hierarchy had discredited itself in the eyes of many working-class Catholics by condemning the New Deal and the CIO. Finally, the ACTU had to contend with Father Charles Coughlin's anti-union followers who were more numerous and vocal in New York than in the steel towns of the Midwest. Coughlin also introduced anti-Semitism into the Catholic anti-Communist cause.[19]

Having attended an ACTU meeting in New York, and then checking out the 1937 CIO convention, Hensler and Rice were aghast. The New York ACTU seemed to be a debating society for dilettantes. Their pilgrimage to the CIO meeting, where they distributed copies of *The Catholic Worker*, was disastrous. As the *Pittsburgh Catholic* reported, New York's Catholic reformers "were being subjected to a barrage of attack and misrepresentation from various sources and yet there was no bitterness and to most of the attacks not even an answer." Good Christians, Hensler and Rice believed, should not be vicious. But still, not to defend their position from the Communist allies of transport worker chief Mike Quill and longshoreman leader

Harry Bridges was ridiculous. Where the New Yorkers prayed for the souls of Quill and Bridges (both Catholic apostates), Hensler and Rice appealed for funds with which to fight the Communists. One 1937 appeal was militant, not prayerful:

> It is a definite fact that Communist agents are active in the field. They are more active than many suspect. They have money, lots of it, they have brains and man power. But they still have not gotten a grip on the rank and file workers, nor have they a grip on the leaders, but if the field be left to them much longer they will get a grip on the whole thing, and then all the "Red Baiters" in creation won't stop them, if they howl till doomsday. If, however, an intelligent Christian social doctrine be intelligently and zealously propagated in the movement the Communists will not have a show. Understand, we see the need for Catholic participation in the movement if there never were such a thing as a Communist, but as things stand now there is need a hundred fold.[20]

That year, Rice gave a speech which endorsed the CIO and rebuked Communists in the labor movement. To the executives of Little Steel who decried the CIO as a tool of the Kremlin, the priest contended the CIO was "not Godless, Communistic, or un-American. It has its roots in Christianity and Americanism. It is taking a step on the road to the building of a new America that will be just, Christian, and in accord with the noblest traditions of our faith and nation." Addressing himself to the Protestant clergy who had preached against the union movement, Rice noted that "the way to fight Communism is not by 'Red Baiting' and 'flag waving.' It is by striving tooth and nail for social justice. If the members of the Christian churches of this country lived up to the teachings of Christ in the matter of justice and charity there would not be one Communist in the United States." Indeed, Rice believed, "the CIO is a bulwark against Communism. The CIO aims to remove injustice and Communism can thrive only where there is injustice. Of course, Rice acknowledged, Communism was a danger to America. "Communists," Rice told his radio listeners, "are working night and day for the success of their ideal. They are zealous, self-sacrificing, tireless workers." However, the priest cautioned:

> When irresponsible characters attack worthy organizations as Communistic they are giving aid to Communism, because they are leading the workers to believe that Communism must be good stuff when so

Fig. 8.   Father Charles Owen Rice, Pittsburgh labor priest and friend of Philip Murray, 1945. (Courtesy of the United Steelworkers of America Archive, Pennsylvania State University Libraries.)

many enemies of the people are its enemies. The workers of this country know in their hearts that the CIO is a good thing, they know that the leaders of it are working for their best interests, they know that it is a powerful foe of suffering and injustice. Efforts to paint the CIO as Red are futile and foolish. Such efforts just aid Communism. The mass of the American workers are untainted by Communism, but if the insane attackers of movements like the CIO keep on with their present tactics we won't be able to say that for long.[21]

There were others who echoed Rice's sentiments. George Schuyler of the *Pittsburgh Courier* despised the Communists. "I disagree with the so-called Reds in dealing with the Negro and also with the advice they give him. I claim that they make the Negro problem worse instead of better by their insane tactics. They give the murderous southern Neanderthals the very opportunity and excuse they are looking for to commit additional homicide." In Johnstown, prior to the 1937 Bethlehem strike, several "strangers" tried to lure steel workers to a meeting. When Anthony Lorditch spoke to SWOC organizer Jim Gent about this meeting, the Catholic labor leader said, "Stay away from it, they're Communists, and they're trying to break up what we're doing." In 1938, at the fifteenth annual convention of B'nai B'rith, the Anti-Defamation League pointed out that "a Communist who was a Jew is now an apostate." Fearful that Jews who joined the Communist Party would provoke an anti-Semitic reaction in America, Rabbi Edward Israel contended that Communism promised "the dictatorship of a hidebound and murderous bureaucracy."[22]

Ignoring Jewish critics of the Soviet Union, Secretary of the Interior Harold Ickes blasted Catholic opponents of the party. In an April 1938 radio broadcast from Chicago, Ickes informed a group of Jewish journalists: "Fascism is the deadly and insidious foe we must prepare to combat. I suspect either the motives or the intelligence of those who would have us marshal our forces against a barely imaginary danger of Communism while fascism thunders at the gate of our citadel of liberty." According to Ickes, Catholics who criticized the Soviet Union, and who jousted against a non-existent Communist foe, were partisans of the fascist Right. (In Ickes's mind, since Jews could not be fascist, they therefore could not be anti-Communist.)[23]

Catholic reformers were shocked to learn that Ickes, and other personalities associated with the Roosevelt administration, felt there were no threats from the Left. After the National Catholic Welfare Conference in March 1938 urged parents not to let their children join the Communist-organized American Youth Congress, Catholics heard from another New Dealer:

Eleanor Roosevelt. She described the American Youth Congress as "an idealistic, hard-working-group" whose attitudes toward Communism were of no concern to her. Eleanor Roosevelt was more inclined to regard Catholics, rather than Communists, as un-American. According to her, American Catholics were under the control of a reactionary Vatican that advanced the cause of domestic and global fascism. In contrast, American Communists struggled for civil rights and economic justice. Moreover, as Eleanor Roosevelt told her family, there was much to admire about the Soviet Union. The Russian people loved Stalin because Communism guaranteed them good jobs.[24]

Undeterred, Hensler and Rice redoubled their efforts to organize unions and combat Communism. The labor priests maintained a frantic pace. In January, Rice spoke to SWOC members at the Polish Hall in Washington, Pennsylvania, the Ancient Order of Hibernians Hall in Hazelwood, and the Lithuanian Hall in Pittsburgh's South Side. Rice also rallied workers at the Croatian Hall in Etna, took part in a civil liberties' demonstration in Bayonne, New Jersey, against the state's antilabor machine boss, and discussed the Catholic conception of social justice with students at Pitt. Where fraternal halls were not available, Pittsburgh's Democratic Party opened its ward clubs to Rice. Writing to other Catholic clergy and lay reformers, Rice urged them not to vote for dishonest politicians simply because they were co-religionists.[25]

Meanwhile, Hensler addressed a SWOC lodge in Donora, Pennsylvania, presented a paper on the "Economic Role of the State" to the Catholic Educational Convention in Louisville, and arranged for John Brophy and Dorothy Day to give talks to six hundred clergy and laity. Attendance at weekly Catholic Radical Alliance functions normally ranged from forty to one hundred people. Both priests sent a stinging rebuke to the Communist president of the Hotel and Restaurant Workers Union, an American Federation of Labor affiliate. Union president Carl Hacker had given a party to commemorate the fourteenth anniversary of Lenin's death. Banners reading "Long Live the Soviet Union" and "Long Live Leninism" greeted Hacker's followers.[26]

February was just as busy. After speaking to SWOC locals in Braddock, Johnstown, and Midland, Pennsylvania, Rice crossed swords with Martin Young, the leader of the Pittsburgh Communist Party. The priest had debated Carl Hacker in late January just prior to a union recall election that Rice helped to instigate. AFL officials rendered the recall election moot by removing Hacker from office. At the New Castle, Pennsylvania, debate Young explained that his organization was just as committed to democracy as

Franklin Roosevelt. He further claimed kinship with American Catholics, contending that Communists were also a minority deeply concerned with abolishing "social inequalities." Rice pooh-poohed Young's assertions and then outlined what he felt was the true nature of Communism:

> The Communists have a definite program of violent revolution. If they are marching with other progressives now that is just because it suits their purpose. They will turn on us when it suits them. . . .
>
> Records show splendid unions which they have ruined after they were firmly in the saddle. A Communist is generally an efficient unionist up to a certain point. He is trained for that purpose. The union is always second to him, the party is first.
>
> If we accept the Communists as normal citizens and allow them to become leaders we are building up trouble. Not the least of the troubles we are building up for ourselves, when we do this, is the encouragement we give to reactionary elements. These people are just looking for a chance to dub every progressive movement alien and Communistic.

Rice's reception was not cordial. Young had stacked the audience with his supporters.[27]

No sooner had Rice tangled with the region's Communist leadership than he found himself locking horns with the ubiquitous Fulton Sheen. The radio homilist came to Pittsburgh, where he broadcast an attack on the CIO. Sheen blamed Murray for the labor violence of 1937 and attacked Pittsburgh's labor priests. Catholic clergy, Sheen argued, should not concern themselves with social reform. Trying to keep his temper with a fellow member of the clergy, Rice responded to Sheen from the pulpit of St. Augustine's Church in the working-class Lawrenceville neighborhood:

> To infer that labor is responsible in whole, or in any considerable part, for the violence that has characterized American industrial disputes is to be decidedly biased and unfair. I would be willing to sit down with Monsignor Sheen and go over one by one the incidents of violence between capital and labor for the past several decades. I would welcome the chance of showing him records of fight after fight provoked by organized capitalist thuggery. Finally, I would go over the roster of the wounded and the dead. They are labor's wounded and labor's dead. We Pittsburghers have too vivid a memory of the Homestead slaughter, the Coal and Iron Police brutalities, the last taxi strike, and

many another incident to have anyone tell us that labor is at fault where there is violence.[28]

Rice aimed his next barbs at laissez-faire capitalism. As he informed his KDKA radio audience on March 19, capitalism was born of the Enlightenment and secular humanism. Declaring that God was dead, inhumane capitalists "pushed the eight beatitudes and the Ten Commandments to the wall." Christianity was not, as the Communists argued, the cause of this state of affairs. True Christians recognized their responsibilities to their fellow men. Celebrating the Feast Day of St. Joseph, Rice noted that this carpenter had been, like the American worker, a "humble cog in an unjust system." Moreover,

> after two thousand years of preaching charity and justice we again have a system endowed with the defects of the one Joseph knew, and with many new, shiny, modern defects of its own. For the world has forgotten much and learned much since then. Usury again rots the social fabric, as of old. The teeming slave population of that day is more than matched by our propertyless, jobless hordes. And what a host of problems, unsolved problems, the machine and mechanical progress have brought: unemployment, over-production, under consumption, super-concentrations of wealth, poverty in the midst of plenty, magnificent factories and wretched homes, a rich nation and an ill fed, ill housed, ill clothed population. Christ, the divine foster son of Joseph, came to a world sick with avarice, cruelty, and selfishness. He lived and died to bring the only remedy that could cure its malaise—justice and charity. Twenty centuries have gone by, and, though millions upon millions honor Christ's name and give lip-service to what he died for, avarice, cruelty, and greed again reign.[29]

To Rice, Christianity was not responsible for the world's injustices. At the same time, Communism, as the bastard twin of laissez-faire capitalism and the offspring of secular humanism, provided no hope for the realization of social justice. The solution to society's ills was Christian democracy—and the CIO was the foundation upon which a moral social order could be built. This was the message Hensler took with him in April when he spoke to the Pittsburgh chapter of the Veterans of Foreign Wars, a group that regarded the CIO with suspicion. Rice, along with Clinton Golden and James Carey, traveled to Schenectady where he assured electrical workers that the CIO was "a good, Christian, necessary thing." With the permission of Albany Bishop

Edmund Gibbons, the Pittsburgh priest toured other New York locales before returning home. To the employees of the Aluminum Corporation of America in New Kensington, Pennsylvania, Rice described laissez-faire capitalism as "un-American and, certainly, un-Christian." More New Deal legislation was necessary, for "sabotage by reactionary legislators has robbed the drive for reform of much of its efficiency." Most important, the priest told his receptive audience, "Christ's concern for the poor and the exploited is a clear command to all His followers to be concerned for them."[30]

Desiring to bring clergy and lay reformers together to discuss politics and economics, the Catholic University organized the first National Catholic Social Action Conference. Milwaukee Archbishop Samuel Stritch, the chair of the Social Action Department of the National Catholic Welfare Conference, played host to forty-six hundred people in May. The three hundred individuals who gave papers came from the ranks of the Church, government, labor, and management. Unlike previous regional Catholic conferences, anti-New Deal businessmen avoided Milwaukee. Ernest Weir of the National Steel Corporation, a hostile participant in Pittsburgh's industrial conference in 1934, lambasted the Milwaukee proceedings. Singling out Hensler for special abuse, Weir told the members of the American Iron and Steel Institute that the Pittsburgher had no right to discuss the social aspects of industry since he was not a businessman. A few weeks before this outburst, Weir met privately with Franklin Roosevelt. Weir denounced Ickes and other friends of the CIO.[31]

Hensler's session at the National Catholic Social Action Conference focused on the steel industry. Bishop Boyle served as chair while Garrett Connors, the vice president of industrial relations at the Sharon [Pennsylvania] Steel Company, David McDonald, and Hensler presented papers. Connors emphasized that the fortunes of labor and management were inseparable; neither could prosper without the other. Stressing the importance of market stability and a happy, well-paid labor force, the Sharon Steel executive expressed his support for unions. Connors then urged the Roosevelt administration to help the cooperative components of the American steel industry in their battle against overseas competitors. Tariffs were necessary, Connors claimed, to protect management and labor from foreign steel makers who were able to sell their product cheaply since they paid low wages and received government subsidies. Ernest Weir was too much of a rugged individualist to have tolerated Connors. The best way to deal with foreign competitors and their less expensive goods, most of Little Steel believed, was to reduce wages.[32]

David McDonald picked up Connors's theme. Praising U.S. Steel, and then citing Pius XI's 1931 encyclical as the guidepost for social reconstruction, Murray's aide turned to Weir:

> Unfortunately, all employers of steel workers did not see eye to eye with the more enlightened in 1937. Some of them tried to stick to the fallacy of "Rugged Individualism"—very rugged on the individual who had to work for them. These employer individualists were simply trying to appropriate to themselves excessive advantages, and desired to leave to their employees the barest minimum necessities to keep soul and body together. Harsh words? Yes, but not nearly so harsh as the blows which they delivered in support of their jungle-born concepts. They desired to be free from the encumbrance of a wage agreement with a labor union whenever they deemed, in their self-assumed omnipotence, that the time had arrived for reducing wages or for perpetrating some other overt act which would result in a degradation of economic and moral standards in the life of a steel worker.

McDonald would never win an award for objectivity, but in rhetoric he was without peer. A silver tongue and a handsome profile made him Murray's heir-apparent. In later years, the news media compared McDonald to an equally glib member of Joseph Kennedy's clan.[33]

More thoughtful than McDonald, Hensler grappled with the related issues of federal regulation, union power, and depressed wages. The priest avoided McDonald's heated language. Hensler abhorred the prospect of protective tariffs that might increase workers' paychecks, but only at the expense of consumers. Turning to the proper role of the federal government in promoting a just society, Hensler observed that Catholic social instruction

> advocates the regulation of industry by the organized industry itself, but allows any measure of governmental intervention that may be found necessary to safeguard the common good. The basic idea of this program is to get the whole industry organized in such a way that it can govern itself for its own good, the good of its customers, and the public welfare. This means, in the first place, bringing together into one organization the employers and the employees of each concern in the industry. . . .
>
> The employees are to be as much a part of the organized industry as the employers. The full aim is to raise them above the status of mere wage earners, to make them partners with the employers in the

performance of a social function, and to have them share finally in ownership, management, and profits.[34]

Hensler offered a vision for American capitalism that neither McDonald nor Connors was willing to accept. Both men desired a strong, economically interventionist government. Their ultimate ends were different. McDonald expected high union wages while Connors wanted great profits guaranteed by protective tariffs. Workers and managers would both win. However, as Hensler realized, the ordinary consumer would find more of his earnings, even if enhanced by the power of collective bargaining, being transferred to Sharon Steel and SWOC. If the consumer was by happenstance of profession, or by individual choice, not a union member, then he would see his limited wages disappear into the pockets of steel workers and executives. Such a situation not only failed to promote the common good in which Hensler believed, but also fed middle-class resentment of unions. Moreover, as a firm believer in the principle of subsidiarity, Hensler could not endorse the erection of a labor-management State. Everyone had to participate in society's governance, including the middle class. Finally, Hensler opposed the extensive federal regulation that Connors and McDonald desired. Unelected, powerful bureaucracies, he felt, cut off ordinary citizens' participation in government. Hensler did not want America to become a capitalist version of the Soviet Union.[35]

While Hensler sought to achieve social justice without, at the same time, erecting a collectivist State, a conservative Democratic congressman from Texas was entering the national political scene. Martin Dies, who had supported legislation to curtail Catholic and Jewish immigration, despised the New Deal. Prior to 1938, however, Dies was an obscure politician. His southern colleagues, who dominated the legislative process by virtue of seniority and the fact that widespread disfranchisement gave them secure electoral bases, did not take Dies seriously. In any event, most southern politicians greatly appreciated the New Deal's agricultural subsidies.[36]

Through his radio addresses, carefully staged public appearances, and cultivation of reporters who were often more liberal than their publishers, Roosevelt dominated the political scene. Moreover, there were 435 congressmen vying for attention. There was only one president, and Roosevelt was articulate and inspiring. In the early years of the Great Depression, Roosevelt also had a national crisis working on his behalf. The majority of Americans cheered his call for struggle and victory. Most important, Roosevelt had Herbert Hoover to kick around. New Deal Democrats ran against Hoover's political corpse in 1934 and 1936. They planned to do so again in 1938.[37]

Unfortunately for Roosevelt, Hoover was not so pungent after six years of New Deal reform. Although Roosevelt had helped millions of Americans, the 1937 recession erased their economic gains. In the span of a few months, the number of unemployed Americans rose from nearly eight million to over ten million, while five billion dollars of the nation's GNP vanished. The class war between the CIO and business added to Roosevelt's difficulties. According to the increasingly sophisticated public opinion polls undertaken by George Gallup and *Fortune* magazine, the 1937 General Motors sit-down strike and the bloody Little Steel battle hurt the president. In 1937, two-thirds of the public advocated punitive action against strikers. Blaming the CIO for fomenting violence, 55 percent of the public in 1938 vowed not to vote for congressmen who received union endorsement. On the first anniversary of the Little Steel strike, 72 percent of Americans informed Gallup that they wanted the Roosevelt administration to shift to the right. Three-quarters of the poll respondents also said that if they had been in Congress they would not have supported every New Deal initiative. The New Dealers suffered a great loss of support in the Northeast and the Midwest—the labor battlefields of 1937.[38]

Any union leader or politician associated with the CIO suffered public censure. In 1937, one-third of Americans expressed approval of John L. Lewis, compared to the two-thirds who thought AFL president William Green was the better labor leader. It was no surprise that Lewis had the least support among upper- and middle-income voters. However, in 1938 just 34 percent of lower-income respondents endorsed the CIO president. Coming from the core constituency of the industrial labor movement, this was disturbing news. Secretary of Labor Frances Perkins, by virtue of her support for the CIO, had the highest negative rating of any cabinet member. Thirty-eight percent of the public in May 1938 rated her performance as poor. Registered Democrats held her in no higher regard. Twice as many Democrats castigated Perkins as denounced the other two controversial cabinet members, Harold Ickes and Agriculture Secretary Henry Wallace.[39]

Congressman Dies found other encouraging signs. Most southern Democrats had grown disgusted with Ickes's efforts to desegregate federal facilities and employ blacks on public works projects. Southerners also felt threatened by the CIO's abortive efforts to organize in Dixie and, like western Republicans, resented the La Follette Committee's hearings on industrial violence. The La Follette Committee understandably roasted Republic Steel executive Tom Girdler when he defended the 1937 Memorial Day massacre in Chicago. However, La Follette opened himself to criticism by employing several Communists on his staff—notably, John Abt and Charles Kramer. A former federal worker, Kramer used the power of the congressional subpoena to look at various companies' records. He routinely leaked information to Wyndham Mortimer and Bob Travis, his allies in the UAW.[40]

If La Follette could use a Senate committee to attack anti-union managers, why could Martin Dies not create a House committee to batter the CIO? The times seemed propitious and, given Father Coughlin's limited support, there was an opportunity for Dies to become the leader of a growing conservative movement. In May 1938, Dies proposed the creation of the House Special Committee to Investigate Un-American Activities. Dies volunteered to be its chair. Realizing that if he was candid about his intentions, Roosevelt's congressional supporters would thwart him, Dies played a clever game. He assured northern liberals that his committee would focus its investigation on Nazi organizations operating in the United States. He also enlisted the support of an influential Democratic congressman, Samuel Dickstein. A Jewish New Yorker, Dickstein viewed right-wingers as potential allies of Hitler. Having no interest in protecting the civil liberties of such people, Dickstein and many New Deal Democrats voted to establish the Dies Committee. Dickstein and La Follette failed to understand that sauce for the goose was sauce for the gander. Dies embarked upon a blood trail, determined to run every Communist or liberal to the ground.[41]

AFL vice president John Frey informed the Dies Committee that 257 CIO and 31 SWOC organizers were Communists. One of the men Frey denounced, a SWOC subregional director named John Dutchman, was a member of Pittsburgh's St. Mary's Assumption parish and an officer in the Grand Carniolan Slovenian Union. Dutchman fired off an angry telegram to Dies: "I am a Catholic, a national officer of a Catholic fraternal organization, and absolutely opposed to any Communistic interference in government or unions." Unfortunately for Dutchman, and the other Catholic SWOC leaders who came under attack, congressional committees may grant special immunities to witnesses. Consequently, antilabor witnesses were exempt from slander prosecution. Most Americans did not realize this, so when labor organizers did not file civil suits the public took it as an admission of guilt.[42]

Several months later, Benjamin Gitlow, the former secretary of the American Communist Party, accused John Brophy of being a subversive. Brophy, according to Gitlow, had promoted Communist efforts to seize the mine workers' union in the 1920s. Deeply offended that the Dies Committee and the press would take the word of a confessed Communist over that of a devout Catholic, Brophy sent a letter to the Texan. The *Pittsburgh Catholic* was one of the few newspapers in the nation to report an extended rebuttal:

I am not a Communist; neither am I a Communist agent as alleged, and never have been. I am and always have been opposed to the philosophy of Communism. No one knows this better than the Communists themselves. If at any time they have expressed approval and apparently supported views and policies for which I have stood, they have done so without advice, consultation, or permission from me.

If you will have this letter read before your committee and placed in its proceedings, I will consider that some little amends have been made for broadcasting the wild, lying, and slanderous statements about me which have emanated from your committee room.[43]

The *Pittsburgh Catholic* felt that it was imperative to expose Dies's reactionary agenda. In a series of editorials written in the summer and fall of 1938, the diocesan newspaper revealed that committee investigator Edward Sullivan was a fallen Catholic who had been active in several anti-Semitic organizations. Addressing Frey's testimony, the *Pittsburgh Catholic* reprimanded Dies, contending that "calumny, detraction, and the bearing of false witness are wrong, and any campaign against subversive movements that involves the employment of such evils cannot be a wholesome thing." The newspaper also condemned Elizabeth Dilling, a right-wing writer who, with the financial assistance of anti–New Deal executives, had published two lurid books, *The Red Network* and *The Roosevelt Red Record*. Dilling charged that Brophy, Father James Cox, and the National Catholic Welfare Conference were part of a vast Communist conspiracy. A favorite source of intelligence for Dies, Dilling had no friends on the editorial board of the *Pittsburgh Catholic*. Her *Pittsburgh Catholic* critics, however, eschewed sarcasm in their responses to Dilling and the committee. The *Pittsburgh Courier* and the Associated Negro Press, a black wire service, were not so gentle. After Dies nominated Lewis and Ickes to an "All International Team of Hate," the *Courier* pointed out that his committee had neglected to include the southern congressional delegation.[44]

Other diocesan newspapers were not as supportive of the New Deal. The *Catholic Telegraph-Register* of Cincinnati praised Rice for his anti-Communist activities, but castigated Roosevelt's "radical advisors," claimed that the president had too much power, and endorsed the Dies Committee. Similarly, the *Catholic Sentinel* of Portland, Oregon, urged Dies to search out and destroy foreign ideologies or "-isms," condemned Frances Perkins for defending Harry Bridges, and called for the end of New Deal relief programs. According to the *Catholic Sentinel*, the WPA had fostered among the poor a dependency upon welfare that was becoming a threat to social stability. Rice

Fig. 9.   John Brophy, SWOC and CIO troubleshooter. Brophy's Catholic faith led him to take on Communists and corporate executives with equal passion. (Courtesy of the United Steelworkers of America Archive, Pennsylvania State University Libraries.)

privately lamented: "The level of stupidity [is] very high in the diocesan press and indeed in all the Catholic press."[45]

As the backlash against organized labor and Roosevelt jelled, Hensler, Rice, and SWOC plotted new political strategies. Elmer Cope, now a SWOC organizer in Rochester, New York, wrote to McDonald in January 1938 urging the union to educate its members in labor history and politics. An ignorant rank and file, Cope warned, could not produce local leaders capable of sustaining the union. The union undertook a major effort to promote worker education that summer: Camp SWOC. Combining recreational activities from archery to volley ball with seminars on labor history and Catholic social thought, Camp SWOC proved enormously popular. Workers, whose impoverished childhood's never included summer camp, spent an enjoyable July in Mt. Davis, Pennsylvania. Cope's friend, Harold Ruttenberg, tore himself away from SWOC's headquarters long enough to serve as general camp advisor. Certainly, Ruttenberg needed a vacation. His economic analysis of the future of the steel industry, published in a February 1938 issue of *The New Republic*, was bleak. Even if the economy fully recovered, Ruttenberg reported, fewer steel workers would be called back to work since recent technological innovations had already eliminated eighty-five thousand mill jobs.[46]

The Mt. Davis campgrounds, built by the Civilian Conservation Corps and managed by the WPA, attracted some notable speakers. After Clinton Golden greeted the campers, John Brophy, "the beloved CIO director," as Ruttenberg called him, spoke. Brophy described the CIO as "a barrier against wage cuts" and pledged that "the next great forward move of the CIO will be in the politically backward South." Two former Pitt professors, Ralph Turner and B. J. Hovde, also appeared at Camp SWOC. Turner, the chair of educational committee of the United Federal Workers (CIO), argued that there would be no lasting economic recovery without a general rise in wages. Only the labor movement, Turner said, could guarantee workers an improved standard of living. Hovde, a high-profile Democratic activist in Pennsylvania, called for increased political activism on the part of SWOC: "Conflicting interest in society [Republican businessmen] make it imperative for labor to take steps to protect itself. When I speak of labor, I mean organized labor. We must either make the capitalist system work by democratic means, or we must set up a better system—again by democratic means." If the campers did not quite get what Hovde thought about anti-CIO businessmen, the professor became more explicit: "Fascism is an effort of a decaying system to perpetuate itself by violent means, if necessary. It is capitalism in the nude."[47]

After Hovde and Turner departed the unionists put on a play, "Coal Black and the Seven Cinders." A parody of the Walt Disney movie "Snow White and the Seven Dwarfs," the Seven Cinders were hard-working coal miners exploited by a wicked boss. Not everyone saw the humor of this production. A group of labor spies from Chicago attempted to plant several bombs at the camp. Luckily for the spies, the FBI quickly took them into custody. The underlings should have counted their blessings. One of the 250 campers, a school teacher employed by the WPA, had been a soldier in the Irish Republican Army. Thanks to his close acquaintance with the British judicial system, he knew how to conduct a fruitful interrogation.[48]

Hensler and Rice also appeared at Camp SWOC. As Rice told the Catholic readers of *The Commonweal*, the Church had to address its message of social justice directly to workers. This was especially important since "communists and leftists of all shades have been making a deal of noise. Condemn them, as we may, for their errors, it is foolish to deny that, in the minds of very many, they stand out as friends of the worker and the poor. Their zeal is magnificent. Their social message, their suggested cures for the world's malaise, abominable." Certainly, no one could fault Hensler for a lack of zeal.

> [The CIO] can secure wage increases in many industries, and maintain present levels, but it lacks the power to increase the percentage of the national income going to the masses of people. It lacks the power because it has nothing to say about prices and production. The control over these important items is still vested in the hands of a small inner group of financial and industrial overlords. They have the power to jump prices every time they increase wages; they have the power to restrict production and employment unless they see opportunities for big profits.
>
> The solution is to break up this highly centralized control by a few over the national economy. The control must be decentralized and shared democratically by every important element in industry. This means that employers should no longer be allowed the whole say in deciding the economic policies of the nation. The power and responsibility of deciding our economic weal must in the future be proportionate, shared by organized labor as well as by organized management.[49]

Although Hensler and Rice were much alike politically, their styles stood in sharp contrast. Like Murray, Hensler sought to keep his rhetoric low-key and his message conciliatory. He did not always succeed, but Hensler invariably returned in his speeches to the idea of the Mystical Body of Christ. Concurring with Leo XIII "that the social question is fundamentally a religious as well as an economic question," Hensler believed that "the basis of social charity is the profound conviction that we all 'are members of a single family and children of the same Heavenly Father, and further, that we are one body in Christ and every one members of another.'" Consequently, Hensler concluded, "if employers and wage earners should take the precept of charity seriously to heart, injustice would be quickly banished, and class hatred would not rear its ugly head."[50]

Rice, on the other hand, friend though he was of Murray, could sound a great deal like Lewis. Addressing SWOC's third annual July picnic in Ambridge, Rice indicated that he would amputate an infected limb from the Mystical Body of Christ:

Unable to realize that their evil day is passed and gone for good, the reactionaries of this country are launching one last desperate effort to maintain their power. They take heart from the fact that the mild reform program of the last six years has hit a snag. But let them reflect that the snag is due to their un-Christian and economically stupid policies, which, extending well over three-quarters of a century, had so debauched and snarled our system that not mild, but drastic, measures are necessary.

They blame the present recession on the New Deal, the CIO, and other mild progressive moves of the past few years. Even a moron, were he intellectually honest, could see that our troubles today are but a partial heritage from the day barely finished, when naked greed ruled undisputed in government and industry.[51]

Murray's confessor was more constrained when the Dies Committee charged that Brophy had journeyed to the Soviet Union in 1926 for some sinister purpose. The telegram Rice and Hensler sent to Dies in the summer of 1938 attested to Brophy's enlightened Catholicism and the fact that the miner had been part of an official American trade union delegation when he went to Russia. Both Dies and the AFL's John Frey would have been well advised to have listened to Brophy's speeches. At a summertime New York rally sponsored by the ACTU, Brophy made it clear he was no Stalinist:

If we Catholics haven't the courage to take over the leadership of the unions and to see that they are directed according to the teachings of the Church, there are others who will step into the positions. It is not enough to talk about social justice and to say, "I am a Catholic and I know the principles of Catholic social justice;" we must get into the fight and earn the right to lead those who are not as well qualified as ourselves.

This was not the rhetoric of the Popular Front. Brophy and the labor priests never considered the Left to be an ally. Even if the anti-CIO Right was enjoying a political resurgence, Christian democrats like Brophy and Rice would not forge an alliance with the Left.[52]

In Detroit, the ACTU, with the blessing of Archbishop Edward Mooney, pledged "to combat Communism, racketeering, and other un-Christian influences with the unions." The New York ACTU initiated a campaign against racial discrimination in the city's unions, contending that Catholics could not condone the persecution of other minorities. Catholic activists also picketed stores in Harlem that refused to hire blacks. Meanwhile, a number of New York transit workers, worried about the power Communists wielded in their union, joined the ACTU. In the columns of the ACTU newspaper, *The Labor Leader*, Hensler exhorted workers to become "educated in Catholic principles to combat the dangerous leadership that Communists and other left-wingers are offering neutral unions." To the textile workers of Utica, New York, Rice urged them to reject revolutionary Marxism:

> We are all brothers, rich man, poor man, worker, capitalist. We are not to hate one another, as individuals or as classes, whatever the provocation.
>
> This does not mean that the worker and his friends are to sit tamely and meekly while they are despoiled of their rights and possessions. It does not deprive them of the right to strive manfully for justice. It does mean that the weapons to be used in the strife are those of nonviolence. It means that workers should have nothing to do with those movements, such as Communism, which believe in violence and class hatred as a matter of course.[53]

No sooner had Rice returned from Utica than he found himself yet again butting heads with Communists and conservative Catholics. Martin Carmody of the Knights of Columbus informed the Vatican daily, *L'Osservatore Romano*, that the CIO was "completely directed by Communist forces." Miffed, Rice called Carmody's charges "wild and unfounded," noting that Phil Murray, David McDonald, Patrick Fagan, and Joseph Timko of the Ambridge SWOC were all practicing Catholics and members of the Knights of Columbus. Turning to Clarence Hathaway, the editor of the *Daily Worker*, Rice rejected the idea of cooperating with Communists. At a fall debate in Pittsburgh that attracted twenty-five hundred spectators, Hathaway advocated the creation of "a broad democratic front of Communists, socialists, trade unionist, of Catholics, Protestants, and others to resist and ultimately destroy the fascist barbarism which today threatens the peace of the world and our democratic institutions." Rice rebuffed the Communist official.

> We will accept the outstretched hand of Communists only when it ceases to be Communist and relinquishes the doctrine and tactics that have put it beyond the pale of normality and ethics. We cannot accept it because in doctrine and tactics we are diametrically opposed. The change in Communism represented by the "outstretched hand" and the "united front" does not alter in any way the fundamental Catholic principles.[54]

Amarillo, Texas, Bishop Robert Lucey, a member of the National Catholic Welfare Conference, rushed to the side of the CIO. In two September issues of *The Commonweal*, Bishop Lucey chided Catholic opponents of the industrial union movement: "In our just determination to stop Communism we must not offend the honest working people who are trying to organize for justice and the common good. . . . Our condemnation of the whole movement brings exceeding great joy to the hearts of the Communists. They want this labor movement for themselves."[55]

The National Catholic Welfare Conference weighed into the fray. On October 14, the bishops issued a statement entitled "Industrial and Social Peace." Expressing the hope that the AFL and the CIO would settle their differences, and that organized labor would survive Communist subversion and conservative persecution, the bishops pleaded for justice:

> We turn to our people and beg of them to study anew the practical implications of the law of love, and to enthrone that law in their hearts. We earnestly beseech them to examine carefully, and to apply conscientiously, the saving principles enunciated in the providential encyclicals of His Holiness, Pope Pius XI. And turning to our separated brethren, in the spirit of Christian charity and brotherly love, we ask them, too, to seek in these encyclicals the common remedy for the harsh conditions of the day. To Catholic labor leaders and unionists, as well as to Catholic employers, we express the profound hope that they will bend their best energies to the realization of the Christian social order envisaged by the Holy Father, to the end that, achieving first a true industrial and social peace at home, we may thus contribute to a lasting peace among all nations.[56]

Achieving "true industrial and social peace" appeared unlikely in 1938. As the state and congressional elections drew near, there were signs that the politics of discord would carry the industrial heartland. Finding their own inspiration from "Snow White and the Seven Dwarfs," anti-union partisans sang a ditty honoring CIO official Sidney Hillman:

> Hiho, Hiho!
> Don't join the CIO!
> And pay your dues to a
> bunch of Jews
> Hiho, Hiho![57]

More serious, the Dies Committee had inaugurated its hearings on Communist infiltration of the Michigan CIO. Dies stacked the witness list with

GM supporters. Detroit's leading newspapers gave extensive, highly favorable coverage to anti-CIO testimony. No one in the White House was surprised. Harold Ickes accurately estimated that 85 percent of the national press was an enemy of the Roosevelt administration. Indeed, many of Roosevelt's foes ran front-page editorials and cartoons savaging the New Deal. For all of that, New Dealers had won decisive elections since 1933. This time, however, Republicans circumvented the White House reporters who had fallen under Roosevelt's spell. Holding congressional hearings in Detroit was one innovative way to deny Roosevelt the ready opportunity to place his own interpretation on the day's events. Conservative publishers also reported only one side of the labor issue and played to the public's fear of foreign subversion. Even newspaper and wire service correspondents who sympathized with Roosevelt turned in damaging stories. In part this was because they did not take it upon themselves to interview the labor organizers and others who stood accused of promoting Communism. Laziness was not the sole reason. Too many CIO and federal employees *were* Communist operatives for reporters to ignore.[58]

The most hapless New Dealer to come under fire from the Dies Committee was Frances Perkins. In one sense the labor secretary was a victim of circumstances beyond her control. Her critics contended that she had encouraged the UAW and SWOC to mount their great strikes. That was untrue. The CIO planned to initiate a national organizing drive in 1937 with or without the blessing of the federal government. As events transpired, it was clear that the CIO did not have Roosevelt's blessing. On the other hand, Perkins had invited attack by opposing congressional calls for the deportation of Harry Bridges. She was convinced that the Australian-born labor leader was not a Communist.[59]

Roosevelt chose not to defend Perkins, recognizing that federal bureaucrats who had no key political constituencies were expendable. However, governors of states critical to the viability of the Democratic Party could not be thrown overboard. The polling data indicated that Michigan governor Frank Murphy was in danger. Roosevelt held a press conference on October 25 urging Murphy's reelection. He also arranged for Paul Anderson, a pro-New Deal writer, to praise Murphy in a national radio broadcast. Anderson was an unfortunate choice. He had written stories on the Detroit hearings for the UAW's newspaper, the *United Automobile Worker*, a Communist-edited publication. His articles for the labor paper, as well as those he wrote for *The Nation*, were just as churlish as those appearing in the Hearst press.[60]

Confronted with a hostile news media, and seeing the support of the Catholic press fading, the New Dealers turned to the organs of the secular

Left. *The Nation* and *The New Republic* were, to many New Dealers, the progressive cheerleaders of social reform. They were mistaken. Freda Kirchwey, the editor of *The Nation*, was a committed Stalinist. The editor of *The New Republic*, Michael Straight, whose family owned the magazine, became a Comintern agent while enrolled at Cambridge University. (For the sake of appearances, *The New Republic* and *The Nation* published articles by non-Communist leftists like Harold Ruttenberg.)[61]

The alliance between the White House and the leftist media did nothing to halt the conservative tide in Michigan. Pennsylvania appeared lost as well. Moe Annenberg, the publisher of the *Philadelphia Inquirer*, waged a relentless war against the Democrats. Distressed by Annenberg's scandal-mongering, Roosevelt encouraged Ickes to attack the publisher. Ickes, who viewed himself as the natural Democratic leader of his native state, delved into Annenberg's business arrangements. The interior secretary discovered that Annenberg was making one million dollars a day from his race track interests. Significantly, Annenberg had failed to pay taxes on this "business."[62]

Skewering Annenberg did not help Pennsylvania Democrats. Lewis had earlier intervened in the state's Democratic primary to advance his own slate of candidates. He gave Republicans much ammunition by assaulting the integrity of David Lawrence, the state chair of the Democratic Party. Paul Block, the Republican publisher of the *Pittsburgh Post-Gazette* and the *Toledo Blade*, among other newspapers, wrote pointed editorials about WPA graft. Although the 210,000 readers of the *Post-Gazette* could scoff at Block's claims that the New Deal was German National Socialism with a smile, they were able to verify his charges against the WPA. Prior to every city, state, and federal election, Pittsburgh's WPA rolls expanded by 1,000 percent. Pennsylvania senator Joseph Guffey expected WPA workers to contribute to, and vote for, the Democratic Party. Frank Kent, a nationally syndicated columnist from Baltimore, provided a damning quote from Harry Hopkins. The WPA director, with four million Americans on his payroll in November 1938, allegedly chortled "Tax, tax, spend, spend, elect, elect" at a Washington-area race track. Whether or not Kent had taken liberties in quoting Hopkins was unclear. As a description of Democratic campaign tactics in Pennsylvania, however, Kent was on the money.[63]

Block did not tout the merits of the Republican candidates. They were the creatures of Moe Annenberg, Liberty League founder Howard Pew Sr., and Joe Grundy, the Quaker master of the Pennsylvania Manufacturers' Association. Rather, the *Post-Gazette* focused on Democratic sins. The conservative publisher also let the *Sun-Telegraph* carry the bulk of the stories alleging criminal activity on the part of David Lawrence. Block did not believe in severing ties to Democrats who, even if Republicans won in 1938, would likely remain influential in regional politics. The *Pittsburgh Bulletin Index* followed Block's lead. Since none of the Republicans came from the Mellon Patch, the society paper gleefully wrote "Pew" under their photographs. It was the season's best double entendre. Even though the *Bulletin Index* snippily referred to Roosevelt as "the Great White Father," the newspaper insisted that Lawrence never accepted bribes. As a rare Democrat who had not taken easy shots at the late Andrew Mellon, the city's Republicans passed on their opportunity to mug Lawrence. Ickes was not so kind. He regarded Lawrence as a typical Irish political hack. Pennsylvania, and the national Democratic Party, Ickes believed, needed progressive Protestant leaders. Ickes forgot that Joseph Guffey and Harry Hopkins were progressive Protestants.[64]

Lawrence made a futile effort to end the worst abuses of the WPA in Pennsylvania. He failed in large measure because of Lewis. The CIO president, through a network of supporters in the UMW, had gained control of many WPA administrative positions. Just as disheartening, the usually supportive *Pittsburgh Catholic* criticized federal relief policies, concluding that "the practice of charity, expressed as interest in the needy and concern for the welfare of our neighbor, is a personal virtue which cannot be turned over to the government." Alarmed, Roosevelt had his operatives canvass Pennsylvania. It was a telling commentary that many of the Democratic and Republican politicians they chanced upon were destined for prison. However, there were more Democrats in danger of being indicted than Republicans. Since neither Democrats nor Republicans could be called paragons of virtue, voters had to keep a body count. The party with the fewest leaders in jail won.[65]

The 1938 midterm elections were a disaster for Roosevelt. Republicans gained eighty-one seats in the House and eight in the Senate. Ominously, Republicans carried blue-collar Canton and Flint. Catholics, disgusted with the violence of 1937 and the presence of Communists in the CIO, did not come to the polls. Pennsylvania—which claimed the second largest pot of electoral votes—was an extremely painful loss. Republicans recaptured the state house and senate and won ten U.S. House seats. That gave them a majority of the Pennsylvania congressional delegation. Moreover, Thomas Kennedy, the Democratic gubernatorial candidate, lost by four hundred thousand votes. Kennedy, a CIO official, as well as lieutenant governor of Pennsylvania, had received Lewis's blessing. Pennsylvania Republicans owed their victories to a resentful, mobilized electorate in the rural Protestant districts. Low voter turnout in the urban Catholic wards finished off the Democrats.[66]

There were any number of political implications stemming from the 1938 elections, among them the fact that the new, more conservative Congress would pass no additional reform legislation. Many commentators, however, missed the most important implication for the future of American politics. Given that the states had not reapportioned their local and federal legislative districts since 1910, urban Catholics had fewer representatives than rural Protestants. Democrats were, therefore, at a disadvantage in trying to capture state legislatures. That fact of life also made it difficult for New Deal Democrats to control their state congressional delegations since, once again, there were more rural than urban House seats. This meant that the urban Democrats, and particularly the CIO, had to concentrate their energies in seizing the White House and—through presidential appointment—the federal judiciary.[67]

Roosevelt obliged his urban political base by expanding the power of the federal bureaucracy. After 1938, CIO leaders would look more to Washington than to their localities for assistance. The federal government, as a liberal Democratic preserve, would increasingly usurp the power of the states and their less liberal officials. American legislative bodies, from Congress to the White House, and the Supreme Court, were becoming hostile camps representing different religious and class interests. Expanding the authority of the federal government through Executive Order and the courts openly served the interests of New Deal constituencies. Conversely, calls for lower federal taxes and the return of authority from Washington to the states played to small-town conservatives who despised the New Deal.[68]

Both Roosevelt and Lewis advocated federal solutions to economic and social problems without realizing that if the government failed to cure every ill known to man, the Democratic Party ran the risk of alienating its constituencies and discrediting reform. Phil Murray and other Catholic Pittsburghers argued that if social reform was to have some chance of success, then cooperation among all parties was required at the local level. That meant making overtures to Protestant Republicans. Moreover, a government that accrued power in order to promote good, would, given human frailties, ultimately produce evil. The secular federal government operated in a moral vacuum, waiting for the ideology of the moment to give it direction. As Hensler and Rice warned, if the CIO bound itself too closely to Washington, it could cease to be an agency to promote the common good. Organized labor would then be just one of many competing interest groups seeking selfish gain at the expense of other citizens.[69]

The concerns raised by the Catholic activists were well-founded. However, as the CIO held its national convention in Pittsburgh, the long-term survival of organized labor appeared in doubt. Many CIO officials believed that there was little choice but to bind labor more closely to the federal bureaucracy. There were additional concerns that promoted a general spirit of rancor among the CIO delegates. (The rancor was unfortunate since the November 1938 convention marked the CIO's official split with the AFL and the adoption of a new name—the Congress of Industrial Organizations.) An embittered Thomas Kennedy called AFL president William Green "an unmitigated liar." The fact that so many AFL officials had gone before the Dies Committee to brand the CIO as Communist-inspired rankled the defeated gubernatorial candidate. Lewis took to the podium and, ignoring the events of the past two years, cried, "The citadel of non-unionism . . . is today almost completely organized."[70]

At Murray's request, Father Rice opened the convention with a prayer that contained a plea for reconciliation as well as a call to arms:

> Oh! Lord and Savior, Jesus Christ. You were once a worker Yourself. We beseech You to bless and prosper those assembled in this convention. May they, leaders of the workingmen, be given the strength to carry on the struggle for justice and security, in spite of overwhelming odds. Give to the ideals that sway this group a successful carrying out. Grant to American labor enlightenment, strength, and unity. Especially we pray for unity that the great labor movement of this country may march forward as one to victory. Grant it victory we pray, for labor's cause is Your cause. May it prosper and carry on its valiant struggle to gain its ends which are the ends of justice, Americanism, and Christianity.[71]

The *Pittsburgh Catholic* editorialized that the CIO "deserves something better than the snarling criticisms to which it has been subjected in to many quarters. . . . It is time to forget the sneers and caviling of those whose motives are anything but disinterested." The editors of the *Bulletin Index* concurred. Prior to the CIO convention, the society newspaper wrote that "SWOC has earned a wholesome public respect for its scrupulous observance of contracts, and notably for its smooth relations with U.S. Steel. Since no organization is much better than its leadership, the half-million members of SWOC owe much of their reputation to the intelligent council and direction of such men as silver-mane, scholarly Chairman Philip Murray and rangy, deep-voiced Eastern Regional Director Clinton S. Golden."[72]

There were other Pittsburghers who were harsher in their assessment of Catholics, the New Deal, and organized labor. Charles Bruce Swift, a Duquesne Light Sub-Station Operator and an officer of the Nazi-inspired Silver Shirts, convened an interesting meeting in November. Gathering thirty prominent businessmen at the Pittsburgh Athletic Club, Swift contended that

the "liberal priests" who sponsored community forums on social reform created "a stamping ground for these damnable Reds." According to the *Bulletin Index*, Swift thought that "the best way to uphold 'Americanism' and
the U.S. Constitution is by driving Jews, Catholics, Negroes, and Reds out
of government and industry." More discreet, Westinghouse executive Andrew Wells Robertson journeyed to Cincinnati where he informed the city's
Chamber of Commerce that "The Rule of Minorities" was destroying America. Catholic, Jewish, and black supporters of the New Deal, Robertson indicated, were driving up the taxes of Protestant businessmen. Implicitly,
Robertson raised the question as to whether such people should be allowed
to vote.[73]

Although Dorothy Day had long argued that the path to social justice did
not run through the secular political arena, she did take note of the midterm
elections. More in sorrow than in anger, Day wrote her eulogy for Governor
Frank Murphy and other defeated friends of social justice:

> By moral force rather than by armed force, these men prevented vio-
> lence and bloodshed and stood out not only against the industrialist
> but against a campaign of public vilification and condemnation. Be-
> cause they resolutely refused to use armed guards against the work-
> ers, and insisted upon arbitration—because they upheld human rights
> above property rights—they were termed spineless and yellow-liver,
> not only by atheistic capitalists but by many of their fellow Catholics.
> Their courage and leadership in public life have been an inspiration
> to others and a message of hope to the workers. May God raise up
> other men like them.[74]

Nineteen thirty-eight had been a year of recrimination. A center of the industrial union movement, as well as an important source of New Deal voters, Pittsburgh was caught up in the bitter battle among conservatives,
Communists, and religious reformers. Hensler, Rice, and Bishop Boyle placed
the moral authority of the Catholic Church behind the steel workers and the
CIO. Arrayed against them were red-baiting corporation executives, angry
Marxists, and, to their great sorrow, elements inside the Church who opposed social reconstruction. If not for their support of Murray, the political
reaction against organized labor would have been entirely successful. Certainly, if not for Hensler, Rice, and other Catholic activists, the Communist
Party might have made greater gains in the CIO. Pittsburgh's Catholic clergy
and laity offered Christian democracy as an alternative to Marxism, laissez-
faire capitalism, and the centralized State. Given the far-ranging scope of

their vision of social justice, Hensler and Rice were fighting on several fronts at once. It would have been hard to have found a social movement at any other period in American history that counted among its foes the likes of Martin Dies, Harold Ickes, James Matles, Fulton Sheen, and Ernest Weir.

While struggling for the soul of organized labor, Murray, David Lawrence, and their clergy allies tried to keep anti-Communist Catholics from abandoning the New Deal coalition. They were largely successful on that score in 1938, but the left-leaning elements within the CIO and the Roosevelt administration were making their organizing efforts among Catholics difficult. Lawrence, Murray, and Rice also failed to persuade small-town Protestants and the middle class that Catholic Democrats were not their enemies. By the end of 1938, the nation seemed bent upon polarization. The legislative prospects for a New Deal reform agenda that would be consistent with the teachings of Leo XIII and Pius XI were dim. Pittsburgh's Catholic social activists had reached an impasse and the cause of social reconstruction appeared lost.

It was evident to Pittsburgh reformers that few Americans—Catholic, Protestant, or Jew—were willing to see themselves as inseparable members of the Mystical Body of Christ. Cultural and class divisions ran too deep. America appeared destined to remain a profoundly disunited nation. Meanwhile, Adolf Hitler and Joseph Stalin were to discover that, as Rice contended, they did have much in common. . . .

# 6

# Confirmation

## Catholic Reformers Confront the Rise of Fascism and the Approach of World War II, 1939–1941

New Dealers in Pittsburgh and Washington learn that the rise of European fascism and Soviet Communism threaten the viability of their electoral coalition. As Bishop Hugh Boyle and fathers James Cox, Carl Hensler, and Charles Owen Rice quickly discover, ethnic-based divisions over political and military developments in Europe threaten the viability of the New Deal coalition. Such divisions also provide anti-Semites like Father Charles Coughlin with yet another opportunity to red-bait SWOC and the CIO. Despite deeply held isolationist beliefs, Pittsburgh's Catholic activists conclude that the United States would have to stop Hitler without, at the same time, helping Stalin. Against this backdrop, Phil Murray, with assistance from Rice and his clerical and lay allies, wrests control of the CIO from a Roosevelt-hating, isolationist-minded John L. Lewis.

Catholic activists recognized that the new Congress would not support social reform. Indeed, conservative Democrats and Republicans hoped to eliminate the WPA and red-bait the CIO to death. On the defensive, Rice and Murray were determined not to yield. At a January 1939 meeting of the Catholic Radical Alliance, Rice minced few words:

Certain legislative and journalistic giants at large today seem to think that the fundamental sickness of the system can somehow be cured by vague shouts for a balanced budget, and very lame and oh, so very, very tiresome jokes about WPA workers sleeping on shovels. Nothing constructive, that I know of, has come from such people in the way of suggestions or plans to cure the deep-seated ills that make unemployment.[1]

Addressing the Catholic Men's Club of St. Patrick's parish in Canonsburg, Pennsylvania, Murray vigorously defended the CIO. Murray, however, rebuked workers who did not combat Communist influence in the CIO:

It was a stupendous task to revamp the principles of organized labor and spread it to the field not enjoying its benefits before, and of course there have been great difficulties and some mistakes. But the charge of "Communism" is intended solely to discredit the movement. Is it Communistic to ask a voice in affairs affecting millions of working people? We do not ask the impossible. We merely ask for a better distribution of the profits which accrue from labor.

If Communism or any other evil philosophy creeps into any group it is because the membership fails to take the interest it should and allows a minority to assume control. Lethargy and indifference are the great dangers to the labor movement as they are to any other cause seeking to reform unjust conditions.[2]

Pittsburgh's labor priests spared no effort to energize the union faithful. In May, Rice returned to Etna's Croatian Hall, where he exhorted SWOC to continue its forward march. At the state CIO convention shortly afterward, the priest brought his angry Irish brogue to Harrisburg: "If the reactionaries have their way, and they seem sure to have it, the sun will once more be blotted out and we shall sink into the miasma of injustice and terrorism, money, position, and privilege will rule in this unhappy state." Sharing Rice's concern, Bishop Boyle announced that the diocese intended to sponsor a summer school on social action and labor organizing. Monsignor John Ryan, Bishop Robert Lucey of Amarillo, and Father Joseph Lonergan of Clairton would be among the participants.[3]

If abandoned by Congress, and held at arm's length by President Roosevelt, Pittsburgh's labor priests stood loyally by the steel workers. SWOC's leaders responded in kind. On February 26, priests and workers gathered at Pittsburgh's Central Catholic High School to pay tribute to Pius XI. Patrick Fagan and David McDonald joined Bishop Boyle in praising the recently deceased pope. As McDonald observed, Pius XI "alone of all men, gave the world a practical program through which industry and the working men and women can solve the all-absorbing economic problems which beset them. The social encyclicals of Pius XI will always be a source of guidance and inspiration to those of us who believe with him that the economic life and the moral life are inseparably interwoven." A few months later, McDonald and Fagan attended the Second National Catholic Social Action Conference. At the Cleveland gathering, McDonald embraced the teachings of Leo XIII and Pius XI while accusing domestic Communists and Nazis of being atheistic and un-American.[4]

Engaged in a desperate battle to save the CIO from conservatives and Communists, the Catholic reformers discovered that there were additional controversies that hobbled the cause of social justice. In 1936, Spanish liberals and socialists, though receiving less than half of the general election vote, forged a coalition government. Conservatives were too sharply divided to put together a cabinet. Spanish militants, who regarded the reform-minded Madrid government as overly cautious, declared war on industrialists, large land owners, conservative peasants, and Catholic clergy. In all, Spanish radicals would execute 6,832 priests and 283 nuns. Outraged, General Francisco Franco led an uprising against a Madrid government that he felt had not done enough to curb the violence-prone Left. Seeing an opening, agents from the Soviet intelligence apparatus, the NKVD, flocked to Spain. Working closely with the NKVD, the Comintern recruited thirty thousand Communists from Europe and America to suppress the "Nationalist" rebellion. Stalin also sent 900 tanks, 1,550 artillery pieces, and 1,000 aircraft and Russian pilots to assist the Spanish "Loyalists." In turn, Hitler and Mussolini supplied Franco with fifty thousand troops. Franco had plunged Spain into a civil war, while enabling Stalin and Hitler to test their military equipment in combat.[5]

Three thousand Americans, among them Steve Nelson, joined the Spanish-bound Abraham Lincoln and the George Washington brigades. Meanwhile the Comintern's allies, from author Ernest Hemingway to Hollywood scriptwriter Lillian Hellman, depicted the Spanish tragedy as a glorious war against Nazism. Prominent Protestant intellectuals concurred. John Dewey of Columbia University, and Reinhold Niebuhr of Princeton's Union Theological Seminary, castigated the Nationalists and urged Roosevelt to assist the Loyalists. Interior Secretary Harold Ickes confided to friends that the Vatican sympathized with the Nationalists because, like Hitler, the Church had a reactionary political agenda. Eleanor Roosevelt was an equally fervent supporter of Madrid. Indeed, with her brother Hall, she sought to ship 150 military aircraft to Spain. Her plan violated the 1935 Neutrality Act, which forbade Americans to provide weapons to combatants. Fortunately for her husband, Congress did not find out about Eleanor's covert operation. Eleanor Roosevelt appeared not to realize the danger ethnic nationalism and religious conflicts like the Spanish Civil War posed to the viability of the New Deal coalition. Catholic reformers and politicians, on the other hand, were increasingly alarmed by overseas developments.[6]

Congressman John McCormack of Boston, and his cardinal, William O'Connell, urged President Roosevelt to ignore the Loyalists. Nevada senator Pat McCarran, a fellow Irishman, helped McCormack keep other Democrats in line. This was not easy. Liberal and Communist intellectuals inside and outside government regarded the Spanish Civil War as a struggle between the anti-Semitic, antidemocratic Right and the progressive Left. Anyone who supported Franco, therefore, was a fascist, and anyone who charged that Spanish radicals had slaughtered thousands of Catholic clergy and leveled hundreds of churches was a liar. Since American Catholics were four times more likely to support Franco than were Protestants, it followed that they must be fascists and liars. This was the line *The New Republic* and *The Nation* had taken. American Communists, although implacable enemies of the Church, had decided after the outbreak of the civil war to mute their rhetoric. The Comintern wished to enhance its position within the CIO and the federal government. If Hitler became too powerful, Stalin would need all of the friends he could get.[7]

Recognizing that Catholics constituted a quarter of the Democratic vote, Roosevelt behaved in a more politically astute (or cowardly) manner than his wife. In 1937, he visited George Cardinal Mundelein in Chicago and delivered an address on foreign policy. The president's Chicago speech reassured Catholics that he had no intention of lifting his embargo on the shipment of weapons to the Loyalists. "America hates war," Roosevelt said, in his most soothing voice. "America hopes for peace. Therefore, America actively engages in the search for peace." Supplying weapons to Madrid, the president argued, would not bring peace to a troubled world. Ironically, the well-intentioned Spanish reformers Eleanor Roosevelt and Harold Ickes wanted to save from Franco were marked for death by the Soviet NKVD. American Catholic leaders insisted that lifting the embargo would only benefit Stalin's side. According to them, there was no democracy to be preserved in Spain.[8]

While many American Catholics regarded the Loyalists as murderous atheists, the *Pittsburgh Courier* took a different tack. In the fall of 1937, the *Courier* proudly recorded the exploits of Ralph Thornton, a black Hill District youth who had become an antifascist machine gunner in Spain. One reporter compared black soldiers in the Lincoln and Washington brigades to "Nat Turner . . . who fought for democracy against slavery and oppression [in the nineteenth century]." Another Hill District youth, Jimmy Peck, was one of four black aviators fighting for the Loyalists. The *Courier* noted that Peck had received an officer's commission. Unlike the United States Army, the Loyalist forces did not practice racial discrimination.[9]

The Catholic Radical Alliance expressed its dismay with the media treatment of the Spanish Civil War. Even though the secular media were largely anti-Communist, they depended upon a handful of correspondents for their overseas information. A number of these reporters, notably Walter Duranty of *The New York Times*, were Communist sympathizers. To ensure that non-Catholics understood the issues, and knew that the League Against War and Fascism—which staged protests on behalf of the Loyalists—was a Communist front, Hensler and Rice dogged the leftist organization. At local Communist rallies in 1937, the Catholic Radical Alliance carried placards reading "We Are Opposed to War, Fascism, and Communism." The activists also passed out sharply worded leaflets:

> The Popular Front in the United States is a Communist device. It started up after the "Reds" got the life scared out of them by the way things turned out in Germany. They switched over night from an active contempt of the labor movement and all things not-ultra orthodox, Communistically speaking, to a sudden love for the labor movement and labor leaders. Like silly fools, droves of "liberals" have fallen for this act. In their respect for the noble Russian experiment they have lost their heads.
>
> That sort of thing has brought a vaguely fascist reaction already. Don't you people see that you are endangering every progressive movement, that you are risking the work of generations of sincere workers for liberty and social justice? The closer "liberalism" unites with Communism (and the stronger Communism, therefore, becomes) the stronger fascism grows.[10]

At its November 1937 national convention in Pittsburgh, the League Against War and Fascism, hoping to sound less leftist, changed its name. It was now known as the American League for Peace and Democracy. Some thirty-five hundred delegates came to the Iron City to listen to B. J. Hovde and theology professor Reinhold Niebuhr praise the Loyalists. According to Niebuhr, capitalist greed and democratic pandering to the masses hobbled American foreign policy.

A curious inhibition seems to prevent the so-called democratic powers from stopping fascist aggression. The reason for this is two-fold—
on the one hand the democratic powers are the great capitalistic
powers and the capitalist forces within these nations are less interested in the preservation of democracy than in the preservation of
capitalism.

On the other hand, insofar as these nations are democratic, their
statesmen are afraid to take the risks which they should take for fear
that the general electorate does not understand the necessity of these
risks.[11]

By 1939, Niebuhr had grown disillusioned with the Communist Party.
Harold Ickes, however, sent an effusive letter to the League for Peace and
Democracy on the occasion of its January 1939 national convention in Washington. The interior secretary praised the organization for its commitment
"to the policy of peace and the policy of democracy." Receiving an invitation
to join the League for Peace and Democracy, Patrick Fagan replied that he
would have "no dealings" with the organization. "What is the difference between a purge by Stalin, Hitler, or Mussolini?," Fagan asked. "They all stand
for slavery, terrorism, and murder." When Franco marched into Madrid in
the spring of 1939, the *Pittsburgh Catholic* breathed a sigh of relief.[12]

Although the majority of citizens did not wish to become involved in another European war, many Americans were not consistently isolationist. An-
glophiles, blacks, Catholics, Communists, and Jews cheered some foreign
leaders and urged diplomatic action against others. Writing in 1939 on black
and white ethnic relations as they pertained to American foreign policy, two
academics made an arresting point:

The relationship of various American minorities to America's foreign
policies has, in fact, always been of great importance even in the time
of peace. America, being the haven of refuge for various social and
political malcontents, has also been the place whence these various
individuals and their organizations have directed their efforts either to
help the lot of the proponents of their cause at home or to help the
struggle against their opponents.[13]

When Mussolini invaded Ethiopia in 1935, the *Courier* took offense.
Ethiopia, after all, was an independent black nation situated among Europe's
African colonies. In turn, hundreds of Italian ethnics in Chicago sent their
gold wedding rings to Mussolini as a gesture of their support for the

Ethiopian expedition. Italian-Americans in New York hoped to give Mussolini $500,000 for medical supplies while fourteen children from Pittsburgh made a special trip to meet the dictator. The outcome of the Ethiopian conflict was never in doubt. Spears and rifles were no match against airplanes and poison gas. Then again, it was difficult for many Americans to shed tears for Ethiopia. The *Courier* did not mention that Ethiopia practiced slavery, terrorized tribal minorities, and was by no stretch of the imagination a democracy. For all of that, though, Catholic reformers could only cringe whenever Italian-American priests praised Mussolini.[14]

While black and Italian leaders clashed over Ethiopia, Croatian-Americans were focusing their attention on Eastern Europe. By 1939, Croatians on both sides of the Atlantic were calling for independence from their Serbian rulers. In Pittsburgh, a powerful ethnic lobby, the Defenders of Croatia, maintained a steady stream of anti-Serbian publications. Ante Doshen, the publisher of Pittsburgh's Croatian nationalist newspaper, the *American Slav*, looked upon Nazi Germany as a potential liberator of the homeland. Maxo Vanka's plans for additional murals at St. Nicholas left no doubt as to his feelings about the accelerating dissolution of Yugoslavia. His new Pittsburgh portraits would include an angel wearing a gas mask, the Madonna fending off a charging soldier, and rows of graves. A civil war was brewing in Yugoslavia. Tragically, some Croatians—the so-called Ustashi—felt so repulsed by the Serbians that they were willing to welcome Hitler as an ally.[15]

The prospects for Czechoslovakia appeared to be no more promising. In 1918, Slovak and Czech delegates had convened at the Pittsburgh Moose Hall on Penn Avenue. At that meeting, Slovaks and Czechs proclaimed their independence from the Austro-Hungarian Empire. Thomas Masaryk, the future president of Czechoslovakia, agreed to what became known as the Pittsburgh Pact, which recognized Slovakian autonomy. Pittsburgh's Slovaks, at great personal sacrifice, then handed Masaryk one million dollars. As Slovak nationalist and labor priest Clement Hrtanek recalled, Masaryk and his aide, Edward Benes, repudiated the Pittsburgh Pact. Czechs dominated the republic economically, militarily, and politically. There was no Slovakian autonomy. In 1933, Hrtanek argued that Czechs and Slovaks were incompatible. "The Slovak soul was always, and is," Hrtanek wrote in the *Pittsburgh Catholic*, "deeply religious, insisting upon accepting the faith, while the Czech soul is very tellingly inclined to [atheism] and rationalism."[16] Hrtanek's hatred of Masaryk was boundless.

> Slovaks, as a deeply religious nation, would not willingly join the irreligious . . . Czechs and be directly governed by Thomas Masaryk,

Fig. 10.   Father Clement Hrtanek of Homestead. Labor priest and Slovak nationalist. (Courtesy of the Diocese of Pittsburgh Archives.)

who betrayed his own Slovak origins . . . to become a Czech; who left the Catholic Church to become a Protestant and finally a superior in the chambers of the Free Masons; who declared that Rome must be judged and condemned; who compared the Catholic Church to a hydra, whose head must be crushed; whose parliament outlawed the existence of God. Would the Slovaks have suspected that Masaryk . . . would become such a capital deceiver and traitor . . . they would never have agreed to have their sovereign nation and their Slovak Fatherland become a part of the new Czecho-Slovak Republic.

As a leading light in the First Catholic Slovak Union of America, the National Catholic Slovak Federation, and the Slovak League of America, when Hrtanek spoke, Slovak-Americans listened.[17]

Hrtanek gave a hearty welcome to his cousin, Monsignor Joseph Tiso, who came to Pittsburgh on two occasions—in 1936 and 1937. A former health minister in the Czechoslovakian government, Tiso was looking for financial and political support in his effort to establish a Slovakian republic. In 1938, Father Hrtanek and thirty thousand Slovak-Americans gathered in Pittsburgh's Kennywood Amusement Park. The Slovaks demanded that Benes, who was now the president of Czechoslovakia, abandon his claims to their homeland. They found an ally in Hitler who wished to annex Czechoslovakia's Sudeten province and acquire its ethnic German population and weapons industry. Benes resisted Hitler's demands, regarding them as a prelude to the dismemberment of Czechoslovakia. To Benes's dismay, his English and French allies had no stomach for a fight. They compelled Benes to accede to Hitler's territorial claims. The *Pittsburgh Catholic* praised the settlement that the British negotiated with Hitler at Munich. As British Prime Minister Neville Chamberlain exclaimed, he had attained "peace in our time."[18]

The Sudetenland crisis gave Monsignor Tiso his opening. On October 31, 1938, Tiso announced that he was now the prime minister of an autonomous Slovakian government. His first action as prime minister was to outlaw the Communist Party and to prohibit the importation of Czech newspapers. The Czechs chose not to recognize Slovakian autonomy. That impasse ended dramatically when Hitler occupied Prague in March 1939. Hitler granted Tiso's request for independence and pledged that Germany would protect Slovakia from its enemies. Tiso did not spell out to his people exactly what Hitler expected the Slovakian government to do in return.[19]

Angered by the support that Slovak-Americans had given to Tiso, the former president of Czechoslovakia came to Pittsburgh. Benes tore into Hrtanek.

Speaking at the Syria Mosque in Oakland, Benes vowed that Slovakia would rejoin the Czech nation once Hitler had departed from the scene. Unwilling to admit that his cousin had made a bargain with the devil, Hrtanek called Benes "a Marxist-Communist political ally with Stalin." The Slovak League of America issued a rousing denunciation of the Czech:

> Dr. Edward Benes is working hand in hand with Communists, and known Communist agitators and propagandists are also aiding his present movement; Dr. Edward Benes himself declared in Chicago that "the only source of true democracy today is Russia." We, not only as Slovak sons and daughters, but above all as Americans, believing in our American democracy, cannot agree or cooperate with the movement of Dr. Edward Benes, who, while enjoying the privileges and protections of our American democracy sees the only true democracy in Communist Russia. We do not wish to have such a democracy in the United States and we certainly do not wish it for our brethren in Slovakia.[20]

The new pope, Pius XII, was distressed by the Slovak situation. *Time* magazine reported that the elevation of a monsignor to the presidency of a nation—"an event believed to be without precedent—was received with anything but rejoicing." Pius XII had already rebuked the Nazi regime when Tiso accepted a military decoration from Hitler in 1939. Beyond distancing the Church from Tiso, however, the Vatican did not condemn the Slovak regime. Although Pius XII disliked Communism and fascism, he could understand why Slovaks preferred the latter as the seemingly less objectionable form of government. Bishop Boyle was in a similar bind. The Pittsburgh bishop detested Nazism, but did not wish to alienate Slovak parishioners by forcing Hrtanek to curb his nationalist prejudices. Worse, important Slovak labor priests, from Joseph Altany in Aliquippa, to Michael Yesko in Brownsville, followed Hrtanek's lead. A breach with Hrtanek possibly meant an ethnic schism in the Church, the steel workers' union, and the Democratic Party.[21]

Father James Cox discovered for himself just how sensitive Boyle was to Hrtanek's feelings. Having played no role in organizing SWOC, and regarding the CIO as too leftist, Cox tried to re-establish his credentials as a friend of labor in 1939. A man with a good heart, but who sometimes exercised poor judgment, he accepted an overture from the International Workers Order. Although he condemned the CIO for employing Communist organizers, Cox inexplicably allied himself with the party's chief front organization in the steel district. The IWO, amazed at its good fortune, announced that the priest would appear at a rally with New York's leftist congressman, Vito Marcantonio. Hrtanek sent a pointed letter to Bishop Boyle:

> Our Slovak priests have been fighting this spread of Communism among our people. I have been doing it for some time. Now they spread their counter claims that we do not know anything: that Father Cox is the only friend of the poor people; that he is with the IWO; that he is going to speak for them on Labor Day.
>
> I protest against this kind of activity of Father Cox. Certainly he must know that the IWO is out and out Communistic. How can he, therefore, back them up?

Boyle ordered Cox to avoid IWO functions.[22]

Significantly, Boyle did not rebuke Cox. His note to Cox, which he attached to Hrtanek's letter, expressed a spirit of exasperation rather than condemnation. Clearly, the bishop was amazed at Cox's lapse of good sense, but he also knew that Hrtanek was on dangerous grounds. Although unwilling to confront the Homestead priest, Boyle did not want the public to think that the American Church had any use for Germany. In June 1939, he gave financial and moral support to the United Jewish Appeal for Refugees and Overseas Relief. A few months earlier, Boyle and the other leaders of the National Catholic Welfare Conference issued a "Condemnation of Bigotry." Quoting Pius XI, the bishops argued that, "It is not possible for Christians to take part in anti-Semitism." Meanwhile, John Brophy and the editors of *The Commonweal* and *The Catholic Worker* joined the national Committee of Catholics to Fight Anti-Semitism.[23]

Of great concern to Brophy and Boyle were the anti-Semitic activities of Father Charles Coughlin. A political cipher since 1936, Coughlin had recently expanded his following by waving the banner of isolationism. Anti-Semitism bound Coughlin's movement together. When Father Denis Fahey wrote an anti-Semitic book, *The Rulers of Russia*, Coughlin distributed the screed in the United States. According to Fahey, Communism was a Jewish conspiracy. Monsignor John Ryan of the Catholic University rebutted Fahey's "scholarship" and chastised Coughlin for spreading racist propaganda. Cardinal Mundelein, in December 1938, had informed a national radio audience that Coughlin did not represent the sentiments of the American Catholic Church. The *Pittsburgh Catholic*, worried about the two hundred Coughlin supporters in the city, editorialized in 1938 and 1939 that anyone who followed the Detroit priest was not a true Christian. Pittsburgh's Coughlinites responded to such criticism by attacking several Jewish shopkeepers and vandalizing a theater showing the antifascist film "Confessions of a Nazi Spy."[24]

Cox found Coughlin's politics so objectionable that he could not remain silent—not that discretion was one of his personality traits. In 1932, while on a religious pilgrimage in Italy, Cox had a chance to meet Mussolini. When American reporters asked Cox for his opinion of the dictator, the Pittsburgher bemoaned the degradation and the loss of human liberty which Mussolini had inflicted upon Italy. *The Christian Century* expressed amazement that a Catholic priest would make such statements. Seven years later, Cox delivered an address in the Dormont, Pennsylvania, Methodist Church. In a spirit of ecumenical harmony that would have been unheard of at the beginning of the Depression, Cox regaled the Protestant audience with his talk on Charles Coughlin, "Hitler's Hatchet Man!":

> *While as Catholics we cannot do anything* to stop Father Coughlin, you may rest assured that all Catholic people and priests are not in sympathy or accord with him. In my humble opinion his attacks upon Jews are abhorrent to everyone who believes in the Fatherhood of God and the Brotherhood of Man. To my way of thinking, it is very bad taste for a priest, a man of God, who preaches love of God and love of neighbor, to either directly or indirectly foster hate on the basis of race, color, or religion. If Father Coughlin is right then the Ku Klux Klan is right and if the Ku Klux Klan is right about the Jews, it is also right about the Catholics and colored people and Father Coughlin thereby condemns himself and all that he represents. . . .
>
> As a Catholic priest I am grieved and humiliated that another Catholic priest is in the vanguard of this Bigot Brigade. He is profaning his pulpit by preaching the pagan doctrine of anti-Semitism. For my part, I choose today to cry out against the sorry spectacle of the Detroit priest, ordained to teach the Love of God, engaged each Sunday over a radio hookup in parroting poisonous Nazi propaganda and huckstering the heresies of Hitler. A Catholic priest become a Storm Trooper! A Coughlin become a Hitler hatchet man![25]

Cox's address, printed in pamphlet form and distributed nationally, generated heated mail. A Wisconsin Catholic accused Cox of promoting Communism. "Are you afraid," she wrote, "[that] the Communists are going to get the upper hand here and that if you side with them and consciously or unconsciously do their bidding you will be spared the persecution which will follow?" Obviously, this Coughlin follower concluded, Cox had swallowed "New Deal and Communist propaganda." An irate Catholic in Pittsburgh sent a blistering letter to Bishop Boyle. She described Coughlin as "an inspiration to all of us. . . . He is the greatest and only teacher of the Church doctrine on the social order of Christ." Given that, she wondered, how could Boyle permit Cox to give more speeches criticizing Coughlin? Worse, how could Boyle then allow Cox to speak on religious tolerance "at a Jewish synagogue"?[26]

The most interesting letters Boyle received came from Coughlin and the Vatican's Apostolic Delegate in Washington, Archbishop Amleto Giovanni Cicognani. According to the Michigan priest, Cox was receiving payments "for the work the Jew wanted him to do on Father Coughlin." Regarding himself as a maligned crusader for social justice, Coughlin threatened to produce documentation proving that Cox was part of a Jewish conspiracy to destroy his reputation. Hoping to end this embarrassing public spat, Cicognani demanded that Boyle punish Cox. Boyle pleaded ignorance but assured the clergymen that he would look into the matter. The Pittsburgh bishop, however, never disciplined Cox for speaking ill of a fellow priest. Boyle also waited nearly four months before responding to the Apostolic Delegate's letter. (By the end of 1939 the Pittsburgh branch of Coughlin's Christian Front fell apart. Pittsburgh's Catholic reformers had stymied the Coughlinites.)[27]

While Cox took on Coughlin, Rice sought to circumvent an anti-Semitic backlash among Catholics. First, he planted the support of the Association of Catholic Trade Unionists behind anti-Communist Jews. At labor rallies and on the radio, Rice emphasized that the battle within labor was between democracy and Communism, not Catholicism and Judaism. (Some Catholics characterized the ideological strife within the labor movement as a struggle between "Isador Communist" and "Joe McUnion." This kind of talk disturbed Hensler and Rice.) Second, in August 1939 Rice gave a special radio address on anti-Semitism.

> Communism is a great stick to beat the Jews. I know from my own experience in labor that the strongest fighters against Communism are Jews. Yet these valiant fighters for Americanism are themselves accused of being Communists, because they have Jewish names. It is stupid and laughable but very dangerous and harmful. . . .
>
> It is poppy-cock to prate of the Jews having killed Christ. We killed Christ, our sins did it. The Jew has no monopoly on sin and has no monopoly on the guilt for Christ's death. Of all the sins that tortured Christ on the cross, be it noted, among the most excruciating were

the sins of hatred and intolerance perpetuated upon His people in His name.[28]

In 1939, anti-Semitism could be found just about everywhere, from WASP-ish officials in the U.S. State Department to Father Coughlin. Following Stalin's directives to forge a Popular Front against Hitler, the Communists branded many isolationists and peace groups as anti-Semitic. Certainly a number of isolationists were anti-Semites who rejected any efforts to coop-erate with the Soviet Union in containing Nazism. They made much of the American Jews who urged President Roosevelt to challenge Hitler. The over-whelming majority of American Jews were not Marxists. However, many Jews appreciated the fact that the Communists, unlike the Democrats and the Republicans, were openly condemning Hitler. That development en-couraged Coughlin to charge that the Jews were seeking to involve America in a war against Germany.[29]

American Catholics were more isolationist than Jews. Interestingly, within Catholic ranks, ethnic Germans and Irish expressed the greatest loathing for the Soviet Union, as well as the strongest desire to avoid war. (They also cared little for Great Britain—America's likely ally in a war against fascism.) Although a few Irish and German ethnics supported Coughlin, most believed that American military intervention would strengthen Stalin's position in Central Europe. There were other Catholics whose religious principles, rather than their anti-Communism, led them to oppose American military inter-vention. The Catholic Worker movement and the Catholic Association for In-ternational Peace—the latter established in 1927 by Monsignor Ryan—were leery of foreign entanglements. By the late 1930s, as Germany, Italy, and Japan pillaged their neighbors, the Catholic Association for International Peace shed its isolationist coloration. The Catholic Worker movement, on the other hand, discerned no transcendent moral reason to abandon its paci-fist principles.[30]

Rice and Hensler belonged to both the Catholic Worker movement and the Catholic Association for International Peace. As the Depression decade progressed, they found themselves torn between their pacifism and growing fear of Hitler. In 1933, Hensler wrote a column for the *Pittsburgh Catholic* in which he contended that "if and when a majority of the people of all na-tions really want peace, their rulers will not be long in setting up the ma-chinery needed to secure and maintain world peace." Sadly, Hensler observed, most people do not want peace. "Narrow patriotism and excessive nation-alism are rampant in every nation," the Pittsburgher sighed. "The interna-tional munitions-makers are busy behind the scenes, and the influence they exert on governments, aided by Jingo newspapers, can only be guessed, never accurately gauged." Five years later, the Catholic Radical Alliance held a large peace rally. Hensler and Rice called for an embargo on the sale of American weapons overseas and opposed the extension of loans to nations at war.[31]

In 1939, the Catholic Radical Alliance was urging the adoption of a twenty-second amendment to the Constitution that would allow Americans to vote directly on whether or not to go to war. The Ludlow Amendment, named after Louis Ludlow, a Democratic representative from Indiana, would strip Congress and the president of their authority to declare war. By a large margin, Pittsburgh's Catholic activists endorsed the amendment. They then accused unnamed federal government officials of trying to involve America in a second world war. Although Roosevelt had quietly lobbied defense-minded Democrats and Republicans to defeat the Ludlow initiative, the president realized that Americans would not tolerate an aggressive foreign policy. According to various public opinion polls, Americans despised the fascist dictators, yet they did not want their president expressing that sentiment aloud. As subsequent polls confirmed, four-fifths of the American electorate wanted peace at any price—short of a direct attack on the United States.[32]

As Hensler and Rice feared, World War II came, ushered in by the Nazi invasion of Poland in September 1939. To the surprise of many Popular Front advocates in America, but not to Catholics, the Soviet Union and Nazi Germany announced that they had signed a nonaggression pact. Stalin quickly invaded eastern Poland, Estonia, Latvia, and Lithuania. Britain and France declared war on Hitler but chose to ignore Soviet aggression. Thousands of Americans abandoned the Communist Party's Popular Front organizations. They no longer believed that the Soviet Union was a defender of exploited people. The Catholic Radical Alliance, its view of Hitler and Stalin as interchangeable tyrants seemingly confirmed, restated the desire not to become involved in a war. Paradoxically, the group also warned that "if Russia and Germany, avowedly anti-Christian, take control of most of Europe the world will be facing a real disaster." On September 4, Rice gave an impassioned radio address on WWSW.

> In order to maintain our neutrality we must remain even mentally neutral. Propaganda will be poured out upon us as it was in the last war [by Britain]. Every effort will be made to induce war hysteria. We must remain aloof. This is an almost superhuman task. It must be done. If we permit our minds to be poisoned with hate we will be mentally and spiritually sick. We will be of no service in restoring sanity to the rest of the world.[33]

A few weeks later, Rice made a radio broadcast in which he praised the first encyclical written by Pius XII, *Darkness Over the Earth*. The pope called for an immediate peace settlement and condemned the totalitarian state. Earl Browder, the general secretary of the American Communist Party, ripped into Pius XII. He accused Pius XII of seeking to establish a Vatican dictatorship in America. The Communist Party that in August 1939 expressed its desire to work with American Catholics in the labor movement, and proclaimed its undying hatred of Hitler, had, one month later, changed its mind. American Communists openly reverted to the anti-Catholic and anticapitalist positions they had enunciated in 1932. Although Hensler and Rice had seen the Hitler-Stalin Pact as an inevitable union between atheistic tyrants, a number of Jewish leftists had not. They quit the party in disgust. Top-ranking Jewish Communists in the CIO like Lee Pressman, however, remained loyal to the party. While Germany may be an anti-Semitic, they argued, Britain and France were worse—they were capitalist.[34]

In December 1939, Stalin attacked Finland. Acting upon the advice of state and treasury department experts, Roosevelt did not break off diplomatic relations with the Soviet Union. Despite that, the American Youth Congress felt that Roosevelt was favoring Finland by loaning money to that war-shattered nation. At a February 1940 rally held on the South Lawn of the White House, the president lost his temper. He informed the students that he did not approve of Soviet aggression, even if he was unwilling to do anything to end it. The Communists booed him. Eleanor Roosevelt, who had arranged for the American Youth Congress to gather at the White House, was horrified. She invited the rally leaders to the Roosevelt home in Hyde Park and gave them a small donation. Then she informed the activists that she could no longer be associated with their cause since they appeared to be helping Hitler by supporting Stalin.[35]

While student radicals organized peace demonstrations, their counterparts in the labor movement were engaged in more serious work. From the moment World War II began, American Communists were leading strikes. The Comintern did not want the United States rearming, or supplying weapons to Great Britain and France. (Although Congress was isolationist, most Democrats and Republicans could see the wisdom of building up America's defenses and revising neutrality legislation in order to profit from Europe's misfortune.) Addressing the rank and file of the United Electrical Workers, the Longshoremen, and the United Automobile Workers, Communist union leaders said that it was time to strike for higher wages. After all, defense orders were ending the Great Depression. While loudly "antiwar," the Communists did not announce their other reason for calling the strikes. The prospect of additional wage increases led UAW members to disrupt aviation production in Flint, Los Angeles, and Milwaukee. Walter Reuther did not condone the UAW strikes of 1940 and 1941.[36]

Even though Phil Murray was enough of an Irish nationalist to keep Britain at arm's length, he was uncomfortable with the isolationist sentiments of John L. Lewis. The CIO president had few qualms about Europe being militarily dominated by Hitler and Stalin. (As Lewis said, "It would be a fearful thing if the British won this war.") Moreover, Lewis was supporting a strike wave larger than the one of 1937 and thereby undermining the defense of the democracies. In April 1940, Murray published an essay in *The Virginia Quarterly Review*. He argued that the CIO was a mature, socially responsible institution. Consequently, strikes were not necessary; labor and management could work out their problems at the negotiating table. With Morris Cooke, an engineer and director of Philadelphia's public works department, Murray elaborated upon his thoughts in *Organized Labor and Production: Next Steps in Industrial Democracy*. Published by Harper and Brothers in 1940, the book rejected class conflict, contended that democracy could not survive without the political participation of workers, and, indirectly, rebuked Lewis.[37]

The events of April and May 1940 forced Murray to walk away from Lewis. With superior planes and tanks, Hitler launched a stunning attack on Belgium, France, and the Netherlands. Within a few weeks, France surrendered, the British retreated to their island, and Italy entered the war on Hitler's side. Believing that his leadership was indispensable to the survival of America and Britain, Roosevelt announced that he would accept an unprecedented third term in office. The president declared a state of emergency, federalized state guard units, and convinced Congress to impose America's first peacetime draft. He also exhorted America to become "the arsenal of democracy." Lewis declared his support for the Republican presidential candidate and accused Roosevelt of warmongering. James Matles of the UE urged the union to go on record against conscription. The UE approved the antidraft resolution by a huge margin. Meanwhile, Ohio's Republican senator, Robert Taft, loudly championed the isolationist position. In 1940, as had been true in 1932, conservatives and Communists united to lambaste Roosevelt while Lewis campaigned for a Republican.[38]

Speaking on a national radio hook-up to thirty million Americans in October 1940, Lewis warned that Roosevelt, if he won reelection, would become a dictator bent upon turning America's sons into "cannon fodder." Dramatically, Lewis pledged to resign as CIO president in the event of a Roosevelt victory. Lewis then vowed that he would carry on his struggle from within the ranks of the United Mine Workers' union. Writing to a friend, SWOC education chief Elmer Cope gave his assessment of Lewis:

> I would say that in so far as the rank and file has an opinion it is not in agreement with Lewis. They are charitable toward Lewis by suggesting that the "Old Fox" has something up his sleeve and is attacking Roosevelt in order to assure the president of industrial support. They cannot believe that Lewis would fight the president who has "done so much for the workers." Of course this is tommyrot—Lewis is quite definitely after FDR's scalp. . . . Lewis is leading a left-wing fight against the New Deal, strange as it may seem. . . . He may be pointing action toward a third party political movement. . . . If this is the case, his methods may bring him to a halt with a much demoralized labor movement drifting away from him.[39]

Murray endorsed Roosevelt. Meanwhile David Lawrence sharpened his knives. The state party boss was still angry with Lewis for having intervened in the 1938 primaries. Lawrence had at least one other cause to detest Lewis. Addressing a group of Pennsylvania Republicans in Philadelphia, Lewis claimed that Roosevelt, rather than Hoover, deserved greater blame for creating the economic crisis of the 1930s. As a newly appointed national Democratic committeeman, Lawrence was not going to permit Lewis's candidate, Wendell Willkie, to win. It was close, but Roosevelt triumphed. A few days later, at the CIO's Atlantic City convention, Lewis made good his promise to resign. The leader did not, however, willingly pass the torch to Murray.[40]

Lewis's allies, as well as his relatives on the CIO payroll, exhorted the union delegates to retain their leader. One of Lewis's men paid a visit to Rice and warned him not to work against the CIO president. Unimpressed, Murray and Rice pushed through a resolution condemning "any policies emanating from totalitarianism, dictatorships, and foreign ideologies such as Nazism, Communism, and fascism." Stalin's pact with Hitler, and Communist-organized strikes in America, had led many CIO members to conclude that the Left cared little for their well-being. As Catholic labor activists contended, the Communists regarded the CIO as merely one of many devices to promote Soviet political and military ambitions.[41]

Not since Terence Powderly, chief of the ill-fated Knights of Labor, had a Catholic led such a great federation of unions. In terms of size and influence, the nineteenth-century Knights of Labor could not be classed with the CIO. Murray's elevation to the CIO presidency paved the way for other Catholics to help shape national economic and political policies. The *Pittsburgh Catholic* showed no restraint in praising Murray. He was, according to the diocesan newspaper, a man "inspired and fortified by a vigorous, unequivocal Catholic faith." Moreover, his "Irish ancestry" and hard life as a humble coal miner, the *Pittsburgh Catholic* observed, prepared him for the task of "consolidating labor's gains, of extending their benefits to all workers and to society in general, [and] of adjusting the new relation of equality between worker and employer so as to promote the welfare of all."[42]

Although Murray and Roosevelt's victories merited celebration, the thoughts of Catholic social activists in 1940 never strayed far from the European war. The National Catholic Welfare Conference had earlier issued a pastoral statement on peace, "Church and Social Order." Bishops Boyle and Alter, among other luminaries of the Church, contended that "the peace which all right-minded men so earnestly desire, must be based upon a comprehensive program of restoring Christ to His true and proper place in human society." There was a fatal flaw in the bishops' reasoning. While American businessmen and workers might be willing to recognize "the law of God," Hitler and Stalin were not. Given that reality, bringing about a just peace in Europe was impossible. The best course of action, then, would be to keep America out of the war and leave Western Europe to the tender mercies of Hitler. Archbishop Francis Beckman of Dubuque, Iowa, who was an ally of Father Coughlin, urged such a policy. Dorothy Day took the same position. Monsignor Barry O'Toole, formerly of the Pittsburgh Catholic Radical Alliance, and later a theology professor at the Catholic University, concurred with Day. He even went so far as to criticize military conscription since an expanded army might be used to fight Hitler.[43]

In contrast to Day and O'Toole, Hensler and Rice had modified their isolationist stances after the Nazi conquest of France. At Rice's prompting in July, the 350 members of the Pittsburgh ACTU endorsed Roosevelt's call to increase defense spending. Two months later, Phil Murray attended the ACTU's national convention in Cleveland. Murray informed his audience that America's war mobilization offered workers an opportunity to better their conditions while cooperating with management and the federal government in the preservation of democracy. Rice concurred with Murray, adding at a Pittsburgh ACTU meeting that the CIO could not tolerate leftist obstruction in the defense industry. "Loyalty to our country comes first," the priest argued, "and if necessary we must lean over backwards to purge Communists from the labor movement."[44]

Paradoxically, Rice and Hensler were destined to be purged themselves— from the Catholic Worker movement. The priests had been encouraging the laity in the Catholic Radical Alliance to discuss the European war. By the fall of 1940, the Pittsburghers had concluded that conscription and a defense build up were necessary. Many ACTU and Catholic Radical Alliance members refused to sell or purchase *The Catholic Worker*, regarding its pacifism as an invitation to invasion by Hitler. Willing to regard Communists as errant brothers, Day had no toleration for Catholic Workers who rejected her pacifist line. In September, the same month in which Coughlin's bishop ordered him to cease his anti-Semitic radio broadcasts, Day fired off a letter to Pittsburgh. She announced that the activist priests and laity were no longer to call themselves Catholic Workers.[45]

Having been expelled from the Catholic Worker movement, Hensler and Rice were welcomed into a new organization: the Committee to Defend America by Aiding the Allies. Founded in 1940, and led by Kansas newspaper publisher William Allen White, the Committee to Defend America had ten thousand members in the Pittsburgh District. Archbishops Lucey and Joseph Schrembs, as well as Monsignor Ryan, joined White's group. In February 1941, Ryan delivered a national radio address calling for Congress to pass legislation that would extend federal loans to the British. Beyond supporting the so-called Lend-Lease Act, Ryan took issue with Day, arguing that a war against Hitler would be morally just. More concretely, fourteen Pittsburgh priests became Army and Navy chaplains in April 1941. Father Cox, despite sore joints and advancing years, asked Boyle for permission to enlist, feeling that he should once again share the hardships that loomed ahead for the young men of his parish.[46]

The Committee to Defend America had a prize catch in Father Rice. As a fervent Irish nationalist, Rice had enormous credibility among Catholic Anglophobes. In a June 1941 radio address given on behalf of the Committee to Defend America, Rice explained why he supported aid to Britain:

> England for all her faults, and they are many, has stood for democracy and freedom in the main, albeit she has often been inconsistent and hypocritical. But under *her* freedom *has* progressed. Don't let us forget that there have not been lacking Englishmen in every generation who have loved Ireland and fought for her and for other victims of injustice.
>
> As for the Nazis—from my reading, from the writings of top-flight Nazis themselves, from personal contact with those who have seen and suffered at first hand, from scanning the anguished protests of two Popes and many cardinals and bishops, I am deeply and firmly

convinced that Nazism constitutes the most coldly efficient, heartless, and brutal enemy that democracy, freedom, and decency, and Christianity have ever known. Just as with marvelous efficiency and success the Nazis undermined the will and courage, and defeated the armies, of the continent of Europe—so they have proceeded and are proceeding to destroy religion and stamp out the image of God in the hearts of men under their sway.[47]

Hitler's attack on the Soviet Union on June 22 dramatically changed the nature of the war and placed American interventionists in an awkward position. Roosevelt gave lend-lease credits to Stalin and privately warned Pius XII not to oppose U.S. aid to the Soviet Union. The president also urged the Soviet Union's American ambassador to publicize the many ways in which Stalin defended religious freedom at home and abroad. Roosevelt made it a point at a press conference to quote from the 1936 Soviet Constitution which guaranteed freedom of religion to all citizens. (That effort did not help Roosevelt's cause since the Soviet Constitution guaranteed freedom *from* religion.) Despite Roosevelt's efforts to improve the image of the Soviet Union, a *Fortune* magazine poll revealed that two-thirds of the American public discerned little difference between Hitler and Stalin. The *Pittsburgh Catholic* was no more willing to trust Stalin, believing that Germany and the Soviet Union would reconcile and renew their war against the West.[48]

Father Rice's July 15 radio broadcast, delivered once again under the auspices of the Committee to Defend America, gave a rather strained defense of Roosevelt's efforts to aid Stalin:

It is a virtual certainty that Hitler will conquer and humiliate Soviet Russia. It is wise policy for us and for England to aid the weaker of the two pestilences. When two scoundrels, who are both a menace to you, start fighting, and when you know that the biggest one is going to come after you when he beats the weakest, the smart thing to do is to cause as much damage to the big one as you can, while he is busy. Because the more you take out of him when he is engaged in fighting, the less damage is he going to be able to do to you. It doesn't mean that we are to have any more use for Soviet Russia today than we ever had. I, for one, don't want to see Soviet Russia beat Germany. I am sure that Germany will beat Russia and I am all for it. But I want them to take a long, long time about doing it and it will be a grand thing for the world if they practically knock themselves out in the process.[49]

With Hitler's eastern offensive, the Communist Party again reversed political course. Now American Communists were vocal proponents of an alliance between the Soviet Union and the democracies. The Communists
decreed that there would be no more strikes since the Soviet Union needed
American weapons. When UE president James Carey ridiculed the party and
lobbied to exclude Communists from holding union office, James Matles and
Frank Emspak declared war. Despite a vigorous campaign by the ACTU, the
Communists persuaded enough delegates at the September UE convention
that they were the victims of a right-wing smear campaign. Had they not led
strikes to increase the wages of the rank and file? Now that they had received
pay increases, there was no need for strikes. The Nazi invasion of the Soviet
Union had nothing to do with the leadership's present opposition to strikes.
Moreover, as Matles and Emspak protested, they believed that UE members
had the right to affiliate with the political party of their choice; that was the
American way. In contrast, Carey was trying to quash free speech—much
like Hitler. Responding to their critics, Matles and Emspak denied that they
were Communists. They also recited Coughlin's anti-CIO record to discredit
their opponents among the Catholic clergy. This tactic only worked in plants
where the Catholic rank and file had not met Hensler and Rice.[50]

Although Murray failed to curb the UE's Communists, he was able to retain Carey as CIO secretary. While the UE battle raged, Murray—at Rice's
prompting—had joined the Committee to Defend the Allies. He became the
only national labor leader, and the nation's most prominent Irish Catholic,
to endorse aid to Britain. As early as 1937, SWOC had condemned Germany,
Japan, and Italy as "fascist aggressors" who slaughtered women and children. Four years later, Murray admitted that war with Germany was inevitable and necessary. At the second national ACTU convention, held in
Pittsburgh, Murray explained a plan he had for recasting America's industrial
relations while building President Roosevelt's "arsenal of democracy." Bishop
Boyle, Fathers Hensler and Rice, and Pittsburgh mayor Cornelius Scully listened intently. The National Catholic Welfare Conference had already endorsed Murray's proposal, collecting the signatures of six hundred Catholic,
Protestant, and Jewish clerical reformers.[51]

The CIO president wanted councils established in every industry that
would be composed in equal parts of union, management, and government
representatives. Such councils would give workers a voice in the operation
of the corporations, ensuring their responsiveness to the economic, educational, and health needs of workers. At the same time, tensions between
workers and managers would be lessened in an atmosphere of cooperation
and shared interests. Government officials would function as mediators un-

til the three groups merged into an industrial trinity. Despite the disastrous 1937 Little Steel Strike, Murray had not abandoned his hope that labor and management could work together in the quest to build a just society.[52]

Murray did not accept the tenets of New Deal liberal pluralism—the belief that economics and politics were the affairs of competing social groups. He did not subscribe to the Marxist view that labor and capital were enemies. Nor was Murray comfortable with the liberal notion that labor and capital should become cooperative monopolies. If irreconcilable enemies, then labor and capital would be locked in a conflict that could only be resolved by a violent workers' revolution. On the other hand, there were serious problems with labor and capital becoming allied trusts. According to historian David O'Brien, in such a situation labor would join "with capital to secure the benefits for the industry as a whole at the expense of the consumer and the common good." Given these considerations, Murray rejected class conflict and urged workers not to become materialistic. Instead, Murray believed that workers and employers were, in Father Hensler's words, indivisible parts of "the Mystical Body of Christ." That body must not be at war with itself for that would prevent Americans from defeating Hitler and achieving the common good.[53]

Washington liberals, as well as congressional conservatives, greeted Murray's initiative with disdain. Neither federal bureaucrats nor corporate executives were willing to surrender any of their power. Most businessmen did not regard their employees as equals. Workers were, as Hensler lamented, simply ciphers on the company's balance sheet. Within the ranks of labor, many unionists opposed any effort at reconciliation with management. They wanted to establish a CIO Political Action Committee. With the labor movement's financial resources and large membership, CIO vice president Sidney Hillman hoped to elect a pliant Congress. Political coercion, not reconciliation, was what too many in the CIO desired in their relationship with corporate America. Roosevelt, recognizing that whatever position he took on the industrial councils plan would alienate one important constituency or another, held his tongue.[54]

In the last weeks of 1941, Roosevelt had been making a heroic effort not to antagonize labor, management, and the general public. He had brought prominent Republicans into his cabinet and appealed for national unity. America could not afford the kind of class and ethnic divisions that had crippled Europe on the eve of Hitler's triumphs. The president's gestures of good will, however, fell upon deaf ears in Pittsburgh's Sacred Heart Parish. Father Thomas Coakley, his disgust with the New Deal having grown deeper since 1937, raged against Roosevelt in his parish newsletter:

The government is scattering billions to the Communist murderers who have closed every church and killed every priest in Russia . . . and to other nations who have ungratefully repudiated the billions we gave them in the last war. . . .

We asked what Americans could expect from the present government, and they told us they were going to give the mothers and fathers of Sacred Heart Parish the privilege of paying super-colossal income taxes, and then having their sons sunk without a trace in the icy waters of the Atlantic, or being run over by a sixty-ton tank on the burning sands of the African desert. And that, mate, is the New Deal!

As Sacred Heart's parishioners gathered for Sunday Mass and read Father Coakley's missive, Japanese planes were flying toward the American Pacific Fleet at Pearl Harbor.[55]

# Requiem

Germany and Italy declared war on the United States three days after the Japanese attack on Pearl Harbor. Although conservative congressmen had opposed American entry into the war, honorable Republicans stood behind Roosevelt. The *Pittsburgh Catholic* welcomed such people as new-found allies in the democratic crusade against evil. Other long-standing friends of reform assured the president that they would do their part. The National Catholic Welfare Conference addressed Roosevelt on December 22:

> We give you, Mr. President, the pledge of our wholehearted cooperation in the difficult days that lie ahead. We will zealously fulfill our spiritual ministry in the sacred cause of our country's service. We place at your disposal in that service our institutions and their consecrated personnel. We will lead our priests and people in constant prayer that God may bear you up under the heavy burdens that weigh upon you, that He may guide you and all who share with you responsibility for the nation's governance and security, that He may strengthen us all to win a victory that will be a blessing not for our nation alone, but for the whole world.[1]

Three thousand Catholic chaplains joined the military while the laity, representing 20 percent of the population, accounted for nearly 35 percent of America's soldiers. In contrast, of the 11,887 conscientious objectors who refused to join the armed forces, only 135 were Catholics. They were Dorothy Day's pacifist remnant. To its credit, the military welded Catholics, Jews, and Protestants into an formidable fighting team. Playboy Paul Mellon and Father James Cox both wore the uniform of their country. Where the Communist Party, the CIO, and the Liberty League had sharpened class and religious animosities, the Army, Navy, and the Marines fostered unity. Once they battled the most racist regimes in human history, the G.I.'s learned to shed some of their prejudices.[2]

War mobilization wrought profound change. The federal government and U.S. Steel financed a $75 million expansion of the Homestead mill. While other mills expanded the scale of their operations, U.S. Steel's Homestead operation was in a class by itself. The Pittsburgh District produced more steel than Germany, Italy, and Japan combined. Prosperity came with the grand opening of "the arsenal of democracy." Then again, industrial pollution returned to the Monongahela Valley. Many small-town G.I.'s who traveled through Pittsburgh were horrified by the sulfur-choked air that blocked out the sun. Worse, the Homestead mill expansion uprooted half of the municipality's population and led to the destruction of 1,363 buildings, 12 churches, and 28 saloons. In a bitter letter to Bishop Boyle, Father Hrtanek observed that St. Ann's Parish had lost two hundred Slovak families. Federal assistance in relocating Homestead's refugees proved inadequate.[3]

In 1942, Clinton Golden and Harold Ruttenberg argued that because of the war, the CIO had an opportunity to advance the union movement. Their book, *The Dynamics of Industrial Democracy*, offered collective bargaining among equals as a way to overcome a legacy of mistrust that had poisoned labor-management relations since the Civil War. Additionally, Golden and Ruttenberg, echoing the sentiments Father Hensler had expressed over the years, pledged "that labor will not combine with industry in unwarranted price changes" in order to benefit CIO members at the expense of the general public.[4]

A year later Golden wrote a provocative essay, "New Patterns of Democracy." He contended that SWOC's successor, the United Steel Workers of America, could promote grass-roots democracy and erase class hatreds. Golden envisioned a postwar social order in which organized labor and management would provide education and an improved living standard to all Americans. Golden concluded his treatise with a warning. If the union rank and file simply demanded fatter paychecks without any thought to the legitimate concerns of business, the long-term survival of America's economy and democracy would be doubtful. Full working-class participation in the nation's political and economic life also entailed responsibility for promoting the common good. Golden began his life as the socialist son of a Baptist minister. By 1943, having worked intimately with Phil Murray, John Brophy, and Patrick Fagan, Golden had absorbed the social teachings of Leo XIII and Pius XI.[5]

If, as Golden and Murray feared, there were workers whose only goal in life was to exact revenge upon their employers for past mistreatment, there were businessmen who were no less irresponsible. While Paul Mellon and his cousin, Richard King Mellon, joined the Army and, in their sincere, awkward manner, learned the folkways of Democrats, other Republicans were behaving badly. On January 30, 1942, L. Ebersole Gaines, the president of the West Virginia Coal Association, slandered Murray:

> Phil Murray, whom Lewis named to the presidency of the CIO [sic], has accepted, after continued repetition, the planted advice of administration sycophants that he is bigger than his maker [Lewis]. Murray has succumbed to the blandishments of the Great White Father [Roosevelt] and now dares to bare his teeth to Lewis. Over night the little terrier imagines he has become a Great Dane. . . .
>
> Labor leaders who are clothed temporarily with political power find it difficult to exercise. It is not strange. There is a reason. Labor leaders rule their unions through the exercise of autocratic powers. They brook no opposition. The politician would lose his shirt at the next election if he attempted the same exercise of arbitrary power that the labor czar wields over his membership.[6]

In 1941, Murray had pleaded with Congress not to pass legislation that would require unions to suspend strikes for a ninety-day "cooling off period." Republicans and southern Democrats ignored Murray. At the same time, the National Labor Relations Board compelled Little Steel to recognize the CIO. Bethlehem and Republic's chieftains were not happy in seeing their congressional gains canceled by federal bureaucrats. Receiving billions of dollars in defense orders was one thing, but being coerced into negotiating with Murray was quite another. With their right hand, some industrialists shook their fists at Roosevelt. With their other hand, they collected the taxpayers' defense dollars.[7]

Frustrated with such intransigence, Sidney Hillman helped create the CIO Political Action Committee (PAC). As Hillman viewed things in July 1943, the CIO had to keep Roosevelt in office for another term and beat back Republican efforts to capture Congress. This meant raising money for Roosevelt and registering CIO members to vote in the 1944 election. Murray preferred labor-management cooperation to the class war that the CIO-PAC and the Right planned to wage. As CIO-PAC chair, Hillman stacked the organization with Communists like John Abt. Even though Len DeCaux and other Communists ridiculed Hillman behind his back, the labor leader wanted to forge a united front against the Republican Party. At a Pittsburgh political rally in October 1944, Murray emphasized that the CIO-PAC was a defensive measure to protect labor from congressional reactionaries. The CIO was not seeking to take control of the Democratic Party or to advance a Communist agenda.[8]

Murray's speech was infused by the very class hatreds he had always condemned. Perhaps the threat a rejuvenated Right posed to the CIO, in addition to the stressful Democratic National Convention in Chicago, had unbalanced Murray. Certainly, the Chicago convention had been an ordeal for Murray. As Pittsburgh's David Lawrence and the other Irish party bosses suspected, Roosevelt was a walking corpse who would not survive his fourth term in office. This meant that Vice President Henry Wallace would be America's point man in negotiating with the Soviet Union.[9]

Lawrence had taken a dislike to Wallace in 1940. Catholic politicians viewed the former agriculture secretary as dangerously sympathetic to the Soviet Union. They also believed that he was mentally unstable. During the 1940 election, Paul Block, the publisher of the *Pittsburgh Post-Gazette*, had acquired copies of Wallace's personal correspondence with his "swami." Block hoped to share Wallace's ramblings on astrology and Communism with Catholic Democrats, but Roosevelt suppressed the correspondence. (FDR threatened to reveal the address of Wendell Wilkie's mistress. Block backed down.) The president then rammed Wallace down the convention delegates' throats. Having no use for politicians who praised Stalin and consulted astrologers, the Irish party bosses moved against Wallace in 1944. They had met Senator Harry Truman of Missouri and concluded that he was a worthy vice presidential candidate. Murray admired Wallace for his pro-labor stance and might have tried to keep him on the ticket. Fortunately for Truman, Lawrence convinced a weary, exasperated Murray that Wallace was not the man to lead the postwar world. It was an upsetting experience for Murray. The CIO leader worried that Truman would prove to be hostile toward organized labor.[10]

Murray's efforts to retain friends in the White House, increase industrial production for the war effort, and answer conservative charges were well-publicized. The CIO leader also denied that the Communist Party exercised enormous influence in the union. Privately, Murray and Rice consulted with each other on a frequent, intimate basis, discussing what to do about their Communist foes. For the duration of the war, both men moved behind the scenes, not attacking their opponents head-on. In a 1942 letter to "Dear Phil," Rice warned Murray that his criticism of the Dies Committee for "witch-hunting" had gone too far. Rice likewise fretted that Murray was receiving false information from the CIO's Washington office.

It was my impression that there is someone close to you who is doing a clever job of running [James] Carey down and it is my impression
that this same individual is doing an equally clever job of building [Frank] Emspak up. I suspect it is the same man who drafted
your anti-witch hunting message, which, forgive me, aided the
Reds.

. . . The Communists probably could not succeed in leading the
American workers astray overnight. They could succeed in poisoning
the whole labor movement and they could become tremendously powerful if they built their men up and tore the others down.

You, Lewis, Hillman belong to one generation of labor leadership.
The important thing is this: When you men pass from the scene, who
will take your places? If [Lee] Pressman and others have their way, it
will be the Emspaks' . . . and [Harry] Bridges'.[11]

Rice was not alone in his fear for the future. Catholics could not ignore the
fact that as victory over Nazi Germany drew near, the Soviet Union was in
a position to dominate Eastern Europe. In 1944, public opinion polls showed
that a number of Catholics were abandoning the Democratic Party which
they saw as too pro-Soviet. Overall, three out of ten voters believed that Roosevelt's reelection would give Communists an enhanced role in the federal
government. Loathing the prospect of a Soviet-dominated Poland, a group
of anti-Communist Catholics organized the Polish-American Congress in
1944. Roosevelt confided to friends that he found the Poles to be "a quar-
relsome people . . . not only at home but also abroad." To deal with the worst
of the domestic fascists and rabid anti-Communists, the U.S. attorney general in 1942 had indicted twenty-six individuals for disseminating "treason-
ous" propaganda. One prosecuting attorney, a supporter of Henry Wallace,
wanted to put Senator Robert Taft of Ohio on trial. The contempt some New
Dealers expressed for the civil liberties of the Right would come back to
haunt them. Further, Roosevelt's resentment of the six million Polish-American voters who tried to influence *his* foreign policy did not bode well for
the health of the Democratic coalition.[12]

On April 15, 1945, the National Catholic Welfare Conference urged America to rebuild the world economically and politically. There could be no return to prewar isolationism. The bishops also issued a warning. Although
Allied cooperation in defeating Nazi and Japanese aggression had been com-
mendable, the United States could not continue its alliance with the Soviet
Union.

Every day makes more evident the fact that two strong, essentially incompatible ways of life will divide the loyalties of men and nations in the political world of tomorrow. They are genuine democracy and Marxian totalitarianism. Democracy is built on respect for the dignity of the human person with its God-given inviolable rights. It achieves unity and strength in the intelligent cooperation of all citizens for the common good under governments chosen and supported by the people. It will advance, expand, and develop our culture. It will maintain continuity with our Christian past. It will give security for our Christian future. Fascism and Nazism, rampant in their might, sought its destruction. Fascism is gone, we hope, forever. And soon Nazism will be only a horrible historical memory.

However, we have to reckon with the active, cleverly organized and directed opposition of Marxian totalitarianism to genuine democracy. This system herds the masses under dictatorial leadership, insults their intelligence with its propaganda and controlled press, and tyrannically violates innate human rights. Against it, genuine democracy must be constantly on guard, quick to detect and penetrate its camouflage. Democracy's bulwark is religion, and justice is its watchword. We entered this war to defend our democracy. It is our solemn responsibility, in the reconstruction, to use our full influence in safeguarding the freedoms of all people. This, we are convinced, is the only way to an enduring peace.[13]

A year later, with the Communist subjugation of Eastern Europe an accomplished fact, the National Catholic Welfare Conference spoke again. This time the bishops chastised Yugoslavia's Marxist leader, Joseph Tito, for imprisoning Archbishop Aloysius Stepinac: "The people of Croatia had but one champion who stood fearlessly in defense of human rights against Nazi and fascist oppression, as he has stood against the tyranny of those now in control. That champion was Archbishop Stepinac." (Stepinac stood accused of having sided with Croatian fascists who had exterminated hundreds of thousands of Gypsies, Jews, and Serbs.) Other voices, which had remained silent on foreign policy issues during the war, could once again be heard. Father Hrtanek and the First Catholic Slovak Union beseeched Bishop Boyle in 1947 to pray for their kinsmen "who are at the present time under the tyrannical reign of the Communist government of" the Czechs. In 1948, Hrtanek denounced Henry Wallace, who was running as an independent presidential candidate. As Communist documents and congressional testimony subsequently revealed, the party provided Wallace with a campaign organization, volunteers, and funds. According to Hrtanek, a Wallace supporter was telling Slovak-Americans that "none of our priests could be made even an auxiliary [bishop] in the largest Slovak centers in the country. Then he spoke of how the progressives [Marxists] in Warsaw and Prague work with effect against the Irish bishops of America, and proposed that the [Communist-front] Slav Congress will do the same for the Slovaks."[14]

Wisely, Hrtanek no longer invoked the name of his cousin. In December 1946, Joseph Tiso went on trial in Bratislava, charged with 113 capital crimes. Among his war crimes, the priest had tortured Czech nationalists, crushed a Slovak uprising against the German occupation army in 1944, and had transported his nation's Jews to the Nazi death camps. *Time* magazine, a bulwark of American reaction against the Soviet Union, could not excuse Tiso's behavior. Tiso, *Time* concluded, was a criminal and a traitor.[15]

On the postwar labor front, Murray and Rice moved decisively against the Communists. The UE split, with James Carey leading the rank and file into a new CIO affiliate, the International Union of Electrical Workers. Only a handful of Communist-led UE locals remained. Rice made sure they were expelled from the CIO. Despising the Catholic labor reformers, David Caute, an academic critic of the Church, contended in 1978 that "the violent epicenter of the anti-Communist eruption in post-war America was the steel city of Pittsburgh." One man who concurred with Caute's sense of history was Communist Party leader Steve Nelson. In 1948 Nelson returned to Pittsburgh in a desperate effort to maintain the party's influence in the CIO. Nelson failed miserably. In his memoirs, Nelson attributed his repudiation to Church and government repression, public hysteria, and anti-Communist propaganda.[16]

As social commentator Richard Krickus noted in 1976, the Communists never won over the majority of workers. Bishop Boyle, Rice, and the National Catholic Welfare Conference had thwarted the party in the early years of the Depression. "Had the Catholic clergy remained indifferent to the plight of the worker, or had the hierarchy adopted a national policy of opposing the CIO," Krickus wrote, "it is likely that the radicals would have achieved greater success with the Catholic white ethnics. The involvement of Catholic clergy in the resurrection of the labor movement had a modifying influence upon the CIO." Nelson and his professorial champions were unable to make the case that the CIO Communists were independent of Stalin's political control. The recent opening of Soviet archives proves that the American Communist Party leaders received money and direction from Moscow throughout the 1930s and 1940s. Moreover, it was difficult for many Americans, Catholic or not, to accept the Popular Front line that the Soviet Union was a worthy

ally against Hitler. It was a difficult line to accept because Hitler could not
have attacked France without first securing Stalin's neutrality in 1939.[17]

Scholars who have had access to the archives of the former Soviet Union,
notably Harvey Klehr and John Earl Haynes, have concluded that the Communists harmed the CIO and the New Deal. Stalin's American allies also provoked a backlash against social reformers. In turn, Democrats went too far
in attacking conservatives.

> Clandestine activities in a democratic polity unavoidably compromise
> those involved. Communists lied to and deceived the New Dealers
> with whom they allied. Those liberals who believed the denials then
> denounced as mudslingers those anti-Communists who complained
> of concealed Communist activity. Furious at denials of what they knew
> to be true, anti-Communists then suspected that those who denied the
> Communist presence were themselves dishonest. The Communists'
> duplicity poisoned normal political relationships and contributed to
> the harshness of the anti-Communist reaction of the late 1940s and
> 1950s.[18]

*Communists rather than left to blame for attacks on ND*

While Catholic activists successfully purged the CIO of Communists, they
largely failed to win blacks over to their side. At the beginning of the war,
Murray directed Carey to investigate ways to end racial discrimination in
hiring. At the CIO's 1944 convention, Auxiliary Bishop Bernard Sheil of
Chicago had exhorted organized labor to battle discrimination. As Sheil
argued,

> American democracy will never come to full flower until discrimina-
> tion against Negroes and Jews and all minority groups is erased from
> our national and personal lives, for of such groups is made the great-
> ness of America.
>
> Any discrimination tears into shreds the solidarity of the human
> race and makes a mockery of the Fatherhood of God and the Broth-
> erhood of Christ. We have asked the Negro and the Jew to fight and
> die for democracy; it would be the basest cynicism to refuse to share
> with them that democracy.[19]

Despite the prohibition against discrimination among its affiliates, as well
as John Brophy and Father Rice's efforts to recruit blacks, the CIO remained
overwhelmingly white. Black workers tended to be hostile toward union organizing efforts. Additionally, many urban blacks were indifferent to CIO

and Church initiatives. In August 1944, Father Thomas Lappan gave Bishop Boyle a sad summary of the St. Vincent de Paul's charitable activities in the Hill District. "The Hill District," Lappan sighed, "was one of [our] failures." Social disorganization abounded while as a moral authority the black church was in a pitiful state. At least one black minister in 1939 had not received a salary for over a year. Father Lappan kept the black Protestant in food and clothing. Worse, crime grew and federal welfare and housing projects had eliminated the need for the Hill District's least disciplined to work. Anguished, Lappan confessed to Boyle that he and the Sisters of Charity had to place their altar and linens under guard.[20]

The inability of Catholic social activists to gain the support of more than a tiny fraction of blacks pointed to a larger problem that the labor priests never solved. SWOC and the CIO were strong only in those sections of the United States where there were a majority of Catholic and Jewish workers. The union movement of the 1930s gained no ground in America's most Protestant region, the South, and had enormous difficulties in midwestern mill towns that had substantial Appalachian-migrant populations. Protestant individualism clashed with Catholic collective action. Only the *coercive* authority of the federal government, propelled by the crisis of the World War II, led to CIO victories in the Midwest's smaller industrial centers. In the industrial metropolises—Chicago, Cleveland, and Pittsburgh—a reformist Catholic Church placed its *moral* authority behind SWOC and the CIO. This was the strength, and the ultimate weakness, of the Depression-era labor movement. The progress of industrial labor depended upon the support of sympathetic Catholic clergy and laity.

As one of the most important industrial centers in America, Pittsburgh was, in many regards, an ideal laboratory in which to examine the social roots of the New Deal. Pittsburgh's working-class population of Catholics, blacks, and Jews made it more culturally diverse than nearly any other American urban center. It was in cities such as Pittsburgh, and in the economically and politically powerful state of Pennsylvania, where the New Deal ended two generations of Republican domination. Out of the ashes of the Republican order came a revitalized Democratic Party. Roosevelt prospered upon a coalition of urban-based minorities and white southerners. While urban Democrats waged tribal warfare among themselves in Boston and New York, Pittsburgh's Catholic politicians, labor leaders, and clergy welcomed all into the fold, regardless of race or religion. The New Deal coalition ruled more successfully—and generously—in Pittsburgh than was true in most urban centers. A Catholic laity and clergy committed to social justice made that development possible.

Pittsburgh was also an excellent place to observe how clergy and laity applied Catholic social instruction to the building of the industrial union movement. There were few cities in America where labor unions came close to exercising the power wielded by Pittsburgh steel workers. That would not have been true had it not been for Catholic clergy who threw their support behind Murray. The CIO gained little ground in Boston and New York, and certainly the Catholic Church of the East often expressed its hostility toward organized labor, the New Deal, and the encyclicals of Leo XIII and Pius XI. Even in the Democratic cities of Chicago and Cleveland—both of which had an activist Catholic clergy—union, party, and Church were not as closely bound together as was the case for Pittsburgh. In Pittsburgh, the Catholic Church, the Democratic Party, and organized labor were inseparable, cooperating entities. SWOC needed the help of the federal government to secure victory in Chicago and Cleveland.

Organized labor did not entirely dominate the Democratic Party organizations in Illinois and Ohio. In Pennsylvania and Michigan it was impossible to ignore the influence that the steel and automobile workers possessed at the state level. (Their influence in Washington was also considerable.) At the same time, Catholic politicians and clergy in Chicago, Cleveland, and Detroit were more discreet than their Pennsylvania counterparts in acknowledging the relationship between religion and government. Unfortunately for the reputation of Catholic social reconstruction, the best publicized clergy activists in 1930s America were not Hensler and Rice. Rather, Father Charles Coughlin and Monsignor Fulton Sheen, both implacable foes of the CIO, garnered the greatest attention in the secular media. Within the Church, and among the Catholic working class, the Pittsburgh activists won the day for the CIO. Organized labor became a significant, national political constituency as a result of New Deal reforms and its alliance with Catholic clerics.

It is important to remember that in the 1930s and 1940s the majority of Catholics were workers. Moreover, much of America's labor force was composed of religious and racial minorities. Catholicism was the glue that bound together a large percentage of the working class. As long as most Catholics remained blue collar, and were denied any educational and economic opportunities to advance themselves, the labor movement had cohesion. Once discriminatory barriers against Catholics fell after World War II, and America enjoyed an unprecedented era of material prosperity, America's largest religious minority became upwardly mobile. Every Catholic who made it into the ranks of the middle class, or who acquired a secular college education, was one less potential CIO member.

We can view the success of organized labor in the 1930s and 1940s as a blip on America's historical radar. The severity of the Depression, the concentration of Catholics in the working class, and the flowering of Catholic social activism in Pittsburgh, made the CIO possible. Once these historical conditions changed, organized labor, and perhaps even the Democratic Party, could not survive. In 1930, three million Americans had joined a labor union. Ten years later, union membership had grown three-fold. By 1950, sixteen million people, or one-third of the work force, were union members. That was the high-water mark. By 1990, union membership plummeted to 16 percent of the work force. The labor movement also declined in absolute numbers, losing three million people between 1990 and 1995. Today, America has more self-employed entrepreneurs than union members.[21]

There is another great irony. Murray, Hensler, and Rice sought to improve the material condition of all laborers. In the long term that material improvement helped transform blue-collar Democrats into middle-class Republicans. However, not everyone who joined SWOC and the CIO left the working class; many remained in the mills, lured by the prospect of generous union wages. America's workers after World War II became the most affluent in the world, acquiring automobiles and summer cottages with the same vigor that they had defeated Germany and Japan. Pittsburgh's steel mills went along with high wages, passing their expenses along to consumers and using tariff barriers to hide from foreign competition. As Hensler and Murray had feared in the 1930s, material gain made workers and managers complacent. By the 1970s, U.S. Steel had lost its competitive edge. Japanese and German industrialists achieved the labor and management cooperation that Pittsburgh's Catholic reformers hoped for, but never realized.

When Monsignor Carl Hensler died in 1984 a joke was wending its way through an economically devastated Homestead. It seemed that several U.S. Steel executives had died and gone to Heaven. St. Peter met the businessmen at the pearly gates and said, "There must be some mistake. You belong in Hell." Later, St. Peter received a phone call from Satan. The devil said, "Do you remember those U.S. Steel executives you sent down here?" St. Peter replied, "Yes, I thought they should be with you. Is there a problem?" Satan responded, "Yeah, there is a problem. They have only been here a week and they have already closed ten furnaces." The downside of enjoying a long and socially meaningful life, as was the case with Hensler, is that you get to see the forebodings you had in your youth come to fruition in your old age.

Those who preceded Hensler in death were, perhaps, more fortunate. In 1951, the Pittsburgh Diocese lost Bishop Boyle and Father Cox. A few days after the 1952 election, Phil Murray passed away. With Dwight Eisenhower's victory, Murray acknowledged that the CIO had become too dependent upon Washington. Now that a pro-business Republican was in the White House, the federal bureaucracy would undercut the CIO as much as possible. Murray had not wanted to wed labor to the government, but secular political considerations had triumphed over Catholic social instruction. Statism became the watchword of labor, as well as the Democratic Party. Pittsburgh's Catholic activists had tried to map a political path away from Communism, laissez-faire capitalism, and the expansive New Deal State. History did not ordain their success.[22]

In 1945, Rice delivered a radio tribute to the labor leader that could have served as Murray's requiem. Duquesne University had given the CIO president an honorary degree at the school's sixty-seventh annual commencement. As the priest observed, Murray

> typifies the best in Americanism and in Catholicism. The things that count for him are his God, his country, and his union.
>
> He said today, when he received his degree, that he believed God had created man and endowed him with an immortal soul and that as a result mankind was the most important thing on the planet. Institutions and nations exist to serve the people and not the other way around; that is what Philip Murray said and that is what he believes and in that belief does he act. His life has been spent in service to his God and his fellow men.

On the day of Murray's funeral, traffic in Pittsburgh came to a halt and church bells rang a dirge.[23]

# Notes

## Abbreviations

AIS      Archives of an Industrial Society, University of Pittsburgh
DPA     Diocese of Pittsburgh Archives, Pittsburgh, Pennsylvania
HCLA    Historical Collections and Labor Archives, Pennsylvania State University
JAHA    Johnstown, Pennsylvania, Area Heritage Association
OHS     Ohio Historical Society, Columbus, Ohio

## Preface and Acknowledgements

1. Patrick J. McGeever, *Rev. Charles Owen Rice: Apostle of Contradiction* (Pittsburgh: Duquesne University Press, 1989); Annemarie Draham, "Unlikely Allies for Unionization: Homestead, Pennsylvania, 1933–1946," M.A. thesis, Indiana University of Pennsylvania, 1984; Liston Pope, "Religion and the Class Structure," *Annals of the Academy of Political and Social Science* 256 (March 1948): 84–95.

2. Gary Gerstle, *Working-Class Americanism: The Politics of Labor in a Textile City, 1914–1960* (New York: Cambridge University Press, 1989), 153–95.

3. Francis L. Broderick, *John A. Ryan: Right Reverend New Dealer* (New York: Macmillan, 1963); David J. O'Brien, *American Catholics and Social Reform: The New Deal Years* (New York: Oxford University Press, 1968), 66–67; McGeever, *Rev. Charles Owen Rice.*

4. Andrew M. Greeley, "What is Subsidiarity? A Voice from Sleepy Hollow," *America* 153 (9 November 1985): 292–95.

## Advent

1. Edward K. Muller, "Metropolis and Region: A Framework for Enquiry into Western Pennsylvania," in Samuel P. Hays, ed., *City at the Point: Essays on the Social History of Pittsburgh* (Pittsburgh: University of Pittsburgh Press, 1989), 181–211.

2. Victor R. Greene, *The Slavic Community on Strike: Immigrant Labor in Pennsylvania Anthracite* (South Bend, Ind.: University of Notre Dame Press, 1968), 2; John Bodnar, Roger Simon, and Michael Weber, *Lives of Their Own: Blacks, Italians, and Poles in Pittsburgh, 1900–1960* (Urbana: University of Illinois Press, 1982), 15; Muller, "Metropolis and Region,"

181–211; Corrine A. Krause, *Grandmothers, Mothers, and Daughters: Oral Histories of Three Generations of Ethnic American Women* (Boston: Twayne, 1991), 1.

3. Kenneth Warren, *The American Steel Industry, 1850–1970: A Geographical Interpretation* (Pittsburgh: University of Pittsburgh Press, 1973), 127, 155.

4. Harvey O'Connor, *Mellon's Millions: The Biography of a Fortune* (New York: John Day, 1933), 383–423; Ronald W. Schatz, *The Electrical Workers: A History of Labor at General Electric and Westinghouse, 1923–1960* (Urbana: University of Illinois Press, 1983), 8–9.

5. Peter George, *The Emergence of Industrial America: Strategic Factors in American Economic Growth Since 1870* (Albany: State University of New York Press, 1982), 174; Anthony J. Badger, *The New Deal: The Depression Years, 1933–1940* (New York: Hill & Wang, 1989), 23.

6. Nora Faires, "Immigrants and Industry: Peopling the 'Iron City,'" in Hays, ed., *City at the Point*, 3–31; Linda K. Pritchard, "The Soul of the City: A Social History of Religion in Pittsburgh," in Hays, ed., *City at the Point*, 327–60.

7. Krause, *Grandmothers, Mothers, and Daughters*, 1; Aviva Gootman, "A Study of Selected Foreign Language Publications in Allegheny County," M.S. thesis, University of Pittsburgh, 1946, passim; Pritchard, "The Soul of the City," 327–60.

8. *Pittsburgh Catholic*, 16 June 1938, 18 May 1939, 18 April 1940; Joseph J. Casino, "From Sanctuary to Involvement: A History of the Catholic Parish in the Northeast," in Jay P. Dolan, ed., *The American Catholic Parish: A History from 1850 to the Present*, 2 vols. (New York: Paulist Press, 1987), 1:37–38, 111.

9. Dolores Ann Liptak, *European Immigrants and the Catholic Church in Connecticut, 1870–1920* (New York: Center for Migration Studies, 1987), 12, 72; John J. Kane, "The Social Structure of American Catholics," *American Catholic Sociological Review* 16 (March 1955): 23–30.

10. Liston Pope, "Religion and the Class Structure," *Annals of the Academy of Political and Social Science* 256 (March 1948): 84–95; Hadley Cantril, "Educational and Economic Composition of Religious Groups: An Analysis of Poll Data," *American Journal of Sociology* 48 (March 1943): 574–79; Mel Piehl, *Breaking Bread: The Catholic Worker and the Origin of Catholic Radicalism in America* (Philadelphia: Temple University Press, 1982), 29.

11. Pope, "Religion and the Class Structure," 84–95; Kenneth T. Jackson, *The Ku Klux Klan in the City, 1915–1930* (New York: Oxford University Press, 1970), 128–29, 133–39, 167, 236–41; Herbert G. Gutman, "Protestantism and the American Labor Movement: The Christian Spirit in the Gilded Age," *American Historical Review* 77 (1966): 74–101. As Gutman and Ken Fones-Wolf, *Trade Union Gospel: Christianity and Labor in Industrial Philadelphia, 1865–1915* (Philadelphia: Temple University Press, 1989), argue, the ultimate failure of the Social Gospel enthusiasts in no way diminishes their efforts to reform laissez-faire capitalism.

12. George, *The Emergence of Industrial America*, 177; William E. Leuchtenburg, *Franklin D. Roosevelt and the New Deal, 1932–1940* (New York: Harper & Row, 1963), 1, 19; Sean Dennis Cashman, *America in the Twenties and Thirties: The Olympian Age of Franklin Delano Roosevelt* (New York: New York University Press, 1989), 146; Schatz, *The Electrical Workers*, 61; Krause, *Grandmothers, Mothers, and Daughters*, 2.

13. George, *The Emergence of Industrial America*, 194.

14. John A. Fitch, *The Steel Workers* (Pittsburgh: University of Pittsburgh Press, 1989), 57–71, 139–49; Bodnar et al., *Lives of Their Own*, 18; S. J. Kleinberg, *The Shadow of the Mills: Working-Class Families in Pittsburgh, 1870–1907* (Pittsburgh: University of Pittsburgh Press, 1989), 9; William Serrin, *Homestead: The Glory and Tragedy of an American Steel Town* (New York: Times Books, 1992), 66–95. Fitch was a contributor to *The Pittsburgh Survey*.

15. Kristi Anderson, *The Creation of a Democratic Majority, 1928–1936* (Chicago: University of Chicago Press, 1979), 29–30, 32, 41–42; John Bodnar, *The Transplanted: A History of*

*Immigrants in Urban America* (Bloomington: Indiana University Press, 1985), 112; George Q. Flynn, *American Catholics and the Roosevelt Presidency, 1932–1936* (Lexington: University of Kentucky Press, 1968) 1–21, 36–60; George Q. Flynn, *Roosevelt and Romanism: Catholics and American Diplomacy, 1937–1945* (Westport, Conn.: Greenwood Press, 1976), xviii–xx; Samuel Lubell, *The Future of American Politics* (New York: Harper & Row, 1952), 28; Raymond E. Wolfinger, "The Development and Persistence of Ethnic Voting," in Lawrence H. Fuchs, ed., *American Ethnic Politics* (New York: Harper & Row, 1968), 163–93; John J. Kane, "The Social Structure of American Catholics," *American Catholic Sociological Review* 16 (March 1955): 23–30.

16. Anderson, *The Creation of a Democratic Majority, 1928–1936*, 34. See Steven P. Erie, *Rainbow's End: Irish-Americans and the Dilemmas of Urban Machine Politics, 1840–1985* (Berkeley and Los Angeles: University of California Press, 1988), Ronald H. Bayor, *Neighbors in Conflict: The Irish, Germans, Jews, and Italians of New York City, 1929–1941* (Baltimore: Johns Hopkins University Press, 1978), and Gerald H. Gamm, *The Making of New Deal Democrats: Voting Behavior and Realignment in Boston, 1920–1940* (Chicago: University of Chicago Press, 1989).

17. Anderson, *The Creation of a Democratic Majority, 1928–1936*, 34; Erie, *Rainbow's End*, passim; Frank Hawkins, "Lawrence of Pittsburgh: Boss of the Mellon Patch," *Harper's Monthly Magazine* 213 (August 1956): 57–61.

18. Gary Gerstle, *Working-Class Americanism: The Politics of Labor in a Textile City, 1914–1960* (New York: Cambridge University Press, 1989); Neil Betten, *Catholic Activism and the Industrial Worker* (Gainesville: University Presses of Florida, 1976); Douglas P. Seaton, *Catholics and Radicals: The Association of Catholic Trade Unionists and the American Labor Movement, from Depression to Cold War* (Lewisburg, Pa.: Bucknell University Press, 1981); Steve Rosswurm, "The Catholic Church and the Left-Led Unions: Labor Priests, Labor Schools, and the ACTU," in Steve Rosswurm, ed., *The CIO's Left-Led Unions* (New Brunswick, N.J.: Rutgers University Press, 1992), 119–37; Lizabeth Cohen, *Making a New Deal: Industrial Workers in Chicago, 1919–1939* (New York: Cambridge University Press, 1990); Joshua B. Freeman, *In Transit: The Transport Workers Union in New York City, 1933–1966* (New York: Oxford University Press, 1989); Ronald Schatz, "Connecticut's Working Class in the 1950s: A Catholic Perspective," *Labor History* 25 (winter 1980): 83–101; Leslie Tentler, "On the Margins: The State of American Catholic History," *American Quarterly* 45 (March 1993): 104–27.

19. M. J. Heale, *American Anti-Communism: Combating the Enemy Within, 1830–1970* (Baltimore: Johns Hopkins University Press, 1990), 106, 116, 173; Stephen J. Whitfield, *The Culture of the Cold War* (Baltimore: Johns Hopkins University Press, 1990), 91–92, 99; David J. O'Brien, *American Catholics and Social Reform: The New Deal Years* (New York: Oxford University Press, 1968), 94–95; Seymour Martin Lipset, "The Sources of the 'Radical Right,'" in Daniel Bell, ed., *The Radical Right: The New American Right* (New York: Anchor Books, 1964), 353, 355; Les K. Adler and Thomas G. Paterson, "Red Fascism: The Merger of Nazi Germany and Soviet Russia in the American Image of Totalitarianism, 1930s–1950s," *The American Historical Review* 75 (April 1970): 1046–64.

20. Whitfield, *The Culture of the Cold War*, 91; Harold L. Ickes, *The Secret Diary of Harold L. Ickes: The Inside Struggle, 1936–1939*, 2 vols. (New York: Simon & Schuster, 1954), 2:86, 390, 423, 586, 650, 705; Alan Brinkley, "The New Deal and the Idea of the State," in Steve Fraser and Gary Gerstle, eds., *The Rise and Fall of the New Deal Order, 1930–1980* (Princeton: Princeton University Press, 1989), 85–121.

21. Richard H. Rovere, "Labor's Catholic Bloc," *The Nation* 152 (January 1941): 11–15; David J. Saposs, "The Catholic Church and the Labor Movement," *Modern Monthly* 2 (May 1933): 225–30; *The Socialist Call* (New York City), 3 September 1938.

22. Bayor, *Neighbors in Conflict*, 90; Flynn, *American Catholics and the Roosevelt Presi-*

*dency, 1932–1936*, xiv, 50–53, 109–13, 128–33; Flynn, *Roosevelt and Romanism*, 4–5, 29, 33–34, 37; Heale, *American Anti-Communism*, 116; John Lewis Gaddis, *The United States and the Origins of the Cold War, 1941–1947* (New York: Columbia University Press, 1972), 52–54; Allen Guttman, *The Wound in the Heart: America and the Spanish Civil War* (New York: The Free Press, 1962), 43; Jose M. Sanchez, *The Spanish Civil War as Religious Tragedy* (South Bend, Ind.: University of Notre Dame Press, 1987), 194; Charles H. Trout, *Boston, the Great Depression, and the New Deal* (New York: Oxford University Press, 1977), 22–23, 259–62; *Catholic Sentinel* (Portland, Ore.), 4 August 1938, 14 August 1938; *Catholic Telegraph-Register* (Cincinnati), 5 August 1938, 12 August 1938.

23. Flynn, *Roosevelt and Romanism*, 54; George H. Gallup, *The Gallup Poll: Public Opinion, 1933–1971*, 3 vols. (New York: Random House, 1972), 1:100–101; John W. Jeffries, *Testing the Roosevelt Coalition: Connecticut Society and Politics in the Era of World War II* (Knoxville: University of Tennessee Press, 1979), 157–58; Jordan A. Schwarz, *Liberal: Adolf A. Berle and the Vision of an American Era* (New York: The Free Press, 1987), 175–215; Henry L. Feingold, *The Politics of Rescue: The Roosevelt Administration and the Holocaust, 1938–1945* (New York: Waldon, 1970); Philip Gleason, "American Catholic Higher Education, 1940–1990: The Ideological Context," in George M. Marsden and Bradley J. Longfield, eds., *The Secularization of the Academy* (New York: Oxford University Press, 1992), 234–58; David S. Wyman, *The Abandonment of the Jews: America and the Holocaust, 1941–1945* (New York: Pantheon, 1985), and *Paper Walls: America and the Refugee Crisis, 1938–1941* (New York: Pantheon, 1985).

Feingold underscored the fact that nearly 23 percent of the Nazi storm troopers were Catholic, a seemingly large proportion until one recalls that the author had mentioned in passing that Catholics represented 43 percent of the German population. Catholics were underrepresented in the Nazi movement and, as Sanchez points out in *The Spanish Civil War as Religious Tragedy*, Pius XI had condemned fascism long before the democracies had done so.

24. Alan Brinkley, *Voices of Protest: Huey Long, Father Coughlin, and the Great Depression* (New York: Vintage, 1983), 86–87, 129–30; David J. O'Brien, *American Catholics and Social Reform: Five Great Encyclicals* (New York: Paulist Press, 1939); Flynn, *American Catholics and the Roosevelt Presidency*, 22–35; John Leo LeBrun, "The Role of the Catholic Worker Movement in American Pacifism, 1933–1972," Ph.D. diss., Case Western Reserve University, 1973; Piehl, *Breaking Bread*, passim; John A. Ryan, "Catholics and Anti-Semitism," *Current History* 49 (February 1939): 25–26.

25. Trout, *Boston, the Great Depression, and the New Deal*, 258–71; Brinkley, *Voices of Protest*, 104–105, 121–22, 176–78, 206, 254–61; Gamm, *The Making of New Deal Democrats*, 154–55; Bayor, *Neighbors in Conflict*, 31, 40–41, 46, 88–91; Erie, *Rainbow's End*, 114–15; Monroe Billington and Cal Clark, "Catholic Clergymen, Franklin D. Roosevelt, and the New Deal," *Catholic Historical Review* 79 (January 1993): 65–82; Lawrence O'Rourke, *Geno: The Life and Mission of Geno Baroni* (New York: Paulist Press, 1991), 203.

## Chapter 1: Pilgrimage

1. Sean Dennis Cashman, *America in the Twenties and the Thirties: The Olympian Age of Franklin Delano Roosevelt* (New York: New York University Press, 1989), 117; Anthony J. Badger, *The New Deal: The Depression Years, 1933–1940* (New York: Hill & Wang, 1989), 22; Roy Lubove, *Twentieth Century Pittsburgh: Government, Business, and Environmental Change* (New York: John Wiley & Sons, 1969), 1–19; Michael P. Weber, *Don't Call Me Boss: David L. Lawrence, Pittsburgh's Renaissance Mayor* (Pittsburgh: University of Pittsburgh Press, 1988), 46; Henry Jones Ford, *The Scotch-Irish in America* (Hamden, Conn.: Anchor Books, 1966), 260–90.

2. Cashman, *America in the Twenties and the Thirties*, 117; *Pittsburgh Federated Press*, 16 November 1932 (Elmer Cope Papers, Box 8, OHS); *Pittsburgh Catholic*, 4 August 1932.

3. *Pittsburgh Federated Press*, 2 November 1931, 9 November 1931, 19 November 1931 (Elmer Cope Papers, Box 8, OHS); *Pittsburgh Catholic*, 14 January 1932.

4. Weber, *Don't Call Me Boss*, 46; *Pittsburgh Federated Press*, 26 October 1931, 5 November 1931, 7 December 1931, 14 December 1931 (Elmer Cope Papers, Box 8, OHS).

5. Lubove, *Twentieth-Century Pittsburgh*, 69; R. L. Duffus, "Is Pittsburgh Civilized?" *Harper's* 161 (October 1930): 537–45; *Pittsburgh Federated Press*, 14 December 1931 (Elmer Cope Papers, Box 8, OHS); *Pittsburgh Catholic*, 13 April 1933.

6. Albert U. Romasco, *The Poverty of Abundance: Hoover, the Nation, the Depression* (New York: Oxford University Press, 1965), 25; Badger, *The New Deal*, 35; David Burner, *Herbert Hoover: A Public Life* (New York: Atheneum, 1984), 199; Harvey O'Connor, *Mellon's Millions: The Biography of a Fortune* (New York: John Day, 1933), 254–55, 302–23, 336–37, 348–51.

7. O'Connor, *Mellon's Millions*, 349–50; *Pittsburgh Post-Gazette*, 1 May 1933; Elmer Cope, "Data Taken from April Applications for Relief, Pennsylvania, 23 April 1933" (Elmer Cope Papers, Box 10, OHS); Otis L. Graham and Meghan Robinson Wander, eds., *Franklin D. Roosevelt, His Life and Times: An Encyclopedic View* (New York: Da Capo Press, 1990), 328–29; Weber, *Don't Call Me Boss*, 107; James Henwood, "Politics and Unemployment Relief, Pennsylvania, 1931–1939," Ph.D. diss., University of Pennsylvania, 1975, 5–8.

8. *Pittsburgh Catholic*, 8 September 1932, 16 March 1933; Sacerdotal Golden Jubilee of the Rev. Ercole Dominicis, 1956 (Ercole Dominicis Papers, DPA).

9. Sacerdotal Golden Jubilee of the Rev. Ercole Dominicis, 1956; Richard Lowitt and Maurine Beasly, eds., *One Third of a Nation: Lorena Hickok Reports on the Great Depression* (Urbana: University of Illinois Press, 1983), 8–14; William E. Leuchtenburg, *Franklin D. Roosevelt and the New Deal, 1932–1940* (New York: Harper & Row, 1963), 13–16; *Pittsburgh Catholic*, 18 August 1932.

10. James R. Cox, Record of Priests, Diocese of Pittsburgh (James R. Cox Papers, DPA).

11. *Pittsburgh Sun-Telegraph*, 20 March 1951; *Our Sunday Visitor* (Indianapolis), 14 July 1974; *Pittsburgh Press*, 28 October 1973; Thomas H. Coode and John D. Petrarulo, "The Odyssey of Pittsburgh's Father Cox," *The Western Pennsylvania Historical Magazine 55* (July 1972): 217–38; Cox, Record of Priests; Dr. H. H. Sullivan letter to James R. Cox, 6 May 1927 (James R. Cox Papers, DPA).

12. Cox, Record of Priests; Coode and Petrarulo, "The Odyssey of Pittsburgh's Father Cox," 217–38; *Pittsburgh Sun-Telegraph*, 20 March 1951; *Our Sunday Visitor*, 15 September 1974; *Pittsburgh Catholic*, 21 March 1935; Victor Anthony Walsh, "'Across the Big Wather': Irish Community Life in Pittsburgh and Allegheny City, 1850–1885," Ph.D. diss., University of Pittsburgh, 1983, 145–57.

13. Elmer Cope letter to A. J. Muste, 12 January 1932 (Elmer Cope Papers, Box 8, OHS); Coode and Petrarulo, "The Odyssey of Pittsburgh's Father Cox," 217–38; *Pittsburgh Sun-Telegraph*, 20 March 1951; *Pittsburgh Catholic*, 11 February 1932, 18 February 1932.

14. Pennsylvania Civil Liberties Committee List of Officers, 1932 (Elmer Cope Papers, Box 8, OHS); Pennsylvania Civil Liberties Committee, The Case of Alfred Hoffman, February 1932 (Elmer Cope Papers, Box 8, OHS); Pittsburgh Civil Liberties Committee, Minutes, 10 March 1932 (Elmer Cope Papers, Box 8, OHS); Pittsburgh Civil Liberties Committee letter to Arthur M. Scully, President Allegheny County Bar Association, 14 March 1932 (Elmer Cope Papers, Box 8, OHS); "Priest Leads Unemployed," *The Christian Century* 49 (17 February 1932): 235; *Pittsburgh Press*, 8 January 1932.

15. Harvey Klehr, *The Heyday of American Communism: The Depression Decade* (New York: Basic Books, 1984), 50–53, 58–59; Harvey Klehr and John Earl Haynes, *The American Communist Movement: Storming Heaven Itself* (New York: Twayne, 1992), 60–62; Daniel

Leab, "'United We Eat': The Creation and Organization of the Unemployed Councils in 1930," *Labor History* 8 (Fall 1967): 300–15; Coode and Petrarulo, "The Odyssey of Pittsburgh's Father Cox," 217–38.

16. Klehr, *The Heyday of American Communism*, 32, 56–58; *Washington Star*, 7 January 1932.

17. Klehr, *The Heyday of American Communism*, 64, 221–22, 308; Pittsburgh Civil Liberties Committee Minutes, 30 November 1932 (Elmer Cope Papers, Box, 9, OHS).

18. *Pittsburgh Post-Gazette*, 10 January 1932; Weber, *Don't Call Me Boss*, 47; Cope letter to Muste, 12 January 1932; Coode and Petrarulo, "The Odyssey of Pittsburgh's Father Cox," 217–38; Jacob Feldman, *The Jewish Experience in Western Pennsylvania: A History, 1755–1945* (Pittsburgh: Historical Society of Western Pennsylvania, 1986), 248–49; Rev. James R. Cox, "Father Cox's Own Story of Jobless March to Capitol," Diocese of Pittsburgh Pamphlet (James R. Cox Papers, DPA).

19. Jo Ann Robinson, "A. J. Muste: Prophet in the Wilderness of the Modern World," in Charles DeBenedetti, ed., *Peace Heroes in Twentieth-Century America* (Bloomington: Indiana University Press, 1988), 147–67; Harry Howe letter to Elmer Cope, 17 August 1932 (Elmer Cope Papers, Box 9, OHS); Klehr, *The Heyday of American Communism*, 15–16, 99, 102–3; John Brophy, *A Miner's Life* (Madison: University of Wisconsin Press, 1964), 211–12.

20. *Pittsburgh Sun-Telegraph*, 5 January 1932; *Pittsburgh Press*, 5 January 1932; Cope letter to Muste, 12 January 1932; Coode and Petrarulo, "The Odyssey of Pittsburgh's Father Cox," 217–38; Paul F. Boller Jr., *Presidential Campaigns* (New York: Oxford University Press, 1985), 223–30.

21. Cope letter to Muste, 12 January 1932; Elmer Cope letter to A. J. Muste, 25 January 1932 (Elmer Cope Papers, Box 8, OHS); Elmer Cope letter to Goldie McCue, 13 January 1932 (Elmer Cope Papers, Box 8, OHS); Robinson, "A. J. Muste," 147–67; Dennis Clark, *The Irish in Philadelphia: Ten Generations of Urban Experience* (Philadelphia: Temple University Press, 1984), 5–6.

22. Cox, "Father Cox's Own Story of Jobless March to Capitol"; Coode and Petrarulo, "The Odyssey of Pittsburgh's Father Cox," 217–38; *Pittsburgh Federated Press*, 11 January 1932 (Elmer Cope Papers, Box 8, OHS); *Pittsburgh Sun-Telegraph*, 5 January 1932; Johnstown *Tribune*, 5 January 1932; Eddie McCloskey Scrapbook (Eddie McCloskey Papers, JAHA); Leuchtenburg, *Franklin D. Roosevelt and the New Deal, 1932–1940*, 71–72.

23. *Pittsburgh Sun-Telegraph*, 5 January 1932; *Johnstown Tribune*, 5 January 1932.

24. Cox, "Father's Cox's Own Story of Jobless March to Capitol"; Coode and Petrarulo, "The Odyssey of Pittsburgh's Father Cox," 217–38; Kenneth Jackson, *The Ku Klux Klan in the City, 1915–1930* (New York: Oxford University Press, 1967), 170–73, 237, 240.

25. Elmer Cope, Personal Notes on Father Cox's March on Washington, 1932 (Elmer Cope Papers, Box 8, OHS).

26. Cope, Personal Notes on Father Cox's March on Washington, 1932; Cox, "Father Cox's Own Story of Jobless March to Capitol"; Gifford Pinchot, "Speech to Father's Cox's Army in Front of Capitol," 6 January 1932 (Elmer Cope Papers, Box 8, OHS); *Pittsburgh Federated Press*, 7 January 1932 (Elmer Cope Papers, Box 8, OHS); *Washington Times*, 6 January 1932; Henwood, "Politics and Unemployment Relief, Pennsylvania, 1931–1939," 5–8.

27. Cope, Personal Notes on Father Cox's March on Washington, 1932; Cox, "Father Cox's Own Story of Jobless March to Capitol"; *Washington Daily News*, 6 January 1932.

28. Cox, "Father Cox's Own Story of Jobless March to Capitol."

29. Cox, "Father Cox's Own Story of Jobless March to Capitol"; *Washington Daily News*, 7 January 1932.

30. Leo Reed letter to Herbert Hoover, 31 December 1931 (James R. Cox Papers, DPA); Lawrence Richey Memorandum to White House Staff, 4 January 1932 (James R. Cox Papers,

DPA); H. P. McInerney Memorandum to Presidential Executive Assistant, 7 January 1932 (James R. Cox Papers, DPA); White House Newspaper Clipping File on Father James R. Cox (James R. Cox Papers, DPA). The documents cited here were originally found in Secretary's Files, James R. Cox, 1931–1932, Presidential Papers, Herbert Hoover Library, Stanford University.

31. *Washington Daily News*, 7 January 1932; Anthony Cave Brown, *The Last Hero: Wild Bill Donovan* (New York: Vintage, 1984), 114–16.

32. *Washington Daily News*, 7 January 1932.

33. *Washington Daily News*, 7 January 1932; Cope, Personal Notes on Father Cox's March on Washington, 1932; Cox, "Father Cox's Own Story of Jobless March to Capitol"; The Father Cox March of the Jobless, Leaflet, 1932 (Elmer Cope Papers, Box 8, OHS); Herbert Hoover, Statement to Father James R. Cox and the Press, 7 January 1932 (James R. Cox Papers, DPA). The Hoover statement was originally found in the Hoover Presidential Library.

34. *Pittsburgh Sun-Telegraph*, 16 January 1932; *Pittsburgh Press*, 17 January 1932; Coode and Petrarulo, "The Odyssey of Pittsburgh's Father Cox," 217–38.

35. Cope, Personal Notes on Father Cox's March on Washington, 1932; Cox, "Father Cox's Own Story of Jobless March to Capitol"; Coode and Petrarulo, "The Odyssey of Pittsburgh's Father Cox," 217–38; *Pittsburgh Sun-Telegraph*, 16 January 1932; *Pittsburgh Press*, 17 January 1932; Message of Governor [Gifford] Pinchot to Mass Meeting of Unemployed at Pittsburgh, 16 January 1932 (Elmer Cope Papers, Box 8, OHS); John Jay Ewers, "Father Cox's Blue Shirts," *The Christian Century* 49 (22 June 1932): 795–97; Weber, *Don't Call Me Boss*, 107.

36. Coode and Petrarulo, "The Odyssey of Pittsburgh's Father Cox," 217–38; Cope, Personal Notes on Father Cox's March on Washington, 1932; *The New York Times*, 17 January 1932; *Pittsburgh Press*, 17 January 1932; "Priest Leads Unemployed," 235.

37. *Pittsburgh Post-Gazette*, 9 January 1932; Coode and Petrarulo, "The Odyssey of Pittsburgh's Father Cox," 217–38; Burner, *Herbert Hoover*, 175, 193, 208, 280; O'Connor, *Mellon's Millions*, 4–5, 36, 318–19.

38. Ewers, "Father Cox's Blue Shirts," 795–97; Coode and Petrarulo, "The Odyssey of Pittsburgh's Father Cox," 217–38; Casimir Orlemanski letter to Herbert Hoover, 20 January 1932 (James R. Cox Papers, DPA). The Orlemanski letter was originally deposited in the Hoover Library.

39. *Pittsburgh Federated Press*, 18 January 1932 (Elmer Cope Papers, Box 8, OHS); "Hodge-Podge of Good-Will," *The World Tomorrow* 15 (14 September 1932): 246; Coode and Petrarulo, "The Odyssey of Pittsburgh's Father Cox," 217–38; Elmer Cope letter to A. J. Muste, 27 April 1932 (Elmer Cope Papers, Box 8, OHS); Father Cox Blue Shirts, leaflet, 1932 (Elmer Cope Papers, Box 8, OHS).

40. Ewers, "Father Cox's Blue Shirts," 795–97; J. J. Lee, *Ireland, 1912–1985: Politics and Society* (New York: Cambridge University Press, 1989), 179–82.

41. Cope letter to Muste, 27 April 1932; Elmer Cope letter to A. J. Muste, 11 October 1931 (Elmer Cope Papers, Box 8, OHS); Elmer Cope letter to A. J. Muste, 6 November 1931 (Elmer Cope Papers, Box 8, OHS).

42. *Pittsburgh Sun-Telegraph*, 22 January 1932; Coode and Petrarulo, "The Odyssey of Pittsburgh's Father Cox," 217–38.

43. Ewers, "Father Cox's Blue Shirts," 795–97; Coode and Petrarulo, "The Odyssey of Pittsburgh's Father Cox," 217–38; "Father Cox's Army at St. Louis," *The Christian Century* 49 (31 August 1932): 1044; Charles O. Ransford, "Father Cox's Hosts Hold Convention," *The Christian Century* 49 (31 August 1932): 1060–61.

44. Andrew J. Krupnick, "Father Cox's Campaign for the Presidency of the United States, Personal Diary, 1932" (James R. Cox Papers, DPA); Coode and Petrarulo, "The Odyssey of Pittsburgh's Father Cox," 217–38.

45. Boller, *Presidential Campaigns*, 231–39; *Pittsburgh Catholic*, 7 July 1932.

46. *Pittsburgh Catholic*, 14 July 1932; Weber, *Don't Call Me Boss*, 52–53; Neal R. Peirce, *The Megastates of America: People, Politics, and Power in the Ten Great States* (New York: W. W. Norton, 1972), 245–47; *Pittsburgh Bulletin Index*, 10 May 1934.

47. *Pittsburgh Press*, 18 October 1932; George Q. Flynn, *American Catholics and the Roosevelt Presidency, 1932–1936* (Lexington: University of Kentucky Press, 1968), 17–18.

48. Andrew Buni, *Robert L. Vann of the Pittsburgh Courier: Politics and Black Journalism* (Pittsburgh: University of Pittsburgh Press, 1974), 178–79, 187, 190–97; Weber, *Don't Call Me Boss*, 48–50.

49. Peter Gottlieb, *Making Their Own Way: Southern Blacks' Migration to Pittsburgh, 1916–1930* (Urbana: University of Illinois Press, 1987), 147–64; Thomas Bell, *Out of This Furnace: A Novel of Immigrant Labor in America* (Pittsburgh: University of Pittsburgh Press, 1992), 330; John J. Bukowczyk, *And My Children Did Not Know Me: A History of the Polish-Americans* (Bloomington: Indiana University Press, 1987), 99.

50. Ronald L. Filipelli, *Labor in the USA: A History* (New York: Alfred A. Knopf, 1984), 164–68; Burner, *Herbert Hoover*, 176; Melvyn Dubofsky and Warren Van Tine, *John L. Lewis: A Biography* (Urbana: University of Illinois Press, 1986), 126; David J. McDonald, *Union Man* (New York: E. P. Dutton, 1969), 66–69; Ronald W. Schatz, "Philip Murray and the Subordination of the Industrial Unions to the United States Government," in Melvyn Dubofsky and Warren Van Tine, eds., *Labor Leaders in America* (Urbana: University of Illinois Press, 1987), 234–57.

51. *Pittsburgh Catholic*, 27 October 1932; Weber, *Don't Call Me Boss*, 53.

52. Kristi Andersen, *The Creation of a Democratic Majority, 1928–1936* (Chicago: University of Chicago Press, 1979), 19–38; Edgar Eugene Robinson, *They Voted for Roosevelt: The Presidential Vote, 1932–1944* (New York: Octagon, 1970), 147; Leuchtenburg, *Franklin D. Roosevelt and the New Deal, 1932–1940*, 17.

53. *Pittsburgh Catholic*, 12 May 1932.

## *Chapter 2: Social Reconstruction*

1. Victor Anthony Walsh, "'Across the Big Wather': Irish Community Life in Pittsburgh and Allegheny City, 1850–1885," Ph.D. diss., University of Pittsburgh, 1983, 152–54; James T. Lemon, *The Best Poor Man's Country: A Geographical Study of Early Southeastern Pennsylvania* (Baltimore: Johns Hopkins University Press, 1972).

2. Bruce Laurie, *The Working People of Philadelphia, 1800–1850* (Philadelphia: Temple University Press, 1980), 35–52; Solon J. Buck and Elizabeth Hawthorn Buck, *The Planting of Civilization in Western Pennsylvania* (Pittsburgh: University of Pittsburgh Press, 1979), 120–24.

3. Francis G. Couvares, *The Remaking of Pittsburgh: Class and Culture in an Industrializing City, 1877–1919* (Albany: State University of New York Press, 1984), 34–35; John N. Ingham, "Steel City Aristocrats," in Samuel P. Hays, ed., *City at the Point: Essays on the Social History of Pittsburgh* (Pittsburgh: University of Pittsburgh Press, 1989), 265–94.

4. Lincoln Steffens, *The Shame of the Cities* (New York: Hill & Wang, 1962), 101; *Pittsburgh Sun-Telegraph*, 15 August 1921, 9 September 1921.

5. Couvares, *The Remaking of Pittsburgh*, 117–18.

6. Couvares, *The Remaking of Pittsburgh*, 99–100; E. Digby Baltzell, *The Protestant Establishment: Aristocracy and Caste in America* (New York: Vintage, 1964), 210, 362–68; Marcia Graham Synnot, "Anti-Semitism and American Universities: Did Quotas Follow the Jews?" in David Gerber, ed., *Anti-Semitism in American History* (Urbana: University of Illinois Press, 1987), 233–71.

7. Kenneth J. Heineman, "The Changing Face of Schenley Park," *Pittsburgh History* 72

(fall 1989): 112–27; Susan P. Ruben, ed., *Thistletalk* 14 (summer 1986), publication of the Winchester-Thurston Alumnae Association, 7; *Pittsburgh Bulletin Index,* 8 February 1934; Thomas Dyer, *Theodore Roosevelt and the Idea of Race* (Baton Rouge: Louisiana State University Press, 1980), 1–68, 143–67.

8. Thomas Bell, *Out of This Furnace: A Novel of Immigrant Labor in America* (Pittsburgh: University of Pittsburgh Press, 1992), 119–208; John Bodnar, *Steelton: Immigration and Industrialization, 1870–1940* (Pittsburgh: University of Pittsburgh Press, 1990), 76–126.

9. Couvares, *The Remaking of Pittsburgh,* 127–31; David Brody, *Steelworkers in America: The Nonunion Era* (New York: Harper & Row, 1969), 231–62; David Saposs interview by Alice M. Hoffman, HCLA, Washington, D. C., 4 May 1966.

10. Baltzell, *The Protestant Establishment,* 202–4; John Higham, *Strangers in the Land: Patterns of American Nativism, 1860–1925* (New York: Atheneum, 1978), 324–30; Brody, *Steelworkers in America,* 254–55.

11. John Brophy, *A Miner's Life* (Madison: University of Wisconsin Press, 1964), 88–89, 176–77, 184–85; Harvey O'Connor, *Mellon's Millions: The Biography of a Fortune* (New York: John Day, 1933), 218–19, 224–25.

12. *Pittsburgh Bulletin Index,* 4 January 1934; *Pittsburgh Federated Press,* 25 April 1932.

13. Saposs interview.

14. Administrative Committee of the National Catholic War Council, "Bishops' Program of Social Reconstruction, February 12, 1919," in Rev. Raphael Huber, ed., *Our Bishops Speak: National Pastorals and Annual Statements of the Hierarchy of the United States, 1919–1951* (Milwaukee, Wis: Bruce Publishing, 1952), 243–260.

15. Bell, *Out of This Furnace,* 411; Clement J. Hrtanek, Record of Priests, Diocese of Pittsburgh (Clement J. Hrtanek Papers, DPA); Annemarie Draham, "Unlikely Allies Fight for Unionization: Homestead, Pennsylvania, 1933–1946," M.A. thesis, Indiana University of Pennsylvania, 1984; Curtis Miner, *Homestead: The Story of a Steel Town, 1860–1945* (Pittsburgh: Historical Society of Western Pennsylvania, 1989), 39, 43.

16. Brophy, *A Miner's Life,* 9, 100, 127, 223.

17. Pat Fagan Interview by Alice M. Hoffman, HCLA, Pittsburgh, Pa., 24 September 1968; Wayne G. Broehl Jr., *The Molly Maguires* (New York: Chelsea House, 1983), 152–362.

18. *Pittsburgh Catholic,* 16 March 1933, 18 May 1933.

19. *Pittsburgh Catholic,* 10 August 1933.

20. *Pittsburgh Catholic,* 31 August 1933, 28 September 1933.

21. Hugh Boyle letter to Thomas Lappan, 5 March 1940 (Thomas Lappan Papers, DPA); Patrick J. McGeever, *Rev. Charles Owen Rice: Apostle of Contradiction* (Pittsburgh: Duquesne University Press, 1989), 23, 60.

22. *Pittsburgh Catholic,* 7 April 1932, 4 May 1933, 9 November 1933, 16 November 1933.

23. Anthony J. Badger, *The New Deal: The Depression Years, 1933–1940* (New York: Hill & Wang, 1989), 201.

24. William E. Leuchtenburg, *Franklin D. Roosevelt and the New Deal, 1932–1940* (New York: Harper & Row, 1963), 53, 174; Badger, *The New Deal,* 206; *Pittsburgh Catholic,* 4 May 1933, 18 May 1933, 31 August 1933.

25. *Pittsburgh Catholic,* 4 May 1933, 18 October 1934, 25 October 1934, 12 September 1935, 21 November 1935.

26. *Pittsburgh Catholic,* 18 May 1933.

27. "Present Crisis, 1933," in Huber, ed., *Our Bishops Speak,* 272–300.

28. Leuchtenburg, *Franklin D. Roosevelt and the New Deal, 1932–1940,* 64–71.

29. Sean Dennis Cashman, *America in the Twenties and Thirties: The Olympian Age of Franklin Delano Roosevelt* (New York: New York University Press, 1989), 154, 162–65; Francis L. Broderick, *Right Reverend New Dealer: John A. Ryan* (New York: Macmillan, 1963), 211–16.

30. Frances Perkins, *The Roosevelt I Knew* (New York: Viking, 1946), 216; *Pittsburgh Catholic*, 3 August 1933; Broderick, *Right Reverend New Dealer*, 215.

31. Perkins, *The Roosevelt I Knew*, 217–20; *Pittsburgh Catholic*, 3 August 1933.

32. Perkins, *The Roosevelt I Knew*, 221; Miner, *Homestead*, 44–45; Arthur Schlesinger Jr., *The Coming of the New Deal* (Boston: Houghton Mifflin, 1959), 143–44.

33. Arthur G. Burgoyne, *The Homestead Strike of 1892* (Pittsburgh: University of Pittsburgh Press, 1982).

34. Miner, *Homestead*, 44–48; Curtis Miner, "Mill Towns, the 'Underworld Fraternity,' and the Working Man: Reconsidering Local Politics and Corruption Within the Industrial Suburb, Homestead, Pennsylvania, 1921–1937," Unpublished manuscript, 1988.

35. Miner, *Homestead*, 44–48; Miner, "Mill Towns, the 'Underworld Fraternity,' and the Working Man."

36. John S. Mayer Affidavit, 29 August 1933 (Clinton S. Golden Papers, Box 5, HCLA); William Green, President, American Federation of Labor, letter to Gifford Pinchot, Governor of Pennsylvania, 30 August 1933 (Clinton S. Golden Papers, Box 5, HCLA); Thomas R. Brooks, *Clint: A Biography of a Labor Intellectual* (New York: Atheneum, 1978), 128–29.

37. David J. McDonald, *Union Man* (New York: E. P. Dutton 1969), 43–44.

38. McDonald, *Union Man*, 58–59; Brophy, *A Miner's Life*, 230.

39. Harvey and Jessie O'Connor interview by Don Kennedy, HCLA, Little Compton, R.I., March 1976; Harvey Klehr, *The Heyday of American Communism: The Depression Decade* (New York: Basic Books, 1984), 44–47, 120–22, 133; Jessie Lloyd O'Connor, Harvey O'Connor, and Susan M. Bowler, *Harvey and Jessie: A Couple of Radicals* (Philadelphia: Temple University Press, 1988), 58–78, 159, 201–3.

40. Harvey and Jessie O'Connor interview; Klehr, *The Heyday of American Communism*, 74; A. J. Muste letter to Elmer Cope, 2 October 1931 (Elmer Cope Papers, Box 8, OHS).

41. William Z. Foster, *Unionizing Steel* (New York: Workers Library Publishers, 1936); Steve Valocchi, "The Unemployed Workers Movement of the 1930s: A Reexamination of the Piven and Cloward Thesis," *Social Problems* 37 (May 1990): 191–205; Brody, *Steelworkers in America*, 214–62.

42. John T. Gillard, "The Negro Challenges Communism," *The Commonweal* 16 (25 May 1932): 96–98; *Daily Worker* (New York City), 27 September 1932; Mark Naison, *Communists in Harlem During the Depression* (Urbana: University of Illinois Press, 1983), 136–37, 309.

43. McDonald, *Union Man*, 76–77.

44. A. J. Muste, Conference for Progressive Labor Action circular, "A Project in Education and Organization Among Steel Workers," 5 February 1932 (Elmer Cope Papers, Box 8, OHS); Elmer Cope letter to A. J. Muste, 1 May 1933 (Elmer Cope Papers, Box 10, OHS); Elmer Cope, "A Critical Analysis of and a Progressive Program for the Amalgamated Association of Iron, Steel, and Tin Workers of North America," 1932 (Elmer Cope Papers, Box 8, OHS); Melvyn Dubofsky and Warren Van Tine, *John L. Lewis: A Biography* (Urbana: University of Illinois Press, 1986), 131–47.

45. *Pittsburgh Catholic*, 4 January 1934, 25 January 1934, 1 February 1934.

46. *Pittsburgh Catholic*, 15 February 1934; J. Joseph Huthmacher, *Senator Robert F. Wagner and the Rise of Urban Liberalism* (New York: Atheneum, 1971), 160–61.

47. *Pittsburgh Catholic*, 22 February 1934.

48. *Pittsburgh Bulletin Index*, 1 February 1934; John P. Hoerr, *And the Wolf Finally Came: The Decline of the American Steel Industry* (Pittsburgh: University of Pittsburgh Press, 1989), 464.

49. *Pittsburgh Bulletin Index*, 21 December 1933, 29 March 1934; Schlesinger, *The Coming of the New Deal*, 142–43, 148–49.

50. *Pittsburgh Catholic*, 26 April 1934; "Rights of Workers to Organize, 12 April 1934," in Huber, ed., *Our Bishops Speak*, 305–6.

51. Carl P. Hensler, Record of Priests, Diocese of Pittsburgh (Carl P. Hensler Papers, DPA); Carl P. Hensler, Curriculum Vitae, 1954 (Carl P. Hensler Papers, DPA); *Pittsburgh Catholic*, "Msgr. Carl P. Hensler," 30 November 1984.

52. Hensler, Record of Priests; McGeever, *Rev. Charles Owen Rice*, 42; Carl P. Hensler letters to Hugh Boyle, 28 June 1930, 26 January 1931, 20 November 1931.

53. *Pittsburgh Catholic*, 26 July 1934, 13 December 1934.

54. *Pittsburgh Catholic*, 4 October 1934, 1 November 1934.

55. *Pittsburgh Catholic*, 15 February 1934, 26 April 1934.

56. Harold L. Ickes, *The Secret Diary of Harold L. Ickes: The Inside Struggle, 1936–1939*, 2 vols. (New York: Simon & Schuster, 1954), 2:86; *Pittsburgh Catholic*, 8 March 1934; Kenneth J. Heineman, "Media Bias in Coverage of the Dies Committee on Un-American Activities, 1938–1940," *The Historian* 55 (autumn 1992): 37–52; Graham J. White, *FDR and the Press* (Chicago: University of Chicago Press, 1979), 27–46.

57. *Pittsburgh Catholic*, 26 July 1934, 30 August 1934.

58. Clinton S. Golden, Application for Government Employment, 1948 (Clinton S. Golden Papers, Box 1, HCLA); Clinton S. Golden, Resume, 1948 (Clinton S. Golden Papers, Box 1, HCLA); Rev. L. Golden Obituary Clippings, 1898, 1899 (Clinton S. Golden Papers, Box 1, HCLA); *Washington Post*, "'Clint' Golden as a Labor Leader Commands Respect of Union and Industry Alike," 13 September 1948; Brooks, *Clint*, 87–127, 138.

59. Brooks, *Clint*, 128–37; Clinton Golden, The Case of George Issoski, 1934 (Clinton S. Golden Papers, Box 5, HCLA).

60. O'Connor, *Mellon's Millions*, 251; Robert C. Alberts, *Pitt: The Story of the University of Pittsburgh, 1787–1987* (Pittsburgh: University of Pittsburgh Press, 1986), 124–83.

61. O'Connor, *Mellon's Millions*, 251–52; Roy Lubove, *Twentieth-Century Pittsburgh: Government, Business, and Environmental Change* (New York: John Wiley & Sons, 1969), 60.

62. O'Connor, *Mellon's Millions*, 251–52; *The Young Socialist* (Pittsburgh), 23 September 1931 (Elmer Cope Papers, Box 7, OHS); *Voice of Revolt* (Pittsburgh), 1931 (Elmer Cope Papers, Box 7, OHS); *The Gadfly* (Pittsburgh), January 1932 (Elmer Cope Papers, Box 7, OHS);

63. "Student Inquiry into Effects of Social and Economic Forces," pamphlet, June 1933 (Elmer Cope Papers, Box 10, OHS); Pittsburgh League for Social Justice, membership List, 1932 (Elmer Cope Papers, Box 8, OHS); Pittsburgh League for Social Justice, pamphlet, 1933 (Elmer Cope Papers, Box 8, OHS).

64. Elmer Cope letter to Communist Party District 5, 5 July 1932 (Elmer Cope Papers, Box 8, OHS); *Pittsburgh Catholic*, 28 February 1935; Harold Ruttenberg, "Pittsburgh Tightens Up," article draft, 1934 (Harold J. Ruttenberg Papers, Box 11, HCLA); O'Connor, *Mellon's Millions*, 252–53; Lubove, *Twentieth-Century Pittsburgh*, 60–61; Rose M. Stein, "Academic Cossacks in Pittsburgh," *The Nation* 141 (24 June 1935): 105–6.

65. Bonnie Fox Schwartz, *The Civil Works Administration, 1933–1934: The Business of Emergency Employment in the New Deal* (Princeton: Princeton University Press, 1984), 114.

66. *Pittsburgh Catholic*, 26 April 1934, 6 September 1934; Arthur Hertzberg, *The Jews in America: Four Centuries of Uneasy Encounter* (New York: Simon & Schuster, 1990), 243; *Pittsburgh Bulletin Index*, 10 May 1934; Michael P. Weber, *Don't Call Me Boss: David L. Lawrence, Pittsburgh's Renaissance Mayor* (Pittsburgh: University of Pittsburgh Press, 1988), 95–101.

67. Weber, *Don't Call Me Boss*, 101; Leuchtenburg, *Franklin D. Roosevelt and the New Deal*, 116–17; *Pittsburgh Catholic*, 8 November 1934.

68. "Call to a National Congress for Unemployment and Social Insurance," Communist Party pamphlet, 1935 (Harold J. Ruttenberg Papers, Box 1, HCLA); Harvey and Jessie O'Connor interview; Harold J. Ruttenberg letter to Robert Lieberman, 4 October 1935 (Harold J. Ruttenberg Papers, Box 1, HCLA); Minutes of the United Front Meeting of all Unemployed Organizations in Pennsylvania, September 20, 1935 (Harold J. Ruttenberg Papers, Box 1,

HCLA); Brooks, *Clint*, 138–39; Charles P. Larrowe, *Harry Bridges: The Rise and Fall of Radical Labor in the United States* (New York: Lawrence Hill, 1972), 32–61.

69. Klehr, *The Heyday of American Communism*, 94, 133; Cashman, *America in the Twenties and Thirties*, 228–29.

70. Otis L. Graham and Meghan Robinson Wander, eds., *Franklin D. Roosevelt, His Life and Times: An Encyclopedic View* (New York: Da Capo Press, 1990), 20–22.

71. Graham and Warner, eds., *Franklin D. Roosevelt, His Life and Times*, 65–66, 132–33, 461–64.

72. Klehr, *The Heyday of American Communism*, 283; Pennsylvania Security League, *Labor Union Record* (Harrisburg), 8 May 1936 (Harold J. Ruttenberg Papers, Box 11, HCLA); Wilson Jerome Warren, "Underneath the Radical Veil: An Examination of a Local of the Unemployed Citizens League of Allegheny County," Doctoral seminar paper, University of Pittsburgh, 1987; *Pittsburgh Catholic*, 14 March 1935.

73. *Pittsburgh Catholic*, 1 February 1934, 7 February 1935, 14 February 1935, 7 March 1935, 26 September 1935; Graham and Warner, eds., *Franklin D. Roosevelt, His Life and Times*, 278–80.

74. Broderick, *Right Reverend New Dealer*, 217–19; *Pittsburgh Catholic*, 21 November 1935; Graham and Wander, eds., *Franklin D. Roosevelt, His Life and Times*, 391–92.

75. Leuchtenburg, *Franklin D. Roosevelt and the New Deal, 1932–1940*, 132–33; Huthmacher, *Senator Robert F. Wagner and the Rise of Urban Liberalism*, 219–20.

76. *Pittsburgh Catholic*, 12 December 1935, 26 December 1935; Graham and Wander, eds., *Franklin D. Roosevelt, His Life and Times*, 274–77; Broderick, *Right Reverend New Dealer*, 218–19; Leuchtenburg, *Franklin D. Roosevelt and the New Deal, 1932–1940*, 144–46.

77. Graham and Wander, eds., *Franklin D. Roosevelt, His Life and Times*, 275; Broderick, *Right Reverend New Dealer*, 220; Huthmacher, *Senator Robert F. Wagner and the Rise of Urban Liberalism*, 190–98; *Pittsburgh Catholic*, 13 June 1935; Harvey Klehr, John Earl Haynes, and Fridrikh Igorevich Firsov, *The Secret World of American Communism* (New Haven: Yale University Press, 1995), 98–106; David J. Saposs, "The Catholic Church and the Labor Movement," *Modern Monthly* 2 (May 1933): 225–30; Saposs interview.

78. Cashman, *America in the Twenties and Thirties*, 235–36; Schlesinger, *The Coming of the New Deal*, 412–14.

79. Ronald W. Schatz, "Philip Murray and the Subordination of the Industrial Unions to the United States Government," in Melvyn Dubofsky and Warren Van Tine, *Labor Leaders in America* (Urbana: University of Illinois Press, 1987), 234–57; Abe Raskin, "Comments," in Paul F. Clark, Peter Gottlieb, and Donald Kennedy, eds., *Forging a Union of Steel: Philip Murray, SWOC, and the United Steelworkers* (Ithaca, N.Y.: Industrial and Labor Relations Press, Cornell University), 113–17.

80. *Pittsburgh Catholic*, 12 December 1935.

81. James P. Shenton, "The Coughlin Movement and the New Deal," *Political Science Quarterly* 73 (September 1958): 353–73; Alan Brinkley, *Voices of Protest: Huey Long, Father Coughlin, and the Great Depression* (New York: Vintage, 1982), 82–123.

82. Shenton, "The Coughlin Movement and the New Deal," 353–73; Brinkley, *Voices of Protest*, 124–42; *Pittsburgh Catholic*, 30 March 1933, 14 March 1935. The *Pittsburgh Catholic* ran a number of stories on Coughlin in 1933, fewer in 1934, and generally ignored him in 1935.

83. *Pittsburgh Catholic*, 2 July 1936, 16 July 1936, 30 July 1936, 6 August 1936; Leuchtenburg, *Franklin D. Roosevelt and the New Deal, 1932–1940*, 179–84; Shenton, "The Coughlin Movement and the New Deal," 353–73; Steven P. Erie, *Rainbow's End: Irish-Americans and the Dilemmas of Urban Machine Politics, 1840–1985* (Berkeley and Los Angeles: University of California Press, 1988), 99, 105, 116–17, 128.

84. Mel Piehl, *Breaking Bread: The Catholic Worker and the Origin of Catholic Radicalism*

*in America* (Philadelphia: Temple University Press, 1982), 67–68, 77; McGeever, *Rev. Charles Owen Rice*, 37–40.

85. Andrew M. Greeley, "What is Subsidiarity? A Voice from Sleepy Hollow," *America* 153 (9 November 1985): 292–95.

## Chapter 3: City of God

1. *Pittsburgh Catholic*, 4 April 1935, 18 July 1935, 1 August 1935, 28 May 1936, 4 June 1936.

2. John J. Appel, "American Negro and Immigrant Experience: Similarities and Differences," *American Quarterly* 18 (1966): 95–103; Suzanne W. Model, "Work and Family: Blacks and Immigrants from South and East Europe," in Virginia Yans-McLaughlin, ed., *Immigration Reconsidered: History, Sociology, and Politics* (New York: Oxford University Press, 1990), 130–59; *Pittsburgh Catholic*, 4 May 1933, 18 October 1934, 25 October 1934, 12 September 1935, 21 November 1935.

3. Thomas Bell, *Out of This Furnace: A Novel of Immigrant Labor in America* (Pittsburgh: University of Pittsburgh Press, 1992), 330; John Bodnar, Roger Simon, and Michael P. Weber, *Lives of Their Own: Blacks, Italians, and Poles in Pittsburgh, 1900–1960* (Urbana: University of Illinois Press, 1983), 188–90; Peter Gottlieb, *Making Their Own Way: Southern Blacks' Migration to Pittsburgh, 1916–1930* (Urbana: University of Illinois Press, 1987), 43, 56–58.

4. Bodnar et al., *Lives of Their Own*, 36, 159–60, 191, 200, 214; *Pittsburgh Catholic*, 28 June 1934, 21 June 1937.

5. Bodnar et al., *Lives of Their Own*, 191, 198–96; Nancy J. Weiss, *Farewell to the Party of Lincoln: Black Politics in the Age of FDR* (Princeton: Princeton University Press, 1983), 183; *Pittsburgh Bulletin Index*, 1 February 1934; Dennis C. Dickerson, *Out of the Crucible: Black Steelworkers in Western Pennsylvania, 1875–1980* (Albany: State University of New York Press, 1986), 56; Gottlieb, *Making Their Own Way*, 29, 69–70; Nicholas Lemann, *The Promised Land: The Great Black Migration and How it Changed America* (New York: Alfred A. Knopf, 1991), 28–32; Nicholas Lemann, "The Origins of the Underclass," Part I, *Atlantic Monthly* 257 (June 1986): 31–55, and Part II, 258 (July 1986): 54–68.

6. Bodnar et al., *Lives of Their Own*, 213–14, 222–23; Roy Lubove, *Twentieth Century Pittsburgh: Government, Business, and Environmental Change* (New York: John Wiley & Sons, 1969), 84–85.

7. Bodnar et al., *Lives of Their Own*, 197, 213, 217, 222–23; Edward C. Banfield, *The Unheavenly City Revisited* (Boston: Little, Brown, 1974), 52–99; *Pittsburgh Courier*, 28 October 1933, 11 November 1933, 21 August 1937.

8. Bodnar et al., *Lives of Their Own*, 199–200; David J. Cuff, William J. Young, Edward K. Muller, Wilbur Zelinsky, Ronald F. Abler, eds., *The Atlas of Pennsylvania* (Philadelphia: Temple University Press, 1989), 165.

9. John Edgar Wideman, *The Homewood Books* (Pittsburgh: University of Pittsburgh Press, 1992), "Damballah," 36.

10. *Pittsburgh Courier*, 28 October 1933, 11 November 1933, 17 July 1937, 21 August 1937, 14 June 1941; Wideman, *The Homewood Books*, passim.

11. *Pittsburgh Courier*, 28 October 1933, 30 October 1937, 27 November 1937, 29 March 1941.

12. Andrew Buni, *Robert L. Vann of the Pittsburgh Courier: Politics and Black Journalism* (Pittsburgh: University of Pittsburgh Press, 1974), 3–42.

13. *Pittsburgh Courier*, 3 July 1937, 20 November 1937, 1 October 1938, 15 October 1938,

5 November 1938, 14 June 1941, 28 June 1941, 5 July 1941; Buni, *Robert L. Vann of the Pitts-burgh Courier*, 174–221; Weiss, *Farewell to the Party of Lincoln*, 96–119, 157–79.

14. *Pittsburgh Courier*, 26 June 1937, 24 July 1937, 31 July 1937; John B. Kirby, *Black Americans in the Roosevelt Era: Liberalism and Race* (Knoxville: University of Tennessee Press, 1982), 132–39; Buni, *Robert L. Vann of the Pittsburgh Courier*, 101.

15. *Pittsburgh Courier*, 3 July 1937, 10 July 1937, 14 June 1941, Buni, *Robert L. Vann of the Pittsburgh Courier*, 249, 251, 262–63.

16. *Pittsburgh Courier*, 30 October 1937; *Pittsburgh Bulletin Index*, 6 October 1938; Kim Lacy Rogers, *Righteous Lives: Narratives of the New Orleans Civil Rights Movement* (New York: New York University Press, 1993), 30.

17. Jacob Feldman, *The Jewish Experience in Western Pennsylvania: A History, 1755–1945* (Pittsburgh: Historical Society of Western Pennsylvania, 1986), 46–47.

18. Robert A. Caro, *The Power Broker: Robert Moses and the Fall of New York* (New York: Alfred A. Knopf, 1974), 30–31; Nora Faires, "Immigrants and Industry: Peopling the 'Iron City,'" in Samuel P. Hays, ed., *City at the Point: Essays on the Social History of Pittsburgh* (Pittsburgh: University of Pittsburgh Press, 1989), 3–31; Linda K. Pritchard, "The Soul of the City: A Social History of Religion in Pittsburgh," in Hays, ed., *City at the Point,* University of Pittsburgh Press 327–60; Arthur Hertzberg, *The Jews in America: Four Centuries of an Uneasy Encounter* (New York: Simon & Schuster, 1990), 147–49.

19. Roger Daniels, *Coming to America: A History of Immigration and Ethnicity in American Life* (New York: Harper Perennial, 1990), 223–24; John Higham, *Strangers in the Land: Patterns of American Nativism, 1860–1925* (New York: Atheneum, 1978), 23; Leonard Dinnerstein and David M. Reimers, *Ethnic Americans: A History of Immigration and Assimilation* (New York: Harper & Row, 1982), 33–35; Ronald Sanders, *Shores of Refuge: A Hundred Years of Jewish Emigration* (New York: Schocken, 1988), 3–26.

20. Daniels, *Coming to America*, 224–26; Corrine A. Krause, *Grandmothers, Mothers, and Daughters: Oral Histories of Three Generations of Ethnic American Women* (Boston: Twayne, 1991), 113–23; Faires, "Immigrants and Industry," 3–31.

21. Krause, *Grandmothers, Mothers, and Daughters*, 113–23; Faires, "Immigrants and Industry," 3–31; Pritchard, "The Soul of the City," 327–60; Feldman, *The Jewish Experience in Western Pennsylvania*, 263; Daniels, *Coming to America*, 228.

22. Faires, "Immigrants and Industry," 3–31; Gerry (Katz) Tanack interview by author, Pittsburgh, Pa., 22 June 1989; Kenneth J. Heineman, "The Changing Face of Schenley Park," *Pittsburgh History* 72 (fall 1989): 112–27; Hyman Richman, "Life on Pittsburgh's 'Hill': Some Views and Values of Jews Who Lived There Before the 1940s," *Pittsburgh History* 74 (spring 1991): 10–19.

23. Rivka Lissak, "Myth and Reality: The Pattern of Relationship Between the Hull House Circle and the 'New Immigrants' on Chicago's West Side, 1890–1919," *Journal of American Ethnic History* 2 (spring 1983): 21–50; Rivka Shpak Lissak, *Pluralism & Progressives: Hull House and the New Immigrants, 1890–1919* (Chicago: University of Chicago Press, 1989), 34–61 108–22; Pritchard, "The Soul of the City," 327–60; Daniels, *Coming to America*, 229–30.

24. *Pittsburgh Catholic*, 21 March 1935; Feldman, *The Jewish Experience in Western Pennsylvania*, 248; Liston Pope, "Religion and Class Structure," *Annals of the Academy of Political and Social Science* 256 (March 1948): 84–95.

25. Pope, "Religion and Class Structure," 84–95; Hadley Cantril, "Educational and Economic Composition of Religious Groups: An Analysis of the Poll Data," *American Journal of Sociology* 48 (March 1943): 574–79; John J. Kane, "The Social Structure of American Catholics," *American Catholic Sociological Review* 16 (March 1955): 23–30; Gottlieb, *Making Their Own Way*, 67–69.

26. David Brody, *Steelworkers in America: The Nonunion Era* (New York: Harper & Row,

1969), 100–101; Karel D. Bicha, "Hunkies: Stereotyping the Slavic immigrants, 1890–1920," *Journal of American Ethnic History* 2 (fall 1982): 16–38; Curtis Miner, *Homestead: The Story of a Steel Town* (Pittsburgh: Historical Society of Western Pennsylvania, 1989); Bell, *Out of This Furnace*, 119–210.

27. Bicha, "Hunkies," 16–38; Thomas G. Dyer, *Theodore Roosevelt and the Idea of Race* (Baton Rouge: Louisiana State University Press, 1980), 123–42; Daniels, *Coming to America*, 220; Victor R. Greene, "Poles," in Stephan Thernstrom, Ann Orlov, and Oscar Handlin, eds., *Harvard Encyclopedia of American Ethnic Groups* (Cambridge, Mass.: Harvard University Press, 1980), 787–803; Victor R. Greene, *The Slavic Community on Strike: Immigrant Labor in Pennsylvania Anthracite* (South Bend, Ind.: University of Notre Dame Press, 1968), 14–23; Charles A. Price, "Appendix I: Methods of Estimating the Size of Groups," in Thernstrom et al., *Harvard Encyclopedia of American Ethnic Groups*, 1033–44; Michael Novak, *The Rise of the Unmeltable Ethnics: Politics and Culture in the Seventies* (New York: Macmillan, 1973), 96–98.

28. Bicha, "Hunkies," 16–38; Dyer, *Theodore Roosevelt and the Idea of Race*, 123–42; "Croats," in Thernstrom et al., *Harvard Encyclopedia of American Ethnic Groups*, 247–56; Karen Johnson Freeze, "Czechs," in Thernstrom et al., *Harvard Encyclopedia of American Ethnic Groups*, 261–72; Michael B. Petrovich and Joel Halpern, "Serbs," in Thernstrom et al., *Harvard Encyclopedia of American Ethnic Groups*, 916–26; M. Mark Stolarik, "Slovaks," in Thernstrom et al., *Harvard Encyclopedia of American Ethnic Groups*, 926–34; June Granatir Alexander, "Staying Together: Chain Migration and patterns of Slovak Settlement in Pittsburgh Prior to World War I," *Journal of American Ethnic History* 1 (fall 1981): 56–83; Rudolph M. Susel, "Slovenes," in Thernstrom et al., *Harvard Encyclopedia of American Ethnic Groups*, 934–42; Price, "Appendix I," 1033–44; Bob Hoover, "Ethnic Warfare Comes to Pittsburgh: Serbs and Croatians Grapple With How to Help Their Ancestral Homeland," *Pittsburgh Magazine* (December 1992): 44–46, 65–70; George Prpic, *South Slavic Immigrants in America* (New York: Twayne, 1978), 33–35, 155–56; George Prpic, *The Croatian Immigrants in America* (New York: Philosophical Library, 1971), 176.

29. Bicha, "Hunkies," 16–38; John Bodnar, *Steelton: Immigration and Industrialization, 1870–1940* (Pittsburgh: University of Pittsburgh Press, 1990), 39, 77–78; Alfred Erich Senn and Alfonsas Eidintas, "Lithuanian Immigrants in America and the Lithuanian National Movement Before 1914," *Journal of American Ethnic History* 6 (spring 1987): 5–19; Ewa Morawska, *For Bread, With Butter: The Life-Worlds of East Central Europeans in Johnstown, Pennsylvania, 1890–1940* (New York: Cambridge University Press, 1985), 272; Novak, *The Rise of the Unmeltable Ethnics*, 77–78.

30. Bicha, "Hunkies," 16–38; Brody, *Steelworkers in America*, 99; David Ward, *Poverty, Ethnicity, and the American City, 1840–1925: Changing Conceptions of the Slum and the Ghetto* (New York: Cambridge University Press, 1989), 124; Dinnerstein and Reimers, *Ethnic Americans*, 35, 41; Daniels, *Coming to America*, 219.

31. Bicha, "Hunkies," 16–38; Krause, *Grandmothers, Mothers, and Daughters*, 145–200; John Bodnar, "Immigration, Kinship, and the Rise of Working-Class Realism in Industrial America," *Journal of Social History* 14 (fall 1980): 45–59; John Bodnar, "Socialization and Adaptation: Immigrant Families in Scranton, Pennsylvania, 1880–1890," *Pennsylvania History* 43 (April 1976): 147–62; Morawska, *For Bread, With Butter*, 187.

32. John Bodnar, *The Transplanted: A History of Immigrants in Urban America* (Bloomington: Indiana University Press, 1987), 144–68; Bodnar et al., *Lives of Their Own*, 76–77; June Granatir Alexander, *The Immigrant Church and Community: Pittsburgh's Slovak Catholics and Lutherans, 1880–1915* (Pittsburgh: University of Pittsburgh Press, 1987), 3–14; Victor R. Greene, "For God and Country: The Origins of Slavic Catholic Self-Consciousness in America," *Church History* 35 (1966): 446–60; Greene, *The Slavic Community on Strike*, 33.

33. Bodnar et al., *Lives of Their Own*, 76–77; Rudolph J. Vecoli, "Prelates and Peasants:

Italian Immigrants and the Catholic Church," *Journal of Social History* 2 (spring 1969): 217–68; Humbert S. Nelli, "Italians," in Thernstrom et al., *Harvard Encyclopedia of American Ethnic Groups*, 545–60; Michael P. Weber, *Don't Call Me Boss: David L. Lawrence, Pittsburgh's Renaissance Mayor* (Pittsburgh: University of Pittsburgh Press, 1988), 50–51.

34. Pritchard, "The Soul of the City," 327–60; Faires, "Immigrants and Industry," 3–31; Joseph J. Casino, "From Sanctuary to Involvement: A History of the Catholic Parish in the Northeast," in Jay P. Dolan, ed., *The American Catholic Parish: A History from 1850 to the Present*, 2 vols. (New York: Paulist Press, 1987), 1:111.

35. Morawska, *For Bread, With Butter*, 9, 268–69; Model, "Work and Family," 130–59; M. Mark Stolarik, "Immigration, Education, and the Social Mobility of Slovaks, 1870–1930," in Randall M. Miller and Thomas D. Marzik, eds., *Immigrants and Religion in Urban America* (Philadelphia: Temple University Press, 1977), 103–16.

36. Pritchard, "The Soul of the City," 327–60; Faires, "Immigrants and Industry," 3–31; John Higham, "Integrating America: The Problem of Assimilation in the Nineteenth Century," *Journal of American Ethnic History* 1 (fall 1981): 7–25; *Pittsburgh Catholic*, 23 May 1935, 21 November 1935, 23 January 1936, 5 December 1935, 22 December 1938, 5 October 1939, 14 December 1939; Greene, "Poles," 787–803.

37. David J. McDonald, *Union Man* (New York: E. P. Dutton, 1969), 31; Lawrence M. O'Rourke, *Geno: The Life and Mission of Geno Baroni* (New York: Paulist Press, 1991), 178; *Pittsburgh Catholic*, 20 July 1937.

38. *Pittsburgh Catholic*, 11 January 1934, 1 February 1934; Kenneth T. Jackson, *The Ku Klux Klan in the City, 1915–1930* (New York: Oxford University Press, 1970), 171.

39. Patrick J. Blessing, "Irish," in Thernstrom et al., *Harvard Encyclopedia of American Ethnic Groups*, 524–45; Daniels, *Coming to America*, 138–40, 108–9, 140–45; John Higham, *Strangers in the Land: Patterns of American Nativism, 1860–1925* (New York: Atheneum, 1978), 26, 60, 79–80; William V. Shannon, *The American Irish* (New York: Macmillan, 1966), 60–85, 151–81.

40. Blessing, "Irish," 524–45; Daniels, *Coming to America*, 136–37, 144–45; Higham, *Strangers in the Land*, 50; Aaron I. Abell, "The Reception of Leo XIII's Labor Encyclical in America, 1891–1919," *Review of Politics* 7 (October 1945): 464–95; Patrick W. Carey, ed., *American Catholic Religious Thought: The Shaping of a Theological and Social Tradition* (New York: Paulist Press, 1987), 41–46; Shannon, *The American Irish*, 60–85.

41. Kane, "The Social Structure of American Catholics," 23–30; Cantril, "Educational and Economic Composition of Religious Groups," 574–79; Pope, "Religion and Class Structure," 84–95; John B. Judis, *William F. Buckley, Jr.: Patron Saint of the Conservatives* (New York: Simon & Schuster, 1990), 17–98; Shannon, *The American Irish*, 392–413.

42. Arthur M. Schlesinger Jr., *The Coming of the New Deal* (Boston: Houghton Mifflin, 1959), 415; McDonald, *Union Man*, 87–99; John Brophy, *A Miner's Life* (Madison: University of Wisconsin Press, 1964), 240–55; *Pittsburgh Catholic*, 12 December 1935.

43. "Statement of Philip Murray," 9 July 1936 (Harold J. Ruttenberg Papers, Box 3, HCLA); Thomas R. Brooks, *Clint: A Biography of a Labor Intellectual* (New York: Atheneum, 1978), 159.

44. Philip Murray letter to Benjamin Fairless, *United Mine Workers Journal*, 1936 (Harold J. Ruttenberg Papers, Box 4, HCLA); Harold J. and Stanley Ruttenberg, "The Silvery Monster," 3 January 1940 (Harold J. Ruttenberg Papers, Box 1, HCLA); Brody, *Steelworkers in America*, 40–41.

45. Brooks, *Clint*, 145, 147, 157, 160–61; Kenneth J. Heineman, "Media Bias in Coverage of the Dies Committee on Un-American Activities, 1938–1940," *The Historian* 55 (autumn 1992): 37–52.

46. Harold J. Ruttenberg letter to Ernest T. Weir, 7 August 1936 (Harold J. Ruttenberg Pa-

pers, Box 11, HCLA); Elmer Cope letter to Harold Ruttenberg, 20 October 1936 (Harold J. Ruttenberg Papers, Box 3, HCLA); Brooks, *Clint*, 160.

47. "We Won't Sign," anti-SWOC leaflet, 1936 (Harold J. Ruttenberg Papers, Box 4, HCLA); James B. Finley, "Mr. American Worker, Warning! Don't Take the Road to the Left," anti-SWOC pamphlet, 1936 (Harold J. Ruttenberg Papers, Box 1, HCLA).

48. Morawska, *For Bread, With Butter*, 216–17, 274–75, 294–95.

49. Brooks, *Clint*, 145; *Pittsburgh Catholic*, 14 September 1933, 5 October 1939; Miner, *Homestead*; John Bodnar, *Workers' World: Kinship, Community, and Protest in an Industrial Society, 1900–1940* (Baltimore: Johns Hopkins University Press, 1982), 119–64.

50. "Philip Murray Answers Letter of Worker Over Radio," *United Mine Workers Journal*, 15 July 1936 (Harold J. Ruttenberg Papers, Box 4, HCLA).

51. Schlesinger, *The Coming of the New Deal*, 483–88; Otis L. Graham Jr., and Meghan Robinson Wander, eds., *Franklin D. Roosevelt, His Life and Times: An Encyclopedic View* (New York: Da Capo Press, 1985), 6–7, 387–88; Michael W. Miles, *The Odyssey of the American Right* (New York: Oxford University Press, 1980), 32; Raymond E. Wolfinger, "The Development and Persistence of Ethnic Voting," in Lawrence H. Fuchs, ed., *American Ethnic Politics* (New York: Harper & Row, 1968), 163–93; George Wolfskill, *The Revolt of the Conservatives: A History of the American Liberty League, 1934–1940* (Boston: Houghton Mifflin, 1962), 207.

52. *Pittsburgh Catholic*, 14 April 1932, 2 November 1933, 25 October 1934.

53. Charles H. Trout, *Boston, the Great Depression, and the New Deal* (New York: Oxford University Press, 1977), 258–71; Alan Brinkley, *Voices of Protest: Huey Long, Father Coughlin, and the Great Depression* (New York: Vintage, 1983), 121–22, 206, 254–61; Gerald H. Gamm, *The Making of New Deal Democrats: Voting Behavior and Realignment in Boston, 1920–1940* (Chicago: University of Chicago Press, 1989), 154–55.

54. Ronald H. Bayor, *Neighbors in Conflict: The Irish, Germans, Jews, and Italians of New York City, 1929–1941* (Urbana: University of Illinois Press, 1988), 31, 40–41, 46, 88–91; Steven P. Erie, *Rainbow's End: Irish-Americans and the Dilemmas of Urban Machine Politics, 1840–1985* (Berkeley and Los Angeles: University of California Press, 1988), 114–15; Brinkley, *Voices of Protest*, 104–5, 176–78.

55. Norman Podhoretz, "My Negro Problem—And Ours," in Edward Quinn and Paul J. Dolan, eds., *The Sense of the Sixties* (New York: The Free Press, 1968), 241–55.

56. O'Rourke, *Geno*, 203.

57. Clifford J. Reutter, "The Puzzle of a Pittsburgh Steeler: Joe Magarac's Ethnic Identity," *Western Pennsylvania Historical Magazine* 63 (January 1980): 31–36.

58. Prpic, *South Slavic Immigrants in America*, 75.

59. "The Murals of Saint Nicholas Croatian Roman Catholic Church," pamphlet, n.d. (in author's possession.)

60. Russell D. Buhite and David W. Levy, eds., *FDR's Fireside Chats* (New York: Penguin, 1993), 73–82.

61. Weber, *Don't Call Me Boss*, 125; Anthony J. Badger, *The New Deal: The Depression Years, 1933–1940* (New York: Hill & Wang, 1989), 249–50.

62. Weber, *Don't Call Me Boss*, 56–64, 115–19, 126; *Pittsburgh Catholic*, 19 July 1934; Priscilla Clement, "The Works Progress Administration in Pennsylvania, 1935 to 1940," *Pennsylvania Magazine of History and Biography* 95 (April 1975): 244–60.

63. Weber, *Don't Call Me Boss*, 127; Clement, "The Works Progress Administration in Pennsylvania, 1935 to 1940," 244–60; Erie, *Rainbow's End*, 127.

64. Pittsburgh Bureau of Parks, *Annual Report of Bureau of Parks, Department of Public Works, City of Pittsburgh for the Year 1938* (Pittsburgh: City of Pittsburgh, 1939); Katz interview; Heineman, "The Changing Face of Schenley Park," 112–27.

65. Feldman, *The Jewish Experience in Western Pennsylvania*, 250; Mark R. Levy and

Michael S. Kramer, *The Ethnic Factor: How America's Minorities Decide Elections* (New York: Simon & Schuster, 1972), 95–121, 140–90.

66. Pope, "Religion and the Class Structure," 84–91; Stolarik, "Immigration, Education, and Social Mobility of Slovaks, 1870–1930," 103–16.

67. Paul Buhle, "Jews and American Communism: The Cultural Question," *Radical History Review* 23 (spring 1980): 9–33; Richman, "Life on Pittsburgh's 'Hill,'" 10–19; Benjamin Ginsberg, *The Fatal Embrace: Jews and the State* (Chicago: University of Chicago Press, 1993), 1–58, 97–144; Lawrence H. Fuchs, "American Jews and the Presidential Vote," in Fuchs, ed., *American Ethnic Politics*, 50–76; David J. O'Brien, *American Catholics and Social Reform: The New Deal Years* (New York: Oxford University Press, 1968), 50–51.

68. *Pittsburgh Courier*, 21 October 1933, 18 September 1937; Celeste Behrend telephone conversation with author, 22 June 1989; Robert C. Weaver and Charlotte Moton Hubbard, "The Black Cabinet," in Katie Louchheim, ed., *The Making of the New Deal: The Insiders Speak* (Cambridge, Mass.: Harvard University Press, 1983), 261–66; Ruth Louise Simmons, "The Negro in Recent Pittsburgh Politics," M.A. thesis, University of Pittsburgh, 1945, 20, 41; T. H. Watkins, *Righteous Pilgrim: The Life and Times of Harold L. Ickes, 1874–1952* (New York: Henry Holt, 1990), 199–201.

69. Simmons, "The Negro in Recent Pittsburgh Politics," 17; Buni, *Robert L. Vann of the Pittsburgh Courier*, 272–75; *Pittsburgh Courier*, 14 October 1933, 4 September 1937; Weber, *Don't Call Me Boss*, 278–79.

70. Edgar Eugene Robinson, *They Voted for Roosevelt: The Presidential Vote, 1932–1944* (New York: Octagon, 1970), 25, 41; Weber, *Don't Call Me Boss*, 120; Simmons, "The Negro in Recent Pittsburgh Politics," 31; Badger, *The New Deal*, 254–55; Weiss, *Farewell to the Party of Lincoln*, 182–83, 196–97, 202–6; *Pittsburgh Catholic*, 7 April 1932, 4 May 1933, 18 May 1933, 9 November 1933, 16 November 1933.

71. *Pittsburgh Catholic*, 24 June 1937, 12 May 1938; *Pittsburgh Catholic*, 6 December 1934, 30 August 1934, 19 November 1936, 15 July 1937.

72. *Pittsburgh Catholic*, 19 November 1936, 26 November 1936.

73. *Pittsburgh Catholic*, 30 July 1936; Dorothy Day, *The Long Loneliness: An Autobiography* (New York: Harper & Row, 1981), 210–11; Mel Piehl, *Breaking Bread: The Catholic Worker and the Origin of Catholic Radicalism in America* (Philadelphia: Temple University Press, 1982), 78.

74. Carey, *American Catholic Religious Thought*, 59–60; Piehl, *Breaking Bread*, 67–68.

75. Piehl, *Breaking Bread*, 115; *Pittsburgh Catholic*, 16 July 1936, 22 October 1936; Day, *The Long Loneliness*, 219; Rosalie Riegle Troester, *Voices from the Catholic Worker* (Philadelphia: Temple University Press, 1993), 126.

76. *Pittsburgh Catholic*, 23 July 1936; Patrick J. McGeever, *Rev. Charles Owen Rice: Apostle of Contradiction* (Pittsburgh: Duquesne University Press, 1989), 42–43.

77. McGeever, *Rev. Charles Owen Rice*, 235–36; *Pittsburgh Catholic*, 4 November 1937, 30 December 1937; Charles Owen Rice, "St. Joseph House of Hospitality," radio address, WWSW, Pittsburgh, Pa., 28 October 1939 (Charles Owen Rice Papers, Box 27, AIS); Charles Owen Rice, "St. Joseph House of Hospitality," radio address, WCAE, Pittsburgh, Pa., 18 January 1939 (Charles Owen Rice Papers, Box 27, AIS); Charles Owen Rice, "St. Joseph House of Hospitality," radio address, WWSW, Pittsburgh, Pa., 4 June 1939 (Charles Owen Rice Papers, Box 27, AIS).

78. F. F. O'Shea letter to Andrew Pauley, 23 December 1938 (Thomas Lappan Papers, DPA); Andrew Pauley letter to F. F. O'Shea, 16 December 1938 (Thomas Lappan Papers, DPA); X letter to Andrew Pauley, October 1938 (Thomas Lappan Papers, DPA); Sister M. Claude letter to Thomas Lappan, 18 October 1938 (Thomas Lappan Papers, DPA); X letter to Hugh Boyle, October 1938 (Thomas Lappan Papers, DPA).

## Chapter 4: Working-Class Saints

1. Pat Fagan interview by Alice M. Hoffman, HCLA, Pittsburgh, Pa., 24 September 1968.

2. Paul F. Boller Jr., *Presidential Campaigns* (New York: Oxford University Press, 1985), 245–56; Louis Stark, "Labor's Civil War," *Current History* 49 (January 1939): 26–28, 42.

3. James A. Wechsler, "Lewis Family Does All Right," *PM* (New York), 26 March 1942; Philip Murray Paycheck, 16 February 1942 (Philip Murray Papers, Box 1, HCLA); John Brophy, *A Miner's Life* (Madison: University of Wisconsin Press, 1964), 281.

4. Fagan interview, 24 September 1968; Melvyn Dubofsky, "Labor's Odd Couple: Philip Murray and John L. Lewis," in Paul F. Clark, Peter Gottlieb, and Donald Kennedy, eds., *Forging a Union of Steel: Philip Murray, SWOC, and the United Steelworkers,* (Ithaca, N.Y.: Industrial and Labor Relations Press, Cornell University, 1987), 30–44; Harold J. Ruttenberg, "Comments," in Clark et al., eds., *Forging a Union of Steel*, 126–30.

5. Brophy, *A Miner's Life*, 137, 151, 172–73; I. W. Abel, "Comments," in Clark et al., eds., *Forging a Union of Steel*, 103–7; Abe Raskin, "Comments," in Clark et al., eds., *Forging a Union of Steel*, 113–17; Ruttenberg, "Comments," 126–30.

6. Brophy, *A Miner's Life*, 282–83; Harvey Klehr, *The Heyday of American Communism: The Depression Decade* (New York: Basic Books, 1984), 162, 229–30, 232, 238, 251, 331; Len DeCaux, *Labor Radical: From the Wobblies to CIO* (Boston: Beacon Press, 1970), 280–81.

7. Juanita Diffay Tate, "Philip Murray as a Labor Leader," Ph.D. diss., New York University, 1962, 9–10, 44–45.

8. Tate, "Philip Murray as a Labor Leader," 50; David J. McDonald, *Union Man* (New York: E. P. Dutton, 1969), 100; Sean Dennis Cashman, *America in the Twenties and Thirties: The Olympian Age of Franklin Delano Roosevelt* (New York: New York University Press, 1989), 237–38.

9. McDonald, *Union Man*, 100–101; Cashman, *America in the Twenties and Thirties*, 238–39; Frances Perkins, *The Roosevelt I Knew* (New York: Viking, 1946), 332–33.

10. Walter Galenson, *The CIO Challenge to the AFL: A History of the American Labor Movement, 1935–1941* (Cambridge, Mass.: Harvard University Press, 1960), 87–88.

11. *Who Was Who in America, 1951–1960*, 10 vols. (Chicago: Marquis Who's Who, 1966), 8:844; McDonald, *Union Man*, 103.

12. McDonald, *Union Man*, 102–4; Tate, "Philip Murray as a Labor Leader," 54.

13. Clinton S. Golden, Memorandum on Undercover Agencies, January 13, 1936 (Clinton S. Golden Papers, Box 1, HCLA); Clinton S. Golden, Memorandum on John J. Mullen, 17 March 1936 (Clinton S. Golden Papers, Box 1, HCLA); Clinton S. Golden, Memorandum on John J. Mullen, 17 April 1936 (Clinton S. Golden Papers, Box 1, HCLA); Clinton S. Golden, Memorandum on W. E. Garrity, 27 April, 1936 (Clinton S. Golden Papers, Box 1, HCLA); John B. Hawkins, Report, 18 April 1936 (Clinton S. Golden Papers, Box 1, HCLA); "M" Report to Clinton S. Golden, 18 April 1937 (Clinton S. Golden Papers, Box 5, HCLA); "M" Report to Clinton S. Golden, 11 May 1937 (Clinton S. Golden Papers, Box 5, HCLA).

14. McDonald, *Union Man*, 104–105; Galenson, *The CIO Challenge to the AFL*, 93–96; Cashman, *America in the Twenties and Thirties*, 232; Tate, "Philip Murray as a Labor Leader," 55–56.

15. Cashman, *America in the Twenties and Thirties*, 232; William E. Leuchtenburg, *Franklin D. Roosevelt and the New Deal, 1932–1940* (New York: Harper & Row, 1963), 242; *Pittsburgh Press*, 3 March 1937.

16. Galenson, *The CIO Challenge to the AFL*, 94; Tate, "Philip Murray as a Labor Leader," 55; McDonald, *Union Man*, 97–98; Klehr, *The Heyday of American Communism*, 231.

17. David O'Brien, "American Catholics and Organized Labor in the 1930s," *The Catholic Historical Review* 52 (October 1966): 323–49; *Pittsburgh Catholic*, 8 April 1937.

18. *Pittsburgh Catholic*, 21 January 1937.

19. Neil Betten, *Catholic Activism and the Industrial Worker* (Gainesville: University Presses of Florida, 1976), 75; *Pittsburgh Catholic*, 17 June 1937; Patrick Renshaw, *American Labor and Consensus Capitalism, 1935–1990* (Jackson: University of Mississippi Press, 1991), 23–24.

20. Dorothy Day, *The Long Loneliness: An Autobiography* (New York: Harper & Row, 1981), 222; Catholic Radical Alliance, leaflet, 1937 (Charles Owen Rice Papers, Box 3, AIS).

21. *Pittsburgh Catholic*, 29 April 1937, 6 May 1937, 13 May 1937.

22. Charles Owen Rice, radio address, "The Dynamite of the Encyclicals," KDKA, Pittsburgh, Pa., 15 May 1937 (Charles Owen Rice Papers, Box 27, AIS).

23. Charles Owen Rice, radio address on the CIO, KDKA, Pittsburgh, Pa., 1937 (Charles Owen Rice Papers, Box 27, AIS); *Pittsburgh Catholic*, 13 May 1937, 20 May 1937.

24. David Brody, *Steelworkers in America: The Nonunion Era* (New York: Harper & Row, 1960), 116–18; Cashman, *America in the Twenties and Thirties*, 240–41.

25. Bruce Williams, "Local Labor History, 1930–1940: The Depression," M.A. seminar paper, University of Pittsburgh, 1993.

26. *Pittsburgh Courier*, 24 July 1937.

27. *Pittsburgh Courier*, 24 July 1937.

28. Galenson, *The CIO Challenge to the AFL*, 103; William D. Jenkins, *Steel Valley Klan: The Ku Klux Klan in Ohio's Mahoning Valley* (Kent Ohio: Kent State University Press, 1990), 65.

29. Galenson, *The CIO Challenge to the AFL*, 104–5; *Pittsburgh Catholic*, 10 June 1937, 24 June 1937; George W. Knepper, *Ohio and Its People* (Kent, Ohio: Kent State University Press, 1989), 375–76, 380; Joshua Freeman et al., *Who Built America? Working People and the Nation's Economy, Politics, Culture, and Society*, 2 vols. (New York: Pantheon, 1992), 2:418.

30. Jenkins, *Steel Valley Klan*, 122.

31. Labor Committee leaflet, National Negro Congress, "Steel Drive Moves Colored People Into Action!" 1937 (Harold J. Ruttenberg Papers, Box 1, HCLA); Labor Committee leaflet, National Negro Congress, "National Negro Congress Supports the Steel Workers Organizing Committee," 1937 (Harold J. Ruttenberg Papers, Box 1, HCLA); *Pittsburgh Courier*, 10 July 1937, 24 July 1937, 31 July 1937, 14 August 1937, 28 August 1937.

32. *Pittsburgh Courier*, 24 July 1937; Booker T. Washington, "Cast Down Your Bucket Where You Are," in Leland D. Baldwin, ed., *Ideas in Action: Documentary and Interpretive Readings in American History*, 2 vols. (New York: American Book Company, 1969), 2:56–57; Jon C. Teaford, *Cities of the Heartland: The Rise and Fall of the Industrial Midwest* (Bloomington: Indiana University Press, 1993), 108.

33. *Pittsburgh Courier*, 24 July 1937.

34. *Pittsburgh Courier*, 10 July 1937, 24 July 1937, 21 August 1937; Curtis Miner, *Forging a New Deal: Johnstown and the Great Depression, 1929–1941* (Johnstown, Pa.: Johnstown Area Heritage Association, 1993), 64–65, 68–69.

35. Ewa Morawska, *For Bread, With Butter: The Life-Worlds of East Central Europeans in Johnstown, Pennsylvania, 1890–1940* (New York: Cambridge University Press, 1985), 180–81; Rev. Ray Starr, "The Strike Situation in the Light of Bible Prophecy," Johnstown, Pa., 1937 (Howard Curtiss Papers, Box 5, HCLA).

36. Anthony Lorditch, Johnstown SWOC, interview by Curtis Miner, JAHA, Johnstown, Pa., 28 April 1993.

37. Lorditch interview; Galenson, *The CIO Challenge to the AFL*, 105; Miner, *Forging a New Deal*, 53–77; Donald S. McPherson, "The 'Little Steel' Strike of 1937 in Johnstown, Pennsylvania," *Pennsylvania History* 39 (April 1972): 219–38; Curtis Miner, "United by Right, Divided by Fear: Johnstown and the 1937 Steel Strike," Film, JAHA, Johnstown, Pa., 1993.

38. Galenson, *The CIO Challenge to the AFL*, 105–6; *Pittsburgh Catholic*, 24 June 1937, 5 August 1937.

39. *Pittsburgh Catholic*, 24 June 1937, 5 August 1937.

40. *Pittsburgh Catholic*, 3, June 1937, 10 June 1937.

41. *Pittsburgh Catholic*, 10 June 1937, 17 June 1937; Patrick J. McGeever, *Rev. Charles Owen Rice: Apostle of Contradiction* (Pittsburgh: Duquesne University Press, 1989), 47.

42. Kenneth T. Jackson, *The Ku Klux Klan in the City, 1915–1930* (New York: Oxford University Press, 1967),170; Thomas Coakley, Record of Priests, Diocese of Pittsburgh (Thomas Coakley Papers, DPA).

43. *Pittsburgh Catholic*, 28 June 1934, 1 July 1937; *Pittsburgh Bulletin Index*, 8 July 1937.

44. McGeever, *Rev. Charles Owen Rice*, 85.

45. *Pittsburgh Catholic*, 1 July 1937; Betten, *Catholic Activism and the Industrial Worker*, 76–77; Roy E. Babcock, "I Knew Him When," *Our Sunday Visitor* (Huntington, Ind.), 15 September 1974.

46. *Pittsburgh Catholic*, 1 July 1937; *Pittsburgh Bulletin Index*, 8 July 1937.

47. *Pittsburgh Catholic*, 1 July 1937; *Pittsburgh Bulletin Index*, 8 July 1937.

48. *Pittsburgh Bulletin Index*, 8 July 1937; *Pittsburgh Catholic*, 8 July 1937.

49. Yale & Towne [Connecticut] Worker, "Communism and the CIO," 3 May 1937 (Harold J. Ruttenberg Papers, Box 1, HCLA); William E. Leuchtenburg, *Franklin D. Roosevelt and the New Deal, 1932–1940* (New York: Harper & Row, 1963), 243.

50. Melvyn Dubofsky and Warren Van Tine, *John L. Lewis: A Biography* (Urbana: University of Illinois Press, 1986), 230–31; Miner, *Forging a New Deal*, 53–77.

51. *Pittsburgh Catholic*, 1 July 1937, 15 July 1937.

52. *Pittsburgh Catholic*, 29 July 1937.

53. *Pittsburgh Catholic*, 29 July 1937, 5 August 1937.

54. *Pittsburgh Catholic*, 22 July 1937.

55. *Pittsburgh Catholic*, 1 July 1937, 15 July 1937, 22 July 1937, 29 July 1937, 19 August 1937, O'Brien, "American Catholics and Organized Labor in the 1930s," 323–49.

56. *Pittsburgh Catholic*, 26 August 1937, 9 September 1937, 16 September 1937.

57. Carl Hensler and Thomas Lappan radio address, KDKA, Pittsburgh, Pa., 19 July 1937 (Charles Owen Rice Papers, Box 27, AIS); *Pittsburgh Catholic*, 19 August 1937, 2 September 1937, 30 September 1937, 14 October 1937.

58. *Pittsburgh Catholic*, 8 July 1937, 9 September 1937.

59. *Pittsburgh Catholic*, 2 September 1937, 16 September 1937, 23 September 1937, 21 October 1937, 28 October 1937, 2 December 1937.

60. *Pittsburgh Catholic*, 2 December 1937, 9 December 1937; Annemarie Draham, "Unlikely Allies Fight for Unionization: Homestead, Pennsylvania, 1933–1945," M.A. thesis, Indiana University of Pennsylvania, 1984, 34.

61. Ralph E. MacIntire letter to Charles Owen Rice, 29 August 1937 (Charles Owen Rice Papers, Box 6, AIS).

62. James McCoy interview by HCLA, Pittsburgh, Pa., 7 November 1968.

63. Harold J. Ruttenberg, "Outline Business Conditions (SWOC Confidential)," 1 November 1937 (Harold J. Ruttenberg Papers, Box 1, HCLA); "The SWOC Sidesteps the Perils of Adolescence," *Newsweek* 10 (27 December 1937): 37–40.

64. First SWOC Convention, "Report of Proceedings, First Day's Session, 14 December 1937" (David J. McDonald Papers, Box 145, HCLA).

65. First SWOC Convention, "Report of Proceedings, Second Day's Session, 15 December 1937" (David J. McDonald Papers, Box 145, HCLA); First SWOC Convention, "Report of Proceedings, Third Day's Session, 16 December 1937" (David J. McDonald Papers, Box 145,

HCLA); First SWOC Convention, "Resolution on Condemnation of Local and State Officials in their Illegal Actions in the Independent Steel Strike, 1937" (David J. McDonald Papers, Box 145, HCLA); Local Industrial Council of the CIO, Minutes, Pittsburgh, Pa., 19 October 1937 (David J. McDonald Papers, Box 145, HCLA); Labor Coordinating Committee, Pittsburgh, Pa., general letter, 1937 (David J. McDonald Papers, Box 144, HCLA); Labor's Non-Partisan League, "I Am the Voice of Labor," leaflet, 1936 (Harold J. Ruttenberg Papers, Box 1, HCLA).

## Chapter 5: Christian Democracy

1. Joan Cook, "John J. Abt, Lawyer, Dies at 87, Communist Party Counsel in U.S.," *The New York Times*, 13 August 1991; Harvey Klehr, *Communist Cadre: The Social Background of the American Communist Party Elite* (Stanford, Calif.: Hoover Institution Press, 1978), 19–69; Harvey Klehr, *The Heyday of American Communism: The Depression Decade* (New York: Basic Books, 1984), 140, 143, 229.
Three recently published works detail the agenda, ideology, and tactics of the American Communist Party. Harvey Klehr, John Earl Haynes, and Fridrikh Firsov, *The Secret World of American Communism* (New Haven: Yale University Press, 1995), is the first volume in a collection of documents from the archives of the former Soviet Union. These detail the working relationship between the CPUSA and the Soviet Union. Two additional works—also drawing upon Soviet archives—further elaborate on American Communism and convincingly argue that anti-Communism was understandable and, with the exception of Joseph McCarthy, justified and responsible: John E. Haynes, *Red Scare or Red Menace? American Communism and Anti-Communism in the Cold War Era* (Chicago: Ivan R. Dee, 1996), and Richard Gid Powers, *Not Without Honor: The History of American Anti-Communism* (New York: Free Press, 1995).
2. Klehr, *The Heyday of American Communism*, 229; Len DeCaux, *Labor Radical: From the Wobblies to CIO* (Boston: Beacon Press, 1970), 8, 223, 238, 263; John Brophy, *A Miner's Life* (Madison: University of Wisconsin Press, 1964), 260.
3. Klehr, *Communist Cadre*, 19–52; Klehr, *The Heyday of American Communism*, 230–31; De Caux, *Labor Radical*, 280–81, 304; George Powers, *Cradle of Steel Unionism: Monongahela, Pennsylvania* (East Chicago, Ind.: Figueroa Printers, 1972), ix–x, 85; Steve Nelson, James R. Barrett, and Rob Ruck, *Steve Nelson: American Radical* (Pittsburgh: University of Pittsburgh Press, 1981), 3–28, 244, 280.
4. Klehr, *The Heyday of American Communism*, 162, 232, 331; Nelson et al., *Steve Nelson*, 3–28; *Pittsburgh Bulletin Index*, 8 July 1937; United States House of Representatives, Committee on Un-American Activities, *Expose of the Communist Party of Western Pennsylvania Based Upon Testimony of Matthew Cvetic, February 1950* (Washington, D.C.: United States Government Printing Office, 1950), 1227.
5. Paul Buhle, "Jews and American Communism: The Cultural Question," *Radical History Review* 23 (spring 1980): 9–33; Klehr, *The Heyday of American Communism*, 70–71, 131, 162–65, 381–84.
6. Hyman Richman, "Life on Pittsburgh's 'Hill': Some Views and Values of Jews Who Lived There Before the 1940s," *Pittsburgh History* 74 (spring 1991): 10–19; Jacob Feldman, *The Jewish Experience in Western Pennsylvania: A History, 1755–1945* (Pittsburgh: Historical Society of Western Pennsylvania, 1986), 240–45; Roger Keeran, "The International Workers Order and the Origins of the CIO," *Labor History* 30 (summer 1979): 385–408 .
7. Keeran, "The International Workers Order and the Origins of the CIO," 385–408; Klehr, *The Heyday of American Communism*, 16–17, 384–85.

8. Ronald L. Filippelli, "UE: The Formative Years, 1933–1937," *Labor History* 17 (summer 1976): 351–71; Klehr, *The Heyday of American Communism*, 233; James Matles interview by Ron Filippelli, HCLA, State College, Pa., 6 May 1968; Ronald W. Schatz, *The Electrical Workers: A History of Labor at General Electric and Westinghouse, 1923–1960* (Urbana: University of Illinois Press, 1983), 14, 74, 170–71.

9. Matles interview; Filippelli, "UE," 351–71; Klehr, *The Heyday of American Communism*, 233.

10. Keeran, "The International Workers Order and the Origins of the CIO," 385–408; Fraser M. Ottanelli, *The Communist Party of the United States: From the Depression to World War II* (New Brunswick, N.J.: Rutgers University Press, 1991), 143, 152; Klehr, *The Heyday of American Communism*, 262; Max Gordon, "The Communists and the Drive to Organize Steel, 1936," *Labor History* 23 (spring 1982): 254–65.

11. Klehr, *The Heyday of American Communism*, 232, 238, 250–51, 384; Harvey Klehr and John Earl Haynes, *The American Communist Movement: Storming Heaven Itself* (New York: Twayne, 1992), 180–81; Klehr et al., eds., *The Secret World of American Communism*, 98–105; Ottanelli, *The Communist Party of the United States*, 139; Jordan A. Schwarz, *Liberal: Adolf A. Berle and the Vision of an American Era* (New York: The Free Press, 1987), 157–59, 175–215; Michael Kazin, *The Populist Persuasion: An American History* (New York: Basic Books, 1995), 324, note 44.

12. *Pittsburgh Catholic*, 16 May 1935, 18 July 1935, 7 November 1935; see also George Q. Flynn, *American Catholics and the Roosevelt Presidency, 1932–1936* (Lexington: University of Kentucky Press, 1968).

13. *Pittsburgh Catholic*, 30 January 1936; Otis L. Graham Jr., and Meghan Robinson Wander, eds., *Franklin D. Roosevelt, His Life and Times: An Encyclopedic View* (Boston: Da Capo Press, 1985), 6–7, 387–88.

14. *Pittsburgh Catholic*, 12 March 1936, 19 March 1936.

15. *Pittsburgh Catholic*, 12 March 1936, 21 May 1936, 3 September 1936, 24 September 1936.

16. *Pittsburgh Catholic*, 24 December 1936.

17. *Pittsburgh Catholic*, 5 August 1937.

18. *Pittsburgh Catholic*, 22 April 1937, 28 July 1938, 19 August 1937; Catholic Radical Alliance, "Catholic Radical Forum," 1937 (Charles Owen Rice Papers, Box 6, AIS); Dorothy Day, *The Long Loneliness: An Autobiography* (New York: Harper & Row, 1981), 220–21; Association of Catholic Trade Unionists, "Statement of Principles," in Aaron I. Abell, ed., *American Catholic Thought on Social Questions* (Indianapolis: Bobbs-Merrill, 1968), 408–14.

19. Day, *The Long Loneliness*, 220–21; *Pittsburgh Catholic*, 26 August 1937; Joshua B. Freeman, *In Transit: The Transport Workers Union in New York City, 1933–1966* (New York: Oxford University Press, 1989), 106, 148–51; Patrick J. McGeever, *Rev. Charles Owen Rice: Apostle of Contradiction* (Pittsburgh: Duquesne University Press, 1989), 45, 50–51; Mel Piehl, *Breaking Bread: The Catholic Worker and the Origin of Catholic Radicalism in America* (Philadelphia: Temple University Press, 1982), 119, 168; Charles Owen Rice interview by Bud and Ruth Schultz, Pittsburgh, Pa., summer 1982 (Charles Owen Rice Papers, Box 13, AIS); Neil Betten, *Catholic Activism and the Industrial Worker* (Gainesville: University Presses of Florida, 1976), 81.

20. *Pittsburgh Catholic*, 17 June 1937, 19 August 1937, 26 August 1937.

21. Rev. Charles Owen Rice, "CIO," radio address, KDKA, Pittsburgh, Pa., 1937 (Charles Owen Rice Papers, Box 27, AIS).

22. Piehl, *Breaking Bread*, 148–49; Andrew Buni, *Robert L. Vann of the Pittsburgh Courier: Politics and Black Journalism* (Pittsburgh: University of Pittsburgh Press, 1974), 238; Richard Gid Powers, *Not Without Honor: The History of American Anti-Communism* (New York: The

Free Press, 1995), 100–103, 156–57; Anthony Lorditch interview by Curtis Miner, JAHA, Johnstown, Pa., 28 April 1993; *Pittsburgh Catholic*, 12 May 1938, 19 May 1938.

23. *Pittsburgh Catholic*, 14 April 1938.

24. Peter Collier, with David Horowitz, *The Roosevelts: An American Saga* (New York: Simon & Schuster, 1994), 271, 357–59; *Pittsburgh Catholic*, 24 March 1938; Eleanor Roosevelt, *This I Remember* (New York: Harper & Brothers, 1949), 200–201; Ted Morgan, *FDR: A Biography* (New York: Simon & Schuster, 1985), 447.

25. Charles Owen Rice, "'Practical' Catholics," *The Christian Front* 3 (March 1938): 37–39; *Pittsburgh Catholic*, 6 January 1938, 13 January 1938, 20 January 1938, 27 January 1938, 12 May 1938; Neil Betten, "Charles Owen Rice: Pittsburgh Labor Priest, 1936–1940," *Pennsylvania Magazine of History and Biography* 94 (October 1970): 518–32.

26. *Pittsburgh Catholic*, 6 January 1938, 13 January 1938, 20 January 1938, 27 January 1938.

27. *Pittsburgh Catholic*, 3 February 1938, 10 February 1938, 17 February 1938, 24 February 1938.

28. *Pittsburgh Catholic*, 3 March 1938; Charles Owen Rice, Response to Fulton Sheen, St. Augustine's Church, Lawrenceville [Pittsburgh, Pa.], 5 March 1938 (Charles Owen Rice Papers, Box 6, AIS).

29. Charles Owen Rice, "Feast of St. Joseph, Patron of the Worker," radio address, KDKA, Pittsburgh, Pa., 19 March 1938 (Charles Owen Rice Papers, Box 20, AIS).

30. Rice, "Feast of St. Joseph, Patron of the Worker"; *Pittsburgh Catholic*, 7 April 1938, 21 April 1938, Charles Owen Rice, "Statement Concerning Aluminum Workers of America, 26 March 1938 (Charles Owen Rice Papers, Box 6, AIS).

31. *Pittsburgh Catholic*, 24 March 1938, 28 April 1938, 12 May 1938, 2 June 1938; Harold L. Ickes, *The Secret Diary of Harold L. Ickes: The Inside Struggle, 1936–1939*, 2 vols. (New York: Simon & Schuster, 1954), 2:295, 326.

32. Garret A. Connors, "The Position of Management in the Steel Industry," in *Proceedings, First National Catholic Social Action Conference, Milwaukee, Wisconsin, May 1–4, 1938* (Milwaukee: Federal Printing Company, 1938), 266–70; *Pittsburgh Catholic*, 19 May 1938.

33. David J. McDonald, "The Position of Labor in the Steel Industry," in *Proceedings, First National Catholic Social Action Conference, Milwaukee, Wisconsin, May 1–4, 1938*, 270–74.

34. Carl A. Hensler, "Christian Principles Applied to the Steel Industry," in *Proceedings, First National Catholic Social Action Conference, Milwaukee, Wisconsin, May 1–4, 1938*, 274–80.

35. *Pittsburgh Catholic*, 21 January 1937, 24 June 1937, 27 January 1937, 17 March 1938, 12 May 1938, 22 June 1939.

36. Kenneth J. Heineman, "Media Bias in Coverage of the Dies Committee on Un-American Activities, 1938–1940," *The Historian* 55 (autumn 1992): 37–52; George Wolfskill and John A. Hudson, *All But the People: Franklin D. Roosevelt and His Critics, 1933–1939* (New York: Macmillan, 1969), 177–91.

37. Heineman, "Media Bias in Coverage of the Dies Committee on Un-American Activities, 1938–1940," 37–52.

38. Heineman, "Media Bias in Coverage of the Dies Committee on Un-American Activities, 1938–1940," 37–52; Hadley Cantril, ed., *Public Opinion, 1935–1946* (Princeton: Princeton University Press, 1951), 754–56, 933; Michael Barone, *Our Country: The Shaping of America from Roosevelt to Reagan* (New York: The Free Press, 1990), 115.

39. Cantril, ed., *Public Opinion, 1935–1946*, 81, 396.

40. Cantril, ed., *Public Opinion, 1935–1946*, 130; Klehr, *The Heyday of American Communism*, 229, 232; Klehr et al., eds., *The Secret World of American Communism*, 96–98; *Pittsburgh Courier*, 7 August 1937, 21 August 1937, 11 September 1937, 18 September 1937.

41. Cantril, ed., *Public Opinion, 1935–1946*, 147; Heineman, "Media Bias in Coverage of

the Dies Committee on Un-American Activities, 1938–1940," 37–52; Kenneth J. Heineman, "A Catholic New Deal: Religion and Labor in 1930s Pittsburgh," *Pennsylvania Magazine of History and Biography* 118 (October 1994): 363–94.

42. Kenneth O'Reilly, *The FBI, HUAC, and the Red Menace* (Philadelphia: Temple University Press, 1983), 40–41; Klehr, *The Heyday of American Communism*, 249; *Pittsburgh Catholic*, 18 August 1938, 25 August 1938.

43. Heineman, "Media Bias in Coverage of the Dies Committee on Un-American Activities, 1938–1940," 37–52; *Pittsburgh Catholic*, 1 September 1938, 21 September 1939.

44. Heineman, "Media Bias in Coverage of the Dies Committee on Un-American Activities, 1938–1940," 37–52; *Pittsburgh Courier*, 19 November 1938; *Pittsburgh Catholic*, 18 August 1938, 1 September 1938; Michael W. Miles, *The Odyssey of the Radical Right* (New York: Oxford University Press, 1980), 25; Klehr, *The Heyday of American Communism*, 486; Leo P. Ribuffo, *The Old Christian Right: The Protestant Far Right from the Great Depression to the Cold War* (Philadelphia: Temple University Press, 1983), 16–17.

45. *Catholic Telegraph-Register*, 5 August 1938, 12 August 1938, 26 August 1938; *Catholic Sentinel*, 11 August 1938, 18 August 1938, 25 August 1938, 15 September 1938; Charles Owen Rice letter to Helen Clark, 30 April 1966 (Charles Owen Rice Papers, Box 9, AIS).

46. Elmer Cope letter to David McDonald, 10 January 1938 (Elmer Cope Papers, Box 13, OHS); Harold J. Ruttenberg, "85,000 Victims of Progress," *The New Republic* 94 (16 February 1938): 37–38; "SWOC Training Camp" report, July 1938 (Elmer Cope Papers, Box 13, OHS); *Pittsburgh Bulletin Index*, 21 July 1938, 6 October 1938.

47. "SWOC Training Camp" report, July 1938.

48. "SWOC Training Camp" report, July 1938.

49. "SWOC Training Camp" report, July 1938; Charles Owen Rice, "Policy and Action," *The Commonweal* 28 (29 July 1938): 366–67; *Pittsburgh Catholic*, 14 July 1938, 21 July 1938, 28 July 1938; Carl P. Hensler, "The Role of the CIO in Economic Reform," 1938 (David J. McDonald Papers, Box 144, HCLA).

50. *Pittsburgh Catholic*, 4 August 1938.

51. *Pittsburgh Catholic*, 11 August 1938.

52. *Pittsburgh Catholic*, 14 July 1938, 18 August 1938.

53. *Pittsburgh Catholic*, 14 July 1938, 11 August 1938; Douglas P. Seaton, *Catholics and Radicals: The Association of Catholic Trade Unionists and the American Labor Movement, from Depression to Cold War* (Lewisburg, Pa.: Bucknell University Press, 1981), 23, 149; Michael Harrington, "Catholics in the Labor Movement: A Case History," *Labor History* 11 (fall 1960): 231–63; Charles Owen Rice, radio address, WIBX, Utica, N.Y., 19 July 1938 (Charles Owen Rice Papers, Box 27, AIS).

54. *Pittsburgh Catholic*, 6 October 1938, 13 October 1938; "Priest Rejects 'Outstretched Hand' in Debate with Communist Editor," Religious News Service press release, 15 October 1938 (Charles Owen Rice Papers, Box 6, AIS); Charles Owen Rice, "Debating the Outstretched Hand," *The Commonweal* 29 (20 January 1939): 351–53.

55. *Pittsburgh Catholic*, 22 September 1938, 20 October 1938.

56. Statement of the Archbishops and Bishops of the Administrative Council, National Catholic Welfare Conference, on "Industrial and Social Peace, October 14, 1938," in Rev. Raphael M. Huber, ed., *Our Bishops Speak: National Pastorals and Annual Statements of the Hierarchy of the United States* (Milwaukee, Wis.: Bruce Publishing, 1952), 320–21.

57. Robert S. McElvaine, *The Great Depression: America, 1929–1941* (New York: Times Books, 1984), 291.

58. Heineman, "Media Bias in Coverage of the Dies Committee on Un-American Activities, 1938–1940," 37–52; Wolfskill and Hudson, *All But the People*, 182, 191; Cantril, *Public Opinion, 1935–1946*, 163–64.

59. Heineman, "Media Bias in Coverage of the Dies Committee on Un–American Activities, 1938–1940," 37–52; Frances Perkins, *The Roosevelt I Knew* (New York: Viking, 1946), 315–19; Stephen Koch, *Double Lives: Spies and Writers in the Secret Soviet War of Ideas Against the West* (New York: The Free Press, 1994), 375, note 50; Klehr et al., eds., *The Secret World of American Communism*, 104.

60. Heineman, "Media Bias in Coverage of the Dies Committee on Un-American Activities, 1938–1940," 37–52; *United Automobile Worker* (Detroit, Mich.), 22 October 1938, 29 October 1938; Paul Y. Anderson, "Fascism Hits Washington: Work of the House Committee to Investigate Un-American Activities," *The Nation* 147 (27 August 1938): 198–99; Paul Y. Anderson, "Loaded Dies Committee," *The Nation* 147 (29 October 1938): 443; Paul Y, Anderson, "Investigate Mr. Dies!" *The Nation* 147 (5 November 1938): 471–72.

61. Koch, *Double Lives*, 174–76, 286, 384, note 73.

62. Paul B. Beers, *Pennsylvania Politics Today and Yesterday: The Tolerable Accommodation* (University Park: Pennsylvania State University Press, 1980), 141–44.

63. Heineman, "Media Bias in Coverage of the Dies Committee on Un-American Activities, 1938–1940," 37–52; J. Cutler Adams, *Pittsburgh's Post-Gazette* (Boston: Chapman and Grimes, 1936), 291–301; *Pittsburgh Post-Gazette*, 13 October 1938; Barone, *Our Country*, 118; Alfred L. Morgan, "The Significance of Pennsylvania's 1938 Gubernatorial Election," *Pennsylvania Magazine of History and Biography* 102 (April 1978): 184–211; Priscilla Clement, "The Works Progress Administration in Pennsylvania, 1935 to 1940," *Pennsylvania Magazine of History and Biography* 95 (April 1975): 244–60.

64. Morgan, "The Significance of Pennsylvania's 1938 Gubernatorial Election," 184–211; *Pittsburgh Bulletin Index*, 3 November 1938; Harold L. Ickes, *The Secret Diary of Harold L. Ickes: The Inside Struggle, 1936–1939*, 2 vols. (New York: Simon & Schuster, 2954), 2:498–500, 695.

65. Thomas H. Coode and John F. Bauman, *People, Poverty, and Politics: Pennsylvanians during the Great Depression* (Lewisburg, Pa.: Bucknell University Press, 1981), 171, 238; *Pittsburgh Catholic*, 18 August 1938.

66. Barone, *Our Country*, 106, 122; Morgan, "The Significance of Pennsylvania's 1938 Gubernatorial Election," 184–211; William E. Leuchtenburg, *Franklin D. Roosevelt and the New Deal, 1932–1940* (New York: Harper & Row, 1963), 271–73.

67. Barone, *Our Country*, 107; Sidney M. Milkis, *The President and the Parties: The Transformation of the American Party System Since the New Deal* (New York: Oxford University Press, 1993), 21–51.

68. Milkis, *The President and the Parties*, 21–51.

69. Milkis, *The President and the Parties*, 21–51.

70. *Pittsburgh Bulletin Index*, 24 November 1938; Leuchtenburg, *Franklin D. Roosevelt and the New Deal, 1932–1940*, 111.

71. *Pittsburgh Catholic*, 17 November 1938.

72. *Pittsburgh Catholic*, 24 November 1938; *Pittsburgh Bulletin Index*, 21 July 1938, 10 August 1939.

73. *Pittsburgh Bulletin Index*, 24 November 1938, 30 March 1939.

74. Dorothy Day, "Decent Poverty the Social Ideal," in Aaron I. Abell, ed., *American Catholic Thought on Social Questions* (Indianapolis, Ind.: Bobbs-Merrill, 1968), 423.

## *Chapter 6: Confirmation*

1. *Pittsburgh Catholic*, 26 January 1939.
2. *Pittsburgh Catholic*, 23 February 1939.

3. *Pittsburgh Catholic*, 9 March 1939, 4 May 1939, 11 May 1939, 22 June 1939.

4. *Pittsburgh Catholic*, 16 February 1939, 2 March 1939, 8 June 1939, 22 June 1939; David J. McDonald, "The Position of Labor in the Steel Industry," in *Proceedings Second National Catholic Social Action Conference, 1939* (Cleveland, Ohio: R. J. McMillan, 1939), 430–35.

5. Jose M. Sanchez, *The Spanish Civil War as a Religious Tragedy* (South Bend, Ind.: University of Notre Dame Press, 1987), 9, 12; Paul Johnson, *Modern Times: From the Twenties to the Nineties* (New York: Harper Collins, 1991), 324–30; Hugh Thomas, *The Spanish Civil War* (New York: Harper & Brothers, 1961), 172–73; F. Jay Taylor, *The United States and the Spanish Civil War* (New York: Bookman Associates, 1956), 21–38, 143–62.

6. Sanchez, *The Spanish Civil War as Religious Tragedy*, 194; Kenneth S. Davis, *FDR: Into the Storm, 1937–1940* (New York: Random House, 1993), 251–53; Harold L. Ickes, *The Secret Diary of Harold L. Ickes: The Inside Struggle, 1936–1939*, 2 vols. (New York: Simon & Schuster, 1954), 2:390, 586, 650, 705–6; Harvey Klehr, *The Heyday of American Communism: The Depression Decade* (New York: Basic Books, 1984), 219–20; Steve Nelson, James R. Barrett, Rob Ruck, *Steve Nelson: American Radical* (Pittsburgh: University of Pittsburgh Press, 1981), 183–239; Stephen Koch, *Double Lives: Spies and Writers in the Secret Soviet War of Ideas Against the West* (New York: The Free Press, 1994), 80, 214, 225, 280–81, 287–89, 291–95.

7. Sanchez, *The Spanish Civil War as a Religious Tragedy*, 186, 194; William E. Leuchtenburg, *Franklin D. Roosevelt and the New Deal, 1932–1940* (New York: Harper & Row, 1963), 220; J. David Valaik, "American Catholic Dissenters and the Spanish Civil War," *The Catholic Historical Review*, 53 (January 1968): 537–46; J. David Valaik, "Catholics, Neutrality, and the Spanish Embargo, 1937–1939," *Journal of American History*, 54 (June 1967): 73–85.

8. Davis, *FDR*, 131–32; Johnson, *Modern Times*, 332–35; Edward R. Kantowicz, "Cardinal Mundelein of Chicago an the Shaping of Twentieth-Century American Catholicism," *Journal of American History* 68 (June 1981): 52–68.

9. *Pittsburgh Courier*, 9 October 1937, 23 October 1937, 6 November 1937, 13 November 1937.

10. *Pittsburgh Catholic*, 5 August 1937, 12 August 1937, 23 September 1937; Catholic Radical Alliance, "Workers Wise Up!!" Leaflet, 1937 (Charles Owen Rice Papers, Box 8, AIS); Wayne Morris, "Stalin's Famine and the American Journalists," *Continuity* 18 (spring/fall 1994): 69–78.

11. *Pittsburgh Sun-Telegraph*, 27 November 1937; *Pittsburgh Bulletin Index*, 6 October 1938; *Pittsburgh Catholic*, 2 December 1937; Klehr, *The Heyday of American Communism*, 47, 102, 110; Guenter Lewy, *The Cause that Failed: Communism in American Political Life* (New York: Oxford University Press, 1990), 172–73.

12. Lewy, *The Cause that Failed*, 174–75; William L. O'Neill, *A Better World: The Great Schism, Stalinism and the American Intellectuals* (New York: Simon & Schuster, 1982), 17, 62, 85, 111, 122, 138, 163, 295, 347–48; *Pittsburgh Catholic*, 12 January 1939, 6 April 1939, 20 April 1939.

13. Joseph S. Roucek and Francis J. Brown, "The Problem of the Negro and European Immigrant Minorities: Some Comparisons and Contrasts," *Journal of Negro Education* 3 (1939): 299–312.

14. Roucek and Brown, "The Problem of the Negro and European Immigrant Minorities," 299–312; *Pittsburgh Catholic*, 27 June 1935; William R. Scott, *The Sons of Sheba's Race: African-Americans and the Italo-Ethiopian War, 1935–1941* (Bloomington: Indiana University Press, 1993), 44–45, 142–43, 249; Johnson, *Modern Times*, 320.

15. George Prpic, *The Croatian Immigrants in America* (New York: Philosophical Library, 1971), 291–320; Philip Jenkins, *Hoods and Shirts: The Extreme Right in Pennsylvania, 1925–1950* (Chapel Hill: University of North Carolina Press, 1997), 212.

16. *Pittsburgh Catholic*, 4 May 1933; *Pittsburgh Bulletin Index*, 11 August 1938.

17. *Pittsburgh Catholic*, 4 May 1933, 5 October 1939.

18. *Pittsburgh Catholic*, 18 June 1936, 23 September 1937, 14 July 1938, 24 November 1938; Alan Bullock, *Hitler: A Study in Tyranny* (New York: Harper Perennial, 1991), 233–83; Davis, *FDR*, 325–45.

19. *Pittsburgh Catholic*, 10 November 1938; Bullock, *Hitler*, 277–83.

20. *Pittsburgh Catholic*, 11 May 1939, 18 May 1939; *Pittsburgh Bulletin Index*, 18 May 1939.

21. *Pittsburgh Catholic*, 14 July 1938, 10 August 1939, 5 October 1939, 24 November 1938; "Priest into President," *Time* 34 (6 November 1939): 24.

22. Hugh Boyle letter to James Cox, 1 September 1939 (James R. Cox Papers, DPA); Clement Hrtanek letter to Hugh Boyle, 30 August 1939 (James R. Cox Papers, DPA); International Workers Order leaflet, "Colossal Labor Day Outing," 1939 (James R. Cox Papers, DPA).

23. *Pittsburgh Catholic*, 8 June 1939, 22 June 1939; Administrative Board, National Catholic Welfare Conference, "In Praise of Christian Democracy Crusade and Condemnation of Bigotry," 29 April 1939, in Rev. Raphael M. Huber, ed., *Our Bishops Speak* (Milwaukee: Bruce Publishing, 1952), 323.

24. Rev. Denis Fahey, *The Rulers of Russia* (Royal Oak, Mich.: Social Justice Publishing, 1939); David J. O'Brien, "American Catholics and Anti-Semitism in the 1930s," *Catholic World* 204 (February 1967): 270–76; John A. Ryan, "Catholics and Anti-Semitism," *Current History* 49 (February 1939): 25–26; *Pittsburgh Catholic*, 11 August 1938, 20 October 1938, 15 December 1938, 3 August 1939; Jenkins, *Hoods and Shirts*, 179.

25. "Father Cox Has a Close-Up View of Mussolini," *The Christian Century* 49 (27 July 1932): 925–26; Father James R. Cox, "Hitler's Hatchet Man!" address delivered before the Dormont [Pa.] Rotary Club in Dormont's Methodist Episcopal Church, 1939 (James R. Cox Papers, DPA).

26. Alice Gremy letter to Hugh Boyle, 2 October 1939 (James R. Cox Papers, DPA); Berniece Muehrcke letter to James Cox, 21 August 1939 (James R. Cox Papers, DPA).

27. A. G. Cicognani letter to Hugh Boyle, 16 June 1939 (James R. Cox Papers, DPA); Charles Coughlin letter to Hugh Boyle, 6 September 1939 (James R. Cox Papers, DPA); Hugh Boyle letter to Charles Coughlin, 26 October 1939 (James R. Cox Papers, DPA); Hugh Boyle letter to A. G. Cicognani, 26 October 1939.

28. Charles Owen Rice, "On Anti–Semitism," radio address, WWSW, Pittsburgh, Pa., 17 August 1939 (Charles Owen Rice Papers, Box 27, AIS); *Pittsburgh Catholic*, 2 March 1939, 13 April 1939, 10 August 1939, 31 August 1939, 7 September 1939; Charles R. Morris, *American Catholic: The Saints and Sinners Who Built America's Most Powerful Church* (New York: Random House, 1997), 213.

29. Lawrence H. Fuchs, "Minority Groups and Foreign Policy," in Lawrence H. Fuchs, ed., *American Ethnic Politics* (New York: Harper & Row 1968), 144–62; Lawrence S. Wittner, *Rebels Against War: The American Peace Movement, 1941–1960* (New York: Columbia University Press, 1969), 17, 25.

30. Fuchs, "Minority Groups and Foreign Policy," 144–62; Alfred O. Hero Jr., *American Religious Groups View Foreign Policy: Trends in Rank-and-File Opinion, 1937–1969* (Durham: Duke University Press, 1973), 21–27; Kevin P. Phillips, *The Emerging Republican Majority* (New Rochelle, N.Y.: Arlington House, 1970), 113–16, 377–78; Wittner, *Rebels Against War*, 13, 19; Charles DeBenedetti, *The Peace Reform in American History* (Bloomington: Indiana University Press, 1984), 129; Patricia McNeal, *Harder Than War: Catholic Peacemaking in Twentieth-Century America* (New Brunswick, N.J.: Rutgers University Press, 1992), 148; Patricia McNeal, "Origins of the Catholic Peace Movement," *The Review of Politics* 35 (July

1973): 346–72; John Leo LeBrun, "The Role of the Catholic Worker Movement in American Pacifism, 1933–1972," Ph.D. diss., Case Western Reserve University, 27–81; John W. Jeffries, *Testing the Roosevelt Coalition: Connecticut Society and Politics in the Era of World War II* (Knoxville: The University of Tennessee Press, 1979), 188.

31. *Pittsburgh Catholic*, 21 December 1933, 24 March 1938, 7 April 1938, 14 April 1938.

32. *Pittsburgh Catholic*, 9 March 1937, 6 April 1937; Davis, *FDR*, 155–56; Hadley Cantril, ed., *Public Opinion, 1935–1946* (Princeton: Princeton University Press, 1951), 163; Robert A. Divine, *The Reluctant Belligerent: American Entry into World War II* (New York: John Wiley & Sons, 1979), 149–50.

33. *Pittsburgh Catholic*, 14 September 1939, 21 September 1939, 26 October 1939; Charles Owen Rice, radio address, WWSW, Pittsburgh, Pa., 4 September 1939 (Charles Owen Rice Papers, Box 27, AIS).

34. *Pittsburgh Catholic*, 16 November 1939; Charles Owen Rice, radio address, WWSW, Pittsburgh, Pennsylvania, 11 November 1939 (Charles Owen Rice Papers, Box 27, AIS); Klehr, *The Heyday of American Communism*, 386–416.

35. Eleanor Roosevelt, *This I Remember* (New York: Harper & Row, 1949), 200–205; Davis, *FDR*, 519–22; Jordan A. Schwarz, *Liberal: Adolf A. Berle and the Vision of an American Era* (New York: The Free Press, 1987), 157–59, 175–215; Peter Collier, with David Horowitz, *The Roosevelts: An American Saga* (New York: Simon & Schuster, 1994), 434–35.

36. Alan Brinkley, *The End of Reform: New Deal Liberalism in Recession and War* (New York: Alfred A. Knopf, 1995), 209; Harry Block interview by Ron Filippelli, HCLA, State College, Pa., 25 September 1967; Wittner, *Rebels Against War*, 23; Harvey Klehr and John Earl Haynes, *The American Communist Movement: Storming Heaven Itself* (New York: Twayne, 1992), 94; Klehr, *The Heyday of American Communism*, 404–5; John C. Cort, "ACTU and the Auto Workers," *U.S. Catholic Historian* 9 (fall 1990): 335–51.

37. Philip Murray, "Labor and Responsibility," *The Virginia Quarterly Review* 16 (April 1940): 267–78; Morris Llewellyn Cooke and Philip Murray, *Organized Labor and Production: Next Steps in Industrial Democracy* (New York: Harper & Brothers, 1940); Nelson Lichtenstein, *Labor's War at Home: The CIO in World War II* (New York: Cambridge University Press, 1991), 46; Robert H. Zieger, *The CIO, 1935–1955* (Chapel Hill: University of North Carolina Press, 1995), 135.

38. Walter Galenson, *The CIO Challenge to the AFL: A History of the American Labor Movement, 1935–1941* (Cambridge, Mass.: Harvard University Press, 1960), 259; Michael Kazin, *The Populist Persuasion: An American History* (New York: Basic Books, 1995), 155; Davis, *FDR*, 528–626.

39. Elmer Cope letter to "Larry," 17 February 1940 (Elmer Cope Papers, Box 13, OHS); Davis, *FDR*, 617–18; Kazin, *The Populist Persuasion*, 155–56.

40. Paul B. Beers, *Pennsylvania Politics Today and Yesterday: A Tolerable Accommodation* (University Park: Pennsylvania State University Press, 1980), 244; Rose M. Stein, "Murray of the CIO," *The Nation* 151 (31 August 1940): 172–73.

41. Rose M. Stein, "Murray to the Rescue," *The Nation* 151 (30 November 1940): 524–26; Rose M. Stein, "A Talk with Philip Murray," *The Nation* 151 (21 December 1940): 629–31; Kenneth J. Heineman, "A Catholic New Deal: Religion and Labor in 1930s Pittsburgh," *Pennsylvania Magazine of History and Biography* 118 (October 1994): 363–94; McGeever, *Rev. Charles Owen Rice*, 98.

42. Kazin, *The Populist Persuasion*, 157; *Pittsburgh Catholic*, 28 November 1940.

43. Administrative Board of the National Catholic Welfare Conference, "Church and Social Order, February 7, 1940," in Rev. Raphael M. Huber, ed., *Our Bishops Speak: National Pastorals and Annual Statements of the Hierarchy of the United States, 1919–1951* (Milwaukee,

Wis.: Bruce Publishing, 1952), 324–43; *Pittsburgh Catholic*, 6 June 1940; Mel Piehl, *Breaking Bread: The Catholic Worker and the Origin of Catholic Radicalism in America* (Philadelphia: Temple University Press, 1982), 194–95.

44. *Pittsburgh Catholic*, 11 July 1940, 5 September 1940, 12 September 1940, 26 December 1940.

45. *Pittsburgh Catholic*, 12 September 1940; David S. Wyman, *The Abandonment of the Jews: America and the Holocaust, 1941–1945* (New York: Pantheon, 1985), 19.

46. James Hennesey, *American Catholics: A History of the Roman Catholic Community in the United States* (New York: Oxford University Press, 1981), 276; Francis L. Broderick, *Right Reverend New Dealer: John A. Ryan* (New York: Macmillan, 1963), 258; *Pittsburgh Catholic*, 13 June 1940, 10 April 1941, 24 July 1941.

47. "Flophouse Father," *Time* 35 (26 February 1940): 54; Patrick J. McGeever, *Rev. Charles Owen Rice: Apostle of Contradiction* (Pittsburgh: Duquesne University Press, 1989), 63; *Pittsburgh Catholic*, 5 June 1941; Charles Owen Rice, "Why Aid England?" radio address delivered under the auspices of the Committee to Defend America by Aiding the Allies, KQV, Pittsburgh, Pa., 12 June 1941 (Charles Owen Rice Papers, Box 9, AIS).

48. John Lewis Gaddis, *The United States and the Origins of the Cold War, 1941–1947* (New York: Columbia University Press, 1972), 40–41; Les K. Adler and Thomas G. Patterson, "Red Fascism: The Merger of Nazi Germany and Soviet Russia in the American Image of Totalitarianism, 1930s–1950s," *The American Historical Review* 75 (April 1970): 1046–64; Robert Dallek, *Franklin D. Roosevelt and American Foreign Policy, 1932–1945* (New York: Oxford University Press, 1981), 296–97; *Pittsburgh Catholic*, 26 June 1941.

49. Charles Owen Rice, radio address delivered under the auspices of the Committee to Defend America by Aiding the Allies, WWSW, Pittsburgh, Pa., 15 July 1941 (Charles Owen Rice Papers, Box 9, AIS); *Pittsburgh Catholic*, 17 July 1941.

50. *Pittsburgh Catholic*, 17 July 1941, 11 September 1941; McGeever, *Rev. Charles Owen Rice*, 112–13.

51. "Resolution on Condemnation of Fascist Aggressors," SWOC Convention, Pittsburgh, Pa., 1937 (David J. McDonald Papers, Box 145, HCLA); Ronald W. Schatz, "Philip Murray and the Subordination of the Industrial Unions to the United States Government," in Melvyn Dubofsky and Warren Van Tine, eds., *Labor Leaders in America* (Urbana: University of Illinois Press, 1987), 244; *Pittsburgh Catholic*, 27 February 1941, 28 August 1941, 4 September 1941.

52. Heineman, "A Catholic New Deal," 363–94; Brinkley, *The End of Reform*, 203–5.

53. Heineman, "A Catholic New Deal," 363–94.

54. Heineman, "A Catholic New Deal," 363–94; Brinkley, *The End of Reform*, 203–5.

55. Brinkley, *The End of Reform*, 175–200; Sacred Heart Parish Newsletter, Pittsburgh, Pa., 7 December 1941 (Thomas Coakley Papers, DPA); Davis, *FDR*, 572–74.

## Requiem

1. *Pittsburgh Catholic*, 11 December 1941; Administrative Board of the National Catholic Welfare Conference, "National Crisis of World War II, 22 December 1941," in Raphael M. Huber, ed., *Our Bishops Speak: National Pastorals and Annual Statements of the Hierarchy of the United States* (Milwaukee: Bruce Publishing, 1952), 350–52.

2. James Hennesey, *American Catholics: A History of the Roman Catholic Community in the United States* (New York: Oxford University Press, 1981), 275–76, 278, 282; Mark Silk, *Spiritual Politics: Religion and America Since World War II* (New York: Simon & Schuster, 1988),

25–26; William Au, *The Cross, the Flag, and the Bomb: American Catholics Debate War and Peace, 1960–1983* (New York: Praeger, 1987), 3–4, 41–42; Patricia McNeal, *Harder than War: Catholic Peacemaking in Twentieth-Century America* (New Brunswick, N.J.: Rutgers University Press, 1992), xi, 1–70; Paul Mellon with John Baskett, *Reflections in a Silver Spoon: A Memoir* (New York: William Morrow, 1992), 183–226; Richard Polenberg, *One Nation Divisible: Class, Race, and Ethnicity in the United States Since 1938* (New York: Viking, 1980), 46–85; Richard W. Steele, "The War on Intolerance: The Reformulation of American Nationalism, 1939–1941," *Journal of American Ethnic History* 9 (fall 1989): 9–35.

3. Curtis Miner and Paul Roberts, "Engineering an Industrial Diaspora: Homestead, 1941," *Pittsburgh History* 72 (winter 1989): 4–25; Clement Hrtanek letter to Hugh Boyle, 7 January 1947 (Clement J. Hrtanek Papers, DPA).

4. Clinton S. Golden and Harold J. Ruttenberg, *The Dynamics of Industrial Democracy* (New York: Harper & Brothers, 1942), 24–27, 52–53, 60–61, 78–79, 88–89, 110–19, 150–53, 324–25, 330–31.

5. Clinton S. Golden, "New Patterns of Democracy," fall 1943 (Clinton S. Golden Papers, Box 1, HCLA).

6. L. Ebersole Gaines, President, West Virginia Coal Association, "The Great Dane and the Scotch Terrier," statement, 30 January 1942 (Philip Murray Papers, Box 1, HCLA).

7. Philip Murray letters to CIO representatives, 25 November 1941, 4 December 1941 (David J. McDonald Papers, Box 33, HCLA); "Analysis of Pending Repressive Anti-Labor Legislation," CIO, 1941 (David J. McDonald Papers, Box 33, HCLA); Harvey Klehr, John Earl Haynes, and Fridrikh Igorevich Firsov, eds., *The Secret World of American Communism* (New Haven: Yale University Press, 1995), 98–106.

8. Steve Fraser, *Labor Will Rule: Sidney Hillman and the Rise of American Labor* (New York: The Free Press, 1991), 495–566; Herbert S. Parmet, *Richard Nixon and His America* (Boston: Little, Brown, 1990), 134–39; Nelson Lichtenstein, *Labor's War at Home: The CIO in World War II* (New York: Cambridge University Press, 1991), 171–77; "Philip Murray's Speech at PAC Meeting," 22 October 1944, William Penn Hotel," text (Philip Murray Papers, Box 1, HCLA).

9. "Philip Murray's Speech at PAC Meeting"; Robert H. Ferrell, *Choosing Truman: The Democratic Convention of 1944* (Columbia: University of Missouri Press, 1994), passim.

10. Ferrell, *Choosing Truman*, 16–17, 20, 44–45, 54–57, Michael P. Weber, *Don't Call Me Boss: David L. Lawrence, Pittsburgh's Renaissance Mayor* (Pittsburgh: University of Pittsburgh Press, 1988), 183–87; Frank Hawkins, "Lawrence of Pittsburgh: Boss of the Mellon Patch," *Harper's Monthly Magazine* 213 (August 1956): 57–61.

11. Charles Owen Rice letters to Phil Murray, 28 January 1942, 26 February 1942 (Charles Owen Rice Papers, Box 16, AIS).

12. Richard Polenberg, *War and Society: The United States, 1941–1945* (New York: J. B. Lippincott, 1972), 48, 208–211; John J. Bukowczyk, *And My Children Did Not Know Me: A History of the Polish Americans* (Bloomington: Indiana University Press, 1987), 91.

13. Administrative Board of the National Catholic Welfare Conference, "World Peace, 15 April 1945," in Huber, ed., *Our Bishops Speak*, 355–60.

14. Administration Board of the National Catholic Welfare Conference, "Injustice of the Trial of Archbishop Aloysius Stepinac, D. D., of Zagreb, Yugoslavia, 30 September 1946," in, Huber, ed., *Our Bishops Speak*, 362–63; The First Catholic Slovak Union, "Resolution of Appreciation to his Excellency the Most Reverend Hugh C. Boyle, D.D., Bishop of Pittsburgh, Pa.," February 1947 (Clement J. Hrtanek Papers, DPA); Clement Hrtanek letter to Hugh Boyle, 10 March 1948 (Clement J. Hrtanek Papers, DPA); Klehr et al., *The Secret World of American Communism*, 12; Harvey Klehr and John Earl Haynes, *The American Communist Movement: Storming Heaven Itself* (New York: Twayne, 1992), 111, 115.

15. "Pride and a Priest," *Time* 43 (17 April 1944): 30; "Journeyman Traitor," *Time* 48 (16 December 1946): 37; "Slovaks: Unhyphenated," *Newsweek* 28 (16 December 1946): 50.

16. David Caute, *The Great Fear: The Anti-Communist Purge Under Truman and Eisenhower* (New York: Simon & Schuster, 1978), 108–10, 216–23, 376–91; Steve Nelson, James Barrett, and Rob Ruck, *Steve Nelson: American Radical* (Pittsburgh: University of Pittsburgh Press, 1981), 298–340; Ronald W. Schatz, *The Electrical Workers: A History of Labor at General Electric and Westinghouse, 1923–1960* (Urbana: University of Illinois Press, 1983), 167–87.

17. Richard Krickus, *Pursuing the American Dream: White Ethnics and the New Populism* (Bloomington: Indiana University Press, 1976), 194; Klehr et al., *The Secret World of American Communism*, 3–19, 105; Klehr and Haynes, *The American Communist Movement*, 92–93; Steven Merritt Miner, "His Master's Voice: Viacheslav Mikhailovich Molotov as Stalin's Foreign Commissar," in Gordon A. Craig and Francis L. Loewenheim, eds., *The Diplomats, 1939–1979* (Princeton: Princeton University Press, 1994), 65–100.

18. Klehr et al., *The Secret World of American Communism*, 106.

19. Bernard J. Sheil, "A Society of Free Men," Address to the Seventh National Convention of the CIO, Chicago, Ill., 20 November 1944 (Harold J. Ruttenberg Papers, Box 4, HCLA); "Murray Orders Study of Negro Job Equality," *CIO News*, 24 August 1942 (Harold J. Ruttenberg Papers, Box 1, HCLA).

20. "Murray Orders Study of Negro Equality"; Thomas Lappan letter to Hugh Boyle, 1 August 1944 (Thomas Lappan Papers, DPA); Office of the Bishop letter to Thomas Lappan, 4 August 1939.

21. Joshua Freeman et al., *Who Built America? Working People and the Nation's Economy, Politics, Culture, and Society*, 2 vols. (New York: Pantheon, 1992), 2:651.

22. *Pittsburgh Sun-Telegraph*, 20 March 1951; Ronald W. Schatz, "Philip Murray and the Subordination of the Industrial Unions to the United States Government," in Melvyn Dubofsky and Warren Van Tines, eds., *Labor Leaders in America* (Urbana: University of Illinois Press, 1987), 234–57; Kenneth J. Heineman, "A Catholic New Deal: Religion and Labor in 1930s Pittsburgh," *Pennsylvania Magazine of History and Biography* 118 (October 1994): 363–94.

23. Charles Owen Rice, "Philip Murray," radio address, WWSW, Pittsburgh, Pa., 3 June 1945 (Charles Owen Rice Papers, Box 16, AIS).

# Bibliography

## Primary Sources

### *Manuscript Collections*

Coakley, Thomas. Papers. Diocese of Pittsburgh Archives.
Cope, Elmer. Papers. Ohio Historical Society.
Cox, James R. Papers. Diocese of Pittsburgh Archives.
Curtiss, Howard. Papers. Historical Collections and Labor Archives, Pennsylvania State University.
Dominicis, Ercole. Papers. Diocese of Pittsburgh Archives.
Golden, Clinton S. Papers. Historical Collections and Labor Archives, Pennsylvania State University.
Hensler, Carl P. Papers. Diocese of Pittsburgh Archives.
Hrtanek, Clement J. Papers. Diocese of Pittsburgh Archives.
Lappan, Thomas. Papers. Diocese of Pittsburgh Archives.
McCloskey, Eddie. Papers. Johnstown (Pennsylvania) Area Heritage Association.
Murray, Philip. Papers. Historical Collections and Labor Archives, Pennsylvania State University.
Pauley, Andrew. Papers. Diocese of Pittsburgh Archives.
Rice, Charles Owen. Papers. Archives of an Industrial Society, University of Pittsburgh.
Ruttenberg, Harold J. Papers. Historical Collections and Labor Archives, Pennsylvania State University.

### *Interviews*

Behrend (Silberstein), Celeste. Telephone conversation with author, 22 June 1989. Author's Files, Lancaster, Ohio.
Block, Harry. Interview by Ron Filippelli, Historical Collections and Labor Archives, Pennsylvania State University. State College, Pa., 25 September 1967.
Fagan, Pat. Interviews by Alice M. Hoffman, Historical Collections and Labor Archives, Pennsylvania State University. Pittsburgh, Pa., 24 September 1968, 1 October 1968, and 8 August 1972.

Katz (Tanack), Gerry. Interviews by author. Pittsburgh, Pa., 5 June 1989 and 22 June 1989. Author's Files, Lancaster, Ohio.

Lorditch, Anthony. Interview by Curtis Miner. Johnstown Area Heritage Association. Johnstown, Pa., 28 April 1993.

Matles, James. Interview by Ron Filippelli, Historical Collections and Labor Archives, Pennsylvania State University. State College, Pa., 6 May 1968.

McCoy, James. Interview by Historical Collections and Labor Archives. Pennsylvania State University, State College, Pa., 7 November 1968.

McDonald, David J. Interview by Helmut J. Golatz and Alice M. Hoffman, Historical Collections and Labor Archives, Pennsylvania State University. Palm Springs, Calif., 20 February 1970.

Murray, Tom. Interview by Alice M. Hoffman, Historical Collections and Labor Archives, Pennsylvania State University. Pittsburgh, Pa., 23 May 1966.

O'Connor, Harvey and Jessie. Interview by Don Kennedy, Historical Collections and Labor Archives, Pennsylvania State University. Little Compton, R.I., March 1976.

Rice, Charles Owen. Interview by Bud and Ruth Schultz. Archives of an Industrial Society. University of Pittsburgh, Pittsburgh, Pa., summer 1982.

Saposs, David J. Interview by Alice M. Hoffman, Historical Collections and Labor Archives, Pennsylvania State University. Washington, D.C., 4 May 1966.

Schmeck, Anthony. Telephone conversation with author, 22 June 1989. Author's Files, Lancaster, Ohio.

Tracht (Blain), Ruth. Telephone conversation with author, 22 June 1989. Author's Files, Lancaster, Ohio.

## Government Documents

City of Pittsburgh. Bureau of Parks. *Annual Report, 1938*. Pittsburgh: City of Pittsburgh, 1939.

City of Pittsburgh. Bureau of Parks. *Annual Report, 1939*. Pittsburgh: City of Pittsburgh, 1940.

United States House of Representatives. Committee on Un-American Activities. *Expose of the Communist Party of Western Pennsylvania Based Upon Testimony of Matthew Cvetic, February 1950*. Washington, D.C.: U.S. Government Printing Office, 1950.

## Newspapers

*Catholic Sentinel* (Portland, Ore.)
*Catholic Telegraph Register* (Cincinnati, Ohio)
*Columbus Dispatch* (Columbus, Ohio)
*Daily Worker* (New York City)
*The Derby* (Johnstown, Pa.)
*Federated Press* (Pittsburgh)
*The Gadfly* (Pittsburgh)
*Hot Saw Sparks* (Pittsburgh)
*Johnstown Tribune* (Johnstown, Pa.)
*Labor Union Record* (Harrisburg, Pa.)
*The New York Times*

*Our Sunday Visitor* (Huntington, Ind.)
*Pittsburgh Bulletin Index*
*Pittsburgh Catholic*
*Pittsburgh Courier*
*Pittsburgh Post-Gazette*
*Pittsburgh Press*
*Pittsburgh Sun-Telegraph*
*PM* (New York)
*The Socialist Call* (New York)
*The Socialist Herald* (Black Lick, Pa.)
*The Torch* (Pittsburgh)
*United Automobile Worker* (Detroit, Mich.)
*Voice of Revolt* (Pittsburgh)
*Washington Daily News*
*Washington Post*
*Washington Star*
*Washington Times*
*The Young Socialist* (Pittsburgh)

## Books

Abell, Aaron I., ed. *American Catholic Thought on Social Questions*. Indianapolis, Ind.: Bobbs-Merrill, 1968.

Adams, J. Cutler. *Pittsburgh's Post-Gazette*. Boston: Chapman and Grimes, 1936.

Bell, Thomas. *Out of This Furnace: A Novel of Immigrant Labor in America*. Pittsburgh: University of Pittsburgh Press, 1992.

Boyer, Richard O., and Herbert M. Morais. *Labor's Untold Story*. New York: United Electrical, Radio, and Machine Workers of America, 1955.

Brophy, John. *A Miner's Life*. Madison: University of Wisconsin Press, 1964.

Buhite, Russell D., and David W. Levy, eds. *FDR's Fireside Chats*. New York: Penguin, 1993.

Burgoyne, Arthur G. *The Homestead Strike of 1892*. Pittsburgh: University of Pittsburgh Press, 1982.

Byington, Margaret F. *Homestead: The Households of a Mill Town*. Pittsburgh: University of Pittsburgh Press, 1979.

Cantril, Hadley, ed. *Public Opinion, 1935–1946*. Princeton: Princeton University Press, 1951.

Cooke, Morris Llewellyn, and Philip Murray. *Organized Labor and Production: Next Steps in Industrial Democracy*. New York: Harper & Brothers, 1940.

Day, Dorothy. *The Long Loneliness: The Autobiography of Dorothy Day*. New York: Harper & Row, 1981.

DeCaux, Len. *Labor Radical: From the Wobblies to CIO*. Boston: Beacon Press, 1970.

Douglas, William O. *Go East Young Man, The Early Years: The Autobiography of William O. Douglas*. New York: Vintage, 1983.

Fahey, Denis. *The Rulers of Russia*. Royal Oak, Mich.: Social Justice Publishing, 1939.

Fitch, John A. *The Steel Workers*. Pittsburgh: University of Pittsburgh Press, 1989.

Foner, Philip, and Herbert Shapiro, eds. *American Communism and Black Americans: A Documentary History, 1930–1934*. Philadelphia: Temple University Press, 1991.

Foster, William Z. *Unionizing Steel*. New York: Workers Library Publishers, 1936.

Gilson, Etienne, ed. *The Church Speaks to the Modern World: The Social Teachings of Leo XIII*. New York: Image, 1961.

Golden, Clinton S., and Harold J. Ruttenberg. *The Dynamics of Industrial Democracy*. New York: Harper & Brothers, 1942.

Huber, Raphael, ed. *Our Bishops Speak: National Pastorals and Annual Statements of the Hierarchy of the United States*. Milwaukee, Wis.: Bruce Publishing, 1952.

Ickes, Harold L. *The Autobiography of a Curmudgeon*. New York: Reynal and Hitchcock, 1943.

———. *The Secret Diary of Harold L. Ickes: The First Thousand Days, 1933–1966*. 2 vols. New York: Simon & Schuster, 1953.

———. *The Secret Diary of Harold L. Ickes: The Inside Struggle, 1936–1939*. 2 vols. New York: Simon & Schuster, 1954.

Klehr, Harvey, John Earl Haynes, and Fridrikh Igorevich Firsov, eds. *The Secret World of American Communism*. New Haven: Yale University Press, 1995.

Kraus, Henry. *The Many and the Few: A Chronicle of the Dynamic Auto Workers*. Urbana: University of Illinois Press, 1985.

Lochheim, Kate, ed. *The Making of the New Deal: The Insiders Speak*. Cambridge, Mass.: Harvard University Press, 1983.

Markowitz, Gerald, and David Rosner, eds. *"Slaves of the Depression": Workers' Letters About Life on the Job*. Ithaca, N.Y.: Cornell University Press, 1987.

Matthews, J. B. *Odyssey of a Fellow Traveler*. New York: Mount Vernon, 1938.

McDonald, David J. *Union Man*. New York: E. P. Dutton, 1969.

McGowan, R. A. *Toward Social Justice*. New York: Paulist Press, 1933.

Mellon, Paul, and John Baskett. *Reflections in a Silver Spoon: A Memoir*. New York: Morrow, 1992.

Mortimer, Wyndham. *Organize! My Life as a Union Man*. Boston: Beacon Press, 1971.

Nelson, Steve, James R. Barrett, and Rob Ruck. *Steve Nelson: American Radical*. Pittsburgh: University of Pittsburgh Press, 1981.

O'Connor, Harvey. *Mellon's Millions: The Biography of a Fortune*. New York: John Day, 1933.

———. *Revolution in Seattle: A Memoir*. New York: Monthly Review Press, 1964.

O'Connor, Jessie Lloyd, Harvey O'Connor, and Susan M. Bowler. *Harvey and Jessie: A Couple of Radicals*. Philadelphia: Temple University Press, 1988.

Perkins, Frances. *The Roosevelt I Knew*. New York: Viking, 1946.

Powers, George. *Cradle of Steel Unionism: Monongahela Valley, Pennsylvania*. East Chicago, Ill.: Figueroa Printers, 1972.

Proceedings, *First National Catholic Social Action Conference, 1938*. Milwaukee, Wis.: Federal Printing, 1938.

Proceedings, *Second National Catholic Social Action Conference, 1939*. Cleveland, Ohio: R. J. McMillan, 1939.

Roosevelt, Eleanor. *This I Remember*. New York: Harper & Brothers, 1949.

Saposs, David J. *Communism in American Politics*. Washington, D.C.: Public Affairs Press, 1960.

Treacy, Gerald C., ed. *Five Great Encyclicals*. New York: Paulist Press, 1939.

Tugwell, Rexford G. *Roosevelt's Revolution: The First Year—A Personal Perspective*. New York: Macmillan, 1977.

Wideman, John Edgar. *The Homewood Books*. Pittsburgh: University of Pittsburgh Press, 1992.

## Articles

Anderson, Paul Y. "Fascism Hits Washington: Work of the House Committee to Investigate Un-American Activities." *The Nation* 147 (27 August 1938): 198–99.

———. "Loaded Dies Committee." *The Nation* (29 October 1938): 443.

———. "Investigate Mr. Dies!" *The Nation* 147 (5 November 1938): 198–99.

Campion, Raymond J. "The Economic Organization of Society and the Mystical Body of Christ." *Journal of Religious Instruction* 4 (March 1934): 608–25.

Clapper, Raymond. "Return of the Two-Party System." *Current History* 49 (December 1938): 14–15.

———. "The Dies Committee: A Necessary Job Badly Done." *Forum* 103 (1940): 155–57.

Cort, John C. "The Association of Catholic Trade Unionists and the Auto Workers." *U. S. Catholic Historian* 9 (fall 1990): 335–51.

Duffus, R. L. "Is Pittsburgh Civilized?" *Harper's Monthly Magazine* 161 (October 1930): 537–45.

Ewers, John Jay. "Father Cox's Blue Shirts." *The Christian Century* 49 (22 June 1932): 795–97.

"Father Cox's Army at St. Louis." *The Christian Century* 49 (31 August 1932): 1044.

"Father Cox Has a Close-Up View of Mussolini." *The Christian Century* 49 (27 July 1932): 925–26.

"Flophouse Father." *Time* 35 (26 February 1940): 54.

Gillard, John. "The Negro Challenges Communism." *The Commonweal* 16 (25 May 1932): 96–98.

Harrington, Michael. "Catholics in the Labor Movement: A Case History." *Labor History* 11 (fall 1960): 231–63.

High, Stanley. "The WPA: Politicians' Playground." *Current History* 50 (May 1939): 23, 25.

"Hodge-Podge of Good-Will." *The World Tomorrow* 15 (9 September 1932): 246.

"Journeyman Traitor." *Time* 48 (16 December 1946): 37.

Lindley, Ernest. "The New Congress." *Current History* 49 (February 1939): 15, 17.

Murray, Philip. "Labor and Responsibility." *The Virginia Quarterly Review* 16 (April 1940): 267–78.

———. "American Labor and the Threat of Communism." *Annals of the American Academy of Political and Social Science* 274 (March 1951): 125–30.

"Pride and a Priest. *Time* 43 (17 April 1944): 30.

"Priest into President." *Time* 34 (6 November 1939): 24.

"Priest Leads Unemployed." *The Christian Century* 49 (17 February 1932): 235.

Ransford, Charles O. "Father Cox's Hosts Hold Convention." *The Christian Century* 49 (31 August 1932): 1060–61.

Rice, Charles Owen. "Practical Catholics." *The Christian Front* 3 (March 1938): 37–39.

———. "Policy and Action." *The Commonweal* 28 (29 July 1938): 366–67.

———. "Debating the Outstretched Hand." *The Commonweal* 29 (20 January 1939): 351–53.

Richman, Hyman. "Life on Pittsburgh's 'Hill': Some Views and Values of Jews Who Lived There Before the 1940s." *Pittsburgh History* 74 (spring 1991): 10–19.

Roucek, Joseph S., and Francis J. Brown. "The Problem of the Negro and European Immigrant Minorities: Some Comparisons and Contrasts." *Journal of Negro Education* 3 (1939): 299–312.

Rovere, Richard. "Labor's Catholic Bloc." *The Nation* 152 (January 1941): 9–15.

———. "J. B. Matthews—The Informer." *The Nation* 155 (3 October 1942): 329–30.

Ruttenberg, Harold J. "85,000 Victims of Progress." *The New Republic* 94 (16 February 1938): 37–38.

Ryan, John A. "Catholics and Anti-Semitism." *Current History* 49 (February 1939): 25–26.

Saposs, David J. "The Catholic Church and the Labor Movement." *Modern Monthly* 2 (May 1933): 225–30.

"Slovaks: Unhyphenated." *Newsweek* 28 (16 December 1946): 50.

Stark, Louis. "Labor's Civil War." *Current History* 49 (January 1939): 26–28, 42.

Stein, Rose M. "Academic Cossacks in Pittsburgh." *The Nation* 141 (24 July 1935): 105–6.

———. "Murray of the CIO." *The Nation* 151 (31 August 1940): 172–73.

———. "Murray to the Rescue." *The Nation* 151 (30 November 1940): 524–26.

———. "A Talk With Philip Murray." *The Nation* 151 (21 December 1940): 629–31.

"The SWOC Sidesteps the Perils of Adolescence." *Newsweek* 10 (27 December 1937): 37–40.

## *Theses and Dissertations*

Brewer, John Howard. "Robert Lee Vann and the Pittsburgh Courier." M.A. thesis. University of Pittsburgh, 1941.

Burns, Jeffrey Mark. "American Catholics and the Family Crisis, 1930–1962: The Ideological and Organizational Responses." Ph.D. diss. Notre Dame University, 1982.

Centola, Kathleen Gefell. "The American Catholic Church and Anti-Communism, 1945–1960: An Interpretative Framework and Case Studies." Ph.D. diss. State University of New York-Albany, 1984.

Draham, Annemarie. "Unlikely Allies Fight for Unionization: Homestead, Pennsylvania, 1933–1946." M.A. thesis. Indiana University of Pennsylvania, 1984.

Emspak, Frank. "The Breakup of the CIO, 1945–1950." Ph.D. diss. University of Wisconsin, 1972.

Fitzpatrick, Walter John. "Places of Worship in Pittsburgh." M.A. thesis. University of Pittsburgh, 1966.

Gootman, Aviva. "A Study of Selected Foreign Language Publications in Allegheny County." M.S. thesis. University of Pittsburgh, 1946.

Halpern, Martin. "The Disintegration of the Left-Center Coalition in the UAW, 1945–1950." Ph.D. diss. University of Michigan, 1982.

Halsey, William Michael. "The Survival of American Innocence: Catholicism in an Era of Disillusionment, 1920–1940." Ph.D. diss. Graduate Theological Union, 1977.

Henwood, James. "Politics and Unemployment Relief, Pennsylvania, 1931–1939." Ph.D. diss. University of Pennsylvania, 1975.

Klingbeil, Kurt A. "FDR and American Religious Leaders: A Study of FDR and His Relationship to Selected American Religious Leaders." Ph.D. diss.. New York University, 1972.

LeBrun, John Leo. "The Role of the Catholic Worker Movement in American Pacifism, 1933–1972." Ph.D. diss. Case Western Reserve University, 1973.

Mortimer, Louis Read. "John Philip Frey: Spokesman for Skilled Labor." Ph.D. diss. George Washington University, 1982.

Robb, Dennis Michael. "Specialized Catholic Action in the United States, 1936–1949: Ideology, Leadership, and Organizations." Ph.D. diss. University of Minnesota, 1971.

Silver, Sarah. "A Study of Newspaper Groups in Allegheny County." M.S. thesis. University of Pittsburgh, 1945.

Simmons, Ruth Louise. "The Negro in Recent Pittsburgh Politics." M.A. thesis. University of Pittsburgh, 1945.

Solomon, Mark Ira. "Red and Black: Negroes and Communism 1929–1932." Ph.D. diss. Harvard University, 1972.

Tate, Juanita Diffay. "Philip Murray as a Labor Leader." Ph.D. diss. New York University, 1962.

Thatcher, Mary Ann. "Immigrants and the 1930s: Ethnicity and Alienage in Depression and On-Coming War." Ph.D. diss. University of California, Los Angeles, 1973.

Thrasher, Eugene C. "The Magee-Flinn Political Machine, 1895–1905." M.A. thesis. University of Pittsburgh, 1951.

Walsh, Victor Anthony. "Across 'The Big Wather': Irish Community Life in Pittsburgh and Allegheny City, 1850–1885." Ph.D. diss. University of Pittsburgh, 1983.

Warren, Wilson Jerome. "Underneath the Radical Veil: An Examination of a Local of the Unemployed Citizens' League of Allegheny County." Doctoral seminar paper. University of Pittsburgh, 1987.

Williams, Bruce. "Local Labor History, 1930–1940: The Depression." M.A. seminar paper. University of Pittsburgh, 1993.

## Secondary Sources

### Books

Alberts, Robert C. *Pitt: The Story of the University of Pittsburgh, 1787–1987*. Pittsburgh: University of Pittsburgh Press, 1986.

Alexander, June Granatir. *The Immigrant Church and Community: Pittsburgh's Slovak Catholics and Lutherans, 1880–1915*. Pittsburgh: University of Pittsburgh Press, 1987.

Allswang, John M. *Bosses, Machines, and Urban Voters*. Baltimore: Johns Hopkins University Press, 1986.

Altenbaugh, Richard J. *Education for Struggle: The American Labor Colleges of the 1920s and 1930s*. Philadelphia: Temple University Press, 1990.

Andersen, Kristi. *The Creation of a Democratic Majority, 1928–1936*. Chicago: University of Chicago Press, 1979.

Au, William. *The Cross, the Flag, and the Bomb: American Catholics Debate War and Peace, 1960–1983.* New York: Praeger, 1987.

Auerbach, Jerold, ed. *American Labor: The Twentieth Century.* Indianapolis, Ind.: Bobbs-Merrill, 1969.

Badger, Anthony J. *The New Deal: The Depression Years, 1933–1940.* New York: Hill & Wang, 1989.

Banfield, Edward C. *The Unheavenly City Revisited.* Boston: Little, Brown, 1974.

Bailey, Harry A., Jr., and Ellis Katz. *Ethnic Group Politics.* Columbus, Ohio: Charles E. Merrill, 1969.

Baldwin, Leland. *Pittsburgh: The Story of a City, 1750–1865.* Pittsburgh: University of Pittsburgh Press, 1981.

———, ed. *Ideas in Action: Documentary and Interpretive Readings in American History, Volume II.* New York: American Book Company, 1969.

Baltzell, E. Digby. *The Protestant Establishment: Aristocracy and Caste in America.* New York: Vintage, 1964.

Barnard, John. *Walter Reuther and the Rise of the Auto Workers.* Boston: Little, Brown, 1983.

Barone, Michael. *Our Country: The Shaping of America from Roosevelt to Reagan.* New York: The Free Press, 1990.

Barton, Josef. *Peasants and Strangers: Italians, Rumanians, and Slovaks in an American City, 1890–1950.* Cambridge, Mass.: Harvard University Press, 1975.

Bayor, Ronald H. *Neighbors in Conflict: The Irish, Germans, Jews, and Italians of New York City, 1929–1941.* Baltimore: Johns Hopkins University Press, 1978.

Bell, Daniel, ed. *The Radical Right: The New American Right.* New York: Anchor Books, 1964.

Belth, Nathan C. *A Promise to Keep: A Narrative of the American Encounter with Anti-Semitism.* New York: Schocken, 1981.

Bencl, Thomas. *Labor, Church, and the Sugar Establishment, 1887–1976.* Baton Rouge: Louisiana State University Press, 1980.

Bernstein, Irving. *A Caring Society: The New Deal, the Worker, and the Great Depression.* Boston: Houghton Mifflin, 1985.

Bernstein, Michael A. *The Great Depression: Delayed Recovery and Economic Change, 1929–1939.* New York: Cambridge University Press, 1989.

Beers, Paul B. *Pennsylvania Politics Today and Yesterday: The Tolerable Accommodation.* University Park: Pennsylvania State University Press, 1980.

Betten, Neil. *Catholic Activism and the Industrial Worker.* Gainesville: University Presses of Florida, 1976.

Betten, Neil, and Michael J. Austin, eds. *The Roots of Community Organizing, 1917–1939.* Philadelphia: Temple University Press, 1990.

Bird, Caroline. *The Invisible Scar: The Great Depression and What it Did to American Life, from Then Until Now.* New York: Longman, 1978.

Bodnar, John. *Workers' World: Kinship, Community, and Protest in an Industrial Society, 1900–1940.* Baltimore: Johns Hopkins University Press, 1982.

———. *The Transplanted: A History of Immigrants in Urban America.* Bloomington: Indiana University Press, 1987.

———. *Steelton: Immigration and Industrialization, 1870–1940.* Pittsburgh: University of Pittsburgh Press, 1990.

————, ed. *The Ethnic Experience in Pennsylvania*. Lewisburg, Pa.: Bucknell University Press, 1973.

Bodnar, John, Roger Simon, and Michael Weber. *Lives of Their Own: Blacks, Italians, and Poles in Pittsburgh, 1900–1960*. Urbana: University of Illinois Press, 1983.

Boller, Paul, Jr. *Presidential Campaigns*. New York: Oxford University Press, 1985.

Brenan, Gerald. *The Spanish Labyrinth: An Account of the Social and Political Background of the Spanish Civil War*. New York: Cambridge University Press, 1988.

Bremner, Robert H. *From the Depths: The Discovery of Poverty in the United States*. New York: New York University Press, 1972.

Brinkley, Alan. *Voices of Protest: Huey Long, Father Coughlin, and the Great Depression*. New York: Vintage, 1983.

————. *The End of Reform: New Deal Liberalism in Recession and War*. New York: Alfred A. Knopf, 1995.

Broderick, Francis. *Right Reverend New Dealer: John A. Ryan*. New York: Macmillan, 1963.

Brody, David. *Steelworkers in America: The Nonunion Era*. New York: Harper & Row, 1969.

————. *Workers in Industrial America: Essays on the 20th Century Struggle*. New York: Oxford University Press, 1980.

Broehl, Wayne G., Jr. *The Molly Maguires*. New York: Chelsea House, 1983.

Brooks, Robert R. *Clint: A Biography of a Labor Intellectual*. New York: Atheneum, 1978.

Brooks, Thomas R. *Toil and Trouble: A History of American Labor*. New York: Dell, 1972.

Brown, Anthony Cave. *The Last Hero: Wild Bill Donovan*. New York: Vintage, 1984.

Buck, Solon J., and Elizabeth Hawthorn Buck. *The Planting of Civilization in Western Pennsylvania*. Pittsburgh: University of Pittsburgh Press, 1979.

Bukowczyk, John J. *And My Children Did Not Know Me: A History of the Polish-Americans*. Bloomington: Indiana University Press, 1987.

Buni, Andrew. *Robert L. Vann of the Pittsburgh Courier: Politics and Black Journalism*. Pittsburgh: University of Pittsburgh Press, 1974.

Burner, David. *Herbert Hoover: A Public Life*. New York: Atheneum, 1984.

Cantor, Milton. *The Divided Left: American Radicalism, 1900–1975*. New York: Hill & Wang, 1978.

Carey, Patrick W. *American Catholic Religious Thought: The Shaping of a Theological and Social Tradition*. New York: Paulist Press, 1987.

Caro, Robert A. *The Power Broker: Robert Moses and the Fall of New York*. New York: Alfred A. Knopf, 1974.

Carter, Stephen L. *The Culture of Disbelief: How American Law and Politics Trivialize Religious Devotion*. New York: Basic Books, 1993.

Cashman, Sean Dennis. *America in the Twenties and Thirties: The Olympian Age of Franklin Delano Roosevelt*. New York: New York University Press, 1989.

Caute, David. *The Great Fear: The Anti-Communist Purge Under Truman and Eisenhower*. New York: Simon & Schuster, 1978.

Charney, George. *A Long Journey*. Chicago: Quadrangle Books, 1968.

Clark, Dennis. *The Irish in Philadelphia: Ten Generations of Urban Experience*. Philadelphia: Temple University Press, 1984.

Clark, Paul F., Peter Gottlieb, and Donald Kennedy, eds. *Forging a Union of Steel: Philip Murray, SWOC, and the United Steelworkers*. Ithaca, N.Y.: Industrial and Labor Relations Press, Cornell University, 1987.

Cochran, Bert. *Labor and Communism: The Conflict that Shaped American Unions*. Princeton: Princeton University Press, 1977.

Cohen, Lizabeth. *Making a New Deal: Industrial Workers in Chicago, 1919–1939*. Cambridge: Cambridge University Press, 1990.

Collier, Peter, with David Horowitz. *The Roosevelts: An American Saga*. New York: Simon & Schuster, 1994.

Coode, Thomas H., and John F. Bauman, eds. *People, Poverty, and Politics: Pennsylvanians During the Great Depression*. Lewisburg, Pa.: Bucknell University Press, 1981.

Couvares, Francis G. *The Remaking of Pittsburgh: Class and Culture in an Industrializing City, 1877–1919*. Albany: State University of New York Press, 1984.

Coy, Patrick G. *A Revolution of the Heart: Essays on the Catholic Worker*. Philadelphia: Temple University Press, 1988.

Craig, Gordon A., and Francis L. Loewenheim, eds. *The Diplomats, 1939–1979*. Princeton University Press, 1994.

Cronin, James E., and Carmen Sirianni, eds. *Work, Community, and Power: The Emergence of Labor in Europe and America, 1900–1925*. Philadelphia: Temple University Press, 1983.

Crosby, Donald F. *God, Church, and Flag: Senator Joseph R. McCarthy and the Catholic Church, 1950–1957*. Chapel Hill: University of North Carolina Press, 1978.

Dallek, Robert. *Franklin D. Roosevelt and American Foreign Policy, 1932–1945*. New York: Oxford University Press, 1981.

Daniels, Roger. *Coming to America: A History of Immigration and Ethnicity in American Life*. New York: Harper Perennial, 1991.

Davis, Kenneth S. *FDR: Into the Storm, 1937–1940*. New York: Random House, 1993.

DeBenedetti, Charles. *The Peace Reform in American History*. Bloomington: Indiana University Press, 1984.

———. *Peace Heroes in Twentieth-Century America*. Bloomington: Indiana University Press, 1988.

Demerath, N. J., and Rhys S. Williams. *A Bridging of Faiths: Religion and Politics in a New England City*. Princeton: Princeton University Press, 1992.

Dickerson, Dennis Clark. *Out of the Crucible: Black Steelworkers in Western Pennsylvania, 1875–1980*. Albany: State University of New York Press, 1986.

Dinnerstein, Leonard, and David M. Reimers. *Ethnic Americans: A History of Immigration and Assimilation*. New York: Harper & Row, 1982.

Divine, Robert A. *The Reluctant Belligerent: American Entry into World War II*. New York: John Wiley & Sons, 1979.

Dolan, Jay P., ed. *The American Catholic Parish: A History from 1850 to the Present*. Volume I. New York: Paulist Press, 1987.

———, ed. *The American Catholic Parish: A History from 1850 to the Present*. Volume II. New York: Paulist Press, 1987.

Draper, Theodore. *The Roots of American Communism*. Chicago: Ivan R. Dee, 1989.

Dubofsky, Melvyn, and Warren Van Tine. *John L. Lewis: A Biography*. Urbana: University of Illinois Press, 1986.

———, eds. *Labor Leaders in America*. Urbana: University of Illinois Press, 1987.

Dyer, Thomas G. *Theodore Roosevelt and the Idea of Race*. Baton Rouge: Louisiana State University Press, 1980.

Edsforth, Ronald. *Class Conflict and Cultural Consensus: The Making of a Mass Consumer Society in Flint, Michigan*. New Brunswick, N.J.: Rutgers University Press, 1987.

Erie, Steven O. *Rainbow's End: Irish-Americans and the Dilemmas of Urban Machine Politics, 1840–1985*. Berkeley and Los Angeles: University of California Press, 1988.

Fehrenbach, T. R. *F.D.R.'s Undeclared War, 1939–1941*. New York: David McKay, 1967.

Feldman, Jacob. *The Jewish Experience in Western Pennsylvania: A History, 1755–1945*. Pittsburgh: Historical Society of Western Pennsylvania.

Ferrell, Robert H. *Choosing Truman: The Democratic Convention of 1944*. Columbia: University of Missouri Press, 1994.

Filippelli, Ronald L. *Labor in the USA: A History*. New York: Alfred A. Knopf, 1984.

Finkle, Lee. *Forum for Protest: The Black Press During World War II*. Rutherford, N.J.: Fairleigh Dickinson University Press, 1975.

Flynn, George Q. *American Catholics and the Roosevelt Presidency, 1932–1936*. Lexington: University of Kentucky Press, 1968.

———. *Roosevelt and Romanism: Catholics and American Diplomacy, 1937–1945*. Westport, Conn.: Greenwood Press, 1976.

Foner, Philip S., and Ronald L. Lewis, eds. *The Black Worker from the Founding of the CIO to the AFL-CIO Merger, 1936–1955*. 7 vols. Philadelphia: Temple University Press, 1983.

Fones-Wolf, Ken. *Trade Union Gospel: Christianity and Labor in Industrial Philadelphia, 1865–1915*. Philadelphia: Temple University Press, 1989.

Ford, Henry James. *The Scotch-Irish in America*. Hamden, Conn.: Anchor Books, 1966.

Foster, James C. *The Union Politic: The CIO Political Action Committee*. Columbia: University of Missouri Press, 1975.

Fraser, Steven. *Labor Will Rule: Sidney Hillman and the Rise of American Labor*. New York: The Free Press, 1991.

Fraser, Steven, and Gary Gerstle, eds. *The Rise and Fall of the New Deal Order, 1930–1980*. Princeton: Princeton University Press, 1989.

Freeman, Joshua B. *In Transit: The Transport Workers Union in New York City, 1933–1966*. New York: Oxford University Press, 1989.

Freeman, Joshua B., et. al. *Who Built America? Working People and the Nation's Economy, Politics, Culture, and Society*. Volume II. New York: Pantheon 1992.

Freidel, Frank, ed. *The New Deal and the American People*. Englewood Cliffs, N.J.: Prentice-Hall, 1964.

Fuchs, Lawrence H., ed. *American Ethnic Politics*. New York: Harper & Row, 1968.

Gaddis, John Lewis. *The United States and the Origins of the Cold War, 1941–1947*. New York: Columbia University Press, 1972.

Galbraith, John Kenneth. *The Great Crash, 1929*. Boston: Houghton Mifflin, 1961.

Galenson, Walter. *The CIO Challenge to the AFL: A History of the American Labor Movement, 1935–1941*. Cambridge, Mass.: Harvard University Press, 1960.

Gamm, Gerald H. *The Making of New Deal Democrats: Voting Behavior and Realignment in Boston, 1920–1940*. Chicago: University of Chicago Press, 1989.

Gans, Herbert J. *The Urban Villagers: Group and Class in the Life of Italian-Americans*. New York: The Free Press, 1982.

Garraty, John A. *The Great Depression: An Inquiry into the Causes, Course, and Consequences of the Worldwide Depression*. New York: Anchor Books, 1987.

George, Peter. *The Emergence of Industrial America: Strategic Factors in American Economic Growth Since 1870*. Albany: State University of New York Press, 1982.

Gerber, David A. *Anti-Semitism in American History*. Urbana: University of Illinois Press, 1987.

Gerstle, Gary. *Working-Class Americanism: The Politics of Labor in a Textile City, 1914–1960*. New York: Cambridge University Press, 1991.

Gottlieb, Peter. *Making Their Own Way: Southern Blacks' Migration to Pittsburgh, 1916–1930*. Urbana: University of Illinois Press, 1987.

Graham, Otis, and Meghan Robinson Wander. *Franklin D. Roosevelt, His Life and Times: An Encyclopedia View*. Boston: Da Capo Press, 1985.

Greeley, Andrew M. *The Catholic Experience: An Interpretation of the History of American Catholicism*. New York: Macmillan, 1967.

———. *The Catholic Myth: The Behavior and Beliefs of American Catholics*. New York: Collier, 1990.

Green, James R. *The World of the Worker: Labor in Twentieth-Century America*. New York: Hill & Wang, 1980.

———, ed. *Workers' Struggles, Past and Present: A "Radical America" Reader*. Philadelphia: Temple University Press, 1983.

Greene, Victor R.. *The Slavic Community on Strike: Immigrant Labor in Pennsylvania Anthracite*. South Bend, Ind.: University of Notre Dame Press, 1968.

———. *For God and Country: The Rise of Polish and Lithuanian Ethnic Consciousness in America, 1860–1910*. Madison: State Historical Society of Wisconsin, 1975.

Guttman, Allen. *The Wound in the Heart: America and the Spanish Civil War*. New York: The Free Press, 1962.

Hamby, Alonzo L. *The New Deal: Analysis and Interpretation*. New York: Weybright and Talley, 1969.

Haynes, John E. *Red Scare or Red Menace? American Communism and Anti-Communism in the Cold War Era*. Chicago: Ivan R. Dee, 1996.

Hays, Samuel P. *American Political History as Social Analysis*. Knoxville: University of Tennessee Press, 1980.

———, ed. *City at the Point: Essays on the Social History of Pittsburgh*. Pittsburgh: University of Pittsburgh Press, 1989.

Heinrichs, Waldo. *Threshold of War: Franklin D. Roosevelt and American Entry into World War II*. New York: Oxford University Press, 1988.

Hennesey, James. *American Catholics: A History of the Roman Catholic Community in the United States*. New York: Oxford University Press, 1981.

Hero, Alfred O., Jr. *American Religious Groups View Foreign Policy: Trends in Rank-and-File Opinion, 1937–1969*. Durham, N.C.: Duke University Press, 1973.

Hertzberg, Arthur. *The Jews in America: Four Centuries of Uneasy Encounter*. New York: Simon & Schuster, 1990.

Higham, John. *Strangers in the Land: Patterns of American Nativism, 1860–1925*. New York: Atheneum, 1978.

———. *Send These to Me: Immigrants in Urban America*. Baltimore: Johns Hopkins University Press, 1984.

Hobgood, Mary E. *Catholic Social Teaching and Economic Theory: Paradigms in Conflict*. Philadelphia: Temple University Press, 1991.

Hoerr, John P. *And the Wolf Finally Came: The Decline of the American Steel Industry*. Pittsburgh: University of Pittsburgh Press, 1988.

Howe, Irving. *World of Our Fathers: The Journey of East European Jews to America and the Life They Found and Made*. New York: Harcourt Brace Jovanovich, 1976.

Huthmacher, J. Joseph. *Senator Robert F. Wagner and the Rise of Urban Liberalism*. New York: Atheneum, 1971.

Jackson, Kenneth T. *The Ku Klux Klan in the City, 1915–1930*. New York: Oxford University Press, 1967.

Jeansonne, Glen. *Gerald L. K. Smith: Minister of Hate*. New Haven: Yale University Press, 1988.

Jeffries, John W. *Testing the Roosevelt Coalition: Connecticut Society and Politics in the Era of World War II*. Knoxville: University of Tennessee Press, 1979.

Jenkins, Philip. *Hoods and Shirts: The Extreme Right in Pennsylvania, 1925–1950*. Chapel Hill: University of North Carolina Press, 1997.

Jenkins, William D. *Steel Valley Klan: The Ku Klux Klan in Ohio's Mahoning Valley*. Kent, Ohio: Kent State University Press, 1990.

Johnson, Paul. *A History of the Jews*. New York: Harper & Row, 1987.

———. *Intellectuals*. New York: Harper & Row, 1988.

———. *Modern Times: From the Twenties to the Nineties*. New York: Harper Collins, 1991.

Jonas, Manfred. *Isolationism in America, 1935–1941*. Ithaca, N.Y.: Cornell University Press, 1969.

Judis, John B. *William F. Buckley, Jr.: Patron Saint of the Conservatives*. New York: Simon & Schuster, 1990.

Kazin, Michael. *The Populist Persuasion: An American History*. New York: Basic Books, 1995.

Keeran, Roger. *The Communist Party and the Auto Workers Unions*. Bloomington: Indiana University Press, 1980.

Kirby, John B. *Black Americans in the Roosevelt Era: Liberalism and Race*. Knoxville: University of Tennessee Press, 1982.

Klehr, Harvey. *Communist Cadre: The Social Background of the American Communist Party Elite*. Stanford, Calif.: Hoover Institution Press, 1978.

———. *The Heyday of American Communism: The Depression Decade*. New York: Basic Books, 1984.

Klehr, Harvey, and John Earl Haynes. *The American Communist Movement: Storming Heaven Itself*. New York: Twayne, 1992.

Kleinberg, S. J. *The Shadow of the Mills: Working-Class Families in Pittsburgh, 1870–1907*. Pittsburgh: University of Pittsburgh Press, 1989.

Klingaman, William K. *1929: The Year of the Great Crash.* New York: Harper & Row, 1989.

Knepper, George W. *Ohio and Its People.* Kent, Ohio: Kent State University Press, 1989.

Krause, Corinne A. *Grandmothers, Mothers, and Daughters: Oral Histories of Three Generations of Ethnic American Women.* Boston: Twayne, 1991.

Krickus, Richard. *Pursuing the American Dream: White Ethnics and the New Populism.* Bloomington: Indiana University Press, 1976.

Larrowe, Charles P. *Harry Bridges: The Rise and Fall of Radical Labor in the U.S.* New York: Lawrence Hill, 1972.

Laurie, Bruce. *Working People of Philadelphia, 1800–1850.* Philadelphia: Temple University Press, 1980.

Lee, J. J. *Ireland, 1912–1985: Politics and Society.* New York: Cambridge University Press, 1989.

Lemann, Nicholas. *The Promised Land: The Great Black Migration and How it Changed America.* New York: Alfred A. Knopf, 1991.

Lemon, James T. *The Best Poor Man's Country: A Geographical Study of Early Southeastern Pennsylvania.* Baltimore: Johns Hopkins University Press, 1972.

Leuchtenburg, William E. *Franklin D. Roosevelt and the New Deal, 1932–1940.* New York: Harper & Row, 1963.

Levenstein, Harvey. *Communism, Anti-Communism, and the CIO.* Westport, Conn.: Greenwood Press, 1981.

Levy, Mark R., and Michael S. Kramer. *The Ethnic Factor: How America's Minorities Decide Elections.* New York: Simon & Schuster, 1972.

Lewy, Guenter. *The Cause That Failed: Communism in American Political Life.* New York: Oxford University Press, 1990.

Lichtenstein, Nelson. *Labor's War at Home: The CIO in World War II.* New York: Cambridge University Press, 1991.

Liebman, Arthur. *Jews and the Left.* New York: John Wiley & Sons, 1979.

Liptak, Dolores Ann. *European Immigrants and the Catholic Church in Connecticut, 1870–1920.* New York: Center for Migration Studies, 1987.

Lissak, Rivka Shpak. *Pluralism & Progressives: Hull House and the New Immigrants, 1890–1919.* Chicago: University of Chicago Press, 1989.

Lowitt, Richard, and Maurine Beasley, eds. *One Third of a Nation: Lorena Hickok Reports on the Great Depression.* Urbana: University of Illinois Press, 1983.

Lubove, Roy. *Twentieth Century Pittsburgh: Government, Business, and Environmental Change.* New York: John Wiley & Sons, 1969.

Marks, Carole. *Farewell—We're Good and Gone: The Great Black Migration.* Bloomington: Indiana University Press, 1989.

Marrus, Michael R. *The Unwanted: European Refugees in the Twentieth Century.* New York: Oxford University Press, 1985.

Marsden, George M., and Bradley J. Longfield, eds. *The Secularization of the Academy.* New York: Oxford University Press, 1992.

McElvaine, Robert S. *The Great Depression: America, 1929–1941.* New York: Times Books, 1984.

McGeever, Patrick J. *Rev. Charles Owen Rice: Apostle of Contradiction.* Pittsburgh: Duquesne University Press, 1989.

McJimsey, George. *Harry Hopkins: Ally of the Poor and Defender of Democracy.* Cambridge, Mass.: Harvard University Press, 1987.

McNeal, Patricia. *Harder Than War: Catholic Peacemaking in Twentieth-Century America.* New Brunswick, N.J.: Rutgers University Press, 1992.

Meier, August, and Elliott Rudwick. *Black Detroit and the Rise of the UAW.* New York: Oxford University Press, 1981.

Miles, Michael W. *The Odyssey of the American Right.* New York: Oxford University Press, 1980.

Milkis, Sidney M. *The President and the Parties: The Transformation of the American Party System Since the New Deal.* New York: Oxford University Press, 1993.

Miller, Randall M., and Thomas D. Marzik. *Immigrants and Religion in Urban America.* Philadelphia: Temple University Press, 1977.

Mills, C. Wright. *White Collar: The American Middle Classes.* New York: Oxford University Press, 1953.

Miner, Curtis. *Homestead: The Story of a Steel Town, 1860–1945.* Pittsburgh: Historical Society of Western Pennsylvania, 1989.

———. *Forging a New Deal: Johnstown and the Great Depression, 1929–1941.* Johnstown, Pa.: Johnstown Area Heritage Association, 1993.

Mink, Gwendolyn. *Old Labor and New Immigrants in American Political Development: Union, Party, and State, 1875–1920.* Ithaca, N.Y.: Cornell University Press, 1986.

Morawska, Ewa. *For Bread, With Butter: The Life-Worlds of East Central Europeans in Johnstown, Pennsylvania, 1890–1940.* New York: Cambridge University Press, 1985.

Morgan, Ted. *FDR: A Biography.* New York: Simon & Schuster, 1985.

Mormino, Gary Ross. *Immigrants on the Hill: Italian-Americans in St. Louis, 1882–1982.* Urbana: University of Illinois Press, 1986.

Morone, James A. *The Democratic Wish: Popular Participation and the Limits of American Government.* New York: Basic Books, 1990.

Morris, Charles R. *American Catholic: The Saints and Sinners Who Built America's Most Powerful Church.* New York: Random House, 1997.

Murray, Harry. *Do Not Neglect Hospitality: The Catholic Worker and the Homeless.* Philadelphia: Temple University Press, 1990.

Naison, Mark. *Communists in Harlem During the Depression.* Urbana: University of Illinois Press, 1983.

Novak, Michael. *The Rise of the Unmeltable Ethnics: Politics and Culture in the Seventies.* New York: Macmillan, 1973.

O'Brien, David. *American Catholics and Social Reform: The New Deal Years.* New York: Oxford University Press, 1968.

O'Donnell, L. A. *Irish Voice and Organized Labor in America: A Biographical Study.* Westport, Conn.: Greenwood Press, 1997.

O'Neill, William L. *A Better World: The Great Schism, Stalinism and the American Intellectuals.* New York: Simon & Schuster, 1982.

O'Reilly, Kenneth, *The FBI, HUAC, and the Red Menace.* Philadelphia: Temple University Press, 1983.

O'Rourke, Lawrence M. *Geno: The Life and Mission of Geno Baroni.* New York: Paulist Press, 1991.

Ottanelli, Fraser M. *The Communist Party of the United States: From the Depression to World War II.* New Brunswick, N.J.: Rutgers University Press, 1991.

Packard, Vance. *The Status Seekers: An Exploration of Class Behavior in America and the Hidden Barriers that Affect You, Your Community, Your Future.* New York: David McKay, 1959.

Parmet, Herbert S. *Richard Nixon and His America.* Boston: Little, Brown, 1990.

Peirce, Neal R. *The Megastates of America: People, Politics, and Power in the Ten Great States.* New York: W. W. Norton, 1972.

Perrett, Geoffrey. *Days of Sadness, Years of Triumph: The American People, 1939–1945.* Baltimore: Penguin, 1973.

Phillips, Kevin P. *The Emerging Republican Majority.* New Rochelle, N.Y.: Arlington House, 1970.

Piehl, Mel. *Breaking Bread: The Catholic Worker and the Origin of Catholic Radicalism in America.* Philadelphia: Temple University Press, 1982.

Piven, Frances Fox., and Richard A. Cloward. *Regulating the Poor: The Functions of Public Welfare.* New York: Vintage, 1972.

———. *Poor People's Movements: Why They Succeed, Why They Fail.* New York: Vintage, 1979.

Polenberg, Richard. *War and Society: The United States, 1941–1945.* New York: J. B. Lippincott, 1972.

———. *One Nation Divisible: Class, Race, and Ethnicity in the United States Since 1938.* New York: Penguin, 1980.

Powers, Richard Gid. *Not Without Honor: The History of American Anti-Communism.* New York: The Free Press, 1995.

Prpic, George J. *The Croatian Immigrants in America.* New York: Philosophical Library, 1971.

———. *South Slavic Immigration in America.* Boston: Twayne, 1978.

Quinn, Edward, and Paul J. Dolan. *The Sense of the Sixties.* New York: The Free Press, 1968.

Ribuffo, Leo P. *The Old Christian Right: The Protestant Far Right from the Great Depression to the Cold War.* Philadelphia: Temple University Press, 1983.

Robinson, Archie. *George Meany and His Times.* New York: Simon & Schuster, 1981.

Robinson, Edgar Eugene. *They Voted for Roosevelt: The Presidential Vote, 1932–1944.* New York: Octagon, 1970.

Rogers, Kim Lacy. *Righteous Lives: Narratives of the New Orleans Civil Rights Movement.* New York: New York University Press, 1992.

Romasco, Albert V. *The Poverty of Abundance: Hoover, the Nation, the Depression.* New York: Oxford University Press, 1972.

Rosswurm, Steve, ed. *The CIO's Left-Led Unions.* New Brunswick, N.J.: Rutgers University Press, 1992.

Sanchez, Jose M. *The Spanish Civil War as a Religious Tragedy.* Notre Dame, Ind.: University of Notre Dame Press, 1987.

Sanders, Ronald. *Shores of Refuge: A Hundred Years of Jewish Emigration.* New York: Schocken, 1988.

Schatz, Ronald W. *The Electrical Workers: A History of Labor at General Electric and Westinghouse, 1923–1960.* Urbana: University of Illinois Press, 1983.

Schlesinger, Arthur M., Jr. *The Age of Roosevelt: The Crisis of the Old Order, 1919–1933.* Boston: Houghton, Mifflin, 1957.

———. *The Age of Roosevelt: The Coming of the New Deal.* Boston: Houghton Mifflin, 1959.

Schwartz, Bonnie Fox. *The Civil Works Administration, 1933–1934: The Business of Emergency Employment in the New Deal*. Princeton: Princeton University Press, 1984.

Schwarz, Jordan A. *Liberal: Adolf A. Berle and the Vision of an American Era*. New York: The Free Press, 1987.

Seaton, Douglas P. *Catholics and Radicals: The Association of Catholic Trade Unionists and the American Labor Movement from Depression to Cold War*. Lewisburg, Pa.: Bucknell University Press, 1981.

Shannon, William V. *The American Irish*. New York: Macmillan, 1966.

Silk, Mark. *Spiritual Politics: Religion and America Since World War II*. New York: Simon & Schuster, 1988.

Sitkoff, Harvard. *A New Deal for Blacks: The Emergence of Civil Rights as a National Issue, The Depression Decade*. New York: Oxford University Press, 1981.

Sleeper, Jim. *The Closest of Strangers: Liberalism and the Politics of Race in New York*. New York: W. W. Norton, 1990.

Sorin, Gerald. *The Prophetic Minority: American Jewish Immigrant Radicals, 1880–1920*. Bloomington: Indiana University Press, 1985.

Sowell, Thomas. *Ethnic America: A History*. New York, Basic Books, 1981.

Stave, Bruce M. *The New Deal and the Last Hurrah: Pittsburgh Machine Politics*. Pittsburgh: University of Pittsburgh Press, 1970.

Steffens, Lincoln. *The Shame of the Cities*. New York: Hill & Wang, 1957.

Steinberg, Stephen. *The Ethnic Myth: Race, Ethnicity, and Class in America*. Boston: Beacon Press, 1981.

Taylor, F. Jay. *The United States and the Spanish Civil War*. New York: Bookman Associates, 1956.

Teaford, Jon C. *Cities of the Heartland: The Rise and Fall of the Industrial Midwest*. Bloomington: Indiana University Press, 1993.

Thernstrom, Stephan, Ann Orlov, and Oscar Handlin, et al. *Harvard Encyclopedia of American Ethnic Groups*. Cambridge, Mass.: Harvard University Press, 1980.

Thomas, Hugh. *The Spanish Civil War*. New York: Harper and Brothers, 1961.

Troester, Rosalie Riegle. *Voices from the Catholic Worker*. Philadelphia: Temple University Press, 1993.

Trout, Charles H. *Boston, the Great Depression, and the New Deal*. New York: Oxford University Press, 1977.

Ward, David. *Poverty, Ethnicity, and the American City, 1840–1925*. New York: Cambridge University Press, 1989.

Warren, Kenneth. *The American Steel Industry, 1850–1970: A Geographical Interpretation*. Pittsburgh: University of Pittsburgh Press, 1973.

Watkins, T. H. *Righteous Pilgrim: The Life and Times of Harold L. Ickes, 1874–1952*. New York: Henry Holt, 1990.

Weber, Michael P. *Don't Call Me Boss: David L. Lawrence, Pittsburgh's Renaissance Mayor*. Pittsburgh: University of Pittsburgh Press, 1988.

Weiss, Nancy J. *Farewell to the Party of Lincoln: Black Politics in the Age of FDR*. Princeton: Princeton University Press, 1983.

White, Graham. *FDR and the Press*. Chicago: University of Chicago Press, 1979.

White, Graham, and John Maze. *Harold Ickes of the New Deal: His Private Life and Public Career*. Cambridge, Mass.: Harvard University Press, 1985.

White, Ronald C., Jr., and C. Howard Hopkins. *The Social Gospel: Religion and Reform in Changing America*. Philadelphia: Temple University Press, 1976.

Wittner, Lawrence S. *Rebels Against War: The American Peace Movement, 1941–1960*. New York: Columbia University Press, 1969.

Wolfskill, George. *The Revolt of the Conservatives: A History of the American Liberty League, 1934–1940*. Boston: Houghton Mifflin, 1962.

Wolfskill, George, and John A. Hudson. *All But the People: Franklin D. Roosevelt and His Critics, 1933–1939*. New York: Macmillan, 1969.

Wood, Forrest G. *The Arrogance of Faith: Christianity and Race in America from the Colonial Era to the Twentieth Century*. New York: Alfred A. Knopf, 1990.

Wyman, David S. *The Abandonment of the Jews: America and the Holocaust, 1941–1945*. New York: Pantheon, 1985.

———. *Paper Walls: America and the Refugee Crisis, 1938–1941*. New York: Pantheon, 1985.

Yans-McLaughlin, Virginia. *Immigration Reconsidered: History, Sociology, and Politics*. New York: Oxford University Press, 1990.

Zieger, Robert H. *The CIO, 1935–1955*. Chapel Hill: University of North Carolina Press, 1995.

## Articles

Abell, Aaron I. "The Reception of Leo XIII's Labor Encyclical in America, 1891–1919." *Review of Politics* 7 (October 1945): 464–95.

Adler, Les K., and Thomas G. Patterson. "Red Fascism: The Merger of Nazi Germany and Soviet Russia in the American Image of Totalitarianism, 1930s–1950s." *The American Historical Review* 75 (April 1970): 1046–64.

Alexander, June Granatir. "Staying Together: Chain Migration and Patterns of Slovak Settlement in Pittsburgh Prior to World War I." *Journal of American Ethnic History* 1 (fall 1981): 56–83.

Appel, John J. "American Negro and Immigrant Experience: Similarities and Differences." *American Quarterly* 18 (1966): 93–103.

Betten, Neil. "Charles Owen Rice: Pittsburgh Labor Priest, 1936–1940." *Pennsylvania Magazine of History and Biography* 94 (October 1970): 518–32.

Bicha, Karel D. "Hunkies: Stereotyping the Slavic Immigrants, 1890–1920." *Journal of American Ethnic History* 2 (fall 1982): 16–38.

Billington, Monroe, and Cal Clark. "Catholic Clergymen, Franklin D. Roosevelt, and the New Deal." *Catholic Historical Review* 79 (January 1993): 65–82.

Bodnar, John E. "Socialization and Adaptation: Immigrant Families in Scranton, 1880–1890." *Pennsylvania History* 43 (April 1976): 147–62.

———. "Immigration, Kinship, and the Rise of Working-Class Realism in Industrial America." *Journal of Social History* 14 (fall 1980): 45–59.

Brody, David. "Labor and the Great Depression: The Interpretative Prospects." *Labor History* 13 (1972): 231–44.

Buhle, Paul. "Jews and American Communism: The Cultural Question." *Radical History Review* 23 (spring 1980): 9–33.

Cantril, Hadley. "Educational and Economic Composition of Religious Groups: An Analysis of Poll Data." *American Journal of Sociology* 48 (March 1943): 574–79.

Clement, Priscilla. "The Works Progress Administration in Pennsylvania, 1935 to 1940." *Pennsylvania Magazine of History and Biography* 95 (April 1971): 244–60.

Coode, Thomas H., and John D. Petrarulo. "The Odyssey of Pittsburgh's Father Cox." *The Western Pennsylvania Historical Magazine* 55 (July 1972): 217–38.

Cunningham, Constance A. "Homer S. Brown: First Black Political Leader in Pittsburgh." *Journal of Negro History* 66 (winter 1981–82): 304–17.

Filippelli, Ronald L. "UE: The Formative Years, 1933–1937." *Labor History* 17 (summer 1976): 351–71.

Freeman, Joshua B., and Steve Rosswurm. "The Education of an Anti-Communist: Father John F. Cronin and the Baltimore Labor Movement." *Labor History* 33 (spring 1992): 217–47.

Gordon, Max. "The Communists and the Drive to Organize Steel, 1936." *Labor History* 23 (spring 1982): 254–65.

Greeley, Andrew. "What is Subsidiarity? A Voice from Sleepy Hollow." *America* 153 (9 November 1985): 292–295.

Greene, Victor R. "For God and Country: The Origins of Slavic Catholic Self-Consciousness in America." *Church History* 35 (1966): 446–60.

Gutman, Herbert G. "Protestantism and the American Labor Movement." *American Historical Review* 77 (1966): 74–101.

Hareven, Tamara K. "The Laborers of Manchester, New Hampshire, 1912–1922: The Role of Family and Ethnicity in Adjustment to Industrial Life." *Labor History* 16 (spring 1975): 249–65.

Hawkins, Frank. "Lawrence of Pittsburgh: Boss of the Mellon Patch." *Harper's Monthly Magazine* 213 (August 1956): 57–61.

Higham, John. "Integrating America: The Problem of Assimilation in the Nineteenth Century." *Journal of American Ethnic History* 1 (fall 1981): 7–25.

Heineman, Kenneth J. "The Changing Face of Schenley Park." *Pittsburgh History* 72 (fall 1989): 112–27.

———. "Media Bias in Coverage of the Dies Committee on Un-American Activities, 1938–1940." *The Historian* 55 (autumn 1992): 37–52.

———. "A Catholic New Deal: Religion and Labor in 1930s Pittsburgh." *Pennsylvania Magazine of History and Biography* 118 (October 1994): 363–94.

Hoover, Bob. "Ethnic Warfare Comes to Pittsburgh: Serbs and Croatians Grapple With How to Help Their Ancestral Homeland." *Pittsburgh Magazine* (December 1992): 44–46, 65–70.

Kane, John J. "The Social Structure of American Catholics." *American Catholic Sociological Review* 16 (March 1955): 23–30.

Kantowicz, Edward R. "Cardinal Mundelein of Chicago and the Shaping of Twentieth-Century American Catholicism." *Journal of American History* 68 (June 1981): 52–68.

Keeran, Roger. "The International Workers Order and the Origins of the CIO." *Labor History* 30 (summer 1979): 385–408.

Leab, Daniel J. "'United We Eat': The Creation and Organization of the Unemployed Councils in 1930." *Labor History* 8 (fall 1967): 300–315.

———. "Anti-Communism, the FBI, and Matt Cvetic: The Ups and Downs of a Professional Informer." *Pennsylvania Magazine of History and Biography* 115 (October 1991): 535–81.

Lemann, Nicholas. The Origins of the Underclass. Part I. *Atlantic Monthly* 257 (June 1986): 31–55.

———. "The Origins of the Underclass. Part II." *Atlantic Monthly* 258 (July 1986): 54–68.

Lissak, Rivka. "Myth and Reality: The Pattern of Relationship Between the Hull House Circle and the 'New Immigrants' on Chicago's West Side, 1890–1919." *Journal of American Ethnic History* 2 (spring 1983): 21–50.

McNeal, Patricia. "Origins of the Catholic Peace Movement." *The Review of Politics* 35 (July 1973): 346–372.

McPherson, Donald S. "The 'Little Steel' Strike of 1937 in Johnstown, Pennsylvania." *Pennsylvania History* 39 (April 1972): 219–38.

Miner, Curtis. "Mill Towns, the 'Underworld Fraternity,' and the Working Man: Reconsidering Local Politics and Corruption Within the Industrial Suburb, Homestead, Pennsylvania, 1921–1937." Unpublished manuscript, 1988.

Miner, Curtis, and Paul Roberts. "Engineering an Industrial Diaspora: Homestead, 1941." *Pittsburgh History* 72 (winter 1989): 4–25.

Morgan, Alfred L. "The Significance of Pennsylvania's 1938 Gubernatorial Election." *Pennsylvania Magazine of History and Biography* 102 (April 1978): 184–211.

Morris, Wayne. "Stalin's Famine and the American Journalists." *Continuity* 18 (spring/fall 1994): 69–78.

Muller, Edward K. "The Legacy of Industrial Rivers." *Pittsburgh History* 72 (summer 1989): 64–75.

O'Brien, David. "American Catholics and Organized Labor in the 1930s." *Catholic Historical Review* 52 (October 1966): 323–49.

———. "American Catholics and Anti-Semitism in the 1930s." *Catholic World* 204 (February 1967): 270–76.

Olson, James. "Gifford Pinchot and the Politics of Hunger, 1932–1933." *Pennsylvania Magazine of History and Biography* 96 (October 1972): 508–20.

Pope, Liston. "Religion and Class Structure." *Annals of the Academy of Political and Social Science* 256 (March 1948): 84–95.

Pozzetta, George E. "Immigrants and Ethnics: The State of Italian-American Historiography." *Journal of American Ethnic History* 9 (sall 1989): 67–95.

Reutter, Clifford J. "The Puzzle of a Pittsburgh Steeler: Joe Magarac's Ethnic Identity." *Western Pennsylvania Historical Magazine* 63 (January 1980): 31–36.

Rosenzweig, Roy. "Radicals and the Jobless: The Musteites and the Unemployed Leagues, 1932–1936." *Labor History* 10 (winter 1975): 52–77.

———. "Organizing the Unemployed: The Early Years of the Great Depression, 1929–1933." *Radical America* 10 (July–August 1976): 37–60.

Schatz, Ronald W. "Connecticut's Working Class in the 1950s: A Catholic Perspective." *Labor History* 25 (winter 1980): 83–101.

———. "American Labor and the Catholic Church, 1919–1950." *International Labor and Working Class History* 20 (fall 1981): 46–53.

Senn, Alfred Erich, and Alfonsas Eidintas. "Lithuanian Immigrants in America and the Lithuanian National Movement Before 1914." *Journal of American Ethnic History* 6 (spring 1987): 5–19.

Shenton, James P. "The Coughlin Movement and the New Deal." *Political Science Quarterly* 73 (September 1958): 353–73.

Tentler, Leslie Woodcock. "On the Margins: The State of American Catholic History." *American Quarterly* 45 (March 1993): 104–27.

Valaik, J. David. "Catholics, Neutrality, and the Spanish Embargo, 1937–1939." *Journal of American History* 54 (June 1967): 73–85.

———. "American Catholic Dissenters and the Spanish Civil War." *The Catholic Historical Review* 53 (January 1968): 537–46.

Valocchi, Steve. "The Unemployed Workers Movement of the 1930s." *Social Problems* 37 (May 1990): 191–205.

Vecoli, Rudolph. "Prelates and Peasants: Italian Immigrants and the Catholic Church." *Journal of Social History* 2 (spring 1969): 217–68.

Ward, Richard J. "The Role of the Association of Catholic Trade Unionists in the Labor Movement." *Review of Social Economy* 14 (September 1956): 79–101.

*Film*

Miner, Curtis. "United by Right, Divided by Fear: Johnstown and the 1937 Steel Strike." Johnstown Area Heritage Association, Johnstown, Pa., 1993.

# Index

Vivid visualities of
   socially concerned priests p. 59
   & good summaries of their
   perspective w/ some verbatim
   statements (but not too much)


Great mutual
Continuity - How many mentions of
   D. Day & Catholic Worker Mov. before
   As explained?


The Assyrian

What's excellent also a problem
   in that the overestimates influence of
   religion as well as recognizing it — 211
   Huge entities in South
   Blacks in labor movement

Assessment of the future of union mov.